FRANCE

LILLE

LAURENCE PHILLIPS

www.bradtguides.com

Bradt Guides Ltd, UK
The Globe Pequot Press Inc, USA

Bradt GUIDES
TRAVEL TAKEN SERIOUSLY

AUTHOR

Laurence Phillips (w laurencephillips.com) has been escaping to France since childhood and has written many and varied guides to the country, including the updated Lazy France guide *Marseillan and a Lot of Languedoc* and a companion to Robert Louis Stevenson's classic *Travels With a Donkey in the Cevennes*. He has been described by the French press as a charming *bon vivant* and by British critics as a witty and entertaining enthusiast. His passion for all things French has fuelled countless BBC radio broadcasts, including Radio 4's *Allez Lille*, and his has been a familiar voice on travel and arts programmes. In France, he has been honoured as a Commander of the Order of St Nectaire cheese and a Squire of the Confrérie des Sacres de la Champagne (although for the latter citation he was inscribed as Madame Laurence Phillips, which possibly makes him a Dame). Three-times winner of the prestigious Guide Book of the Year award from the British Guild of Travel Writers, including laurels for this book, he combines wanderlust with a love for theatre and work as a critic, playwright and songwriter, and has written for the Royal Shakespeare Company. His stage work has clocked up more travel miles than the author, being performed on four continents, from the West End to the South Pacific.

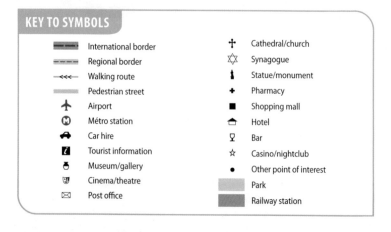

KEY TO SYMBOLS

▬▬▬	International border	✝	Cathedral/church
▬ ▬ ▬	Regional border	✡	Synagogue
◄◄◄	Walking route	⚲	Statue/monument
▬▬	Pedestrian street	✚	Pharmacy
✈	Airport	■	Shopping mall
Ⓜ	Métro station	⌂	Hotel
🚗	Car hire	♀	Bar
ℹ	Tourist information	☆	Casino/nightclub
🏺	Museum/gallery	●	Other point of interest
🎭	Cinema/theatre		Park
✉	Post office		Railway station

Fifth edition published September 2024
First published 2004
Bradt Travel Guides Ltd
31a High Street, Chesham, Buckinghamshire, HP5 1BW, England
www.bradtguides.com
Print edition published in the USA by The Globe Pequot Press Inc,
PO Box 480, Guilford, Connecticut 06437-0480

Text copyright © Laurence Phillips, 2024
Maps copyright © Bradt Travel Guides Ltd, 2024; includes map data ©
OpenStreetMap contributors
Métro map copyright © UrbanRail.net (R Schwandl), 2014
Photographs copyright © Individual photographers (see below), 2024
Project Manager: Elspeth Beidas
Cover research: Pepi Bluck, Perfect Picture

ISBN: 9781804691014

British Library Cataloguing in Publication Data
A catalogue record for this book is available from the British Library

Photographs © individual photographers and organisations credited beside images;
picture libraries credited as follows: Alamy.com (A); Dreamstime.com (D); Hauts-de-
France Tourisme (HDFT); Shutterstock.com (S)

Front cover Vieille Bourse (Hemis/A)
Back cover, clockwise from top left Citadelle (MisterStock/S); Euralille (MisterStock/S);
mussels being cooked at the Braderie (MisterStock/S); La Piscine, Roubaix (Laurent
Javoy/Hello Lille)
Title page, clockwise from top left The Christmas big wheel on Grand' Place
(Prosiaczeq/D); baguettes at Paul (SuperStock); pont de la Citadelle (world8/S);
La Vieille France *estaminet* (Maria Studio/S)

Maps David McCutcheon FBCart.S. FRGS

Typeset by Ian Spick, Bradt Travel Guides
Production managed by Gutenberg Press Ltd; printed in Malta
Digital conversion by www.dataworks.co.in

Paper used for this product comes from sustainably managed forests, recycled and
controlled sources.

ACKNOWLEDGEMENTS

Special thanks to my dining partners in Lille for letting me reveal their secret tourist-free tables; to those generous readers who emailed me with their own stories of this special city; to Vera Dupuis, her heirs and successors, especially Bruno Cappelle (later at the Louvre-Lens), Audrey Chaix and Sélic Lenne for their unstinting support; and to Delphine Bartier, formerly at the late lamented CDT Nord and her colleagues in the wider Hauts-de-France region, including Benoit Guilleux; to the editorial team at Bradt for reining in my ramblings, airbrushing my grammar and granting me the illusion of fluency; to my family and friends for bearing with me as I disappeared on yet another culinary and cultural expedition; and of course to my parents, Di and Ronald Phillips, for getting out the car and ferrying me from table to table, and wallowing in cholesterol when, as usual, the clock and the calendar said we'd never finish the infinite mealtime of summer.

DEDICATION

To Stéphane Fichet
who has had to endure my lyrical appreciation of so many fine meals,
without the joy of actually passing a fork from plate to palate!

LIST OF MAPS

Contents

• Citadelle

© Bradt Travel Guides Ltd

ZOO
page 215
In the grounds of the Citadelle, the zoo is an ideal (and free) family treat, and a charming digression from a country walk in the Bois de Boulogne.

Église
Ste Cathérine ✝

• Zoo

Jardin Vauban

BOULEVARD DE LA LIBERTÉ

CITADELLE
page 190
Louis XIV's classic five-sided fortress, built and governed by royal military architect Vauban, remains a working garrison standing in the city-centre park and woodland.

RUE NATIONALE

Église
Sacré Cœur ✝
RUE NATIONALE

Palais R

RUE NATIONALE

BOULEVARD DE LA LIBERTÉ

RUE SOLFÉRINO

WAZEMMES MARKET
page 176
If you miss the annual Braderie, then make sure you visit the Sunday flea market in a lively, up-and-coming quarter.

Palais des
Beaux-Arts

Wazemmes
Market •

RUE SOLFÉRINO

Église
St Pierre et ✝
St Paul

PALAIS DES BEAUX-ARTS
page 184
France's second museum after the Paris Louvre with Flemish, Renaissance and Impressionist galleries.

GRAND' PLACE
page 195
The main hub and social rendezvous where Vieux Lille opens out to the modern shopping district. The square is overlooked by a statue of the city's goddess.

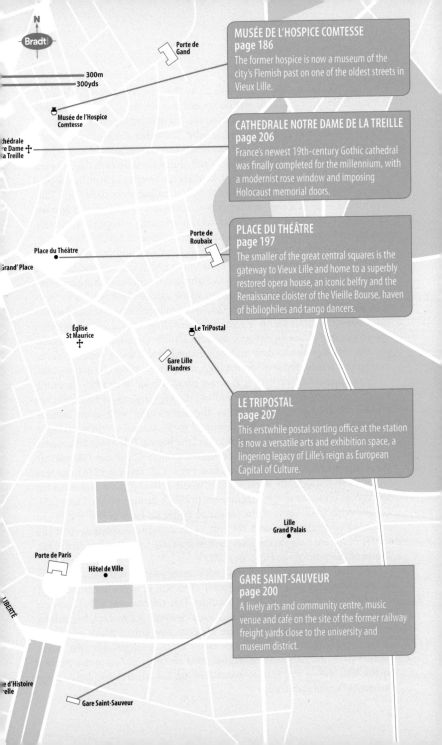

Bradt

300m
300yds

Porte de Gand

Musée de l'Hospice Comtesse

Cathédrale Notre Dame la Treille

Place du Théâtre

Grand' Place

Porte de Roubaix

Église St Maurice

Le TriPostal

Gare Lille Flandres

Lille Grand Palais

Porte de Paris

Hôtel de Ville

LIBERTÉ

e d'Histoire elle

Gare Saint-Sauveur

MUSÉE DE L'HOSPICE COMTESSE
page 186
The former hospice is now a museum of the city's Flemish past on one of the oldest streets in Vieux Lille.

CATHEDRALE NOTRE DAME DE LA TREILLE
page 206
France's newest 19th-century Gothic cathedral was finally completed for the millennium, with a modernist rose window and imposing Holocaust memorial doors.

PLACE DU THÉÂTRE
page 197
The smaller of the great central squares is the gateway to Vieux Lille and home to a superbly restored opera house, an iconic belfry and the Renaissance cloister of the Vieille Bourse, haven of bibliophiles and tango dancers.

LE TRIPOSTAL
page 207
This erstwhile postal sorting office at the station is now a versatile arts and exhibition space, a lingering legacy of Lille's reign as European Capital of Culture.

GARE SAINT-SAUVEUR
page 200
A lively arts and community centre, music venue and café on the site of the former railway freight yards close to the university and museum district.

How can you fail to fall in love with a city that erects a statue to a lullaby? Although the *Internationale* was composed in Lille, the song the townsfolk took to their hearts was *Le P'tit Quinquin*, a sentimental *patois* melodrama of a poor lacemaker and her weeping baby. The statue, ravaged by a million scrambled cuddles and kisses, is a working-class *Madonna and Child* to melt the hardest of hearts. The town clocks still chime the tune each day at noon.

For years, Lille was France's best-kept secret. Despite charming cobbled streets, broad Flemish squares and the richest art gallery outside Paris, Lille was tucked away in a coal-mining region, scorned by Parisians and ignored by tourists. Then came Channel Tunnel trains linking Europe's key capitals, and the city was reborn. Lille may have a population of barely 233,000 but, with over a million in the greater metropolitan area and literally millions more people now living within an hour of the city, it is an unofficial capital in its own right, deservedly chosen as European Capital of Culture in 2004.

Decades later, Lille2004 can be seen as the catalyst Lille needed to kick-start yet another renaissance: more than a dozen brand new and wonderfully inventive arts centres set up in remarkable buildings in and around the city; the reopening of one of France's most beautiful opera houses; a calendar packed with reasons to dine and dance until dawn; and a programme of performance, from Shakespeare to tango, to rival any capital city in the world.

Proof came with the very first street party. We all wore white as exotic images were projected on to the milling throng. Organisers had expected around 200,000 people to take to the streets and were quite frankly astounded when the best part of a million good-natured revellers managed to squeeze into central Lille. I tried to surf the human tide to see a thousand musicians perform the opening concert (Berlioz's *Chant des Chemins de Fer*, composed for the arrival of the first Paris–Lille train in 1846), but was swept away towards the main squares where artificial snow accompanied partygoers en route to the magnificent firework display by the Esplanade. *Les showgirls* (and boys) of the lamented Folies de Paris performed in the Chamber of Commerce, and the rest of us danced 'til dawn around the flames of square Foch, in the pink light of the Gare Lille Flandres and to the sound of *chansons* at the Hôtel de Ville.

That first year was punctuated with many such explosions of high-octane bonhomie and the theme-party tradition is now confirmed as an essential part of city life in the 21st century. Like the Maisons Folies, the new TriPostal centre, the now reinvented Saint-Sauveur goods yard, beautifully restored churches, and the promise of more new urban parks, weekends of merrymaking are the long-term legacy of an unforgettable year. Eight million party animals can't be wrong! 2004 certainly pulled in the punters to the last, with a respectable 300,000 filling the squares and beyond for November's final knees-up.

Then came the decision – the party was not over. Cue Lille3000 (page 208), a biennial mini-me to the original festival. From an opening season in 2007 that brought a million visitors to the city and India to Flanders – with the rue Faidherbe most memorably lined with elephants – it has continued to grow with every subsequent incarnation, now wooing 2 million sensation seekers every couple of years. Alongside this, international sporting events – from football and rugby championships to the 2025 Tour de France – provide further encouragement to flex the community's cultural muscles.

Even without an official excuse, a glance at the listings magazines promises hundreds of events any Saturday night, from national theatres and concert halls to smoky dives, film festivals and rock happenings. As for art, Lille can barely contain its national and international treasures: the cultural map embraces towns for miles around, and not just the outpost of the Louvre in Lens. Picassos and Braques have packed out the Musée d'Art Moderne at the Villeneuve d'Ascq campus for years; Roubaix's Piscine is home to a truly eclectic and thrilling art collection, worth a day or two of anyone's life; and Matisse's private pictures are an essential drive away at Le Cateau-Cambrésis. Tourcoing is now second home to the Institut du Monde Arabe. In Lille itself, museums include the Palais des Beaux-Arts, France's second collection after the Louvre, with its wickedly wonderful Goyas and splendid Renaissance treats, its deep-red walls and high ceilings being the perfect backdrop to a veritable banquet of masterpieces from the Impressionists to Rubens' majestic *Descent from the Cross*. Perhaps while away a weekend hour in a re-imagined natural history museum once quaintly dated with suspended skeletons and tableaux of taxidermy.

Elsewhere this might be the stuff of stuffiness, but in such a youthful and exuberant university town there is always a definite buzz in the air, the vitality of youth amid improbably quaint 17th- and 18th-century elegance.

Whether in Lille to meet up with friends, or just to celebrate your own special weekend; whether lifting a *bière blanche* in an *estaminet* or raising your fork in a Michelin-starred restaurant; admiring Old Masters in a museum or breaking bread with a young artist in their studio; among crowds packing Grand' Place on a midsummer night's free rock concert or listening to a chamber recital in a Baroque salon: wander, wonder and wallow in a corner of the world that has always been a capital city of culture. Let music follow your footsteps into history, let your taste buds tempt you from your chosen path. Let lunch segue into dinner, Art Deco streets lead you to the talents of tomorrow and the sounds of a lone midnight saxophone from an open window in the lamplight blend into a bedtime serenade in a city that, more than any other, knows the value of a great lullaby.

Laurence Phillips
e lolly@laurencephillips.com
X @LazyFrance

HOW TO USE THIS GUIDE

SYMBOLS These indicate the location of venues/sites/sights listed in the book:

🚇   Closest métro or tram stop, or other public transport

🍵   Entrance fee

◎   Grid reference

MAPS *Find the city maps from page 257.*

Keys Alphabetical keys cover the locations of places to eat and drink featured in the book. These may be found on page 263.

Grids and grid references Map grid references are listed in brackets after the name of the place or sight of interest in the text, with page number followed by grid number, eg: (◎ 260 C3). In the eating and drinking listings in *Chapter 7*, the map page number, grid reference and number of listing in the key is given as follows: ◎ 261 G4 ❶.

PRICES

Restaurants The price range included in this guide indicates options ranging from a basic set menu to indulgent à la carte. Where applicable, listings have a price code based on the average price of a three-course meal or, where a traditional three-course menu is not available, on the cost of a typical meal. All menu prices were verified within a few months of each other, so use them as a comparative guide. See page 90 for price codes.

Hotels Hotel room prices are based on the walk-in rate for a double room in high season. Prices quoted in the text were correct at the time of going to press. See page 66 for price codes.

LILLE AT A GLANCE

Location Northwest France, 45 minutes' drive from the Channel coast. By rail it is 35 minutes from Brussels, 1 hour from Paris and 1 hour 40 minutes from London.

Climate Average temperatures: winter 6°C; spring and autumn 14°C; summer 23°C. For weather forecasts, check online weather services or dial ✎ 08 92 68 02 59

Population 232,741 in the city; 1,085,199 in the greater metropolitan area

Language Predominantly French; also some Flemish. A composite patois Ch'ti may also be heard (page 251)

Religion Principally Roman Catholic; also Protestant, Muslim and Jewish (page 53)

Currency Euro

Exchange rate £1 = €1.19, US$1 = €0.93 (August 2024)

Time GMT/BST +1 hour

International telephone code +33

Public holidays 1 January, 1 May, 8 May, Pentecost Monday, 14 July (national day), 15 August, 1 November, 11 November, 25 December

School holidays One week at the end of October, two weeks at Christmas, two weeks in February, two in spring, the whole of July and August

1

Contexts

INTRODUCTION TO THE CITY

When French mayors go to French Mayor School, they all learn several key buzzwords. By far the most popular is the phrase 'Carrefour de l'Europe' ('The Crossroads of Europe'). The crossroads of the silk route, the wine route, the tin route, even, I presume, the beetroot route. Almost every town in the country claims to have been, at some stage in its history, at the crossroads of Europe. A well-known resort on the Atlantic coast once seized the honour in a triumph of civic pride over orienteering. With so many mayors declaring crossroad status, the historic map of the Continent must have resembled a particularly virulent tartan.

Pierre Mauroy, unique among his mayoral colleagues (and now immortalised with the original rue de Paris renamed in his honour), claimed the rank as a goal rather than mere heritage. Lille's mayor for 29 years, until handing his flaming torch in 2001 to Martine Aubry, Mauroy was most famously President Mitterrand's first prime minister. Like Mitterrand, Thatcher and Reagan, his was an iron will, and so, when the Channel Tunnel rail link was agreed, Pierre Mauroy persuaded the world that the shortest distance between two points was a right angle. Thus the Eurostar route was swung in an arc to create a new European hub. With a flourish of the presidential and prime-ministerial pens, Lille was transformed, Cinderella-like, from the depressed centre of a mining district with 40% unemployment to France's third most powerful financial, commercial and industrial centre by the turn of the millennium.

Mauroy's successor is equally worthy of the mantle that she inherited. Nearly a quarter century into her own reign, Aubry's socialist credentials are unquestionable: the blood of Jacques Delors courses through her veins; she was the firebrand who seared the cause of women's rights on the national consciousness; and she is still cheered to the gables during gay pride parties and cultural events alike. By managing to cobble together a left and centre coalition, she survived the political minefields of the local elections and retained control of the city despite the rise of Marine LePen and the far right.

But this corner of France, birthplace of the legendary Charles de Gaulle, has a tradition of social-reforming politicians. Jean Lebas, whose name

graces the principal street of nearby Roubaix, was a much-loved mayor of that town, whose valour in two world wars is still spoken of with reverence, as is his institution of paid holidays for factory workers, introduced when he served as minister of works in the pioneering government of Léon Blum. Lebas died a hero, deported by the Nazis.

Politically, Lille may be French, but it was most famously the old capital of Flanders. Perhaps the town's heritage, being variously and successively Flemish, Burgundian, Spanish, Dutch, French, German, French, German and French again, might have inspired Mayor Mauroy's ambitious vision to create the future of Europe in a town that had long been dismissed as a broken yesterday, arguing that in an era of Eurostar, Thalys and TGV, geography should no longer be determined by distance but by time. These days, Paris, Brussels, Amsterdam and even London might be legitimately classed as the suburbs.

And so Lille, best-kept secret in the world, with a current population of almost 233,000, became one of the great capital cities of Europe. She may not be the capital of any nation-state, but a morning, weekend or lifetime in her company proves without doubt that Lille is the capital city of life. With its high-flying business community and university campuses, Lille is where Europe comes to party. A former director of the Opéra de Lille once told me how (in the halcyon pre-Brexit era) he would nip between Germany and Britain to arrange meetings with soloists and musicians during the working day, and how he mixed and matched choruses, soloists and orchestras from around Europe. After all, he argued, audiences pop over from Cologne, Brittany and Kent; why not the performers? His successor doubtless agreed, and the first opera to be staged after the house's renovation was a co-production with the Théâtre de la Monnaie, Brussels's famous opera house.

The opera is not the only lure in town. With legendary Goyas, Impressionists and Dutch masters at the Palais des Beaux-Arts, a national theatre, ballet company and orchestra, not to mention scores of smaller theatres and music venues, Lille may offer a Saturday night sensation-seeker as much as any town ten times the size. Serious shopping, from couture to the flea markets, pulls in bargain hunters and the money-no-object fraternity alike. Good food, great beers, cider and locally distilled *genièvre* are the recipe for a legendarily good-natured northern welcome. I was not the first, nor the last, stranger to find myself lost in the old town, ask for advice in a bar and be personally escorted by the locals to my destination, with handshakes and good wishes all round.

Perhaps this attitude is born of Lille having discovered the secret of eternal youth. With estimates of up to 150,000 students living in both the town and the dormitory suburbs of the campus of Villeneuve d'Ascq, 42% of

◀ 1 Pastel-coloured houses in the charming backstreets of Vieux Lille (page 41).

2 Place du Théâtre (page 197) illuminated in all its glory.

the local population is younger than 25 (27% under 20). Every year brings a new influx of first-time residents to be wowed by the city, youngsters from all over France, and from Europe and beyond, studying at arts, business, journalism and engineering faculties. Lille hands over to these same *arrivistes* the responsibility of producing the annual *Ch'ti* guide. The *Ch'ti* (named for the local patois) is produced by the business school and is the most comprehensive local directory you will ever find anywhere. Each year a fresh editorial team spends 12 months visiting every establishment in town. With honest, often witty reviews of every shop, photocopy bureau, bar, club and restaurant in Lille and the metropolitan area, the *Ch'ti* is a veritable bible. Until a belated awakening during the mid 1990s, the guide even rated local red-light streets with details of nearest cash and condom dispensers. And prior to the Covid pandemic, *Ch'ti*'s spring launch came with a free music festival in the centre of the city – a two-day party. Check out the number of 'C' symbols on stickers in each restaurant window for an indication of the *Ch'ti* rating (C–CCCCC).

As such an international melting pot, it is sometimes easy to forget that Lille is also a real modern-day capital city. It is capital of a European metropolitan area that embraces the former manufacturing towns of Roubaix and Tourcoing and urban areas straddling the Belgian border. It is also capital of the sprawling new Hauts-de-France region (that merged the north with Picardy), home to the first new Louvre museum at Lens, the only branch outside Paris of the Institute of the Arab World in Tourcoing, and the royal and imperial court of Compiègne, with the Channel ports and tunnel only an hour's drive away.

Although the heritage of the region is generously displayed on the tables of Lille, this is also a country of tomorrows, with wonderfully ambitious projects breathing new life into the old mining district. Perhaps no more so than in Lille, where the uncompromisingly modern Euralille district stands comfortably next to the Flemish squares and Art Deco shopping streets. In other cities the grafting of a new high-tech glass-and-chrome futurescape on to an historical landscape would jar like UPVC double glazing on a thatched cottage or ill-fitting dentures in a favourite smile. Lille's newest quarter, from the old railway station to the *périphérique* ring road, settles easily by its classical neighbour. Architect Rem Koolhaas was given free rein over the transformation of 70ha of city-centre wasteland reclaimed from the army. His brief: to create a city of the 21st century to greet the high-speed trains. This continues to mutate into new business, administrative and conference districts with contemporary residential projects emerging each season in the hinterland beyond Euralille and the casino. Glass and chrome do not define all new architecture in the city, however – since the Maisons Folies projects and Lille3000 adventures (page 208), abandoned industrial and civic buildings are being redefined as exciting new public spaces.

This Lille Europe quarter is just one of the many welcomes that Lille showers on its visitors. If Grand' Place is forever on the verge of a party, Vieux Lille is a portal to times past, the Citadelle and Bois de Boulogne a living legacy of the Sun King, and the marketplaces of Wazemmes and Solférino the pulse of modern life.

Walk back towards your hotel in the late evening, tripping down the *pavé* of the old town towards the magnificent belfry, passing illuminated ornate scrollwork and carvings over the shopfronts. Look around you as crystal lights reflect a hundred diners, families, friends and lovers. Then surrender to temptation and head to brasserie tables or jazz cellars to steal another hour or two of the perfect weekend.

Lille, capital of the past and beacon of the future, has found her time. As any self-respecting mayor would say, 'Welcome to the crossroads of Europe.'

HISTORY

Lille is a European capital of culture. In its time it has also been capital of Flanders, belonged to the Austrians, Spanish and Dutch, been governed by the royal families of Portugal and Constantinople, and served as the ducal seat of Burgundy, 500km due south. As this guide went to press, it was French.

Nestling in a loop of the River Deûle and its canals, and cornered by Belgium, Lille, in the administrative *département* of Nord, is capital of Hauts-de-France. This new region (uniting the former Nord-Pas-de-Calais and Picardy regions) takes in the Côte d'Opale sweep of the Channel coast from the Belgian border, via the ports of Dunkerque, Calais and Boulogne, stretching past the resort of Le Touquet and through the cathedral city of Amiens and the battlefields of the Somme, reaching as far south as the 'Paris' airport at Beauvais and the Auvers sur Oise landscapes that inspired Van Gogh. It also includes the ancient areas of Artois, Hainaut and French Flanders. Always at the front row of history, this is home to Henry V's Agincourt, Henry VIII's Field of the Cloth of Gold and, more recently, those Flanders fields and the Armistice Forest of Compiègne of World War I. Vimy Ridge lies beside the town of Arras and Hitler's V2 rocket bunker, now a museum of war and space, outside St-Omer. Napoleon stood on the cliffs and planned an invasion of Britain (which never happened) and Louis Blériot looked across the same expanse of sea and planned his historic flight across the Channel. Lille has mattered since at least 1066, when l'Isle (The Island) was mentioned in a charter listing a charitable donation by Baudoin V, Count of Flanders, who owned a fortified stronghold on the site of the present Notre Dame de la Treille. At this time, Grand' Place was already a forum. In 1205, at the time of the Crusades, Count Baudoin IX was crowned king of Constantinople, and his daughters were raised under the protection of the French king, Philippe Auguste. The eldest, Jeanne, married Ferrand of Portugal. As the English and the Holy Roman Empire united with Flanders against France, the French captured Lille after the Battle of Bouvines, in 1214, and the city was given to Jeanne.

Throughout this time Lille had been earning its living through trade. The upper and lower Deûle rivers did not meet, so merchants from Bruges and Ghent, en route to major fairs in Champagne and beyond, were obliged to unload their barges and push carts through the town centre in order to continue their journeys. This staging post evolved into a market town, and textiles and fabrics changed hands, the city even giving its name to some products: Lisle socks – ever wondered where that name came from?

In 1369, Marguerite of Flanders married the Burgundian duke Philippe le Temoin. His ducal successor Philippe le Bon moved the Burgundy court to Lille in 1453 with the construction of the Palais Rihour. Less than a quarter of a century later, in 1477, Lille was handed over to the Hapsburgs when Marie de Bourgogne married Maximilien of Austria. Since the Hapsburgs were as pan-European as you can get, the Spanish King Charles V took on the mantle of emperor and therefore Lille and the Low Countries were considered part of Spain.

Of course, it wasn't too long before France came back into the picture – a couple of centuries after the Hapsburgs first got their hands on the city. In 1663 Maria-Theresa of Spain married Louis XIV, France's Sun King, who, claiming his wife's possessions in northern Europe, set about protecting the dowry, with the great architect Vauban building the fortifications that we know today. The famous five-pointed star-shaped Citadelle and the residential Quartier Royal that dominate Vieux Lille were created during the golden era of construction that began in 1667. During its seasons of favour as a Royal Town, the garrison was governed by both Vauban himself and another swashbuckling hero, d'Artagnan.

This was not the end of the shuttlecock identity saga. From 1708 to 1713, Lille was occupied by the Dutch in a war over the Spanish succession and, in 1792, 35,000 Austrian troops laid siege to the town. However, Lille remained in French hands and took its rightful place in the agriculture and education revolutions of the mid 19th century, with the completion of the main railway line to Paris in 1846 and Louis Pasteur becoming first dean of the Faculty of Science in 1854 (page 189).

In July 1888, a local wood-turner, Pierre Degeyter, embodied Lille's spirit of social reform and revolution when, in the long-demolished Bar La Liberté in the old Saint-Sauveur district, he sang for the very first time the music that he had composed for Eugène Pottier's socialist anthem *L'Internationale*, a song that in the century to come would change the world forever.

---

1 The modern Euralille district is the city's newest quarter. 2 Beer is a key element of the warm northern welcome. 3 The Palais des Beaux-Arts (page 184) is a bedrock of the city's thriving arts scene. 4 Lille's five-pointed star-shaped Citadelle (page 190) was built in the 17th century. ▶

In two world wars Lille held out against the invading German armies for three days, both in 1914 and in 1940. Some 900 houses were destroyed during World War I. During the Nazi occupation, the city's most renowned son, Charles de Gaulle, famously led Free France from London.

In 1966 the Communauté Urbaine made Lille the capital of a cluster of towns in the wider region, and in 1981 Mayor Pierre Mauroy became prime minister, laying the seeds of a public transport renaissance. The world's first driverless, fully automated public transport system, the VAL métro, was inaugurated in 1983; ten years later the TGV brought Paris within an hour of the city. In 1994, the Channel Tunnel Eurostar service enabled the new Europe quarter to become a continental hub. The 20th century ended with the reopening of the Palais des Beaux-Arts, France's second national gallery, and the completion (a century behind schedule) of the cathedral.

The 21st century began with Mauroy handing over the city to Martine Aubry and Lille becoming European Capital of Culture in 2004. With characteristic forward planning and boundless optimism, the decision was made to continue the celebrations long past the date that Lille relinquished the European title. Lille3000, a programme of biennial culture festivals, hit the ground running, with world-class arts events and grand gestures. The party is over, so long live the party.

MODERN LILLE

France's fourth-largest city and third financial centre, river port, medical research centre and industrial zone is an unlikely success story. The area was crippled by unemployment during the 1960s and 1970s when traditional mining and manufacturing industries declined, yet revived its fortunes in the age of the TGV. Until 2016, Lille was capital of the Nord-Pas-de-Calais region. Now it is the principal city of a vast super-region, Hauts-de-France, stretching from the Belgian border almost as far south as Paris, with a population of over 6 million across five *départements*: Aisne, Nord, Oise, Pas-de-Calais and Somme.

A legacy of centuries of textile manufacturing is the city's current status as the centre of Europe's mail-order industry. Lille is also the principal textile-trading area in France. There are more law companies based here than anywhere else outside Paris, and it is the second city for insurance companies.

By contrast, the city's huge transient student population, coupled with the region's socialist heritage, means that, unusually in a city with such a large business community, left-wing causes are very much to the fore. Even during recent elections, thanks to some creative alliances with moderate-centre parties, Lille managed to avoid the swing to the far right that affected many other towns and cities in France. Regular marches, protests and rallies criss-cross the city, from Hôtel de Ville to Grand' Place and the stations, sometimes with a carnival air about them.

THE FUTURE

A green park for the centre of Lille itself and the reinvention of an abandoned railway yard brought a breath of fresh air to a former city car park, and Maisons Folies (page 210) continue to rejuvenate towns across the region. The slag-heaps of these old mining communities first grabbed the popular imagination as a year-round ski resort, then took on a near-Parisian cachet as nearby Lens, previously only really known for its Sang et Or football team, was plucked from obscurity to open France's second Louvre museum (page 238). This satellite of the world's most famous museum now houses up to 700 of the nation's greatest art treasures in a rule-breaking exhibition space folded into the landscape of the former Théodore Barrois pit-head: the northern talent for reinvention continues apace. In Lille itself, the neglected southern quarters behind the conference and casino district have been reborn with new open spaces and attractions and a grimy goods yard in the city centre has evolved into the St-So district, centre of bustling life. The next new public space to emerge in the heart of town may yet be the stunning Chamber of Commerce building under the iconic belfry by the main squares – signature venue of many an arts festival. The *Gault&Millau* gastro guide's early predictions that the next generation of great chefs will emerge from the cobbles of Vieux Lille have proved deliciously correct. Don't forget to bring an appetite for fine food, convivial drinking and, above all, life itself.

2

Planning

SUGGESTED ITINERARIES

Also check out the city overview on page 41 before deciding where to stay/planning an itinerary.

IF YOU ARE STAYING ONE DAY
- Walk through Vieux Lille
- Have a coffee or meal on the main squares
- Treat yourself to an excellent lunch
- Spend at least an hour at the Palais des Beaux-Arts
- Stroll round the Vieille Bourse
- Go shopping: the old town for something special; the streets around Grand' Place or Euralille for more practical purchases
- Taste a selection of freshly brewed beers at Les Trois Brasseurs before catching the train home

IF YOU ARE STAYING TWO DAYS
Day one
- Vieux Lille – and the Musée de l'Hospice Comtesse
- The Palais des Beaux-Arts
- Browse the bookstalls at the Vieille Bourse
- Wander through the magnificent churches
- Start your evening on Grand' Place and enjoy a performance at the opera, theatre or jazz club before hitting the late-night bars
- Have at least one bistro or brasserie meal with a local beer, and indulge yourself with a gastronomic treat at one of the gourmet restaurants

Day two
- Start the second day with breakfast at Paul or a walk in the Bois de Boulogne
- Shop for bargains: midweek at Roubaix discount outlets; Sunday morning at Wazemmes market

- Explore the wider district for half a day: take the train to Lens for the amazing new Louvre, or tram to Roubaix and La Piscine, or perhaps the modern art collection at Villeneuve d'Ascq
- Or simply visit the smaller museums back in Lille itself, such as the Maison Natale Charles de Gaulle, or catch an event or exhibition at one of the Maisons Folies

IF YOU ARE STAYING THREE DAYS OR MORE Do all of the above, but give yourself a full day away from central Lille to discover the attractions of the Métropole. Perhaps you might hire a car to visit Le Cateau-Cambrésis to see Matisse's own art collection and home movies. Or walk through the trenches and see the Canadian National Memorial at Vimy Ridge. Or travel further south to the many sites of the Battle of the Somme, or cathedral cities in Picardy, such as Amiens. If your French is up to it, do take yourself to the theatre or a cabaret show.

And, if your visit includes a summer Sunday, do not miss the tango at the Vieille Bourse (page 202).

TOURIST INFORMATION

Before leaving home, visit w france.fr which links to the French national tourist office in your own country. There are also regional tourist offices (see below), so do check these if you are looking to explore Lille's surroundings. For details of the tourist office in Lille itself, see page 49.

Hauts-de-France
w hautsdefrancetourism.com. For information on the wider region (including themed package breaks & battlefield tours).

Pas-de-Calais w pas-de-calais-tourisme. com. For information on tourism & travel in the neighbouring *département* of Pas-de-Calais.

RED TAPE

European Union (EU) nationals need carry only a valid identity card or passport. For nationals of non-EU countries, including the UK, passports are required. Nationals of some countries require visas. Check with the nearest embassy or consulate when planning your trip (taking into account the time it may take for visas to be issued).

Following Brexit, UK citizens are now considered third-country nationals and face more restrictions to travel. This includes being limited to a maximum of 90 days within the Schengen area of the EU in any 180 day period. UK passports may also now only be used for travel up to 3 months before the tenth anniversary of issue, so a renewed passport carrying an extra 6 months from a previous passport may be invalid in the EU nine months before its official expiration – so do check before your trip. Note that,

Lille2004 was merely a shop window for a city with a talent for late-night partying. Several themed weekends inaugurated for the festivities have become regular events, and each year sees a string of *incontournables* – the unmissable happenings that make the perfect excuse for a trip to Lille.

JANUARY

Big Wheel on Grand' Place Until mid-Jan. Lingering legacy of the Christmas market.
January sales Mid-Jan–mid-Feb. Dates & authorised discounts announced by the government.
Hip Open Dance Festival w flow.lille.fr. Hip-hop dance festival.

FEBRUARY

Lillarious w lillarious.com. Comedy festival.

MARCH

SériesMania w seriesmania.com. TV drama box sets convention.
Jazz En Nord Marq-en-Baroeul w jazzenord.com
Lille Half Marathon w semimarathon-lille.fr

APRIL

European Cinema Festival w eurofilmfest-lille.com
Paris–Roubaix cycle race w letour.com/paris-roubaix
Fortified towns open day Lille's Citadelle & other walled towns of the region open their doors to the public.
Waka Afro-urban dance festival.

MAY

La Louche d'Or w lalouchedor.com. Soup festival in Wazemmes.

Wazemmes l'Accordéon w flonflons. eu. International accordion festival.
Nuit des Musées Late-night museum weekend.
Armistice Day 8 May, VE Day.

JUNE

Lille Piano Festival Mid-Jun w lillepianosfestival.fr
Lille Pride Weekend w lillepride.fr. Fun across the city with free concerts.
Fête de la Musique 21 Jun. Musical events take place throughout Lille.

JULY

Bastille Day 14 Jul. Much partying in the streets as summer holidays officially begin with fireworks & dancing for the French National Day.
Summer sales Late Jun–mid-Jul. Dates & authorised discounts announced by the government.

AUGUST

Foire aux Manèges Fairground rides on the Esplanade.
Sunday evening tango at Vieille Bourse See page 202.

SEPTEMBER

Braderie de Lille First weekend. Europe's biggest market – see page 174.
Lille Short Film Festival w festivalducourt-lille.com

National Heritage Days Third weekend. Across France, private buildings open their doors to visitors for a celebration of history & heritage.

OCTOBER
Street Food Festival
w lillestreetfoodfestival.com
Tourcoing Jazz Festival
w tourcoing-jazz-festival.com

NOVEMBER
Bière à Lille Aka BAL w bierealille.com. 90-plus breweries take part in Lille's annual beer fest.

Circus Festival w cirque-lille.fr. Troupes & performers from all over the world come to Lille.

DECEMBER
Christmas market Browse the craft stalls on place Rihour or take a ride on the big wheel on the Grand' Place.
Braderie de l'Art Roubaix w labraderiedelart.com. For 24hrs non stop, artists come together to breathe new life into old objects – recycled wares can sell for anything between €1 & €300!

The Christmas market on place Rihour

BENOÎT GUILLEUX/HDFT

Planning RED TAPE

2

15

from the first half of 2025, citizens of visa-exempt countries, including the UK, USA, Canada and Australia, will be required to pay a fee and obtain an ETIAS travel authorisation (w travel-europe.europa.eu/etias_en) in order to enter France. A new Entry-Exit System (EES; w travel-europe.europa.eu/ees_en) is also to be introduced, to replace the requirement for stamping passports. Check before you travel.

Since Brexit, previously informal arrangements for bringing goods from France into the UK no longer apply. So, no more loading the car with supplies for a family wedding. Duty Free rules allow travellers 4 litres of spirits, 18 litres of still wine, 42 litres of beer and 200 cigarettes. There is a limit of £390 on other goods. Travellers under 17 have no duty-free allowance and must pay any taxes on wines etc. Duty may be paid online 72 hours before arriving in the UK – see w gov.uk/bringing-goods-into-uk-personal-use for more details.

Narcotics, some pornographic material, illegal drugs, weapons, live plants and ivory may not be carried across borders. Travellers visiting wartime battlefield sites (page 242) should be careful about bringing home souvenirs. When grenades or similar memorabilia are discovered by X-ray machines at Eurostar security, the entire Lille Europe station may be evacuated. For passengers already at platform level, this can mean being boarded on the next available train, no matter the destination. You might end up in Marseille or Paris instead of London. I found myself in Brussels when booked to St Pancras.

Travellers from outside the EU must take heed of duty-free regulations for importing goods into France and make a customs declaration and pay duty on items with a value of over €300 if arriving by car or train (or €430 by plane). Strict rules apply for bringing in food from the UK. For customs advice in France telephone ✆ 01 53 24 68 24 and in the UK ✆ 0300 200 3700.

If you lose your passport, contact your consulate immediately. Most of these are to be found in Paris, although Canada has consular officials in Lille (page 49). Replacement passports may be reissued in France. However, if you are travelling within the EU (even if not an EU national) you may, under certain circumstances, be allowed to travel without your passport, subject to discretion of the airline, carrier and immigration authorities, should you have acceptable photo ID.

TIME

From the end of March through to the end of October, Continental European Time changes from GMT+1 to GMT+2.

GETTING THERE AND AWAY

BY TRAIN Eurostar, from the UK, is a fabulous way to travel to Lille: 80 minutes from London St Pancras International. Each 400m-long Eurostar train can carry up to 560 standard-class and 206 first-class passengers from London to the heart of Lille in 18 air-conditioned carriages. Two train managers and teams of uniformed stewards look after passengers, welcoming arrivals and reminding would-be smokers that the entire train is ciggie-free. Two bar-buffet carriages, modelled on TGV bars, have space to stand and chat over a drink. Baby-changing rooms are at each end of the train, and there are toilets in all carriages. Pricier seats are spaced three abreast, one single, one pair; in standard class, two pairs. Groups of four passengers may book seats around a table. Be aware, not all standard-class tickets sold as 'window' seats are actually next to a window: around four places in each carriage are in fact against a solid wall. Regular passengers with a good book may not mind, but first-timers and anyone who thrills to a view will be disappointed, so do check that your window seat actually has a window, if only for the thrill of arriving back at the new London terminus. You should be able to change your seat online after booking if needed.

In late 2024, the three classes of travel were renamed: Eurostar Standard, Eurostar Plus and Eurostar Premier (business class). All fares are now flexible and tickets may be exchanged at no cost (other than difference in fare) as often as you like up to an hour before travel, and are fully refundable up to seven days before your trip. Premier tickets may be refunded up to two days after scheduled travel. There are self-print, save to phone/app and ticket-on-departure options for online reservations, while phone bookings incur a £12 supplementary charge. Eurostar Plus and Premier passengers enjoy more spacious accommodation and a meal served at their seats during the journey. For Eurostar Plus passengers, this will usually be a light main course and dessert with wine; Premier travellers may indulge in a three-course menu designed by chef-restaurateur Raymond Blanc, with welcome glass of champagne and a choice of wines served with the meal. The quality of onboard food is pretty good – an improvement on previous years. Vegetarian and other dietary requests may be made online up to 48 hours in advance. For an inexpensive upgrade from standard class, consider travelling with a tour operator since deals usually include hotel accommodation. You may also upgrade in one direction or find day-trip and weekend promotional rates. Bargain lead-in one-way fares can be found for under £40, but these are often snapped up fast and mostly available for off-peak travel.

Eurostar's first make-over, courtesy of France's pet designer Philippe Starck, restyled the carriages before the move from Waterloo to St Pancras and regular 'relookings' have punctuated the decades since. Crew uniforms have ranged from golden age purser style to an unwise dress-down look that muted the glamour that marked out Eurostar as special. The recent merger of Eurostar with continental operator Thalys saw original blue and yellow accessories replaced with navy and plum. Despite whims of fashion, onboard staff remain as professional, helpful and charming as ever. Most of the current fleet is made of the new e320 trains. These have extra facilities for travellers with disabilities (page 33), and variable seat pitches (even in standard class), adjustable by around 2 inches, to make journeys more comfortable for tall, pregnant or elderly passengers. A few original e300 trains have also been refurbished. Since seating and even carriage configuration is different on the two trains, should your booking be changed at the last minute, you will be reissued with a new ticket at the station. An extra 50 trains have now been commissioned to increase capacity.

There has been much talk of other train operators launching rival services from St Pancras International. However, in the short term, it is unlikely than any of these will stop at Lille. Initial interest is for non-stop capital-to-capital routes only.

A major casualty of complex Brexit border rules (page 13) has been the shutting down of two international stations in Kent. Ebbsfleet Station (off junction two of the M25 near Bluewater shopping centre) had a car park like a medium-sized continent, expressly built for Eurostar travellers. Ashford Station, close to the tunnel entrance, just 1 hour from Lille, opened to boost a local cross-Channel economy. When flooding cut off St Pancras from the international network over Christmas 2023, trains that might otherwise terminate at Ebbsfleet (20 minutes from London) could not be used. In 2024, Eurostar confirmed no services would run from the Kent stations for at least another two years due to border control complications. Meanwhile, MPs continue to lobby in Parliament for Ashford and Ebbsfleet services to be restored.

Likewise, a hugely popular direct summer service from St Pancras to the South of France, stopping at Lille for passport checks, was not renewed in 2020.

Eurostar and high-speed continental services from Paris, Brussels, Amsterdam, Cologne and other key European cities arrive at Lille Europe station, with some additional Paris services at nearby Lille Flandres. For onward bookings from Lille, SNCF, the French rail company, has online booking facilities (see opposite). Click the link for *prems* deals: discount advance-purchase tickets to print or download to your phone. Rail Europe also sells all tickets, and Interrail/Eurail offers passes for unlimited rail travel across Europe (see opposite). Note that French trains have dedicated compartments banning mobile phones.

Tickets Tickets may be purchased directly from Eurostar, as well as from SNCF and Rail Europe (which also offer internal European tickets for Eurostar's mainland continental services, French TGV and regional trains). Unless you are buying a package deal including accommodation, it is easiest to order directly online or by phone. The St Pancras Eurostar ticket office has closed, but you may still buy tickets in person from two customer service podiums just before the check-in desks at the Pancras Road entrance to the station.

Eurostar ☎ 03432 186 186 (UK), 08 36 35 35 39 (France) w eurostar.com. Book online, as telephone reservations are subject to a £12 surcharge (except for wheelchair bookings – see page 33).

Rail Europe w raileurope.com. Established in the US in 1932 & now running SNCF's international services, as well as selling tickets across UK & Europe & Interrail/Eurail passes for unlimited travel on Europe's rail network. This is the only option for buying through-ticketing from UK regional stations to Lille.

SNCF ☎ 36 35 (from France) or from abroad +33 184 94 36 35 w sncf-connect.com. French national railway operator.

Arriving at St Pancras

By public transport The combined Kings Cross-St Pancras underground station has several exits to St Pancras International – follow the signage for the Eurostar. By national rail, St Pancras's domestic platforms, mostly on the upper level, serve destinations north of London including Derby, Nottingham and Sheffield; on the lower level platforms run Thameslink trains linking Bedford, Luton, St Albans, Gatwick and Brighton, as well as suburban stations in north and south London. The HS1 high-speed line that sends the Eurostar to the tunnel also brings passengers from Kent on SouthEastern's Hitachi high-speed bullet trains. The East Coast mainline, serving all stations from Scotland and Yorkshire, has its terminus next door

ST PANCRAS

Returning to St Pancras is always an occasion. As the train pulls out of the tunnel that sweeps under the Thames and the city itself, the view across the regenerated lands of the King's Cross goods yards is a feast of promise. Note the Grand Union Canal with its basin at the new Kings Place concert venue, the protected wildlife reserve at Canley Street, the British Library compound, and the barcoded skyline of London, from the old Post Office Tower to the Gherkin and the Shard and the plinthed pyramids of Docklands. Reigning supreme are the Gothic spires of St Pancras itself. Glide through the new glass box of the station's extension to the splendid archway of the original Barlow Shed, ironwork now picked out in a British sky blue, the magnificent span perched on the warm red brick-and-white stone walls. For some passengers, the centrepiece is the lumbering statue of snogging giants looming over the platforms in chunky impersonation of a cinematic farewell. For me, despite the neon scrawl of a Tracey Emin embellishment, the station clock itself is the more potent symbol of the timeless thrill of arrival and departure, of the tender kiss of parting and the balmy embrace of return. And sculpture-wise, the more modest John Betjeman statue by the Champagne Bar holds the true spirit of the place.

2

at Kings Cross Station. West Coast trains arrive at Euston, half a mile along the Euston Road, from where you can walk or catch a bus or tube to St Pancras; bus stops are outside the front of the station.

Alas, Eurostar no longer offers through ticketing from local stations in other UK cities and towns. This was really useful, as it allowed passengers to take the next available Eurostar train should domestic trains be delayed. Fortunately, Rail Europe (w raileurope.com) still issues a single ticket from your local station in England, Scotland or Wales to Lille and beyond. Otherwise, you have to pay £44 to rebook the next Eurostar.

By car or taxi There is a pick-up and drop-off point on Pancras Road, right outside the Eurostar station entrance, and there is a taxi rank on the other side of the station on Midland Road. If driving to St Pancras from outside the London Congestion Charge zone, don't panic if the one-way system takes you across the Euston Road, rather than letting you turn right in front of Kings Cross in order to get to the Eurostar entrance on Pancras Road. Stick with the directions, cross the main road to turn after the former Scala cinema and you will not be charged! There is an underground car park if you are in no rush to leave.

Station maps and more information can be found at w stpancras.com.

Onboard meals Eurostar Plus and Premier travellers' meals are served at their seats (page 17) and, for all passengers, there is a Eurostar Café buffet car offering a range of hot and cold snacks. An alternative to the trek to the food counter for those encumbered with luggage, small children or delicious lethargy is an onboard picnic. St Pancras International station boasts two Marks & Spencer food stores, offering a range of salads, snacks, sandwiches and sushi. A tip: when the branch opposite the Eurostar check-in is busy, nip along to the larger M&S store (next to Boots the Chemist) at The Circle by the domestic section of the station. A smaller selection of snacks is available from Boots. For more upmarket picnicking, Fortnum & Mason's tea shop on the ground floor concourse (page 22) sells its famous hamper travel baskets. There is also a branch of Waitrose at King's Cross station over the road. For a similar treat on the return journey, Lille's Carrefour hypermarket (page 177) is located just across the parvis François Mitterrand from the station. As well as obvious pâtés, cheeses, breads and sandwiches, this store has platters of prepared crudités and dips as a healthy option – at the back of the food hall, by the fresh veg. Otherwise, pick up sandwiches, sushi and snacks from any of the metro-mini-supermarkets in the city. Do make sure that food on your outward journey complies with Brexit rules. Since the UK opted out of EU

◀ 1 & 2 London's St Pancras station makes a glamorous departure point for the Eurostar to Lille.

St Pancras International is a true destination station in its own right. It lives up to its dramatic architecture and, appropriately for the UK's premier link to mainland Europe, this is a continental-style *Grande Gare*. Just as Paris's Gare de Lyon has its celebrated *belle époque* Le Train Bleu restaurant, so St Pancras has four flagship dining places – the Midland Grand Dining Room in the revived and reopened St Pancras Hotel and, on the station concourse, the old Booking Office, Searcey's St Pancras Brasserie and the already legendary **Champagne Bar**. The latter encompasses around 100m of fizz, with a breathtaking selection of champagnes, from a £16 glass of house brut to a Dom Pérignon White Gold 1995 at £6,500 a jeroboam. Naturally, the Grand Terrace setting along a stretch of platform is impressive. Spectacular railway-cathedral architecture soaring above the Barlow Shed, restored in all its 19th-century glory, is a perfect setting for toasting a journey, turning travel into an occasion. An all-day menu features the obvious indulgent accompaniments to bubbly. Here, even without an onboard upgrade, you can start your trip to Lille with flair: perhaps a full English afternoon tea of sandwiches, scones, cake and nice pot of Darjeeling with a glass of bubbly.

While the Champagne Bar has its all-day menu, its sister **St Pancras Brasserie** is the choice for hearty appetites, with full breakfast menus starting around £20 (champagne versions almost twice the price). Romantics might opt for the full caviar, salmon and champers for €135 for two. There's also Sunday brunch with jazz at £65 each.

Once the main Gilbert Scott-designed building was returned to its majestic splendour as one of Britain's greatest ever railway hotels, the St Pancras Hotel restaurant was named in the architect's honour by starry chef Marcus Waring. Covid saw an end to the Waring regime, however, and the brasserie restaurant has since been re-baptised as the **Midland Grand Dining Room**, serving set menus under £40 and à la carte around double that. The other upmarket brasserie, **Booking Office 1869**, is housed in the original Gothic booking hall, with almost ecclesiastical wooden ticket offices and celebrated russet brickwork. Here, lavish main courses are in the £20–50 range, while the buffet breakfast costs £25 and sundry eggy mains around £20.

A newer and more affordable option is **The Hansom**, the hotel's lounge restaurant, reclaimed from the original cobbled courtyard where Victorian arrivals would once have hailed a horse-drawn cab. Here, between the iconic external walls of the old building, order fish and chips or beef shin ravioli for £22.

For a flavour of the quarter itself, rather than the anticipation of travel (remember, St Pancras has always been the blurred boundary of King's Cross and Bloomsbury), the original station pub from the terminus's humbler days retains a local feel. Now known as The **Betjeman Arms** (after the poet, Sir John, who long campaigned for the station's preservation and whose statue by Martin Jennings is far more evocative of the spirit of the place than the Brobdingnagian lovers under the clock), it serves British gastro-pub grub to international sports fans and locals on match days. Enjoy pretty tasty food and a top wine list – plus good views across Pancras Road, just like those from the business class lounge for privileged travellers.

Also on the upper concourse, behind the famous statue of the lovers kissing, are a branch of Carluccio's Italian restaurant and MI+ME, which serves gourmet burgers and milkshakes. In the lower level Circle shopping area are Yo Sushi, the Japanese conveyor-belt eatery, and two branches of coffee shops familiar from the streets of Lille: Le Pain Quotidien (by Eurostar Arrivals) and Paul (opposite the sushi bar). The newest *petit-dejeunererie* here is **The Breakfast Club** (opposite Eurostar Departures), just yards from where a real greasy spoon once served carbs to cabbies. The first station branch of the uber-trendy 'traditional' caff chain offers a Full English fry-up at around £17, avocado on toast for a tenner and a vegetarian shakshouka at £13. Should your pre-travel routine involve a truly British cup of tea with all the requisite daintiness, stop off at **Fortnum & Mason** on the ground floor, where an all-day menu also offers authentic Welsh rarebit (before you experience the ubiquitous Lille brasserie reinvention) and you might even buy a classic wicker food hamper for your journey – subject to Brexit food rules, of course (page 16).

At least a dozen other cafés and food outlets may be found on the main St Pancras International concourse. And even a takeaway coffee may be enjoyed around the public pianos, including one right by Eurostar arrivals and departures. Alternatively, cross Pancras Road to King's Cross Station to indulge in a range of superb eateries, from the station hotel brasserie to pizza chains and more, at the vast and impressive food court.

Betjeman Arms Upper Concourse 020 3040 7158 w thebetjemanarms.co.uk
The Booking Office 1869 Upper Concourse 0207 7841 3566 w booking-office.co.uk
Fortnum & Mason Ground floor main concourse 020 7734 8040 w fortnumandmason.com
The Hansom St Pancras Renaissance Hotel 0207 7841 3566 w thehansom.co.uk

Midland Grand Dining Room St Pancras Renaissance Hotel 0207 7341 3000 w midlandgranddiningroom.com
Searcys St Pancras Grand Brasserie & Champagne Bar Upper Concourse 0207 870 9900 w stpancrasbysearcys.co.uk

food standards in April 2024, British dairy and meat products, including sandwiches, may be confiscated by the authorities.

Cash and carry St Pancras International sites most of its facilities before Eurostar check-in, so left luggage and bureau de change should be checked out in the main station, where a bigger range of shops includes Fortnum & Mason, John Lewis, Hatchards and Hamleys, as well as a wide range of perfume, fashion and high street outlets, from Boots and WHSmith to Marks & Spencer. Europe's longest champagne bar, more than a dozen restaurants (page 22) and pub grub, burgers and lighter options are also 'landside'. Free Wi-Fi is available across the station.

Eurostar's terminal is housed in the exquisitely reconceived undercroft of the splendid Victorian Gothic station. The restoration work is simply stunning, especially to those of us former 'locals' who recall this area from evening dog walks as the province of taxi repair shops and earthy greasy spoon caffs. The departure lounge has its own café and restaurant-bar, Wi-Fi and a bank of workstations. As well as books, magazines and newspapers, you may buy last-minute greetings cards at WHSmith to post in the mail box at the information desk.

Holders of top level Eurostar frequent traveller cards, AmEx or Business class tickets have an excellent private lounge with complimentary refreshments, juice-bar, newspapers and mobile phone chargers.

Passport control, customs and security Eurostar terminals run passenger security screening similar to that found at airports. Early plans for onboard passport inspections were overtaken by more traditional checks at the station. Newer changes to immigration rules since Brexit mean it takes much longer to pass through immigration and passport checks, due to the new UK Entry/Exit System (EES) and ETIAS visa waiver scheme (page 13). The original 30 minutes before departure check-in time was scrapped in 2024, with the introduction of facial and fingerprint scanning booths for non-EU travellers. These may be found before the check-in queues at St Pancras. The more complex processes mean check-in should now be around 90 minutes before departure – longer at peak times. Biometric control gates have been installed for those who have already been scanned, but visa and waiver checks still take time. Even before the EES booths arrived, extra time required for pre-boarding procedures meant fewer seats available for sale on each train (well over 100 empty places) in order to meet timetable demand. So do check with Eurostar when to check in. Two cases and one extra piece of hand luggage are allowed per person. Knives and other restricted items must be registered before travel.

BY CAR From Great Britain you must cross the Channel or the North Sea, either by boat or through the Channel Tunnel on Le Shuttle. Most ferries ply the busy route from Dover to Calais, with journey times averaging 90 minutes; the tunnel claims a 35-minute crossing on the same route. However, you must also allow for check-in times, queuing and visits to the terminal buildings. DFDS ferries run from Newcastle to Amsterdam (16½ hour crossing) and P&O ferries from Hull to Rotterdam (11 hours), each with a 3–4-hour drive through Holland and Belgium to Lille.

Best value is often to be found with inclusive hotel and travel package deals from tour operators. Otherwise, you can find bargain cross-Channel fares at w ferrysavers.co.uk and w aferry.com.

Cross-Channel operators

Le Shuttle ☎ 3443 353 535 (UK), 08 10 63 03 04 (France) w eurotunnel.com. Eurotunnel operates Le Shuttle Channel Tunnel service for motorists. At the terminal near Folkestone, motorists are directed to drive aboard trains that carry cars through the tunnel. Easy & by far the most efficient route, since you need not even leave your vehicle. Of course, ferries offer a wider range of entertainment, with restaurants, bars & children's play areas, but the advantage of the tunnel is the saving of time & effort. Wi-Fi in the terminal. Certainly, least-stressful option travelling with pets.

DFDS ☎ 0344 848 6090 (UK), 08 09 54 18 91 (France) w dfds.com. Regular crossings between Dover & Dunkerque with journey time around 2 hours, & Dover & Calais at 90 minutes. Newcastle–Amsterdam route (see above). Reliable online chat customer service enquiry option.
P&O ☎ 01304 44 88 88 (UK), 03 66 74 03 25 (France) w poferries.com. Biggest fleet & largest ships on Dover–Calais route. Round-the-clock service means passengers may turn up at the port & drive straight aboard. Also operates Hull–Rotterdam.

After the crossing From Boulogne, Calais or Dunkerque take the A16 then A25 motorways (signposted to Lille). From Amsterdam/Rotterdam, follow motorways A19 to A17. Remember, some Belgian motorway signs may list Lille by its Flemish name, Rijsel.

BY AIR In addition to the following options, flights to Brussels Airport connect with a rail link to Lille in around 40 minutes (page 61).

Lille Lesquin Airport w lille.aeroport. fr. For domestic & continental European & African flights, to & from around a dozen French cities & over 30 European destinations. The airport is 8km from city centre, with a regular shuttle bus to Euralille station district (page 61).
Roissy Charles de Gaulle airport w parisaeroport.fr. Visitors from UK regions or beyond Europe may fly direct to Paris's Roissy-Charles de Gaulle Airport

& take the 51min TGV train to Lille from the station within terminal 2B. Air France (w airfrance.com) sells TGVAir through-air/rail tickets to Lille from most international & intercontinental airports. Budget-conscious travellers may book a €10 ticket on the no-frills OuiGo train from the airport to Lille Flandres (54mins).
Beauvais Airport w aeroportparisbeauvais. com. Beauvais is technically within the Hauts-de-France region, with Ryanair flights

from Belfast, Birmingham, Edinburgh, Leeds, Bradford & Manchester. It's worth considering only if you plan to rent a car for exploring the southern half of the region, as otherwise the journey by rail to Lille takes more than 3hrs & means changing trains.

TRAVELLING WITH PETS

Dogs and cats with an EU-issued pet passport may still travel freely between Great Britain and France. However, while British authorities continue to recognise EU paperwork, since Brexit, only UK passports issued before 2021 are valid for travel within the EU. All other dogs and cats now require an **Animal Health Certificate (AHC)** issued by a government-licenced British vet no more than 10 days before leaving Great Britain. The animal must previously have been microchipped and vaccinated against (and blood tested for) rabies. The AHC is only valid for a single trip, returning to Great Britain within four months. The certificate will usually cost £200–300 per animal per trip, and additional charges for blood tests may apply. Specialist AHC services close by the ports in Kent may issue a certificate up to the day of travel for around £100 – search online for options. If you stay in France longer than four months, you will need a to get a separate **Great Britain pet health certificate** issued by an authorised EU vet within 10 days of arrival back in the UK. Different rules apply to travellers to and from Northern Ireland and the Republic of Ireland.

Most cross-Channel ferries carry your pets at a modest fee (usually between £20 and £30 for each leg of the journey) on condition the animal stays in the car throughout the journey. P&O has introduced an onboard pet lounge where you may travel in comfort with your dog (no cats) in a convivial bar area, with complimentary refreshments for you and an outdoor exercise area for your pet. On the DFDS Newcastle–Amsterdam ferries, you may choose the option of a private pet-friendly cabin. I prefer to travel on Eurotunnel's Le Shuttle, where you must remain in the car with your pets for the entire journey. Whichever way you travel, you will need to go to a dedicated pets check-in before boarding.

You may not travel with your pet on Eurostar, nor as a foot passenger on the ferries. However, there is now a private minibus service, Le Pet Express (w lepetexpress.com), that will take you and your pet across the Channel on Le Shuttle. Pick up and drop off at rail stations in Kent and Calais for a price of around £170 each way. You may sit next to the onboard cage, where your dog or cat will be kept during the journey, then continue by train from Calais to Lille.

Check with your hotel in Lille regarding policies and prices for staying with pets. And once in the city, bear in mind that only small dogs (in a basket or carrier) may travel on public transport.

For more detailed rules regarding travel for pets, see w gov.uk/taking-your-pet-abroad.

VETERINARY CLINICS

Clinique Vétérinaire Gambetta 80-82
rue Masséna ♀ 262 C1 ✆ 03 20 30 75 11
🕐 08.00–19.00 Mon–Fri, 08.00–18.00 Sat
🚊 République Beaux-Arts; rue Gambetta to
rue Solférino to rue Masséna. English spoken.

Clinique Vétérinaire de Lille St Maurice 112 rue du Faubourg de
Roubaix ♀ 259 K3 ✆ 03 20 06 58 20
w cliniqueveterinairelillesaintmaurice.
chezmonveto.com 🕐 08.00–19.30 Mon–Fri,
08.00–14.30 Sat 🚊 Gare Lille Europe/St-
Maurice Pellevoisin

HEALTH

No inoculations are required to visit France. Citizens of EU countries should carry an EHIC (European Health Insurance Card), available from post offices. This enables travellers to claim reimbursement of medical and pharmaceutical expenses in the event of illness or accident. UK citizens no longer qualify for the EHIC card, but a Brexit-era GHIC card, available via w nhs.uk/using-the-nhs/healthcare-abroad/apply-for-a-free-uk-globalhealth-insurance-card-ghic, covers emergencies and limited urgent medical care. Reciprocal arrangements for on-going or non-urgent treatment are no longer included. Holders of either card will need to pay up front for doctors' appointments, nurses' visits and prescriptions. Show your EHIC or GHIC and request the necessary paperwork for a refund when you return home. Generally, approved GP consultations cost around €25 and home (or hotel) visits by nurses €10.

UK and other non-EU travellers should arrange necessary private travel insurance before their trip. Insurance is recommended for all travellers (even from EU countries) to cover additional costs such as repatriation or extra nursing care.

Note that some medications legally sold in your home country may not be permitted in France. If so, you may need to bring a letter from your prescribing physician.

See page 53 for emergency phone numbers.

TRAVEL CLINICS AND HEALTH INFORMATION A full list of current travel clinic websites worldwide is available on w istm.org. For other journey preparation information, consult w travelhealthpro.org.uk (UK) or w wwwnc.cdc.gov/travel (USA). All advice found online should be used in conjunction with expert advice received prior to or during travel.

PHARMACIES Pharmacies are an excellent resource for advice on injuries and medical conditions and can provide lists of local GPs and nurses. They are easily identified by the green-cross sign and open usual shopping hours. Close to stations and the central area, you'll find three pharmacies along rue Faidherbe, and a smaller shop in Euralille opposite Carrefour supermarket.

On the corner of rue Solférino, close to the bars of Les Halles, the Grande Pharmacie des Halles has a dispensary open 24 hours a day, seven days a week (non-medical sales and services only during regular trading hours). Details of out-of-hours opening are posted in pharmacy windows, or may be obtained from police. Prescriptions dispensed after 20.00 may incur €2–8 surcharge.

Grande Pharmacie de France 12 rue Faidherbe ♀ 261 J5 ✆ 03 20 63 11 11 ⏱ 09.00–19.30 Mon–Sat 🚊 Gare Lille Flandres

Grande Pharmacie des Halles 99 rue Solférino ♀ 262 D1 ✆ 03 20 54 02 74 🚊 République Beaux-Arts. Pharmacy counter open 24/7.

Grande Pharmacie de Paris 1 pl de la Gare ♀ 261 K6 ✆ 03 20 06 20 64 ⏱ 08.00–20.00 Mon–Sat 🚊 Gare Lille Flandres

Pharmacie Casetta 35 rue Faidherbe ♀ 261 J5 ✆ 03 20 06 16 31 ⏱ 07.30–21.00 Mon–Fri, 08.00–22.00 Sat 🚊 Gare Lille Flandres

Pharmacie du Centre Euralille shopping centre (opposite Carrefour) ♀ 259 H4 ✆ 03 28 38 18 08 ⏱ 09.00–20.30 Mon–Sat 🚊 Gare Lille Europe

ACCIDENT AND EMERGENCY

Emergency Department (A&E) Centre Hospitalier Régional Universitaire de Lille, 2 av Oscar Lambret ♀ 262 B5 ✆ 03 20 44 59 62 w chu-lille.fr 🚊 CHU Eurosanté. The University Hospital Centre is a cluster of 9 hospitals on a large campus, with a 24hr emergency department at the Hôpital Roger Salengro within the complex.

La Maison Médicale de Garde de Lille-Métropole 24 bd de Belfort ♀ 259 J8 ✆ 03 20 87 74 33 ⏱ 20.00–midnight Mon–Fri, 08.00–midnight Sat, 08.00–20.00 Sun 🚊 Porte de Valenciennes or Porte de Douai.

Evening & weekend emergency GP doctor service. Close to local hospitals.

Service d'Odontologie Caumartin du CHU de Lille Pl de Verdun ♀ 258 A8 ✆ 03 20 44 43 55, out-of-hours helpline (18.00–23.00): 06 73 59 21 85 ⏱ 08.30–11.00 & 13.45–16.00 Mon–Fri 🚊 CHU – Centre O Lambret. Emergency dental services.

SOS Médecin 3 av Louise Michel ♀ 259 H8 ✆ 0826 46 91 91 (premium rate) w sosmedecins-lille.fr 🚊 Porte de Douai. Out-of-hours emergency medical assistance. Open 24/7; no appointment required.

WHAT TO TAKE

Apart from Marmite (and you'll probably find that in the '*cuisines du monde*' aisle at the supermarket), there is virtually nothing essential that you could wish to take that cannot be found in Lille. Perhaps the only exception is plug adaptors. Electricity in France is 220 volts; appliances use two-pin plugs. Adaptors are available from airport and station shops before travel.

1 The *estaminets* of Lille offer traditional home cooking. 2 A visit to the Palais des Beaux-Arts (page 184) can be afforded on most budgets. ▶

MONEY AND BUDGETING

CURRENCY The euro constantly plays dynamic games of cat and mouse with sterling and the US dollar. The single European currency is divided into 100 cents (sometimes referred to locally by the old French term *centimes*). Notes are valued at €5, €10, €20, €50, €100, €200 and €500. In practice, many shops may refuse to accept the three largest denominations – you can change higher-value notes at banks or supermarkets. Coins are worth 1, 2, 5, 10, 20 and 50 cents. A good way to get rid of too much heavy loose change is to use self-service cash checkout machines in supermarkets and fast-food outlets. All notes bear uniform designs featuring architectural images, but coins carry national emblems (monarchs' heads for Spain and Belgium, the Irish harp, sundry symbols of the French Republic, Leonardo da Vinci's works for Italy). No matter what the motif, all coins, like banknotes, may be used anywhere in the euro zone.

BUDGETING As befits a student city with exclusive shops, Lille may be savoured by all budgets. But how much money should you expect to spend? Of course, these prices do not include shopping for clothes, jewellery, etc. But that said, I have been as thrilled by an unexpected find at Wazemmes market as others have been at Bulgari and Cartier!

Rock bottom If you really want to keep your hand from straying into your pocket you can manage on as little as €75 per day – by staying at a hostel, eating one inexpensive set meal at a modest bar or restaurant and making your own breakfast. Bread costs around €1 a loaf; cheese, pâté, water and beer are quite cheap at markets and supermarkets. Don't use public transport – sit outside and enjoy people-watching on the squares and visit those sites that do not charge for admission.

Modest Expect neither hardships nor extravagances at €100 a day. Using online hotel promotions, a basic hotel room could cost you as little as €30 per person per night. Allow yourself €45 for meals, including a delicious set menu at lunchtime (when restaurants are cheapest), a *flammekeuche* (page 112) or *moules-frites* evening meal and a couple of beers or coffees around town. You'll have change for sightseeing and public transport.

Fun A daily allowance of €200 gives you a better hotel room, and budgets for a delicious lunch and a good brasserie or bistro dinner, drinks at cafés and bars around town and a good deal of sightseeing and travel.

Indulgent Spend €250+ each day, and enjoy a good three-star hotel room, a gastronomic set menu, a hearty lunch, a good day's sightseeing and an evening out.

Extravagant From €400 upwards you'll be able to afford a luxury hotel room, an à la carte meal at a Michelin-starred restaurant twice a day and as much shopping as the chauffeur can carry!

3

Lille for Visitors with Limited Mobility

Philanthropic may have been the adjective linking the centuries of Lille but, despite a tradition of hospices for the poor and needy, jumble sales for servants and retirement homes for Renaissance hookers, you can't get over the sheer ubiquity of the cobbles. Just as the *pavés du nord* play havoc with the bruised bottoms of thousands of cyclists each season, so those stones and steps lining the old quarter provide a challenge for wheelchairs, walking frames and sticks. No wonder one mercifully short-lived trend in the noughties was for oxygen bars with flavoured air pumped to guests through masks. Having personal experience of walking these streets with zimmer frames, rollators, sturdy crutches and canes before graduating to a wheelchair, I can testify to the awkwardness of the city centre (just try crossing the place Lion d'Or without catching your wheels between uneven cobble stones).

The wider city is not off-limits. It's replete with user-friendly central pedestrianised streets, well laid-out parks and flat access to cinemas, and most restaurants around squares and side streets have heated outdoor terraces in the off season. Shopping malls are well equipped, so a restaurant table near those or stations provides a practical alternative to the toilet problem.

PLANNING A TRIP

The national tourist office website (w france.fr) has some info: follow links via *Practical information*. Shamefully, its only official guide for tourists with disabilities has not been published for ten years. Advice from the

AVOIDING THE COBBLES

Best tip for surviving the cobbles: pick up the Navette Vieux Lille (page 57) on place Rihour, opposite the métro lift from platforms to street. Plan your trip in advance, and board using the ramp. NVL's circular route has stops within a couple of hundred yards of most destinations.

local tourist office is also limited, and at the time of writing there was still no comprehensive information covering all aspects of your trip. An earlier campaign, by the Association Tourisme & Handicaps (w tourisme-handicaps.org), launched a series of four logos indicating facilities for those with auditory, visual, mobility and learning disabilities; these symbols may still be found in some listings publications as well as on stickers at venues. All transport providers and most hotels have information on their websites. Be aware, however, that there is no wheelchair/scooter hire at Lille Tourist Office, so you will need to organise everything before leaving home.

GETTING THERE AND AWAY

BY RAIL Of course (as very few major organisations understand), there are many and varied limits and levels of mobility. Transport authorities often lump all differently abled travellers as 'wheelchair users'. It's easier to book trains or planes for a wheelchair user; persons of restricted mobility who may perhaps be able to walk a few metres on the flat with a frame or stick, but not climb into a railway carriage without a ramp, nor board a plane without level access, might face long interrogation and explanations as some booking clerks do not have a preordained keystroke on their reservation software that recognises a disability not involving wheels. Pack any official papers recognising your disability – UK travellers, laminate DWP award letters.

Eurostar's **St Pancras Station** is well equipped to support passengers with disabilities, with lifts to all levels and a gentle sloping travelator to platforms for those with powerful brakes. Customer assistance staff in light blue uniforms are on hand throughout the wider station. Eurostar travellers should request assistance at time of booking. With special fares for wheelchair users (and companion if required), this may be arranged when making telephone reservations (as with most transport operators, the telephone booking fee is waived for travellers with disabilities). Otherwise, booking online, choose your train, tick the wheelchair symbol from the eventual drop-down menus when selecting passenger numbers to ensure the correct discounted fares are displayed, book your ticket, then phone to confirm assistance. A second ticket at the same reduced fare is available to one travel companion/carer. A designated check-in/welcome counter is at the far left of the queue for departures; ask concourse staff to be fast tracked to this desk. With pre-booked assistance, you will be escorted through security and passport control to the departure lounge, then later accompanied to the platform, with ramps provided for boarding. Solo travellers should check in advance as to whether station staff are trained to push their particular model of manual wheelchair. A quiet waiting area in the lounge, close to the information desk, is reserved for passengers requiring assistance. At busier times you may be invited to wait in a peaceful corner of the business lounge.

3

Evolution of language when referring to mobility continues apace. In my teens, I would thrill to romantically heroic images evoked by the word *mutilé* printed above reserved seats on trains. For many years, *handicapé* was the universal adjective/noun. Today's correct terminology is PMR (*Personnes à Mobilité Reduite*). By the way, the French word *mobilité* has little to do with disability – it is a generic term for getting around and transport options.

Service at St Pancras has improved considerably in recent years. and is now up to the high standards set at Lille Europe station.

Onboard the train, there are two designated spaces in each Business and Standard Premier compartment. The newer e320 trains have the easiest turning circle, especially when preparing to disembark, and an adapted WC allows easy access/transfer for wheelchair users. Only passengers who can walk 200m without assistance may opt to travel in other carriages. In-carriage display panels are designed for visually impaired passengers. Always double-check that the requested ramp is actually in the right place on the platform at each end of the journey. Onboard train and platform staff are generally lovely, kind and helpful, and not at all patronising. Contact Eurostar directly for information (page 19).

In France, the excellent semi-privatised service Accès Plus has evolved as **Assist'en Gare**. The station assistance team will be on hand to meet your train at **Lille Europe,** with the ramp already set up. An agent will accompany you to the next stage of your journey or take you to the most convenient station exit. During renovation works, the central Voyageurs Handicapés desk was moved to a former lost property office in Hall 1 by a rear exit with no step-free access to and from the street – you had to use the main central lifts and then make your way to the back of the station. Happily, a new, fully accessible welcome lounge is expected to return in late 2024 to the main concourse by the Eurostar check in. Assistance for return trips should automatically be booked by Eurostar, but it's worth checking when you arrive in Lille.

Lille Europe has a good system of lifts to platforms and street – although be aware of two alternative exits from the station. Should the lift *down* to parvis Mitterrand/Euralille be out of order, take another lift *up* to viaduct level and walk/trundle back down avenue le Corbusier. The rear entrance from Hall 1 (parvis de Rotterdam) has no lift to/from street level.

Lille Flandres' Assist'en Gare desk is slightly harder to find. Tip: do not use the main station entrance, as the specialist reception is opposite platform 16, closer to the taxi rank entrance by Euralille mall on avenue Willy Brandt. Platforms are at street level and there are further entrances are on rue de Tournai and place des Buisses. Métro and tram access and the public transport information centre are all on lower level. Instead of the escalator, look for lifts from the station building or street. **Do not use** the Gare Lille Flandres exit from the first floor of Euralille. This leads to a footbridge with no step-free access to platforms.

If using any other trains during your stay, it's best to book assistance in advance, which can be done up to three months ahead. Otherwise, contact Assist'en Gare in person an hour before travelling to arrange help. Proof of disability may be requested.

Advisers can also help plan your journey, and even suggest alternative routes and facilities. A mini-boutique in the Lille Europe office offered a range of travel accessories from plasters to notebooks and condoms – refreshing to have our humanity recognised! Arrive at the lounge/reception 30 minutes before departure to be accompanied all the way to reserved seats on the train. Train managers will be informed of your requirements, and a team member waiting at your destination should you book onward travel in France. On TGV, choose a duplex train if possible and ask to be put in a lower-level carriage with an elevated floor. This mini-platform system makes for dignified and comfortable boarding in a wheelchair, with no need for a heavy ramp. If your train is delayed or journey disrupted, call the helpline ☏ 09 72 72 00 65. Passengers with hearing disabilities will receive an emergency number to text in the email confirmation of their booking. A videochat option for those who prefer to sign uses only French sign language, not BSL.

Assist'en Gare ☏ 3212 (in France), +33 (0)9 72 72 00 92 (from outside France) w garesetconnexions.sncf/en/customer-service/PRM-train-station-assistance-service ⏱ 08.00–20.00

BY CAR Ferry and Channel Tunnel operators are very helpful. Explain your requirements when booking (page 25) and arrangements may be made for your car to be parked onboard near a lift , with flat/wheelchair access to passenger lounges. Arrive an hour before departure. Le Shuttle is the easiest option, with no need to leave the car during 35-minute crossing. However, the train toilets are not wheelchair accessible, so use the terminal's facilities before departure.

BY AIR Let airlines know special requirements at the time of booking. Lille's airport has lifts and ramps for access to aircraft, adapted toilets and telephone kiosks, and supplies wheelchairs. There are ten designated parking spaces near the terminal.

GETTING AROUND

PUBLIC TRANSPORT The Ilévia website (page 57) is useful for journey planning. It has basic information for specific needs in English and links

to downloadable brochures; click *Réseau Ilévia* then *Accessiblité de Réseau*. The *infos traffic* link on the top right of the page has details of delays and any issues with station lifts. There's also an Ilévia app (page 57) that's worth downloading. And passengers with hearing impairments can download the **acce-o app** (w app.acce-o.fr/client/ilevia), which transcribes speech and offers live LSF (French sign language) video interpretation. Station staff wearing red gilets (Les Welcomers) are trained to offer assistance to travellers with mobility issues.

Métro and trams The métro system is excellent: level platforms and lifts from street to booking hall to platform level at every station. Double-width automatic gates allow wheelchair users access without waiting for assistance. On platforms, wait by the glass door with a wheelchair logo, as it indicates the carriage most likely to have space for your chair. Officially, wheelchair users have priority, though at peak times the carriage may be too crowded. Be prepared to wait for the next train or the one after. Ideally, prepare an alternative bus route as back up. All stations are announced through the onboard PA system, helpful for visually impaired passengers.

Tram platforms are fully accessible, though wheelchair users are advised not to use the two rear doors at Gare Lille Europe due to the gap between tram and platform. Sirens/flashing lights warn of doors closing.

Warning: do not try to use escalators instead of lifts if unable to climb conventional stairs. I was once stranded between platforms and concourse when a down escalator only took me partway to train level and there was no up escalator to return me to the ticket-office level. Two staff answered my SOS and a very slow and undignified rescue followed.

Buses All buses across the Métropole now have ramps and at least one wheelchair space (newer vehicles have two). Signal to the driver should you require the ramp (usually rear or central door); some buses have a blue button by the adapted door for passengers to summon the ramp.

At bus stops, wait by the yellow markings on the pavement indicating ramp locations. Passengers and drivers are very helpful when it comes to using your ticket or pass, and drivers often ask your destination stop to be sure the ramp is put out before other passengers use the doors. After 22.00, you may ask drivers to stop between official stops, at the most convenient point for your destination.

The Navette Vieux Lille bus is a boon if you find cobbles in the historic centre a challenge too far. Board at Rihour station (♀ 261 H6), then get on

◀ 1 The cobbles of Vieux Lille provide a challenge for wheelchairs, walking frames and sticks. 2 Pavement cafés and restaurants are usually accessible. 3 Gare Lille Europe provides assistance for travellers with disabilities on arrival in Lille. 4 The Opéra can seat guests with limited mobility at all performances.

and off at will, flagging down the bus anywhere along the route once in the oldest quarter. Be warned, though: minibus ramps are notoriously unreliable and on more than half the occasions I have tried boarding, ramps wouldn't work. Be prepared to wait 10 minutes for the next bus.

The airport shuttle bus has a wheelchair lift.

DRIVING AND PARKING Blue badges issued in any EU country may be used in France. Informal arrangements since Brexit allow UK drivers to park in designated bays, but you may still need to pay for parking. Print/laminate this French notice to display beside your UK badge: w disabledmotorists.eu/download/parking_cards/notice_france.pdf.

OVERGROUND RAIL Assist'en Gare (page 34) will help with train journeys across the region. As well as both Lille Europe and Lille Flandres, the service is also available at most town stations in the region including Amiens, Arras, Boulogne Ville, Calais Frethun, Calais Ville, Douai, Dunkerque, Lens, Saint-Omer, Tourcoing and Valenciennes. Ask about accessibility at rural stations before travelling. Passengers with OuiGo budget bookings (€10 to Disney or Roissy airport) should check if the booking is for a TGV or *classique* train – *classsique* is not wheelchair accessible.

ACCOMMODATION

In France, the definition of accessible hotel rooms can be flexible. I booked a room 500km south of Lille, fully adapted with handrails in the en suite and other international standard facilities. However, it was on an upper floor with no lift. Assume most B&Bs and *chambre d'hôtes* will not be fully accessible unless specifically classified as such in official listings. Some self-catering *gîtes* in the wider region feature on the Association Tourisme & Handicaps website (page 33). Nonetheless, Lille has many adapted and accessible rooms. All new establishments are required to offer full accessibility – so no worries in the emerging quarters. However, even if they have not been granted the official label, chain hotels (eg: Ibis, Holiday Inn, Novotel) have reasonably accessible rooms on request and most can provide properly adapted accommodation. Remember to detail your precise requirements when booking, and do not be afraid to specify requests relating to your own situation. Many apartment and suite options (and most new or converted hotels) have wet-room bathing options with no step to the shower. One slightly older hotel provided a wide enough bathroom in a standard room, yet the WC was so impractical that I had to use facilities at the nearby station. Some rooms may have extra-wide doors, yet no place for a wheelchair beside the bed for easy transfer. Do check for updates, since many hotels are undergoing a rolling programme of improvements.

Be warned that lifts in some older, taller hotels may not reach the ground floor. Extra questions to ask when booking include: does the lift run from street level to the room with no steps? Can it take a wheelchair? Is there flat access to the breakfast room? Some establishments, such as Calm Appart'hôtel (page 80) and Urban Hotel (page 78), have inventive mobile platforms to carry guests with disabilities up steps not served by the main lift. Always call to check on the day of arrival that this is not out of order. And be warned, some gates and front doors may be hard to negotiate from a wheelchair. The *Accommodation* chapter (page 65) has first-hand reports on particularly good facilities at specific hotels, but these ticked most boxes: Barriere (page 67), Citadines (page 80), Hilton (page 73), Ibis (page 86), Mama Shelter (page 75), Moxy (page 76), Novotel Suites (page 81), Okko (page 77), De La Treille (page 70), Urban (page 78) and Why (page 78).

EATING AND DRINKING

The annoying truth is that most seriously *gastronomique* addresses come complete with doorstep. But, if a helping hand with one or two steps can be arranged, nothing is impossible. Phone ahead to ask about access before booking; plenty of restaurants are worth considering (if you can cope without needing the loo). Pavement terraces abound and most listed restaurants and brasseries on squares will serve meals outdoors, many with heated terraces in winter or spring. The brasseries opposite Lille Flandres station serve meals outside, just across the road from the station with its 'facilities'. New food courts in shopping complexes also have access to adapted WCs, as do restaurants in or by hotels, museums or public buildings. A handful of out-of-town eateries have official access ratings but, again, a phone call will tell just how accessible a restaurant, café or club may be. Sometimes, there is just one step, but more establishments are now investing in ramps. I carried my own small lightweight portable ramps when reviewing for this guide. As ever, be warned: no matter how easy it is to get into an establishment in Vieux Lille, the cobbled street itself may still be the challenge. The *Michelin Red Guide* to France now features a wheelchair symbol indicating hotels and restaurants with sensible facilities/access for visitors with disabilities.

NIGHTLIFE

Underground cafés and cellar bars bring unique problems. Theatres and nightclubs often have a side entrance, however – as always, call in advance. The Opera house can seat guests with limited mobility at all performances (subject to availability) and has audio-described options for those with visual impairments. A complex network of lifts takes patrons through backstage and front-of-house for an escorted adventure between the booking office (only accessible entrance) and your eventual seat. Théâtre du Nord on

3

Grand' Place is also accessible, with a lift from the ground floor. A street-level lift and reserved seating is available at the Nouveau Siècle concert hall. Likewise, special arrangements can be made for audience members with disabilities at Zenith and Grand Sud concerts and arena shows. The Gymnase and Verrière theatres are also totally accessible, and the multiplex cinemas around rue Béthune are easy to use – just check the situation for individual screens before handing over your cash. Fortunately, many pop-up events and club or party nights take place in fully accessible public spaces, at converted venues such as the Maisons Folies or outdoors, with just the everyday trials of cobbles to cope with.

MUSEUMS AND SITES

New spaces, Maisons Folies, and recent conversions and renovations are mostly accessible. Sometimes a step-free route may miss out a gallery or take you past exhibits in a different order than usual. Older museums have their own challenges, but a phone call usually results in assistance viewing at least part of a collection. Sometimes, an alternative entrance is revealed. Request *parcours handicapé* itineraries for alternative routes through these museums (often featuring hidden lifts). Visually impaired visitors can contact museums for details of tailor-made visits, allowing hands-on exploration of exhibits.

Most sites and memorials relating to the World Wars have excellent facilities, usually designed around the needs of military veterans. Museum websites in our listings usually provide full accessibility details.

4

Practicalities

THE CITY: A PRACTICAL OVERVIEW

Lille has grown somewhat since its early years, when it was clustered around the site of today's Notre Dame de la Treille. First, Louis XIV built his fortress on a virtual island in the River Deûle and commissioned a residential quarter next to the old trading district. As it sprawled in all directions, the city swallowed up neighbouring districts – those quarters that still bear the names associated with their own histories. On maps you will see **Lille Centre** around the main squares, with the university-lined boulevards known as **Vauban Esquermes** stretching westward; to the south are **Wazemmes**, **Moulins** and **Lille Sud**; eastward is the **Fives** district; and to the north are **Vieux Lille** and **St-Maurice Pellevoisin**. The neighbouring communes of **Lomme**, **Lambersart**, **La Madeleine** and **Hellemmes** are now very much part of Lille itself.

Lille is surprisingly compact and very easy to explore on foot – that is, if you are wearing your sturdiest walking shoes rather than the stylish footwear sold in a dozen exclusive emporia in the hilly and cobbled old town. Even without using the excellent public transport system, you can cross from one side of the central area to another in 15 minutes. To make life even easier for readers, we have divided the centre of Lille into four easily distinguished zones:

VIEUX LILLE Vieux Lille is a very special place. It's all looming gables, cobbled streets, and intoxicatingly wonderful street names promising golden lions, hunchbacked cats or freshly minted coins at every turn. Since the principal roads were laid out in sweeping arcs to protect the long-forgotten castle on the site of the old castrum fortified camp, and many other streets were reclaimed from canals, no map will ever satisfactorily convey the geography of the place.

The first-, second- or even fifth-time visitor should be prepared to surrender to fate and banish any dreams of short cuts. Getting lost is among the greatest pleasures that Lille has to offer its visitors, with so many entrancing little shops selling antiques, fragrant soaps and sumptuous linens that every journey brings its own diversions. Don't try to second-guess the map: turning left, left, left and left again, may not bring you back to where you started. Vieux Lille is hilly, and with some streets reclaimed from canals, you may actually end up on a road 20m below the pavement you were expecting!

From central Lille it seems that all roads lead to the old quarter. The Parc Matisse may be the short cut from the station, and the Alcide archway on Grand' Place might seem an obvious entrance. However, the most comfortable introduction is from the rue de la Bourse by the distinctive belfry on place du Théâtre. A few paces lead to rue de la Grande Chaussée; an iron arm above the corner shop will point you in the right direction. Charles, Comte d'Artagnan, lived at numbers 20 and 26. Turn right along rue des Chats Bossus and admire the fabulous Breton Art Deco mosaic frontage of the former L'Huîtrière restaurant. Continue across the place du Lion d'Or to the 17th-century rue de la Monnaie. Named after the royal mint, this is the oldest street and has many of the original traders' emblems above the regimented shopfronts. Like the rues Royale and Basse, it wraps around the cathedral, following the line of the moat. Houses of red Armentières brick and white Lezennes stone have doorways adorned with cherubs, cornucopia and wheatsheaves, all painstakingly restored in the 1960s.

Rue de la Monnaie links the market square of place du Concert with the main hub of the old town, place du Lion d'Or and the adjacent place Louise de Bettignies. The latter was named for a local heroine, a spy who died at the hands of the Germans in World War I (page 216). Number 29 is the Demeure Gilles de la Boë, a handsome Baroque house dating from 1636 that once overlooked the inland port. Lille's name derives from its original position as an island between the upper and lower Deûle rivers, and the wealth of Vieux Lille comes from the thriving trade between merchants who plied the two routes between Paris and the Low Countries.

Furthest north of the town centre is the Quartier Royal, an elegant residential district commissioned by King Louis XIV, who fell in love with the town when the Citadelle was built. These roads were built to link the marketplaces of the centre with the fortress in the woods of the Bois de Boulogne.

The quaint narrow streets of Vieux Lille today feel wonderfully safe, with cheery multi-generational groups in animated discussion, well-dressed couples window-shopping arm-in-arm on the narrow pavements, and traffic insinuating turns at a snail's pace, ensuring the quarter's refined charm never slips into stuffiness. Mind you, the indiscreet presence of those who walk the streets for more professional reasons beyond the old Porte de Gand is

1 Place du Général de Gaulle is affectionately known as Grand' Place to locals. 2 Vieux Lille is a warren of cobbled streets filled with enticing distractions. 3 The district around the stations is the heart of the city's business community. 4 The Wazemmes quarter is centred around its market. ▶

a reminder that any town with a continuing military presence can never become too prissy! Decades ago, the kerbside trade in earthy encounters was the only truly thriving *métier* of the old town, but as Lille reclaimed its streets, art dealers and restaurateurs moved into the renovated buildings to create the enchanting realm of refinement that we know today.

Carnality on the plate and in the boudoir are not the only tastes catered for in this other world of 17th- and 18th-century houses and shops. No-one should miss the pretty pleasures of saying 'I wish' to the latest fashions on rue des Chats Bossus, and 'I will', 'I do', 'I can't help myself' to the unrivalled confections of Pâtisserie Méert on rue Esquermoise, just a whim and drop of the willpower away from Grand' Place.

GRAND' PLACE TO RÉPUBLIQUE Absolutely everything that matters in Lille begins on Grand' Place, from sunrise over Vieille Bourse's morning market selling uncut antiquarian books, to shirtsleeved lunchtimes on the terrace of the Coq Hardi. You will not find the name Grand' Place on any map or street sign – the square has long been officially dubbed Place du Général de Gaulle, yet locals still prefer its old, familiar name. The central column is a virtual sundial of life in the city. Carrier bags from FNAC and Furet du Nord rest on tables during the 'any time, coffee time' of a contented shopper. Afternoon rendezvous by the fountains flow into evenings at the Théâtre du Nord, its posters proudly proclaiming a new season of Shakespeare, Pinter and Molière. Bars, beers and bonhomie beckon from all directions, but the goddess standing on her central column draws everyone back for a dawn onion-soup breakfast at a late-night restaurant.

The square is bounded by performing arts, with theatre dominating the south side and, to the east, a picture-book opera house on place du Théâtre; westward, the circular Nouveau Siècle building is home to the Orchestre Nationale. Many weekends see displays or entertainment on Grand' Place itself. Perhaps a bandstand will have been erected for a concert, or a marquee set up to house an exhibition sponsored by the local paper, *La Voix du Nord*, whose elegant building dominates the square.

The main commercial districts of Lille fan out from Grand' Place, like a giant compass where all roads lead to shopping: chain stores, multiplex cinemas and boutiques, from traditional *chapellerie* to a magic wand emporium, line rues de Béthune and Neuve. Since traffic was barred from these streets in 1973, visitors have been able to admire Art Deco architecture above shopfronts in a pedestrianised triangle between the stations, place de la République and those city squares. Along rue Faidherbe, formerly home to inexpensive shoe and wedding dress shops, you now find grand pharmacies and chain restaurants; the wide rue Nationale has Printemps, the last Parisian department store still standing (page 178); and northward, beyond the once-upon-a-time perpendicular-style belfry of the Chambre de Commerce, hide the picture-perfect boutiques and galleries of Vieux Lille.

Walk along the wide, traffic-free shopping streets south of the square and you'll reach the Palais des Beaux-Arts – the very magnet that pulls the world to place République, providing an abundance of inspiration and fulfilment. How many visitors realise that the museum is but a gateway to the one-time Latin Quarter of Lille, a 19th-century haven of culture and learning? The boulevard de la Liberté was laid out when the original city walls came tumbling down in the mid 19th century. Named for the Empress Eugénie, this was an essential address for well-to-do families enriched by the Industrial Revolution. Textile barons and their ilk competed to build grand and grander mansions with grand staircases for grand gestures and grander entertaining, some with their own private theatres for after-dinner opera at home. The boulevard itself decants into Parc Jean-Baptiste Lebas, gateway to the revived Saint-Sauveur station (page 200), music venue and cultural melting pot, last vestige of the long-demolished Saint-Sauveur district and home to the early 20th-century Hôtel de Ville and its belfry. This is where old and new meet.

Place de la République itself is poised between the museum and equally grand Préfecture, which was based on the design of the Paris Louvre. Notice the emblems on each wing: an eagle for the Second Empire, the letter N for Napoleon III. At the centre of the gardens is a stepped arena, providing a stage for musicians and a well of natural light for the métro station.

MARKETS: GAMBETTA TO SOLFERINO Lille is a market town, never more so than during the **Braderie** of the first weekend in September (page 174). For 48 hours non stop, the entire city sets out its stalls on doorsteps, pavements, trestles and pitches. Recycle your children's clothes for a few pence, rediscover stolen goods from that break-in in May and swap Deco uplighters for 1960s lava lamps in a tradition that dates back to the city fathers granting servants the right to earn money by selling their master's cast-off clothing once a year. A hundred kilometres of stalls appear every year, the métro runs all night long, and every hotel room for miles around is booked months in advance. The Braderie never sleeps and brasseries compete to sell the most *moules* and create the highest pile of shells on the pavement outside the front door. A special map-guide is published to be picked up at the tourist office.

Since the event is held only once a year, a happy alternative takes place every week in the **Wazemmes** quarter, 15 minutes' walk or two métro stops from the town centre. This is the market of markets and a Sunday morning institution (page 176). A smaller food market is held each Wednesday and Saturday at place Sébastopol, where the Théâtre Sébastopol dominates the square. An entertaining explosion of architectural styles – Renaissance, Moorish, classical and sheer pantomime – this people's playhouse provides popular boulevard entertainment. From populist playtime one can turn to intellectual reflection, as roads south lead to the former Faculté des Lettres, once a centre of study, reflection and tolerance. The Protestant temple and synagogue may be seen on rue Angellier. While the secular university is now

ALIAKSANDR ANTANOVICH/S

OANDERSON/S

JORDAN TAN/S

based outside the town centre to the north, boulevard Vauban is home to the Catholic university campus.

Between the two city-centre seats of learning, rue Solférino, the centre of Lille's student nightlife, is the starting point for any serious partying (page 152).

STATIONS/HÔTEL DE VILLE Not one station but two. The 30-year-old Europe station looks like an airport terminal and welcomes both TGV and Eurostar. Dominated by the boot-shaped Crédit Lyonnais building, this is the heartland of a new international business community. The emerging Parc Matisse, constructed on land hived off by the military, is scattered with hints of early fortifications. The paved piazza of the parvis Mitterrand has been claimed by a generation of skateboarders, microscooter aces and mountain bikers.

Across the square is Euralille shopping centre, indoor alternative to the rest of the city. A few yards along, avenue le Corbusier is a public transport hive: underground are two métro stations and the tramway to Roubaix and Tourcoing, while at street level one finds the bus stops, taxi ranks and the original 19th-century station serving all points local and beyond, and all speeds under and over *très grandes*.

The older Gare Lille Flandres was Paris's original Gare du Nord, moved brick by brick and stone by stone for the railway line's royal opening. The town elders, not wishing to appear satisfied with the capital's leftovers, insisted on building an extra storey on to the station façade to create an even more imposing frontage. The first train to arrive at the station was greeted by the Bishop of Douai, who blessed the locomotive, and by Hector Berlioz conducting the town band in a specially composed concerto. Today, the place seems less grand, just the typical terminus hive of bars, cafés and eateries clustered around the fountains at the front of the station. Weekends see soldiers from the garrison flirt with students from the universities. After a while, the incongruous sight of a young lad with a sub-machine gun at his belt, composing text messages on his Samsung phone, seems perfectly normal. At the side of the station, on rue de Tournai, eating is cheap with *frites* and burger counters. Seamier services are available behind the line of brasseries facing the station, with flesh offered shrink-wrapped in cellophane in shops and in lycra on pavements around rues de Roubaix and Ponts de Comines. Flandres station itself has been remodelled as a contemporary commuter hub, complete with an underground métro concourse with hairdressers and snack bars for the passing rush-hour trade.

Close to the motorway intersections of the ring road, Lille Grand Palais is a huge exhibition arena. Here, Zenith auditorium hosts major rock concerts

◀ 1 The city tourist office is housed in the ducal Palais Rihour. 2 *La Voix du Nord*, the daily local newspaper, has an impressive office on Grand' Place. 3 Cathédrale Notre Dame de la Treille is a beautiful place of worship.

and lavish musicals such as *Les Misérables*, and is the place to see international superstars like Eric Clapton or Elton John. Civil servants and employees of global financial institutions share the surrounding sparkling office buildings with hermetically sealed-in mini-marts, coffee shops and restaurants. Linking Grand Palais to Euralille is a fresh new residential quarter being built at a bewildering pace around the big, brash, glass casino.

Between this and the stations is the Saint-Sauveur district (page 200). Further out to the east and across the railway lines is the district of Lille-Fives, which grew up as a town in its own right. Fives has its own brass bands, festivals and customs, including a wine harvest festival every autumn, when micro vineyards produce *vin de Fives*.

Cutting a swathe from the *gares* to République is the broad, only slightly seedy rue du Molinel, a boulevard wide in its aspiration and an un-grand ribbon of otherness and improbable neighbours: Catholic schools rubbing shoulders with kebaberies; travel agencies selling weeks in north Africa alongside artistic florists selling miniature topiary opposite nail bars and religious bookshops; the long-forgotten *schmutter* trade recalled by long-closed textile traders and occasional bespoke tailors and wedding couturiers. The fluctuating fortunes of the Molinel are told by many regeneration attempts on a thwarted Monoprix supermarket at the station end of the road, and the new generation Tanneurs shopping mall and Kitchen Market urban food court where rue Pierre Mauroy bisects the main road. This is also where the latest reinterpretation of the Monoprix thrives anew.

The other walk, along avenue le Corbusier from Lille Europe past the old station, then along the rue Faidherbe to Grand' Place and the old town, is a gentle turning back of the clock as the architecture rewinds through 21st, 20th and 19th centuries to the 18th and 17th; 400 years of optimism, confidence and faith in the future, respecting the past.

TOURIST OFFICE

Lille tourist office in the magnificent remains of the ducal Palais Rihour offers a friendly welcome with multilingual staff who provide advice on sightseeing and excursions, and help with hotel bookings. Since the closure of the regional and *départemental* tourist offices across the road, this is now a one-stop shop for advice on making the most of the city and surrounding area. Shelves of free leaflets and brochures may seem bewildering, but pick up essentials: a good, free, fold-out city map and a listings magazine. Bulkier hotel, dining and shopping directories are no longer printed, since up-to-date information is available on the tourist office website, together with a current *agenda* (diary) of events. Staff will browse or print pages for you to take away. Also check in here for all-inclusive city pass deals (page 60); these and other transport passes can be bought from the information desk, which also sells specialist guide books. Hosted walking tours of the city may be booked here as well, which rendezvous outside the building. The hour-long minibus tour of Lille (strongly recommended) also departs by the main entrance – for prices and information, see page 61.

Lille tourist office   Palais Rihour,
pl Rihour ♀ 261 H6 ☎ 03 59 57 94 00
w lilletourism.com ⏱ 10.00–12.30 &
13.30–17.30 ☒ Rihour

CONSULATES

IN LILLE

Canada 30 av Emile Zola ♀ 259 K1 ☎ 03 20
14 05 78

IN PARIS

Australia 4 rue Jean-Rey, 75015 ☎ 01 40
59 33 00

Ireland 4 rue Rude, 75016 ☎ 01 44 17 67 00
New Zealand 103 rue de Grenelle, 75007
☎ 01 45 01 43 43
UK 35 rue du Faubourg Saint-Honoré, 75383
☎ 01 44 51 31 00
USA 4 av Gabriel, 75008 ☎ 01 43 12 22 22

BANKS AND MONEY MATTERS

Some shops and fast-food outlets now have cash payment machines for coins and notes as an alternative to credit cards.

BANKS There are branches all around town, with most major French banks on rue Nationale. They generally open Monday–Friday 10.00–17.00 (some close noon–14.00); some branches also open Saturday 10.00–13.00, and some close Monday. Banks shut earlier on the eve of holidays. ATMs (*distributeurs automatiques de billets*) are widely available around town (even within 100m of place Lion d'Or in Vieux Lille); most accept Visa and MasterCard, as well as Cirrus and Maestro debit cards.

CURRENCY EXCHANGE Bureaux de change can be found in some banks and post offices, and in department stores, railway stations and airports. Caution: while exchange rates may be fixed, commission rates are flexible (these should be clearly indicated). For more on the euro, see page 30.

CREDIT CARDS Visa and MasterCard are both widely accepted, and American Express and Diners may be used in many tourist and business areas. Depending on the card, you may withdraw up to €300–400 at ATMs and banks. Since Covid, contactless payment limits have risen to €50 per transaction. Should you lose your card, notify the issuing bank as soon as possible to block fraudulent charges. Keep a note of your credit card number in case of such an eventuality.

VAT AND TAX REFUNDS France charges value-added tax (TVA in French) at 20% on most purchases. Food, drink, transport and books are taxed at just 5.5%, while newspapers and medical items from pharmacies have an even lower rate of 2.1%. Non-EU residents over the age of 15 and staying less than six months in Europe may claim refund of TVA on purchases of more than €100 at any one store. **Printemps** has a dedicated counter to handle this (page 178): budget for a rebate of around 16.5% on the purchase price, and add 30 minutes to your shopping time to process. Staff will provide a VAT refund form for you to show customs (within three months of date of purchase) when leaving France or the last EU country you visit. Check in 30 minutes early to allow extra time for this, with your purchases handy for inspection. Customs will stamp the form, which then needs to be mailed back to the shop within six months. Refunds are credited back to your card. It's a bit of a palaver, but hey – those French wedding dresses and tableware? It's worth it!

TIPS AND SERVICE Restaurant must include service charges (15%). However, it is traditional to round up the total in restaurants and bars when paying in cash, leaving small change behind. Hotel porters expect €2–5, and chambermaids an appropriate gratuity. Tip taxi drivers 10–15% of the fare, hairdressers 15% or round up to the next zero, cloakroom attendants €1 and public lavatory attendants around 50 cents. In some cinemas and theatres, you might be expected to tip the usher between 50c and €1 when escorted directly to your seat.

COMMUNICATIONS

INTERNET With mobile data and roaming packages, demand for traditional cyber cafés has fallen dramatically. There are Wi-Fi hotspots around town at mainline and key métro stations, including Lille Flandres, République Beaux-Arts, Roubaix-Téléport and Tourcoing Centre. Many restaurants, bars and cafés have unsecured Wi-Fi, and hotels and B&Bs usually offer internet connection (check when booking). Larger hotels typically have a 'business centre', even if it's just a desk with computer and printer, for downloading and printing boarding passes. Remember that French keyboards differ slightly from the English QWERTY layout, so type slowly and carefully! Co-working spaces around town include WOJO at Le 31 (former Galleries Lafayette, rue Béthune; page 178), while the lounge at Okko Hotel (page 77) has a full business workspace with complimentary refreshments available by the hour, half or full day.

MEDIA
Press UK daily papers are widely available, as is the *International Herald Tribune*. Outside Paris, France prefers to get news from regional rather

than national papers. The local daily, *La Voix du Nord,* offers the essential low-down on everything happening in the region, with good national and international coverage too. Once an underground wartime Résistance news-sheet, it is now the key news source, publishing editions for each town in the north of France from its distinctive office on Grand' Place (page 195). Read over breakfast at your hotel, or sitting in a central café or bar to look cool and local as you check listings and entertainment news. You can also browse online before travelling at w lavoixdunord.fr, though much of the site is now blocked by a paywall.

Other notable French newspapers include *Le Figaro,* a popular middle-market national daily; *Le Monde,* the national daily paper of record; *Libération,* the left-wing tabloid of choice for intellectuals and students; and *Nord Éclair,* a local weekly published in Roubaix. Free dailies such as *20 Minutes* (w 20minutes.fr/lille) and *MetroNews* (w metronews.fr) are distributed at stations and shopping centres.

Sortir, a free weekly listings magazine for Lille and the wider region, is published each Wednesday and is available at hotel receptions, many bars and the tourist office. *Going Out,* a free bimonthly arts and eating magazine, can be picked up from bars and restaurants and features interviews with local restaurateurs and Hollywood stars.

Radio Local news can be heard on 94.7FM and the university campus station on 106.6FM. Motorway traffic is on 107.7FM and BBC Radio 4 can be picked up in Lille on 198LW.

TV Lille's own TV channel, BFMGrand Lille – the local wing of the main digital rolling news station BFM TV – has a good breakfast show and programming from events around the city. Watch before your trip at w **bfmtv. com/grand-lille.** Other regional news and weather bulletins can be found on France 3. In the morning, tune in to France 2 for *Télé Matin,* a news and arts programme. Weather reports are at 06.55, 07.25, 07.55 and shortly before 08.40.

Mainstream French TV channels offer loads of franchise music 'talent' contests, *Big Brother*-type reality shows, emotional food series (reality heartstring-pulling blended with recipes), wildlife documentaries and endless discussion programmes featuring people in brightly lit studios wearing strong primary colours. The bilingual French and German arts channel Arté is well worth watching. M6 has reality TV, youth culture and dubbed US series. Canal Plus is a subscriber cable channel showing films, drama and sport. Hotels may offer English-language news, usually CNN or BBC World, and occasionally Sky News. The national state-owned rolling-news channel France24 broadcasts three streams: French, Arabic and English. Some hotel smart TVs may allow you to connect to Netflix and log into your own account, but be warned that subscription streamers may not let you watch certain films/series outside your home country. Other hotels allow you to cast to the TV from your phone.

POSTCODES Most central Lille addresses use the postcode (zip code) 59000. Some streets on the edge of the centre are 59800. Since the principal code covers most of any urban area in France, GPS navigation within French towns and cities should be based on street names rather than postcodes.

POST OFFICES At post offices you can buy stamps, post letters and parcels and receive your mail *poste restante*. The main office is at boulevard Carnot (♀ 261 J4), but you can also buy stamps from tobacconists, kiosks and bars displaying the red cigar *tabac* symbol. Letterboxes are painted yellow. Post offices are generally open 08.00–18.30 Monday–Friday, 08.00–noon Saturday.

TELEPHONES Payphones in restaurants and bars may accept coins, with street kiosks mostly a thing of the past. Calls from hotels are invariably quite expensive. Ask reception for rates per unit, and be sure to also check length of each unit: sometimes it can be as little as 15 seconds! Okko (page 77) offers €10 credit towards calls. Use free hotel internet for WhatsApp, Skype or similar web calling.

Mobile phones Foreign mobile phones connect to France Telecom's Orange or rival networks. There are no roaming charges for EU citizens travelling between EU countries. For UK citizens post-Brexit, most mobile providers offer free roaming voluntarily – but check with your operator to make sure this applies to you before going. Similarly, in respect of data, certain providers have a cap on your usage, so it is worth checking with your provider pre-departure to avoid running up an unwanted bill. Should your phone be unlocked or you have a dual SIM option, you can alternatively buy a French pay-as-you-go SIM card from a supermarket or post office. Usually under €10, many include free international calls and texts.

Dialling When calling France from outside the country, use the country code (33) and omit the first 0 of the listed number. To call international numbers from France, dial 00 then the country code and number (omitting the first 0). Within France, dial the ten-digit telephone number. For operator-assisted dialling, key in 00+33+country code.

Country codes

Australia 61
Belgium 32
Canada 1
France 33
Ireland 353

New Zealand 64
UK 44
USA 1

Useful telephone numbers

Emergency services in English 112 (police, fire, ambulance)
Ambulance 15
Car pound 03 75 83 40 83
Duty doctor 03 20 33 20 33
Fire 18
Hospital & medical emergencies 36 24 (see also page 28)
Lost property 03 75 83 40 83
Operator 12
Police (emergency) 17
Police (all other matters) 03 62 59 80 00
SOS (English-language crisis line) 01 46 21 46 46
Weather (France) 32 50

WORSHIP

A full list of churches and other places of worship is available at the tourist office (page 49).

(Anglican) Christ Church Rue Lydéric 262 H3 03 28 52 66 36 bus L5 to Liberté then rue Hazebrouk to rue Lydéric
(Jewish) Synagogue 5 rue Angellier 262 G4 03 20 52 41 59 Bus L5 to Liberté then turn on bd Lebas to rue Jean Bart to rue Angellier
(Muslim) Grande Mosquée de Lille 59 rue de Marquillies 262 B5 03 20 53 02 65 Métro 2 to Porte d'Arras, then bus CITL to Faubourg d'Arras, & walk rue Hénaux to rue de Marquillies
(Roman Catholic) Cathédrale Notre Dame de la Treille 261 J3. See page 206 & other churches listed on page 204.

TRAVELLING WITH CHILDREN

Like any city, Lille may be paradise for kids, or a nightmare for parents. It is just a matter of planning your day.

PRACTICALITIES Breastfeeding in public is legal and generally accepted in French cities. Although fewer French mothers choose to breastfeed than in other European countries, there is now no stigma nor any pressure to hide away! Department stores and shopping malls have toilets and baby-changing facilities. If you've not brought essential equipment with you (or your low-cost airline charges a fortune for extra luggage), then you can hire buggies, cots, high chairs, etc from w location-de-poussette.fr, to collect from Maison ZD (220 rue Jean Jaurès, Villeneuve d'Ascq). Many hotels

OPENING HOURS

Opening hours for specific sights are covered in the relevant chapters. For **restaurants**, see page 92; for **shops**, page 158; for **museums**, page 184.

and apartments can provide cots/high chairs and Euralille offers half-price buggy hire to holders of their loyalty card. Vieux Lille has cobbled streets and its shops and restaurants may have steps, so follow tips in *Chapter 3* if pushing a pram or buggy during your stay. Public transport is adapted for buggies as well as wheelchairs, with lifts to platforms and ramps on buses.

EATING AND DRINKING Families eat together in French cities, so there shouldn't be any problems at mealtimes, besides the limited lunch hour window. Most restaurants have a children's menu. To avoid the ubiquitous chicken nuggets or *steak hachée* (tell the kids it's a burger), try **Brasserie André** (page 101), where youngsters are given a more sophisticated choice, or sample a tailor-made gastronomic menu for under-10s at **Rouge Barre** (page 121). In central Lille, if the weather is good enough, sit outside at a table on the terrace. Most child-friendly museums and attractions have a family-orientated restaurant, and the **St So café** (page 93) has plenty of family-based activities.

ATTRACTIONS AND OUTINGS Museum welcome desks often provide kids' activity packs , offering interesting and enjoyable things to do. They will also suggest a child's itinerary and exhibits that youngsters will enjoy. Supervised activities, workshops and games take place in most museums on Wednesdays and Saturdays. Traditionally, Wednesday afternoons were school-free in France, although since 2014 many schools have stopped giving pupils the afternoon off.

On rainy days, consider the **Planetarium** at Villeneuve d'Ascq (page 231), easily reached by métro. Wednesday and Saturday parent and child screenings are held at local cinemas such as **L'Hybride** (page 143), with films for over-fives, while physical and virtual fun for kids and adults alike can be found indoors at **Hall U Need** (see opposite) and the **Musée de l'Illusion** (page 190).

Bookshops are enjoyable: **Le Big Le Moi** book café (page 159) schedules storytime workshops, while **Le Bateau Livre** (page 158) stocks only titles that will appeal to the under-16s. So, find a picture book or easy reader for the youngest, or challenge the others to attempt a J K Rowling or Stephanie Meyer in French. Should you need to dangle a bribe over a young Potter fan, a magic wand from a wizarding shop (page 170) might ensure best behaviour throughout the trip.

In good weather, you've plenty of parks to discover (page 215). The **zoo** (page 215) by the Citadelle is always worth a visit, and is walking distance from **Jardin Vauban's** puppet theatre and **Cita Parc's** rides for younger children. If staying a while in Lille, there are regular direct trains from Lille Europe station to **Disneyland Paris** (**w** disneylandparis.com). Even better: there's no need to drag the kids and their accessories across the capital, as Marne La Vallée-Chessy Station is in the theme park itself. The train from Gare Lille Europe gets there in just over an hour; from Gare Flandres could take 40 minutes longer. OuiGo budget trains (page 62) have fares from €10 each way. If you have a car, **Parc Astérix** is the fully French theme park alternative, 180km south, within the Hauts-de-France region (w parcasterix.fr).

Cita Parc 1 av Mathias Delobel ♀ 260 C2 ☎ 21 88 14 14 w cita-parc.fr ⏰ Mar–Oct 11.00–19.00 weekends & school hols (18.00 low season), 14.00–19.00 Wed (18.00 low season) 🚌 Bus L5 to Champ de Mars. Sucessor to former Parc des Poussins, with slides, rides carousels & swings at a children's mini theme park by the zoo in the Bois de Boulogne (page 215). Rides for small children include a woodland train, carousels & a gentle nursery-slope version of a roller-coaster. Pay €3 for 1 ride, €25 for 10 tickets or €17 for a day pass. Trampolines for bouncing off excess energy or the side effects of too much candyfloss & fizzy drinks.

Hall U Need 26 rue Félix Faure, Saint André Lez Lille ♀ 261 G1 ☎ 03 59 61 38 60 w halluneed.com ⏰ noon–midnight Tue–Thu, noon–01.00 Fri, 11.00–02.00 Sat, 11.00–midnight Sun, school hol hours vary 🚌 Bus L90 to Sainte Helene, follow bd Carnot. Ignore the pun, come for the fun. Not an exclusively kids' attraction, but as genuinely welcoming to the after-work crowd here for the beer or students having a blast before the clubs open as to a family celebrating a 12th birthday. A teen hangout as well as a safe space for families, this massive gaming zone in a converted factory has everything from toddler play park to full-size bowling alley, VR experiences, family-friendly escape games & old-school wooden bar diversions such as shuffleboard. Race model classic cars 20 laps around the track, play table football or pinball, loiter in a video arcade or hang out on the summer terrace. Free admission, but pay per play. Top up a rechargeable card or wearable tag to control the family budget. Not a cheap day out, but great way to let off steam indoors & has appeal to all ages. Under 16s must be accompanied. Bar & restaurant (€12 kids menu); if coming with kids, make it an afternoon outing. The space is accessible to all, & differing abilities are catered for.

Théâtre de Marionnettes du Jardin de Vauban Jardin Vauban, 1 av Léon Jouhaux ♀ 260 C4 ☎ 03 20 42 09 95 w lepetitjacques. fr ⏰ Apr–Oct weekends & school holidays 🚌 Bus 12 to Champ de Mars 🎫 €6. Generations of children have known Monsieur Rameau's Goat House (Chalet des Chèvres – page 217), where a puppet theatre stages the many exploits of le Petit Jacques as the marionette has countless adventures. Each season brings a good selection of stories, so you may come back more than once. Performances last around 50 minutes.

5

Local Transport

MÉTRO, TRAMS AND BUSES

MÉTRO A superb métro system ties in with trams and buses. The unmanned VAL métro is completely automated, and runs on two ever-expanding lines crossing central Lille and serving the suburbs and metropolitan area. Central métro platforms are sealed off from tracks by sliding glass doors that open when trains come to a standstill. En route to suburbs, trains swoop and soar from underground tunnels to futuristic tracks high above the countryside and motorways – sit at the very front for a true fairground-attraction experience.

Métro lines in France have no names: just numbers and platforms indicated by the terminus. Thus, Line 1 will be either 4 Cantons/Stade Pierre Mauroy or CHU Eurosanté, and Line 2 CH Dron or St Philibert.

TRAMS Twin tramways run out to Roubaix and Tourcoing, passing the pretty Parc Barbieux. On a sunny day, it makes a particularly pleasant alternative to the underground. Métro/tram services run 05.15 to midnight (from 06.20 weekends).

BUSES The city bus network covers the areas of the old town that no métro could possibly reach, since much of Lille is built on land reclaimed from canals and waterways. From principal bus stops in the streets around Gare Lille Flandres, services fan out to outlying districts of the MEL European Metropolitan District, even crossing the Belgian border. Buses generally run from 05.30 to 21.00, though some services (including **Liane** lines to suburbs and neighbouring towns and some city routes into the old centre) continue until midnight. Most late-night routes depart from place de la République or Gare Lille Flandres. Line 9 gets you back from Vieux Lille after dinner.

A **weekend night bus** runs half-hourly Thursday–Saturday from the last métro (usually around 01.00) until the full network kicks in first thing in the morning. N1, from Lille Porte de Douai to 4 Cantons, takes in bus stops at Jeanne d'Arc, Philippe Lebon, Masséna, Sacré Cœur (return only – outbound stops at National) to Gare Lille Flandres, Gare Lille Europe and République Beaux-Arts, linking bar and club quarters with main hotel districts.

While most bus routes merely skirt the Vieux Lille historic centre, a welcome addition to the fleet is the **Navette Vieux Lille (NVL)**. Using the value ZAP fare (page 60) for single journeys, these minibuses run every 10–15 minutes between 07.00 and 21.00 from outside the métro and tourist office on place Rihour. It runs on a loop taking in the squares, Vieux Lille from place Lion d'Or and looping through rue de Gand (except in summer when the road is pedestrianised), the garrison district on the edge of the city, back through the Royale and Voltaire quarters and out to the Citadelle, returning to the starting point via rues de la Barre and Bouchers. An invaluable aid to exploring cobbled streets of the oldest part of town, the hail-and-ride service may be boarded anywhere along the route in Vieux Lille, not just bus stops, and you should ask the driver to drop you at a convenient point. Regular price tickets are valid for 1 hour after the first swipe, so you may get 2 or 3 hops out of them.

Since a road traffic calming scheme removed bus routes from Grand' Place to rue Nationale, only NVL links place Rihour and the squares to Vieux Lille. For hotels and restaurants based in this area, I suggest you take the métro to place Rihour and either cross the squares to the old town or use the NVL. Otherwise, route 9 from Gare Lille Flandres runs to place Lion d'Or.

INFORMATION AND ADVICE Ilévia (03 20 40 40 40 w ilevia.fr) has an excellent online journey planner; click '*Itineraires*' to research a route by bus, tram, métro and/or rail. Transport maps can be collected from stations, the tourist office or Ilévia agencies. Ilévia no longer publishes paper timetables; instead, use the app or request a printout from one of the Agences Ilévia information desks. There are three agencies in central Lille.

Agences Ilévia

Gare Lille Flandres Métro level 261 K6 07.00–19.00 Mon–Fri, 08.00–18.30 Sat Gare Lille Flandres. In the métro interchange hall beyond the ticket barriers. You will need a ticket or pass to enter the zone or ask to be buzzed through from the ticket gate intercom.

Gare Lille Flandres Place des Buisses 261 K6 10.00–17.00 Mon–Fri Gare Lille Flandres. Side entrance to Gare Lille Flandres, by taxi rank.
République Beaux-Arts 262 E1 10.00–17.00 Mon–Fri République Beaux-Arts. Underground ticket hall.

TICKETS AND PASS PASS Traditional tickets are now a thing of the past. All travel, from a single journey across town to a day pass, season ticket or *carnet* for ten journeys, now only requires a simple smart card – the Pass Pass. If you already have a Pass Pass branded *Transpole* (issued by the previous transport agency) this may still be valid to be recharged (page 58).

Whatever your mobile phone, you may buy single bus tickets for €2 simply by texting the word BUS to 93089. The ticket you received via SMS message is for buses only and not valid on métro/tram services.

Lille is working hard to support women travellers, as well as travellers with a disability or those who are potentially vulnerable. Not only does Ilévia support the international Ask for Angela campaign (page 150), but after 22.00, bus passengers may ask to be dropped off at a convenient point between official stops.

Pass Pass types A PasPass is fully rechargeable across town (or online for holders of a Carte Personelle with the Easy Card app) and available in three forms.

Ticket Rechargeable (20c – refunded on fifth recharge) This cardboard smart card is the simplest option for visitors, available from all outlets and rechargeable up to ten times. Download single tickets, *carnets* for multiple journeys, day passes, and even ZAP tickets (page 60). Several people may travel on the same card at the same time and you may lend it to friends.

Carte Non-Personnalisée (€2) A versatile option for all ticket types, and may be used by several people travelling together or lent to a friend. Virtually unlimited recharges.

Carte Personelle (€4) A plastic smart card for one person's use. Ideal for regular users and season-ticket holders, even those signed up for bike and car hire. Order online at w ilevia.fr.

Where to buy Buy Pass Pass cards from vending machines at métro stations and certain bus stops, or pick one up at a *tabac* (tobacconist/newsagent) displaying the Ilévia or Pass Pass logos. They are also available at any Ilévia agency or ticket office. At Gare Lille Europe, you can collect a basic *ticket rechargeable* or *carte non-personnalisée* pass from the métro ticket machine on the same level as the station concourse. It's best to buy a simple *carnet* for your first purchase – that will get you and your party safely to the hotel! There are more than 200 ticket machines across the network and 60 recharging points at stations and key bus stops.

How to use Card readers and validation screens are found at entrance gates to platforms, escalators and lifts on the métro, and close to doors on buses and trams. Hold your Pass Pass over the screen (do not swipe, it will

1 The striking République Beaux-Arts métro station. 2 Trams run beyond the city to Roubaix and Tourcoing. 3 Bright red V'Lille bikes are available for hire across town. 4 Gare Lille Flandres has links to Paris and Brussels airports and beyond. ▶

Lille City Pass allows you to travel on all trams, métro and bus services, and provides free admission to 27 major museums and attractions in Lille and neighbouring towns, as well as guided city tours (page 49). The three-day option adds another 11 sites in the wider region with free travel on RER local trains in the Nord and Pas-de-Calais *départements*. It also offers discounts on concert, theatre, opera and ballet tickets. The pass costs €25 for one day, €35 for two days or €45 for three days, and may be bought at many hotels, any local tourist office, or by calling 03 59 57 94 00; alternatively, book online at booking.lilletourism.com for a 10% discount. The site and museum pass is activated on your first museum or site visit and the separate transport pass clocks on with your first journey.

not register) and wait for the beep and tick symbol to appear on the screen. If a cross appears and the buzzer sounds, try again. If you have bought discount ZAP tickets (see below) for specific journeys, press the ZAP button on the card reader before placing your Pass Pass on the screen. When travelling with friends and using just one Pass Pass, hold your card and key in the number of passengers.

When transferring between bus/tram/métro, remember to present your card on each leg of the journey (no need to update passengers numbers when in a group). You will not be charged when the second or third mode of transport is a continuation of your original journey.

Failure to validate your card results in a €5 fine. Travelling without a Pass Pass or ticket incurs a €100 fine (€50 if settled immediately).

Prices Tickets cost around €1.80 for any journey on the métro/tram/bus network and allow travel in one direction, changing from métro to tram to bus if necessary, without buying another ticket. They are valid for 1 hour from first to last validation. *Carnets* of ten tickets are better value at €15.40, and full-day Pass Journée tickets offer unlimited travel for around €5.30 for one day, €9.60 for two days, €12.80 for three days or €18.10 for 7 days (each day is a full 24 hours from the moment of first use, so if you buy your pass at 19.00 you may use it the following day until the same time).

There are also a couple of lesser-known bargains to consider: the Pass Soirée, for travel after 19.00 until the night bus network stops in the morning, is just €2.45. And, if taking only short trips of less than three métro stops, such as to Wazemmes market, or if you wish to use the Navette Vieux Lille for one trip only, you could buy a reduced-price ZAP ticket at €1.15. Should you plan to stay around Grand' Place and Vieux Lille, you are not likely to use much public transport, since the métro does not serve the old town (although buses reach a surprising number of streets there). In that case you may be better off using the occasional ticket rather than day or weekend passes. If plans involve trips out to Roubaix, Tourcoing or Villeneuve d'Ascq, or a few cross-city runs to and from the markets, however, a carnet between friends or a day card would be better value. Note that regular overground SNCF rail services (such as the journey to Lens for the Louvre) are not included in regular network tickets/passes, but your Pass Pass may cover park and ride services.

During the two days of the Braderie (page 174) a special Pass Braderie gives unlimited travel on public transport across the metropolitan area. Similar deals may be offered from noon until late on National Music Day (21 June).

If you are staying a while in Lille, or are a student at the university, check on the on Ilévia website to discover alternative discount options.

APP All travellers should download the Ilévia app for live traffic information, timetables and journey planner. This is not to be confused with the Pass Pass Easy Card app for downloading tickets and recharging passes – Easy Card requires specific android phones with an active NFC reader, and is only recommended for regular or long-stay visitors.

LOST PROPERTY If you have lost an umbrella, wallet, sunglasses or domestic pet on any bus, tram or métro, call ☏ 03 20 81 43 43.

TOUR BUS

See the sights in the shortest possible time by taking take the 1-hour minibus city tour (☏ 03 59 57 94 00 w booking.lilletourism.com/city-tour.html). Buses leave at 10.30, noon, 14.30 and 16.00 Tuesday–Sunday from outside the tourist office on place Rihour, and provide a decent multilingual audio-visual commentary. Tickets cost €16 (€14 online), or are free for under-6s and holders of the City Pass. It is wheelchair accessible.

AIRPORT TRANSFERS

BY BUS A shuttle bus links Lille Lesquin Airport (8km out of town) with the main Lille stations, stopping a few steps from Gare Lille Flandres, by place des Buisses. The journey time is around 20 minutes. A single fare costs €8, and a return €14; buy tickets from the driver or online at w flibco.com, where you will also find timetables. Buses depart from stop 'B' outside the airport arrivals hall.

Alternatively, use Ilévia public transport for just €1.80, taking bus 68 from the airport to 4 Cantons (Stade), then métro 1 to central Lille.

BY TRAIN High-speed trains link central Lille to Paris Roissy Charles de Gaulle Airport (CDG) in 51 minutes and Brussels Airport in 38 minutes.

Services run from Lille Flandres and Lille Europe stations, and prices vary considerably – check online at **w** sncf-connect.com. An alternative rail option from CDG is to take the low cost Ouigo (**w** ventes.ouigo.com) train to Lille Flandres for €10, with a journey time of 54 minutes.

TAXIS

Taxis may be found at clearly marked ranks and, if you are very lucky, hailed in the street. The main ranks are outside the Lille Europe and Lille Flandres stations. Remember: when you book a taxi, the meter starts ticking from the moment of your call, not from the time and place you board the cab. Licenced taxis can be booked by calling 03 20 06 06 06 or 03 20 56 19 19. You may also book an Uber.

CAR HIRE

Most international car-rental agencies have desks at Lille Europe station and the airport, offering discount rates through airlines and rail companies. However, it may be cheaper to rent a car from one of the smaller companies in town. **Rent a Car** (113 rue du Molinel 262 H1 03 20 40 20 20 **w** rentacar. fr), a five-minute walk from Gare Lille Flandres, has low rates for one- or two-day rentals. Online bargains can also often be found at **w** auto-europe. co.uk and other travel consolidation sites.

Avis **w** avis.com

Budget **w** budget.fr

Europcar **w** europcar.com

Hertz **w** hertz.com

Sixt **w** sixt.fr

PARKING Lille boasts 11,800 secure parking spaces in huge underground and multi-storey car parks tucked around the central area. Check with the tourist office for current rates as prices vary from site to site – usually from around €2 per hour. For street parking, check payment options and rules on the *horodateur* (meter). Blue badge users, see page 38.

Always check with your hotel for preferential rates. When shopping at Euralille, Carrefour supermarket checkout staff will stamp your ticket for free or reduced-rate short-term parking. If you stay out of town and use public transport, you can park for free at Porte des Postes, CHU Eurosanté, St Philibert and 4 Cantons.

Most car parks close at 01.00; some central locations are open 24/7 (see opposite). Two have limited hours: Parking Grand Place (3 pl Charles de Gaulle 07.00–midnight Mon & Wed–Fri, 07.00–01.00 Tue & Sat, 07.00–22.00 Sun) under the square charges €28 per 24 hours, while Parking Rihour Printemps (pl Rihour 08.00–21.00 Mon–Sat), next to the tourist office, charges €23.20 per 24 hours, mainly for department store shoppers.

Rue Bethune Pedestrian zone 6, rue de la Rivierette. €21/24hrs.
Noveau Siècle Pl Pierre Mendes. €14.70/24hrs.

Euralille 13 av Le Corbusier. €33.50/24hrs.
Parking-Republique Bd de la Liberté. €15/24hrs.

CITROËN 2CV HIRE

Tradi'balade 28 pl du Général de Gaulle ♀ 261 H5 ☏ 03 20 51 10 29 w tradibalade. com ⏲ 10.30–12.30 & 14.00–19.30 daily 🚊 Rihour. Rent a classic open-topped Citroen 2CV at €159/day, or be chauffeured around on a personalised city tour from €33 pp in the iconic French car. Office based behind the Vieille Bourse between the main squares. Also bookable through the tourist office.

CYCLING AND SEGWAYS

Hire a bike at one of the many pick-up-and-drop-off points by railway stations. You will usually be asked to leave a returnable deposit of around €300, which can be organised by credit card. Ask at the tourist office for maps of cycle routes around Lille, or perhaps book an hour with a local greeter (see below). For itineraries outside the city, see page 250.

BIKE HIRE

V'Lille w ilevia.fr/v-lille. These bright red bikes are available for hire across town, from €1.80/day or €7.70/week. To access them you need to register with a €200 refundable deposit, which can be done online or in person at an Ilévia agency (page 57) or any Station V'Lille equipped with a credit card reader. Use the screens at the docking station or the app to get

PHONE A FRIEND – LES GREETERS EN NORD

No matter how enjoyable the guidebook or how informative the pamphlet, nothing matches the experience of being personally escorted around somewhere new by a local. Meet Les Greeters en Nord: a dozen or so volunteers from Lille, Roubaix and the villages and towns of the Nord *département* who love their county and are delighted to share their tips, secrets and stories in person. Book an hour or so with a local 'greeter' and arrange for a personalised tour, tailor-made to suit your own interests. During the week, greeters may be university lecturers, customs officers, architects or shop workers, but they give up their spare time for free to introduce visitors to the area. Some specialise in museums, history or the arts, others enjoy cycling in the countryside or walking the cobbled streets of old villages. In Lille itself, Eric, Franck, Geneviève, Jean-Pierre, Sylvie and Valérie share the honours. To book, visit the website at w greeters.fr/nord and either choose by greeter or theme.

SKATEBOARDING

The parvis François Mitterrand (259 H4) outside Gare Lille Europe has been popular with skaters, both inline and on boards, for 20 years. However, the youth of Lille went a stage too far when skaters adopted guerrilla building tactics one night in 2014 and concreted ramps and half pipes on the central reservation and kerbs of a main road in the business district, turning a dual carriageway into a skate park – causing rush hour chaos.

started: you will receive a user code & PIN to retrieve a bike. There are 260 docking stations on the network (full list on website & app), mostly at métro stations & by sights & popular streets & squares, as well as beyond the city limits. Outside Gare Lille Flandres (261 K6) is a good place for first check in, as it's close to *agences llévia* if you have any problems. Choose option VLS (V'Lille Libre Service) for casual non-residential use; longer-stay residents may choose monthly or annual rentals &

even electric bikes. If your journey is less than 30mins, the ride is free; you just pay €1.35 for each extra 30mins in the saddle. So if you pick up the bike at the main station, cycle to Palais des Beaux-Arts & park at rue Inkerman, there's nothing extra to pay. If, after the museum, you wish to head off to the old town, that can easily be done within a free 30-min cycle. You might then ride back to the Rihour brasseries in a few mins. Help & advice is available from llévia customer service.

BIKE TAXI

Happy Moov m 06 24 16 08 18
w happymoov.com. Rickshaw taxi service in the city centre. Prices start from €5 for the regular taxi service, or you can take a guided

city tour for €20–40. Rickshaw ranks are at pl Rihour, pl des Buisses (Gare Lille Flandres) & parvis François Mitterrand (Gare Lille Europe).

SEGWAY HIRE

Mobil'Board 06 60 97 74 52
w mobilboard.com. Alas, since the expansion of V'Lille bike scheme, the Segway-for-hire option offered by official public transport providers is no more. A private company has taken over the tradition, with 2–3 hour Segway training sessions on Champs de Mars & around town from €45 & guided tours from €70. This is, of course, the somewhat retro sci-fi way to

travel. Sway backwards or forwards to steer while standing on what looks like a garden roller pretending to be a hovercraft. Naturally, France has decided that the universal name Segway is too anglophone and has introduced the official noun *gyropede* instead. The name is even less likely to catch on than the transport itself. In Lille, it has already been modified to *gyropode*.

6

Accommodation

In a city where hospitality comes as standard, stories of northern welcomes are legendary. I only regret that one offbeat gem closed its doors just too early to be included in this guide: a B&B run by a former *madame* who, after years of service to the garrison, had ultimately transferred her attentions from the bed to the breakfast. Friends told me that many men who had visited the establishment as soldiers in their youth, and partaken fully of the fleshly delights on offer, had returned in later years with their families for a more orthodox *accueil*. Nonetheless, there are still plenty of unconventional treats to be discovered in and around Lille. Early editions of this guide included such eccentric options as a luxurious bedroom in a distillery devoted to the memory of Napoleon, while today you'll find rooms within historic monuments ranging from the former Faculty of Pharmacy in Louis Pasteur's 19th-century university to an imposing religious building originally established as a retirement home for the early garrison's ladies of the night.

Chambre d'hôte is a particularly Gallic twist on bed and breakfast and, as well as our choice of the most welcoming homes (page 85), it is good to check the latest B&B lists published by the tourist office. **Self-catering** is well worth considering if you are planning a longer stay. As budget becomes a bigger factor in most travel plans, apartment hotels are springing up close to stations and main tourist areas. Considering a couple could have to add €100–200 for hotel breakfasts over a long weekend, a working kitchen and proper fridge is a plus, and the option of going to restaurants just once a day can help make a city break more affordable. Supermarkets and restaurants will often deliver and Lille has great local markets for fresh food if you fancy recreating gourmet masterworks with a two-ring hob and microwave! In the countryside, consider the charms of a *gîte* (page 82).

Should you choose a **city-centre hotel**, take my tip. Unless staying in one of the larger hotels with a grand breakfast-buffet selection – in which case you should eat heartily and later opt for a simple baguette, pâté and cheese lunchtime picnic – forego the standard hotel breakfast, usually costing around €10–20 on top of the room rate. Instead, make your way to the main Paul bakery (page 133), on the corner of rue Pierre Mauroy and place du Théâtre. In the magnificently tiled surroundings of this fabulous shop, enjoy an excellent *petit déjeuner* of fresh-baked bread, homemade jams, and superb coffee or tea, or sinfully sensational hot chocolate. Other good breakfast options include Le Pain Quotidien (page 131) and the lobby of L'Hermitage Gantois (page 72).

Mobility-restricted guests should be aware that some older hotels, especially around the Flandres station, may not have lift access from the street level to the bedrooms – so always check when booking if you have issues with stairs (page 39).

HOTELS

ARBRE VOYAGEUR 45 bd Carnot 📍 261 K4 📞 03 20 20 62 62 w hotelarbrevoyageur.com
🚊 Gare Lille Flandres, then Bus 10, 14 or 50 to Lycée Pasteur
Some come for the good night's sleep, others, blessed with perfect metabolism, for the chocolate and *crème pâtissière*-based alchemy wielded by the hotel's master pastry chef Louis Stempin. You don't even have to dine at his on-site Jane restaurant for the sweet fix as the hotel has its own cake shop, Le Colibri, which also sells artisanal breads and attracts locals seeking breakfast treats to take home. The hotel, in a former Polish consulate building, unashamedly seduces guests lured to Lille by the city's gastronomic reputation, enticing them to brasserie dining room Ma Reine with classic northern dishes, also available for delivery or takeaway. Which is perhaps why more people know of the Arbre Voyageur than actually stay there. Rooms (from €120–400) are modern without being offensive, although the trend for full-height clear glass walls between bathroom and bedroom means friends sharing will either become more than friends or need the services of a chiropractor to deal with the long-term effects of looking the other way. Mind you, since the most expensive room has a jacuzzi, perhaps the easiest way of preserving modesty would be actually to share a bath and hope the bubbles do their thing while keeping your toes turned resolutely inwards. Other distractions include Apple TV, video on demand, all current Bluetooth-style treats, complimentary nibbles in the mini bar and espresso machines. That sought-after breakfast at the hotel costs around €20. €€€

ART DÉCO EURALILLE 110 av de la République, 59110 La Madeleine ♀ 259 J1 ✆ 03 20 14 81 81 w hotel-artdecolille.com ⛭ Romarin

Rechristened to name-check the district around Gare Lille Europe, the hotel is actually beyond the ring road. But while La Madeleine is officially outside central Lille, the hotel is a lot closer to the Eurostar station than most officially designated town-centre establishments. It's just 5 minutes' walk from Lille Europe (turn left on to bd Pasteur and right into av de la République), or you can take any tram leaving Lille Europe towards Roubaix or Tourcoing. The hotel is opposite the Romarin tram stop. It's smart and modern, with more than a nod towards the Art Deco style of its name – the reception area, with helpful and charming staff, is dominated by a coloured glass ceiling – and bedrooms are neat and stylish. Rooms €85–350. €€

BARRIÈRE 777 pont de Flandres ♀ 259 J5 ✆ 03 28 14 45 00 w hotelsbarriere.com ⛭ Gare Lille Europe; lift or escalator to bd Turin, then walk along the boulevard to pont de Flandres

The coast comes to town with architect Jean-Paul Viguier's dramatic evocation in glass of an ocean liner berthed on the skyline. Perched on a bridge above the new Europe quarter, this wedge of glass and chrome, both casino resort and 5-star city destination, has a deceptively small, cool and fragranced hotel lobby humming with gentle efficiency and discretion. Beyond, it connects to the bolder bigger casino foyer (page 142): heavy velvet drapes herald the gaming rooms and a theatre that hosts regular floorshows, from star concerts to musical revues. The rest of the hotel's public spaces are lower key, with artwork inspired by local architectural landmarks – a suggestion of regional heritage to contrast with the international sheen and polish of the Riviera-Vegas-style casino wing. Being able to dine out, catch a live performance and then take the lift upstairs to bed is like being on that cruise without ever leaving dry land.

Even the smallest bedroom, paradoxically dubbed the *chambre supérieur*, is pretty spacious, with a king-sized bed and leather/suede seats. Suites are bigger than the average home in Lille. The interior design is by Pierre-Yves Rochon, better known for London's Savoy and Paris's George V. Despite a pretty palette blending mauves and olive greens, massive windows (featuring

ONLINE DEALS

In an age of comparison sites, official room rates bear little relation to what you may actually need to pay, other than during conventions and conferences. Check hotel websites for special offers, or visit the sites below for last-minute deals with discounts of 30–70% – often you can find a 4-star room priced at less than the budget chains. Search, using budget or location parameters, for your given dates or check for promotions at a specific hotel.

Agoda w agoda.com
Booking.com w booking.com
Expedia w expedia.com
Hotels.com w hotels.com
Lastminute w lastminute.com

LateRooms w laterooms.com
Trivago w trivago.com
Voyage Privé
w voyage-prive.com

Accommodation HOTELS

6

electric blinds to cheat dazzling sunlight) allow the outdoors to upstage the décor. Roomy bathrooms have both overhead and hand-held showers, lots of large towels, bathrobes and slippers. There are plenty of sockets to charge phones and devices bedside the bed or at the desk. This even includes a socket inside the safe, so you may continue charging when away from the room. A hospitality tray of kettle and upmarket teabags can be found in standard rooms, while suites boast Nespresso machines. Mobility challenges are well catered for: adapted bathrooms have no hint of the clinical, more than enough space to manoeuvre, and a practical seat for showering. One of three lifts from the lobby has all buttons within reach of a wheelchair user. Pampering beyond the bedrooms can be done at the health spa, gym and sauna. Rooms upwards of €170, suites much pricier. €€€€

BRUEGHEL 3–5 parvis Saint-Maurice ♥ 261 J6 ☏ 03 20 06 06 69 w hotel-brueghel.com
🚆 Gare Lille Flandres; left into rue de Priez & walk round the church
The least-known and most charming of the central hotels, this little gem is very much a word-of-mouth favourite. Tucked away in a quiet pedestrianised street between the old Gare Flandres and the shops of the centre, the hotel faces the church of St Maurice (page 204), which hosts excellent classical concerts and summer Sunday afternoon organ recitals. Inside a cosy reception area, an authentic 1920s cage lift takes guests Noah-fashion, two-by-two, to the bedrooms – though you may wish to forego the lift just once to browse an excellent collection of paintings, prints and posters on each landing. Rooms are styled to combine minimalism with comfort: think wrought-iron mirrors, picture frames from salvaged wood and classic bathrooms. Pick up a leaflet advertising the hotel's luxurious sister establishment, Le Château de Mazan in Provence, former home of the Marquis de Sade (imagine the room service). €€

CARLTON 3 rue Pierre Mauroy ♥ 261 J5 ☏ 03 20 13 33 13 w carltonlille.com 🚆 Rihour; walk from place Rihour to place du Théâtre
As with Cliveden in the UK, no account of this hotel is complete without a breath of scandal. Until a decade or so ago, this was best known as a provincial grand hotel of the old school, with the usual 4-star comforts liberally dispensed – while the Couvent des Minimes (see opposite) has the higher profile in the package-tour brochures, the Carlton has always enjoyed an enviable location on one of the key corner sites in the very centre of town, a chime away from the belfry of the Chambre de Commerce. However, in the wake of the notorious Dominique Strauss-Kahn affair, which dramatically cut through the presidential ambitions of the former head of the IMF, the hotel became the setting for the next high-profile political sex scandal, with tales of escorts and VIPs from top cops to politicians, and DSK himself was called in for interview among the red-faced A-listers.

With Louis XV-influenced rooms costing €135–650 and suites soaring skyward price-wise, before booking it is always worth asking for any weekend promotions (all above board, I hasten to add) that may easily halve the bill. An experience at any price is a stay in the panoramic rooftop cupola duplex suite, actually inside a turret dome, with arguably the best view in town: overlooking the squares, the Vieille Bourse, the opera house and the first cobbled alleys of Vieux Lille. There are wide picture windows on one level, quaint round windows on the other, and a plasma TV should you ever tire of looking out on the city. An en-suite spa bath adds to the feeling of luxury and romance – no need to mix with the lower castes in the hotel's main sauna.

Apart from the new panoramic bar The View, the public areas may seem slightly stuffy, but this is what the French consider British Club and therefore the height of sophistication. If buffet breakfast at €20 is not included in the deal, then home-baked treats *chez* Paul (page 133) are just yards away. Private parking available. Wi-Fi. €€€

CHAGNOT 24 pl de la Gare ♀ 261 K6 ☏ 03 20 74 11 87 w hotel-chagnot-lille.com 🚆 Gare Lille Flandres

Nudged up to 3 stars, Chagnot's surprisingly comfortable and quiet (if bland and compact) rooms sit next to Gare Lille Flandres and above the Trois Brasseurs. The slowest lift in Christendom serves an astonishing 75 bedrooms, but be warned: as with so many of the hotels around the stations, the elevator does not go all the way down to the ground floor. Rates begin from around €60. Rather than the €13 breakfast tray on the roof terrace, perhaps grab a quick coffee at the bar next door then work up an appetite with an amble into town for hot chocolate and fresh bread. As a reassuring plus, luggage lockers are available at €2–4 should you need baggage storage after checkout. €

CLARANCE 32 rue de la Barre ♀ 261 F3 ☏ 03 59 36 35 59 w clarancehotel.com 🚌 Bus L5 from Gare Lille Flandres to Champ de Mars then bd Vauban to Square Daubanton to rue de la Barre

Twinkle, twinkle, Michelin star… Within months of opening its doors, and thanks to an award-winning chef in the dining room, this five-star hotel came to dominate the firmament of Vieux Lille. An authentic 18th-century *hôtel particulier*, once a private home of the nobility who clustered around the royalist ghetto, the house is a mini gated estate in the cobbled centre, with front and rear courtyards, discreet lawn and terrace. There's even a garden of raised beds providing herbs, seasonal fruits and vegetables to the kitchen. The house has been exquisitely renovated, with contemporary touches highlighting classic architecture: elegant columns, fine parquet floors and ironwork on balustrades and staircases are all bathed in bright light from the dazzling white walls. While the hub of the house is its dining room, La Table (page 122), fine dining should also be served with a good night's sleep, so bedrooms benefit from high ceilings on the lower floors or, in the loft suite, converted from attic *chambres des bonnes* (servants' rooms), a complex cats' cradle of beams. The purity of the white paintwork is challenged by some bolder statements in the contemporary soft furnishings that are used throughout. Le Pavillon, a new block of six urban-style modernist rooms, has more recently been added to the main house. When paying between €230 and €650 a night for the bedroom, you are unlikely to flinch at a €35 bill for breakfast. €€€€€

COUVENT DES MINIMES 17 quai du Wault ♀ 260 E3 ☏ 03 20 30 62 62 w alliance-lille.com 🚌 Bus L5 from Gare Lille Flandres to Nationale, 10-min walk along rue Nationale to sq Foch & through the square to the pond

Just behind the gardens of the square Foch, in a quiet waterside street a short walk from the Citadelle and on the banks of a dock built in the mercantile age of Charles the Bold, the high walls of the Couvent de Minimes are testament to four centuries of change. Indeed, continued refreshment of the décor has made the hotel a much more attractive place than the sterile venue it was on first conversion in the early 1990s. Then, when I visited, the old cloister of this listed

17th-century monastery building had been smothered in glass and chrome and muzzled by an atrium and mezzanine piano bar, and the core of what might have been a charming and tasteful conversion had the air of an airport hotel. Thus the gentle strains of George Gershwin were generally muted by my murderous thoughts towards the architect or corporate philistines who conceived and executed the original project. Perhaps I was being unfair or unduly sensitive. On revisiting, the personality of the building has since re-emerged, and the old walls now dominate the newer touches. In any case, the current incarnation has greater dignity than that allowed over the previous 200 years: when the religious order was disbanded by the Revolution, the Couvent de Minimes saw service as a uniform warehouse to the garrison across the water. Happily, successive make-overs have brought out much of the original charm, not least the sophisticated brick vaulting from craftsmen who built the monastery back in 1622. Well-equipped and very comfortable bedrooms have evolved into relaxing and aesthetically pleasing bolt holes from city life. Service is courteous and efficient and all is as one would expect of an establishment of this quality, including the usual four-star perks of €20 big buffet breakfasts in the morning, aircon in the summer, and minibars and muzak all year round. Most major hotel guides wax lyrical about the place, and the Lille business community swears by it. Live jazz evenings are *très décontracté*, and the restaurant in the glazed courtyard is well respected by discerning locals. The hotel room rate fluctuates from under €150 up to €350 and *demi-pension* deals are also available. €€€€.

DE LA PAIX   46 rue Pierre Mauroy ⚲ 261 J6 ✆ 03 20 54 63 93 w hotel-la-paix.com 🚆 Gare Lille Flandres; cross to rue Faidherbe, then left on rue des Ponts de Comines to rue Pierre Mauroy
This is a family-run gem, just around the corner from Grand' Place. Its rooms are devoted to great artists, and rather than merely flaunting a few predictable prints in the bedrooms and lobbies, walls are graced with neatly framed posters from lesser known exhibitions around the world. You may share your room with Van Gogh, Lautrec or Magritte, or perhaps spend time getting to know a less-vaunted talent. Of course, the hotel provides great inspiration to visit the many museums and galleries in and around town. Slightly larger 'Club' rooms have a lounge zone with soft furnishings for flopping after shopping, though each floor of the hotel boasts a residents' lounge by the lift, where one may admire in-house exhibitions. Some guests might find the en-suite shower rooms smaller than expected. You may register online for a free basic breakfast, but the main branch of Paul's bakery (page 133) is just along the road. Extremely helpful staff are on duty day and night, and the room rate is competitive (the hotel website promises to beat any online offer from the consolidators). Now upgraded from two to three stars. €€

DE LA TREILLE   7–9 pl Louise de Bettignies ⚲ 261 J3 ✆ 03 20 55 45 46 w hoteldelatreille. com 🚌 Bus 9 to Lion d'Or
What a difference a decade makes. When I first stayed here it was an anachronism, a standard, internationally smart, clean and bland hotel in the most charming historic quarter of town. More recently, I have been seduced and won over by a smart, rolling makeover that has turned a city break-brochure favourite into a hideaway at last worthy of its picturesque setting. Previously,

---

1 The infamous Hotel Carlton (page 68) overlooks the squares of central Lille.
2 A courtyard at L'Hermitage Gantois (page 72), Lille's first five-star hotel. 3 The Moxy (page 76) is housed in the university's former Faculty of Medicine and Pharmacy. ▶

you chose this address only for its location in the very heart of the old-town bustle: the famous cathedral Notre Dame de la Treille is just behind the hotel, and across the way, through a doorway by a craft shop, is the unexpected reward of the Hospice Comtesse. Today's entrance and light, bright reception area are welcoming, and bedrooms, renovated in smart beiges and greys, have contemporary Baroque-inspired curves and decorative swirls, neatly straddling the period setting and 21st-century expectations. Some rooms are quite compact, but no less comfortable; others (pricier) have space for couples. Smaller single rooms are ideal for those who just use the hotel for sleeping and spend their weekend enjoying all the city has to offer. An adapted room for guests with disabilities was part of the first refit. The architecture- and horticulture-inspired framed prints on bedroom walls may also be seen in the breakfast room and reception lounge – a useful venue for welcoming friends over coffee before slipping out to hit the shops and attractions of the district. Otherwise, simply looking out from a bedroom window towards rue de Gand and down to place du Lion d'Or provides a perfect appetiser to an evening on the town. Private (yet pricey) parking option available on request. Rooms €80–200; breakfast from around €14. €€

GRAND 51 rue Faidherbe 261 K5 03 20 06 31 57 w grandhotellille.com Gare Lille Flandres; turn right on to rue Faidherbe
A clean, modestly priced hotel on the main thoroughfare from the stations to the squares. Rooms are bright if a teensy bit tight on space, which is fine if you intend to spend most of your time out exploring the town and saving the extra money for a special meal. Soundproofed windows come as standard. Pay a tad more for the *chambre grand confort* with room to manoeuvre and a nice big bathtub. Cheery, welcoming reception staff. Rooms €68–400. €

GRAND HÔTEL BELLEVUE 5 rue Jean Roisin 261 H5 03 20 57 45 64
w grandhotelbellevue.com Rihour
Never mind the postal address, this hotel has double-glazed rooms on Grand' Place itself, giving a thrilling goodnight view of a city at play. No mere onlooker, however, the hotel has long played an active role in Lille's musical heritage – not just because the brass plaque by the entrance announcing the address as the Brazilian Consulate might inspire dreams of Latin nights and carnival costumes. Ever since the evening a young Mozart played in one of the building's original salons (the nine-year-old prodigy stayed here for four weeks with his father Leopold when he was taken ill en route from England to the Netherlands), the building has enjoyed much dabbling in the arts. A function room occasionally doubles as a theatre and breakfast is served in the Vivaldi room, whatever the season. The reception area adds a hint of a flourish to the décor, while rooms attempt to blend slightly garish, boxy high-street furniture with classic period pieces. The marbled en-suite facilities add a certain indulgence to prices that are comfortably lower three-star (€100–300) for a four-star address. €€

L'HERMITAGE GANTOIS 224 rue Pierre Mauroy 262 H2 03 20 85 30 30
w hotelhermitagegantois.com Mairie de Lille; walk westward along av du Président Kennedy & turn left on to rue Pierre Mauroy
Lille's first five-star hotel is more than just a place to rest your weary head, it is a veritable restorative for the soul. Now with a full spa and swimming pool for pampered guests, in its new

incarnation within the Marriott Bonvoy Autograph Collection, it remains one of the best-kept secrets in the city, an unmissable site in its own right and architecturally a consummation devoutly to be wished. Before the turn of the 21st century, most visitors saw number 224 as little but an imposing 15th-century gable on the walk from central Lille to the Porte de Paris remnant of the original city walls (page 199). To locals, it always had a special place in their hearts as the Hospice Gantois, a hospital and old people's home, its courtyard a peaceful haven and escape from the bustle of everyday life. The institution was founded in 1462 as the St John the Baptist Hospice by wealthy merchant Jean de la Cambe, better known as Jean Gantois. His other main claim to philanthropic fame was in establishing a rest home for retired sex workers, and this legacy of health care for the poor (irrespective of their lifestyles) continued until 1995 when the hospice, a listed building since 1923, finally closed its doors. This cluster of religious and secular buildings was then united by architect Hubert Maes into an exciting celebration of one of the few survivors of the long-demolished Saint-Sauveur quarter. An imaginative revival of street façades gives not a clue to the thrilling marriage within: contemporary design ties the knot with a respect for history, beamed ceilings, panelled walls and smart tiled floors. Former dormitories and wards make way for 67 bedrooms and suites, clustered around four courtyards. Rooms are nicely equipped and bathrooms well proportioned. Even if you can't afford to stay the night or go for the full €25 breakfast, remember the central atrium bar is open to everyone. Flop in a comfy sofa and gaze heavenward through glass at the architectural harmonies or spend some time relaxing in the sauna. Among the eclectic treasures housed within the hotel are sundry vintage medical instruments (including a 1926 X-ray machine) and the body of the hospice's founder, buried in the chapel. Tuesday mornings see tours of the building (a bonus, since this listed building used to open to the public on but two days a year). You may sneak peeks at the courtyards, chapel and other gems of the ground floor when you take the coffee and *croissant* bar breakfast or afternoon tea. A classic wine list at around €12 a glass is the perfect way to toast the original general manager Danielle Gey, whose wit and perception in hand-picking an excellent staff proved the lady from Biarritz was blessed with the typically Lillois wisdom to unite old walls with young minds. Raise a second glass to her successor André Grosperrin, who oversaw the extension of the hotel to a new annexe next door without losing the charm of the original buildings. One trick of discreet revisionism makes me chuckle: the principal ballroom has been renamed the Salle des Hospices, the original title being considered unsuitable for the hospitality industry. Since Jean Gantois's day it had been better known locally as the Salle des Malades! Wi-Fi. Rooms €200–1,250. €€€€

HILTON 335 bd de Leeds ♀ 259 J3 ☏ 03 20 42 46 46 w hilton.com 🚇 Gare Lille Europe
Until recently this was the Crowne Plaza, one of those conference-type hotels standing slap on top of the Eurostar station. But, after an interregnum in the guise of Hotel Lille-Euralille, late 2024 had it emerge with a new identity as a fully fledged Hilton Hotel. The iconic copper façade remains, but gone are the interior browns and beiges and transparent plastic chairs of its Philippe Starck design era, replaced by comfortable and sensibly designed rooms, smart woodwork and muted shades, all befitting a modern traveller, passing through or staying put for business or leisure. Rooms feature USB sockets by beds for phone charging, new bathrooms with good strong showers and (finally) strong enough Wi-Fi. If you prefer a well-maintained room more practical than quirky, you may be in the shower within 3 minutes of the train pulling into the Gare Europe. Simply go up the escalator from the platform, cross the road and check in to a room with a view over the city.

A new team, cannily blending industry experience with the cream of youthful enthusiasm from the better hospitality colleges, provides a welcome that is easy and natural. The lobby bar-lounge no longer feels like an executive waiting room but a genuine hangout for a mixed bag of ages, with holiday makers and locals mingling alongside obvious business delegates. The barman knows his local beers, gins and whiskies, and the professional and friendly restaurant staff, aware of the conference market and city-hopping timetable, can genuinely time your last lunch in Lille to your Eurostar departure from the station downstairs (*café espresso et l'addition* to departure gate check-in within 5 minutes). Good local recipes and provender feature on the menu. Budget €115–400 for your room and expect little change from €20 for a delicious and more than decent breakfast, unless your online deal throws it in for free. €€€

KANAÏ 10 rue de Béthune ♀ 261 H6 ☏ 03 20 57 14 78 w hotelkanai.com ⬚ Rihour; take rue Vieille Comédie to the corner of rue de Béthune
Well known to night owls, this centrally located hotel in a noisy district has clean, modest-sized rooms smartly (or garishly) tinged with mauves, and fresh, sharply designed shower rooms. Above the shops in the lively pedestrianised zone and with no lifts to take you up two or three spiral flights of stairs to bed, the place is nonetheless popular with a younger crowd and presided over by very welcoming and efficient reception staff. Surprising L'Occitane freebies and *de rigueur* espresso machine (here deploying Café Richard pods) give a pretty good indication that the management is aware of what is being offered by pricier and starrier establishments elsewhere. Prices for the smallest rooms start at the €75 mark off-season. If TV in the rooms is not your distraction of choice, borrow a book from the lobby shelves. The breakfast buffet is locally sourced, with ingredients delivered to the hotel by bike, backing up the green credentials. Late-night room snacks are of the gastro variety, arriving in sealed jars, and produced by Michelin chefs under the Boco label. €€

LILLE CITY 57 rue de Béthune ♀ 261 H7 ☏ 03 20 12 96 96 w lillecityhotel.com ⬚ République Beaux-Arts; follow pl Béthune to rue de Béthune
Formerly of the Mister Bed budget chain, Lille City is a recently refreshed and surprisingly affordable hotel inside a faded mini mall of mostly shut-down streetwear outlets. A glass door within leads to a lift to the hotel reception, breakfast room and urban terrace. Rooms are spread over two floors and tend to be small but basic, with good quality linens and reasonably sized bathrooms. There are few plug sockets though, so once your phone is being charged bedside, you'll need to unplug the TV should you want to use any other appliances. Working on my laptop, I never got to test the telly options. Forewarned, bring a recommended multi-plug adapter with you, or pick one up from Monoprix round the corner. Listed as accessible, all floors are served by modest sized lifts, though a heavy front door can be a challenge from a wheelchair. Even officially adapted bedrooms are tight on space with no easy transfer from chair to bed, so depending on ability/needs ask specific questions before booking. There was no spare socket in the only wheelchair-wide part of the room for charging a chair battery, so you might need to drag the cable into the shower-room. The shower and WC area is very easy to use, though. Staff, from management to cleaners, are extremely friendly and helpful. The standard buffet breakfast may be eaten indoors or on a terrace, and there is a basic hot food and beer option for night owls, though late-night brasseries may be found just a few minutes from the hotel. Prices often

start under €60, but contact the hotel directly to guarantee a price-match discount on any online offers from booking sites. €

LILLE EUROPE Av le Corbusier 📍 259 H4 📞 03 28 36 76 76 **w** hotel-lille-europe.com 🚉 Gare Lille Flandres

Nestling between the two main railway stations, this *hôtel de la gare de nos jours* in the original Euralille building was originally commissioned as a two-star, hotel, before being launched as a three-star. Which explains how it squeezes in 97 bright, light and euphemistically cosy bedrooms, with bedside phone charging and mini bars, plus espresso units in Premium rooms. Bathrooms have bright lighting and either tubs with glass screens or strong showers. However, loos are in a snug niche with very limited elbow room. Furniture in accessible rooms folds away for wheelchair access, and what family rooms lack in size, they make up for with two bathrooms. Front rooms have great views towards the park, while quieter rooms at the back look over the rooftops of Euralille. In contrast to such compact, smart and functional bedrooms and the tiny street-level reception area, the showcase feature of the hotel is a massive double-height, glass-wrapped breakfast room and lounge, designed by Jean Nouvel (architect of the new Louvre in Abu Dhabi) and poised above Euralille's main entrance. Sweeping views take in Parc Matisse across the Le Corbusier bridge between the stations, and the panoramic early morning bustle as northern France goes to work in the city. Here, you may savour one of Lille's very best value hotel breakfasts at around €14. The cold buffet features excellent plump, buttery, crispy and flaky *croissants* and *pains au chocolat* from one of the city's premium bakeries, along with meats, cheeses, hard-boiled eggs and fresh fruit. Local treats include chicory as a coffee alternative. Help yourself to real coffee and juices then saunter to a table by those huge showcase windows. I love the hotel's can-do approach to challenges: once, when there were problems with the Wi-Fi, I was offered a pocket 4G fast router to use out and about in the city as well as in the room, so saving on phone data charges. Many of the helpful front desk team have been at the hotel for years. Room rates begin at €60 in quiet season. €

MAMA SHELTER 97 pl Saint Hubert 📍 259 H4 📞 03 59 82 72 72 **w** mamashelter.com/lille 🚉 Gare Lille Flandres; walk down av Le Corbusier & turn right into rue des Connoniers

'Are you seeing anyone special?' 'Are you eating enough?' 'Let me look at you properly.' OK, the receptionist does not actually utter the phrases. Yet, the corporate Mama hug that hangs in the air might be a tad overwhelming if you were not expecting it. This hip and cool in-joke of a brand is all embracing and all welcoming, with the fictional declaration that 'Mama Loves You' appearing everywhere from merchandising at reception to lipstick messages on mirrors and Post-It notes in the fridge. Close by the stations, this is a perfect first stop: take the lift to your room to be greeted by homely touches that'll make you feel like a student back from uni, including carnival masks hanging over the bedside lamp, a bottle of apricot juice, and even a Tupperware container of homemade cookies. What I especially liked was the furled umbrella in the room, acknowledging the climate of northern France, and useful for nipping out to the métro station across the way. Rooms are comfortable with enough sockets and lights, and movies to stream if you don't fancy going out. The hotel can also bring your night out to you, with the restaurant hosting live music as well as regular DJ nights. (I was seriously impressed by a singer delivering next-level blues and soul one Saturday, who sent shivers down the spine with everything from 'Stand By Me' to a slow and sultry 'Barbie Girl'). An excellent nutritious, mouthwatering and varied €21 breakfast takes over the bar/dining room the morning after, followed by an American Roadhouse-style menu at lunch and dinner which attracts family and after-work crowds that outnumber resident guests. Surprisingly, there's no hot drink facility in the €100+ bedroom (this is an infuriating trend at the coolest new places), and while you may order a coffee, tea or hot chocolate from the bar downstairs, you pay each time. I nipped to Euralille opposite and bought a cheap kettle for under €10. Members of the Dis-loyalty card scheme may claim up to 50% off room rates and 10% discount on meals. €€

MERCURE LILLE CENTRE GRAND PLACE 2 bd Carnot ♀ 261 J4 ✆ 03 20 14 71 47

w all.accor.com 🚊 Gare Lille Flandres, then walk or take bus 10, 14 or 50 to Lycée Pasteur
This dear old diva loitering behind the stage door of the opera house has finally dropped her maiden name and fallen in corporate line, announcing herself as the Mercure. Previously known and loved as Le Royal, now she works under the colours of a global brand. Until recently somewhat faded and slightly worn, following her first serious face-lift when the Opéra itself was rejuvenated for Lille2004, this chain hotel with a friendly provincial welcome has been spruced up anew for the renaissance of a long-ignored corner beside the place du Théâtre. With its good-sized bedrooms, spacious en-suite bathrooms and smart new look, this acquisition of the Accor group is no longer the forgotten hotel of Lille. Perfectly poised at the junction of the old and new towns, it's a short walk from the station and handy for the fun of a night on the town and a day at the heart of the city. The breakfast room/bar is now open all day, serving *charcuterie* platters and wine in the evening as an alternative to the coffee, juice and pastries of the morning. Bright, air-conditioned rooms come with huge windows and even bigger blow-up photos behind the beds, as well as Wi-Fi and cable TV. Rooms from €110 ever upwards. €€

MOXY 3 rue Jean Bart ♀ 262 F4 ✆ 03 59 61 40 40 w marriott.com/fr/hotels/lilox-moxy-lille-

city 🚊 République Beaux-Arts or bus L5 to Liberté
Just stop to drop your jaw before passing through the grand iron gates of this hotel and take in the majesty of the building. This is not merely a bed for the night, it is Lille's architectural and cultural heritage. Just along the way is the wonderfully camp homage to local hero Louis Pasteur (page 189), first dean of the Faculty of Sciences, and here, in the heart of the university district, cheek by jowl with SciencesPo and the library, is the original Faculty of Medicine and Pharmacy. A cherished part of the local heritage register, the listed red-brick building resembles a majestic 19th-century railway terminus, complete with mosaics and clockface on its façade. If the outside quickens the heart, within all is studied San Francisco cool, featuring retro radios and turntables on the shelves of a lounge/co-working space (bar cocktails behind reception). In truth, this youthful vibe reflects the wider quarter of 19th-century university buildings, whose historical significance is ignored by throngs of convivial undergraduates and distracted dons. The buzz is as friendly inside as the pedestrians are outside. Away from the street art and flophouse kitsch of the lobby and bar, the surprisingly small bedrooms are far more minimalist, with metal and wood industrial décor, cages as wardrobes, very comfortable beds and plenty of tech (cast your phone to the TV screen). Yet no desk or mini-bar/coffee platter. When questioned, reception staff referred to the hotel's conviviality first policy: all typing and sipping should be done in communal public spaces rather than the bedroom, and they would be delighted to make you a nice hot

drink. Nonetheless, it is annoying to have to get dressed and shod in the middle of the night to shell out €4 for an emergency cuppa when you are not in the party mood. Or to settle down to compose your emails at excellent lobby workstations when surrounded by revelers during an evening drinks reception. This policy might be seen by less charitable souls as a money spinner for the bar. On the plus side, you'll find reliable lighting, USB sockets and excellent blackout blinds in bedrooms, and really good bathrooms with power showers and comfy towels. A fitness and ironing space echoes the school's-out, let-your-hair down mood. The breakfast is good for the star rating/budget. Accessible rooms have only just enough space to park your chair but very well-designed and easy-to-use shower rooms and WC. Room rates start around €100 and rise from there. €€

OKKO LILLE CENTRE   13 rue d'Amiens 📍 261 H6 📞 03 20 48 19 40 w okkohotels.com
🚇 Rihour; take rue de Béthune to Le 31 then turn left into rue d'Amiens
Confession time: I originally decided to stay here as I rather liked the idea of spending a night in a department store. Taking the biggest slice of the former Galeries Lafayette (now known as Le 31; page 178), filling up three floors of the building, is an hotel quite unlike any other in Lille. Its past life means fabulously high ceilings in spacious, bright and attractive bedrooms, but otherwise there's no hint of what was there before, so you'll never know whether you are laying down your head in the former handbags or glad rags department. Aside from the universal issue of negotiating heavy fire doors and a need to stretch to reach the beside lamp, this has one of the most practical accessible rooms in the city: wheelchair users have plenty of space to turn around, get in and out of bed, set up any equipment and appliances, and access the impressive bathroom. Even the make-up/shaving mirror is fixed at sink height; only the tissues and hairdryer are out of reach, remedied by a call to housekeeping.

There are many extras to be appreciated, including €10 worth of international and unlimited domestic landline and mobile phone calls. But the biggest plus is the brand's trademark Le Club, which doubles as the breakfast room for a frankly delicious €20 buffet start to the day, with even gluten-free bread and pastry options. And who needs a hospitality hot drinks tray in the bedroom with this 2nd-floor airline-style lounge, where soft and hot drinks are free all day long? Especially when those hot drinks include top-end Palais des Thés loose teas with self-tying teabags (I had dried mint and green tea) and barista-quality coffee from the coffee machine, offered alongside fresh and dried fruits and nuts. There is even a chilled water dispenser to fill your own bottles. The light and airy space is lounge, library, office and business centre, and all opens into a big bar and terrace. Between 18.30 and 20.30 in the evening, you'll receive a complimentary plate of local *charcuterie*, cheeses or vegetarian hummus/tapenade alternative if you pay for a craft beer or wee dram. While bedrooms have a truly excellent foldaway connected workstation, Le Club and the terrace make an attractive co-working space where you may use the printer (even the house PC), make photocopies, and enjoy hot and cold running refreshments. My tip to anyone with a laptop to-do list staying elsewhere is to skip the breakfast option in your own hotel across town and come here first thing. Non-residents get to enjoy the generous breakfast and day's full use of the facilities for €30 (there are also hourly and half-day options). Hot food may include a superior *croque monsieur* (Poilâne artisan bread, ham and 18-month aged Comté cheese) at €14. There's no need to join the fashionable gym in Le 31 complex downstairs to work it off, since the Okko's own fitness room overlooks the terrace and helpful reception staff will work out a running/jogging circuit from the hotel for you. All this in a great location between the shopping and entertainment district, the squares, and the Beaux Arts cultural attractions. Seasonal room rates €100–450. €€

URBAN HOTEL 48b rue de Valenciennes ♀ 259 J8 ☏ 03 20 92 50 57 w urbanhotel.fr
🚊 Porte de Valenciennes; follow bd Belfort to rue Trevisse, pl Guy de Dampierre then rue de Valenciennes
Next to the Salvation Army building in a street of factory conversions and century old redbrick terraces, Urban provides a Best Western-branded *bienvenue* to the renaissance of a grand mansion, once home to 19th-century mill owner M. Pouillet. The ground floor is satisfyingly opulent, with an imposing staircase wrapped around a dinky glass elevator, and an extravagantly lavish dining room, Rococo, that has become a food destination in its own right (page 120). Recently, all 40 bedrooms over four floors underwent a discreet renovation project, and while they still lack the vintage kitsch of the public rooms, there are no more glaring 1990s anachronisms, just standard smart décor with espresso and tea-making facilities. Beds are firm and comfortable and surrounded by ample power sockets. Well-lit bathrooms have big mirrors and hairdryers, and boast strong showers and dispensers of citrus shampoo and soap gels. More spacious deluxe rooms, with sitting areas, have bathtubs rather than showers. Comfy, spacious adapted rooms on the ground floor have a folding stool and grab rails in a roll-in shower, and are soundproofed from the busy Rococo restaurant along the corridor. There is a tiny wheelchair lift from street level to the lobby and another serves the basement breakfast room. The advantage of an hotel on St-So side of town, away from obvious tourist or business hot spots, is getting so much more for your money. Although if you recall the spacious free-to-guests spa, big enough for a cabinet meeting, alas it is now just a memory – closed during Covid, never to reopen. Nonetheless, a large outdoor courtyard lounge has comfy seating and tables and a smokers' area, and there is now a garden too. A VIP Box photobooth at reception (with dressing up accessories) takes guests' selfies and will post to your Insta or print them out as a souvenir. Free car parking for 20 cars, first come first served. €€€

WHY HOTEL 7 sq Morisson ♀ 261 G6 ☏ 03 20 50 30 30 w why-hotel.com 🚊 Rihour; walk past the tourist office & sq Morisson is on your left
Not just a Best Western hotel but arguably the Very Best Western. This boutique hotel converts a dull concrete office block on the wrong side of place Rihour into a rather lovely pamper palace within walking distance of everything. The reception desk might be made from glazed-over vintage kitchen cabinets, but bottles and cases of quality champagnes feature in display cases by the lift on each floor and facilities include a mini gym. My bedroom was a modest-sized, lozenge-shaped sanctuary with huge circular windows, top-branded soaps and plenty of treats and distractions. Welcome nibbles included mini Mars, Snickers and Bounty bars, a plate of pastel-shaded macaroons and a little tub of Haribo sweets to cover all comfort food cravings and inspire sugar rushes. A smart Nespresso machine and iPad dock suggests the target market. The bathroom has a wooden sink (triumph of design over function) and a peek-a-boo shower with full voyeur potential, thanks to one wall being a full-length window in prime line of sight from the pillows on the bed – although there are venetian blinds to tease or temper exhibitionism with modesty. The firm, high-level bed itself was the most comfortable I have enjoyed in Lille. On the ground

floor, the Why Dinette restaurant spills into a glazed terrace, popular with local office workers (page 123). A professional team glides between the front-of-house zones, lounge and reception with the neo-kitsch self-awareness of the décor, reminding visitors that, despite the veneer of informality, this is still a quality deal. Breakfast at €18 in the restaurant is imaginative yet familiar, with delicious *pain au chocolat* and excellent country-grain breads. Hot food on my visit included creamy mushrooms, which were simply scrumptious, with smoked salmon atop toasted *brioche*. The ubiquitous Nespresso also makes an encore appearance at the buffet, along with a great range of imaginative fruit juices, fine jams and honeys, and a choice of quality butters. Rooms €115–1,200 (suite with decked roof terrace). €€€

SELF-CATERING

Aparthotels are a great way to enjoy the basic services of a hotel, with the freedom of your being in your own home – so no need to pay for each breakfast, lunch and dinner of your stay in Lille. Budget-conscious travellers may cook for themselves, saving restaurant experiences for the occasional evening, and true foodies can try to recreate a great restaurant dish for themselves with fresh produce from local markets.

As well as the establishments listed below, and other apartment chains with branches a little farther out from the centre, you may find city-centre self-catering options in private homes from around €300 per week. See page 85.

ADAGIO ACCESS LILLE VAUBAN 17 rue Colson ♀ 260 B5 ☏ 03 20 15 43 43 w adagio-city.com 🚌 Bus Citadine from Gare Lille Flandres to Sacré Cœur, then walk along rue Nationale & it's the first right into rue Colson

I needed a little persuasion to return to this address a few years back. When, many moons earlier, the building had been simply student digs, I had spent the longest of long weekends here, first abandoning the dodgy bed in favour of the floor and finally rushing out to budget shops to buy my own bedlinen. Thankfully, those demons are now laid to rest and I've been back several times. Here cleanliness is next to good-night's-sleepliness, and the place is an excellent value, spotless and welcoming self-catering option. Rebranded by current owners Accor from sundry interim corporate identities, it now serves holidaymakers and business guests as efficiently as it continues to host a cheerful student population in the heart of the halls of residence district. Behind what looks like a basic apartment block, in a side street beyond the Solférino that links rue Nationale to boulevard Vauban, is a warren of pathways connecting a chain of buildings, all home to studios and one-bed apartments with decent internet access. Some accommodation is still reserved for the university, but other flats are designed for visitors. Good-sized rooms feature kitchenettes with a microwave, hob, filter-coffee machine and fridge, with sliding doors to the bedroom in larger units. A ground-floor bar serves optional breakfasts and here student residents mingle with visitors. Reception staff are very friendly and helpful, and there is an underground car park (pay extra). It's ideally suited to night owls since the place is around a 15-minute walk home from the restaurants of the old town and less than 10 minutes from the bars of the Solfé. Get to know the bus network, as walking to the nearest métro is not easy – though several bus routes from the stops on both main roads will take you to and from République Beaux-Arts in 5 minutes or so. The distance from Lille Europe keeps rates surprisingly low. Rooms from around €60 per night. €

ADAGIO LILLE CENTRE GRAND PLACE 76 rue de l'Hopital Militaire ♀ 261 G5

📞 03 74 09 03 01 w adagio-city.com 🚇 Rihour; walk rue du Palais Rihour, past tourist office to rue de l'Hôpital Militaire

Lille now has a second Adagio aparthotel (see page 79 for the first), this time tagged as Grand Place and much more centrally located, within walking distance to most attractions. Borrow toasters and other appliances from the lobby to enhance your studio or apartment lifestyle. €

CALM APPART'HOTEL 2 rue des Buisses ♀ 261 K5 📞 03 20 15 84 15 w appart-hotel-lille.

com 🚇 Gare Lille Flandres; walk down rue des Buisses behind the Napoleon bar

Lille3000 launched a new wave of aparthotels, including this one located just yards from the Gare Flandres, behind more traditional station hotels. Sharing premises with a youth hostel, it has a young, fun vibe with smart full-length black-and-white photos in the lobby and walls covered with those random English phrases you might find on a French teenager's T-shirt or souvenir mug. Reception is at street level, and each member of the team I met during my few days here was as helpful and charming as the last. A pneumatic folding platform at the side of the few steps to the hotel lift is groaned and creaked into service for guests with mobility issues, and a conventional elevator takes you to bedrooms, each equipped with kitchenette. Reflecting its standing as a budget version of trendier neighbours, the *de rigueur* Nespresso machine was a communal affair on my visit, in a hallway seating area by the lift rather than in the bedroom (and we paid per capsule). A take-away style breakfast was offered at €12, but trumped by guest initiative. On my first morning, I walked to the coffee shops by the station, dithered between American-style grandes with muffins and the local option, and spent a few euros on take-away *café crème* and *croissant* from Paul's nearest sandwich stall counter. By day two, I had visited Carrefour hypermarket to pick up a pack of ground coffee, a carton of milk for the room fridge and some *brioche* for the larder, as well as a plastic filter cone and huge pint-sized coffee mug. Interestingly (perhaps a sign of the cutting-edge clientele), and despite no official in-room coffee option, an aerosol of balsamic vinegar was provided. Most basic rooms are a fair size, with excellent bathrooms, comfy beds and pleasant grey shaded décor. Larger (and larger still) bedrooms, up to a vast 40m^2 (bigger than a flat in Paris) come with both bathtub and shower. Rooms €70–350. €€

CITADINES CITY CENTRE LILLE 83 av Willy Brandt ♀ 259 H4 📞 03 28 36 75 00

w citadines.com 🚇 Gare Lille Flandres; av le Corbusier to Euralille, then left on to av Willy Brandt

In the Euralille building, and opposite the Tripostal exhibition space, this central self-catering option was the first to offer competitively priced studios and larger apartments with well-equipped kitchenettes and extra facilities, from adequate buffet breakfast (but why pay extra when you have your own kitchen?) to a launderette. Studios start from under €100 per night in quiet season, rising to double when busier, with reductions for weekly bookings. There's also the option of a slightly higher rate for those requiring a full hotel package, with daily maid service. Otherwise, pay the basic price and use the dishwasher, vacuum cleaner and ironing board provided. Security is pretty good, with front doors locked and guests given private entry codes if the main desk is unmanned. A very helpful reception team and basement parking are among the bonuses. €€

EDGAR SUITES 10 pl de la Gare 259 G4 07 68 42 28 28 w edgarsuites.com
Gare Lille Flandres

Still a work in progress when last I passed by, the renovation of the old Hotel Faidherbe by the station may yet become a top-end aparthotel experience. Interior designer Léonie Alma Masson was inspired by the 1920s façade to create ten two- or three-bed apartments, fully equipped with everything from egg whisk and cafetière to hotel-quality linens on the queen-sized beds. There's no on-site receptionist, but guests will be given the mobile number of a personal manager to meet them on site and be on call throughout the stay. Looking forward to my first visit.

NOVOTEL SUITES GARE LILLE EUROPE Bd de Turin 259 J4 03 20 74 70 70
w novotel.accor.com Gare Lille Europe; cross bd de Turin from the station

A great concept by the Accor chain, this aparthotel opposite the Credit Lyonnais tower on the edge of town is a reinvention of the hotel room concept. It offers an L-shaped space, with bedroom and bathroom at 90 degrees to the living space, and each area may be separated by sliding divider screens. An extra divan by the table/workstation allows a friend to crash for the night. Amenities include internet, TV, movies and music on demand, free local phone calls, and fridge, microwave, Nespresso and kettle in each room. Boutique Gourmande chill cabinets in the reception area stock salads, soups, desserts and ready meals. Mornings in the bar lounge see nutritionally balanced breakfasts at around €19. Good accessible rooms, to tick most boxes. Budget €105–500 per night. €€

RESIDHOTEL LILLE VAUBAN 69–71 bd Vauban 260 B5 03 28 82 24 24
w residhotel.com Bus L5 from Lille Europe to Universite Catholique

A new name (it was formerly known as Cosy's), same value budget studios and apartments, close to parks and the Citadelle in the Catho student quarter, yet still an easy walk down the Solfé to nightlife. Flats sleep one to five people and are efficiently equipped with a standard two-hob and microwave kitchenette combo, with separate workstation and basic TV channels. Brown wood veneer dominates a colour scheme of rich reds and greys. The optional communal breakfast is basic, but if you are staying more than one night, prepare your own in the room. There are pizza places nearby if you don't want to cook in the evening. Lower prices reflect the location away from the métro network, but bus stops outside reception link the apartments to stations and République. Off-peak studio rates often start at under €60, otherwise around €100 should cover it. €

SÉJOURS & AFFAIRES 271 av Willy Brandt 259 H5 03 20 04 75 51 w sejours-affaires.fr Gare Lille Flandres; walk along av le Corbusier to Euralille, then left on to av Willy Brandt

Don't be seduced by the Franglais implication of the name; this is not a love nest, as much as a collection of self-contained studio and one-bed flats, for the budget end of the business travel market, with a fair smattering of student digs as well. Less a hotel-style complex than neighbouring Citadines, this slightly pared-down version has key collection during working hours from a busy office rather than a traditional reception desk. Its small but well-equipped apartments are in the Euralille Towers. There's a breakfast option in the mezzanine bar – but with coffee maker, crockery and fridge in the room, why bother? It's situated right next door to the Carrefour entrance to the shopping mall (by the green pharmacy sign), making it very convenient for bringing in your own food and drink. Internet option available. Sometimes found on bargain listings as 'Les Estudines'. Budget €60–110 per night. €

HOSTELS

Hostels are excellent value for travellers on a budget, with bunk beds available in shared rooms sleeping four, six or more. Unlike most hotels, these have washing machines available to guests and often the option of preparing a picnic lunch for the day ahead

AUBERGE DE JEUNESSE STÉPHANE HESSEL 235 bd Paul Painlevé ♀ 259 H8
📞 03 20 57 08 94 w hifrance.org/auberges-de-jeunesse 🚇 Porte de Valenciennes
The best-value accommodation in Lille is the official Youth Hostel, if you don't mind sharing a room and have a membership card from a recognised national Youth Hostel Association. Recently

GÎTES

Self-catering *gîtes* are a great way to get to know a region, and the *département* of Nord has a huge range of privately owned holiday homes in the countryside within easy reach of the city. You can drive to the Ilévia car parks at the end of the métro lines and travel by public transport into the centre. You may also find self-catering apartments in the city centre. From €500–800 per week for four people, or €400+ for a couple, it is almost unbeatable value. Be aware, though, that basic prices may not include bed linen/towels.

Outside Lille, in villages within the greater metropolitan area, you may find *gîtes* in farm buildings from as little as €300 per week, with the average around €350. Or perhaps the *péniche* barge La Bigoudène moored on the canal at at Wambrechies (from €85/night) might take your fancy. Consider basing yourself even further afield, at an hour or so from the city, perhaps along the Côte d'Opale, or inland around the Monts de Flandres, along the battlefield remembrance circuit or the protected natural woods and parkland of Hainaut and the Avesnois.

To be at one with the environment, check out the **Gîtes Panda** brand in the protected countryside of the Avesnois or Scarpe-Escaut Natural Regional Park: eco-friendly accommodation approved by the World Wide Fund for Nature. Extras to help understand the natural setting are included, from binoculars and suggested walks to jam-making or trout-fishing excursions relocated to a spanking new, ultra eco-friendly building, rooms have one to six beds and cost from €20 pp per night. You may book or check in until midnight. €

THE PEOPLE 109 rue Saint-André ♀ 261 G1 ☎ 03 20 06 06 80 ⓦ thepeoplehostel.com
🚌 Bus 10 from Gare Lille Flandres to rue de Magasin

In most hostels, you may learn to speak French with a Scandinavian or Australian accent. After all, these places are where we meet up with fellow backpackers from around the world. However, this address in Vieux Lille, formerly known as Gastama, is a bit different: you are as likely to strike up a conversation with someone who lives around the corner as your Norwegian or Tasmanian gap-year student en route between Paris and London. Think of this almost as a neighbourhood nightspot with beds, since the street-level bar is a seriously popular hangout in the old town. A range of beers, from the Baltic to the Med, outnumber the *bières de Flandres*, and some weekend nights it's the mojitos and tequila slammers that set the tone for the evening. Accommodation-wise, there are dormitories with pine-framed and curtained bunk beds lined up against the red-brick walls of the loft, as well as a range of private and family rooms – with en-suite facilities – to rival local hotels. There is accessible accommodation and you'll find laundry facilities, too. Dormitory beds cost from €20 and private rooms from around €60; weekend rates are usually one or two euros higher than midweek. The inexpensive breakfast is a euro less if you book it on arrival. Tip: bring your own padlock for the dormitory locker, rather than paying for one at reception. €

with the property's owners! A *gîte* at **Féron**, in the Avesnes, meanwhile, is in a restored old village that has developed into something of an artists' colony. Here, Florence Beaurant teaches visitors her skills as a glassblower, and fellow artists open studios and workshops to showcase work restoring old paintings, creating ceramics or basket-weaving. Other artists direct their talent towards the table: village *boulanger* Mario bakes organic breads, and café-bar proprietor David serves locally brewed Flanders beers. Perhaps hire donkeys to explore the parkland.

Most recommended homes will be members of the associations **Gîtes de France du Nord** (ⓦ gites-de-france-nord.fr) or **CléVacances** (ⓦ clevacances.com), with comfort ratings indicated respectively by the number of ears of corn or keys. These organisations rate and inspect all properties listed. As a rule, prices do not include bedlinen and towels, which may be hired locally (reserve in advance), as most guests prefer to pack their own and save the cost for an evening out. Some *gîte* prices are exclusive of electricity, for which a supplementary charge may be payable. Others are all-inclusive. See online listings for details including accessibility, Wi-Fi and whether pets are welcome. Information brochures and booking details are available from Lille Tourist Office (page 49) or Hauts-de-France tourism (page 13), which has a selection of treehouses and wooden caravans to choose from.

6

BED AND BREAKFAST

The local tourist office (page 49) has updated lists of B&B establishments.

LE COMPTOIR INDUSTRIEL   19 rue Malus ♀ 259 F8 ☏ 06 63 44 38 91 w comptoir-industriel.com ☒ République Beaux-Arts or bus L5 to Liberté; at the end of the boulevard turn right on to bd Jean Lebas & take 2nd right to rue Malus

If bohemian luxe is a thing, then look right here: a *fin-de-siècle* studio workshop, hidden behind the Natural History Museum in the heart of the university quarter, converted into two fabulous loft-style studios. Cross a courtyard koi carp pond and settle into either the ground floor or first floor apartment. Inside each you'll find a king-size bed and some witty post-industrial furnishings, but the main room is dominated by a good-size jacuzzi spa. It is walking distance from museums, the central shopping quarter and even the lively Solfé district. Breakfast is included in the price, and there's an extra option of dining in with a homecooked *table d'hôte* meal for €30 per person. With an eye on romance, your hosts allow an extra hour in bed for honeymooners or can even set up all you need for a marriage proposal. Rooms €200–240. €€€€

LA COUR SOUBESPIN   30 rue Sainte Catherine ♀ 261 F2 ☏ 06 95 21 20 61 w cour-soubespin.fr ☒ bus L5 to Liberté, then bus L1 to Colpin; on Façade de l'Esplanade go left on rue Colpin then right on rue Sainte-Catherine

It is quite impossible to walk down the residential streets at the back of the old town, once the conviviality of the bars and restaurants starts to trickle away beyond the confluence of the rues Royale and Angleterre, without trying to imagine the interiors of those neat redbrick terraced houses, almost gingham checked with white mortar. What would it be like to live in one of these homes? Well, now you may find out. As much a mini *gîte* as a conventional *chambre d'hôte*, La Cour Soubespin is the doll's house option. A dinky little courtyard alleyway hides a trio of tiny one-bedroom red brick cottages, tucked away far enough from the main road for a good night's sleep. The smallest (Chez Gigi) would only fit a couple, while the other two also have a sofa bed in the living rooms for two more guests. The kitchenettes are decently equipped for breakfast, with a hob, microwave, kettle and espresso machine. Each morning, the owners themselves deliver a breakfast hamper of tea, coffee, milk, juice, jams and pastries. Nightly rates from €120. €€€

L'ESPLANADE   42b Façade de l'Esplanade ♀ 261 F1 ☏ 03 66 96 93 86 w esplanadelille.com ☒ Bus L5 to Liberté, then bus L1 to Colpin

Those who miss their weekends at the old Maison du Jardin Vauban might enjoy another home on the edge of the old town. Only, instead of the eccentric taxidermy and colonial souvenir clutter of the old house, here you may enjoy a deep inhalation of spacious calm. This lovely, bright and spacious building in the leafiest corner of Vieux Lille is a haven of minimalism and modernity, situated right on the Esplanade to the canal, overlooking another stretch of joggers' parkland around the Citadelle. Just around the corner from the original royal quarter, and a brisk 10–15-minute walk from the attractions of the centre, this charmingly refreshed 19th-century

◀ The eye-catching exterior of the Auberge de Jeunesse Stéphane Hessel, the city's official youth hostel.

As well as the very individual charms of the hotels reviewed here, the international hotel chains are well represented in town and across the greater metropolitan area.

The Accor group (Sofitel, Novotel, Mercure, Ibis, etc) alone has around 2,000 rooms in the district. This is just a selection of chain hotels in the central areas; there are plenty more to choose from on the corporate websites of the hotel groups.

Several other budget hotels can be found in the streets around Gare Lille Flandres station. The tourist office (page 49) publishes an online list of all registered hotels in and around town, and offers a booking service.

CAMPANILE

Lille Sud rue Jean Charles Borda ♀ 262 B5 ☎ 03 20 53 30 55 w campanile-lille-sud-chr.fr

HOLIDAY INN EXPRESS

Lille Centre 75 rue Léon Gambetta ♀ 262 E2 ☎ 03 20 42 90 90 w hotel-hiexlillecentre.com

IBIS

Lille Centre Grand-Place 21 rue Lepelletier ♀ 261 H4 ☎ 03 20 06 21 95 w ibis.com/lille **Lille Gares** 29 av Charles Saint-Venant ♀ 261 K7 ☎ 03 28 36 30 40 **Lille Roubaix Centre** 37 bd Gl Leclerc, 59100 Roubaix ☎ 03 20 45 00 00 **Lille Tourcoing Centre** Centre du Général de Gaulle, rue d'Havre, Tourcoing ☎ 03 20 26 29 58

Lille Villeneuve d'Ascq Grand Stade, rue des Victoires, Villeneuve d'Ascq ☎ 03 20 91 81 50

IBIS STYLES

Lille Centre Gare Beffroi 172 rue Pierre Mauroy ♀ 261 J8 ☎ 03 20 30 00 54 w ibis.com/lille

KYRIAD

Lille Centre 21 pl des Reignaux ♀ 261 K5 ☎ 03 28 36 51 18 w kyriad.com

NOVOTEL

Lille Aeroport 55 route de Douai, Lesquin ☎ 03 20 62 53 53 w novotel.com **Lille Centre Gares** 49 rue de Tournai ♀ 259 H5 ☎ 03 28 38 67 00 **Lille Centre Grand Place** 116 rue de l'Hôpital Militaire ♀ 261 F5 ☎ 03 28 38 53 53

family home draws an expanding regular clientele with its huge windows and spacious modern bedrooms, complete with shiny top-end shower rooms. The breakfast area and reception rooms are an ever-evolving art gallery, displaying works by up-and-coming artists. While you may prefer to saunter into town for restaurants, the proprietors are happy for guests to invite the restaurants to come to them. Simply stay home and set up a table for two in the rather grand breakfast salon and enjoy Deliveroo or Uber Eats orders from your favourite chef. €€€

LA MAISON BLEUE 21 rue Charles Quint ♀ 262 B2 ☎ 03 20 12 99 37 w lamaisonbleuedelille.e-monsite.com 🚇 Gambetta; from rue de Flandre turn right into rue du Marché to rue Charles Quint

This takes me back to my earliest *chambre d'hôte* stays in Lille, not too far from here. In the livelier Wazemmes district, La Maison Bleue is a traditional northern French B&B in a real home, with two guest rooms, one extravagantly floral, the other a classic shade of blue. Both have sturdy traditional wooden beds and are decorated with finds from family travels that echo the famous local *brocantes*, from Sunday's fleamarket around the corner to the annual festive weekend. There's lovely period stained glass in the windows and a separate guest sitting room, away from the bustle of a host family preparing its kids for school. €€

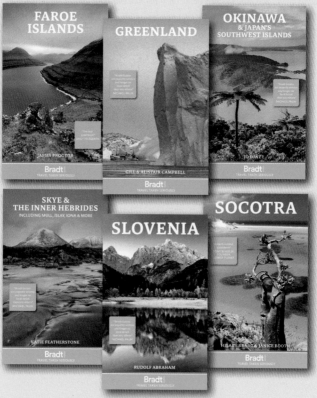
 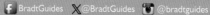

7

Eating and Drinking

Food and drink matter in Lille. The best argument of the day is deciding where to eat – a tavern serving savoury tarts with fresh-brewed beers; an old-fashioned traditional brasserie; gastronomic elegance with starched linens and eloquent menus to set the pulse racing; or a moody jazz café by the city walls.

There are so many flavours to be discovered that one mealtime is simply not enough. From one table to the next, you may segue from that which makes Lille French and that which sets it so very much apart. Regional specialities are a happy blend of the Flemish and northern French styles. Dishes may feature the cheeses of Mont des Cats and Maroilles, *genièvre* juniper gin, the famous Blanche de Lille white beer and other local brews, all tickled with local wisdom to transform the simplest of ingredients into something special.

Waterzooï, on many a menu, is a stew usually of freshwater carp, tench and pike; rabbit may be prepared with prunes; and winter warmers include the *hochepot* casserole of meats and market-garden vegetables, and the ubiquitous *carbonnade à la Flamande* simmered in beer, onions and brown sugar. Year-round favourite *potjevleesch* is a white-meat terrine, usually of chicken or rabbit. If all is reminiscent of Belgian comfort food, remember that Lille's borders have shifted almost with the tides.

Even more Belgian is that most traditional of budget meals, a pot of mussels served with a heap of chips. *Moules-frites* are an institution here, the single menu served during the Braderie (page 174), when piles of shells outside restaurants are the most photographed icon of the *rentrée*. Sausage lovers should seek out *Cambrai andouillette*, rated as among the best in France. *Welsh* is a peculiarly northern reinvention of Welsh rarebit, usually served in a soup bowl: cheddar-style cheese melted in beer and drenching a hidden slice of bread and (generally) ham, sometimes with an egg; always with chips. See individual brasserie or bistro reviews to discover the myriad variations on this cardiovascular white-knuckle ride.

To round off any meal, modern chefs make ice cream and sorbet with local flavourings: *fleur de bière*, gin and the ubiquitous *chicorée*. Traditional desserts include *tarte au sucre* and a local variation of bread-and-butter pudding known as *pain perdu*.

Easy to forget, with all these local flavours, that Lille is in France. Fortunately, almost every other region is represented with a restaurant or five to offer the flavours that lure most visitors across the Channel in the first place. Breton *crêperies* ward off summer snack attacks, and a browse through the following pages should lead you to specialities of Bordeaux and the southwest, and Lyon and the southeast. So, great steaks, *confit de canard*, truffles and *foie gras* are never too far away. And never forget that Lille is still a port, the third most important river port in France, very close to the big fishing fleets of the Channel. Fresh fish is on every menu: Dover sole and cod are among local catches, while tuna, salmon and sea bass feature in every chef's party pieces.

A new locavore movement celebrates produce sourced as close to the table as possible, and many leading chefs now forego even tomato and peppers out of season in favour of root vegetables plucked from the soil within half an hour of the kitchen. That said, influences from further afield are also taking up residence on many menus. As well as exciting ethnic innovations in food courts (page 126), Canadian fast food *poutine* (page 97) has found its way on to bistro and brasserie specials boards across town. But standard northern classics still reign supreme.

What to drink: might I suggest a beer (page 132)? Lille is a great brewing region, with some *brasserie* restaurants serving draught created in-house. It would be a waste to order a standard multinational brand

RESTAURANT PRICE CODES

Average price of a three-course meal. Where a traditional three-course menu is not available, we have based the price code on the cost of a typical meal instead.

€€€€€	Over €70
€€€€	€50–70
€€€	€35–50
€€	€20–35
€	Under €20

However, these ratings are not to be considered definitive. Even a €€€€ or €€€€€ designated restaurant may have a lunch deal to suit the seriously budget-conscious. In France, all restaurants are obliged to display their prices outside the front door, and most will offer a set-price meal deal. Very expensive restaurants often have a far cheaper *prix-fixe* menu at lunchtimes, usually featuring two, and occasionally three, courses, at half the above price code for free-range dining. See individual restaurant reviews for prices.

when the breweries around Lille create such memorable ales. These were once limited mainly to Ch'ti, La Goudale or Trois Monts, but nowadays a dazzling selection from myriad microbreweries can be found around town. A traditional lager is known as a *bière blonde*. Be guided by your waiter or barman and go with the seasonal specialities: in March, order the *bière de mars*, for one month only, a sprightly and heady affair; at Christmas, the spicy and fruity *bière de Noël* is a treat; at any time, but unbeaten as a summer cooler and quencher, the cloudy white *blanche de Lille*, served with a slice of lemon, is simply heavenly. For a bit of an extra kick, try beer brewed by the Wambrechies *genièvre* distillery.

Genièvre, a Dutch-style juniper gin, is distilled in and around Lille (page 233) and is a popular chaser, flavouring or mid-meal *trou* (to be gulped in one to clear the digestive system for more food). The base of many a house cocktail, it was once popular as a Chuche Mourette, blended, like a *kir*, with *crème de cassis*.

Whether due to Covid, the economy or simply the lure of retirement, the past several years have seen many favourite dining rooms close their shutters for the last time. Apart from the legends À l'Huîtrière and Aux Moules (page 106), physical landmarks such as the Compostelle and Les Remparts (in the actual Port de Gand gatehouse to the city itself) no longer receive the hungry and appreciative. Jean Luc Jermond had already hung up his toque at the original Le Sebastopol when his lauded *confrères* around town folded their napkins and stepped away from the city. If I miss Monsieur Jean's parlour above the main branch of Paul's, it is not necessarily for the food, but the trappings of a two-star Michelin chef, slumming it in a parlour above a branch of Paul's bakery. This departure marked the beginning of the end of an era of confusing dish descriptions. Marc Meurin's *velouté de chou-fleur, saumon fumé et caviar de Hareng* suggested *du Barry* soup with fishy garnish. In reality, smears of the anticipated warm cauliflower soup barely covered the bottom of a vast white bowl, but served as a groundsheet for lavish piles of superior-grade smoked salmon – to be eaten with a spoon! This was a regime of lavish staff to punter ratios: orders taken by a brace of highly professional secretary-bird waitresses, a lowly minion to brush away crumbs and food itself presented by an improbably perpendicular waiter.

The heirs and successors of these garlanded mantels offer a more stripped-back approach to service and cooking. The careers of the best-known *enfants terribles*, messieurs Ladeyn, Pourcheresse and Ramon, are celebrated on page 120; their contemporaries in the reviews and listings that follow. Still to check out on my next visit (you may yet beat me to it) are La Braque in Vieux Lille, project of another *Top Chef* laureat Damien Laforce, emerging from under Ladeyn's wing, and exploring further around Lambersart, notably Ismaël Guerre-Genton's l'Empreinte.

BUDGETING

I lingered long, mused much and pondered hard over how to categorise the restaurants of Lille. Unlike hotels, it is not really fair to classify the eateries of the town by price, since a good value set-menu lunch at even a famous gastronomic restaurant can often cost less than grazing à la carte in a bistro. So do not be hidebound by the restrictions of these listings since, should you fancy just a main course at a pricier restaurant, it may still work out cheaper than three courses at a mid-range restaurant. Nonetheless, the listings ahead also feature a reality check with the rates for a free-range food-fest.

Almost every restaurant offers special lunchtime deals between €25 and €40 per person, with many having a two- or three-course suggestion either side of €20. Be warned: the lowest-priced menu is usually served only at lunchtimes, so if you fancy good food and are worried about how far your euros will stretch, go for a big meal in the middle of the day and aim for something lighter in the evening. And unfortunately, inexpensive set meals may not be suitable for people with special dietary requirements. Non-meat eaters, for instance, may have to pay much more à la carte than their companions happy with the *plat du jour*! Restaurant prices include all taxes and service charges; it is customary to leave a small tip (usually loose change) to reward good service (page 50).

Brasseries are ideal for those who would rather just have one course instead of the pricier menu, and make a lively option for kicking off or rounding out an evening on the town. Check out the bar and café options at midday for a filling sandwich or *plat du jour*.

OPENING HOURS

Most restaurants open for dinner around 19.30–22.00 or 23.30, and lunch 12.30–14.00. City-centre bars usually stay open until after midnight, generally closing between 01.00 and 02.00. Where establishments open or close later than usual, it is mentioned in the text. With the exception of all-day and late-night brasseries, it is advisable to telephone in advance to make a reservation for dinner after 22.00 or for late lunches. Gastronomic restaurants may even shut down for two to four weeks in summer or a month in winter. And you will have far fewer places to choose from on a Sunday evening.

WHERE TO EAT AND DRINK

Bistro, brasserie or fine-dining room: to be honest, they are all restaurants. I have highlighted those that offer traditional bistro and brasserie fare or style, or that offer a typical Lillois, Flemish or French atmosphere. Other restaurants listed may be trendier or more traditional, but each establishment offers something different. However, in recent years the trend towards '*Bistronomie*' has blurred the boundaries between bistro, brasserie and even fine dining so much that you are as likely to find a *choucroute*, *andouillette* sausage or *Welsh* at a fine dining restaurant as in its traditional setting, and cross-cultural international fusion has become confusion in the other direction. So browse through the reviews in all categories before deciding where to lunch or dine. Lille's wine bars and *estaminets*, originally intimate bars in the front or back room of a village house, are also well worth thinking about. Also consider **Maisons Folies** (page 210) in town and around the region for the opportunity to break bread with the artists of Lille and beyond.

BISTROS AND ESTAMINETS

L'ARRIÈRE PAYS 47 rue Basse 261 H4 03 20 13 80 07 w arrierepayslille.fr
Rihour; Navette Vieux Lille to rue Basse
Essentially, this is a local bakery selling loaves of artisan sourdough (*pain au levain*) and *focaccia*. But its lovely dining rooms (red-brick décor upstairs, classic style downstairs) are simple and modern, respecting the period of the building, and provide a perfect excuse to taste the wares at brunch/lunch/teatime. Open sandwich tartines (France's answer to a ploughman's lunch) here include a €10 Oh My Duck (*magret de canard* with fig confit, brie, walnut and honey). Pastas are around €12 and a fixed-price lunch of daily dish and dessert with drink should set you back under €15. €

LE BARBUE D'ANVERS 1bis rue Saint-Étienne 261 H4 03 20 55 11 68 w barbuedanvers.fr closed Wed & Sun Rihour; take rue Roisin into rue de Pas & right on to rue Saint-Étienne
Hidden behind a high wall, the Barbue has presented classic Lillois fare to an appreciative mix of after-work colleagues, uni friends and quieter couples for two decades, yet its talent has only recently being recognised with a plaque as a Maitre Restaurateur. It still serves both *estaminet* and restaurant appetites; early days saw local Wambrechies gin (page 233) liberally sprinkled over duck dishes, while today's preferred boozy ingredient is local beer, with the legendary *carbonnade flamande*, previously infused with gingerbread, now billed as *à la bière Deconinck*. Vegetarians should find an acceptable risotto on the seasonal menu. You might not easily find a traditional *moules-frites* on every visit, but a contemporary gastro tweaking of classics won't be too far away. There's an impressive array of local gins and beers at the bar as well as a modest wine list. No set-price menu. Starters under €10, mains in the €20s. €€€

BISTROT DE ST SO Gare Saint-Saveur, bd Jean-Baptiste Lebas 259 G8 03 20 32 05 42 w bistrotdestso.com 11.30–23.00 Wed & Thu, 11.30–01.00 Fri & Sat, 11.30–21.00 Sun
Lille Grand Palais or bus 14 from Gare Lille Flandres to Lille-Lebas
The bistro-café-bar at St So, the former Saint-Sauveur railway station turned arts centre and community hang-out (page 200), has a great programme of live music events. Drop in for a coffee or local beer, snack and quick fix of popular culture; afternoons are family-friendly, switching to a bit of a party vibe by evening. Choose fish or meat of the day with starter or dessert for €18. Half-size portions for kids. Check gig guide online. €€

7

BISTROT DES TOQUÉES Les Toquées de la Cuisine, 110 quai Géry Legrand ♀ 260 A6 ⊕
☏ 03 20 92 03 21 w lestoquees.com ⏰ lunch Tue–Sat, dinner Thu–Fri 🚌 Bois Blancs or bus 18 to
Piscine M Dormoy, then av Butin to quai Géry Legrand
A pleasing little oddity, this bistro is part of a waterfront cookery school a good half-hour from
the stations and more than a walk from the centre. Budget perhaps €80–90 for evening menus
indulging in delectables such as oysters with caviar or scallop *carpaccio,* before a game or farmyard
main course, or €35 for two-course lunches. If you've not the time to indulge in a full lunch hour,
pick up a take-away midday meal from the *épicerie* for under €35 and enjoy lobster caviar and
perhaps a truffled *croque monsieur* at your desk. €€€€€

CHEZ LA VIEILLE 60 rue de Gand ♀ 261 K2 ⊕ ☏ 03 28 36 40 06 w estaminetlille.fr
⏰ closed Sun & Mon 🚌 Bus 9 to Lion d'Or; cross pl Louise de Bettignies to rue de Gand
Franck Delobelle may not be a grandmother, but his welcome is as warmly old-fashioned as the
wooden tables and hop-decked beams of this cheery Flemish dining room. From the crockery
on shelves above the seats to the traditional wooden toys and games in the window, La Vieille
is very much in the tradition of homely conviviality that marks out this popular *estaminet* by
the master hosts of Au Vieux de la Vieille (page 99) as the real McCoy rather than fashionable
reinvention as urban-rustic retro fad. Here, food is of exclusively seasonal regional standards
– warm stews in winter and tasty flans in summer – all prepared to old country recipes and
tasting as though stirred by a granddaughter under the watchful eyes of a matriarch. Black
pudding and apple *tatin* or chicken with Maroilles cheese are among winter warmers. The
genuinely house beer is Les Sept Péchés. Main courses come in at €15–20, with three-course
free-range dining from €35. €€€

LE COQ HARDI 44 pl du Général de Gaulle ♀ 261 H5 ⊕ ☏ 03 20 55 21 08 w coq-hardi.fr
🚌 Rihour; walk to Grand' Place
An institution on Lille's main square for donkey's years, the tables spreading out across the *place*
are better known than the small restaurant behind them. In fact, it was only the ominous grumble
of winter weather that led me to check out the restaurant itself. Small but perfectly busy, with
service on two floors, Coq Hardi is unashamedly basic and rustic. Inside are untreated wooden
ceilings, sacks of baguettes inside the front door and a constant flow of customers keen on value-
for-money lunching. Huge portions are the order of the day, whether *andouillette de Cambrai avec
frîtes* or a *tartare aux deux saumons,* served ready-mixed or with the additional ingredients on the
side. Most *plats* are €14–16. In sunshine, take a big bowl of *moules* or a huge summer salad and
lunch outdoors for well under €20, indulging in good old-fashioned people-watching at this key
corner between the old town and *la place.* €€

LA DUCASSE 95 rue Solférino ♀ 260 D6 ⊕ ☏ 03 20 57 34 10 w laducasse.fr 🚌 République
Beaux-Arts or bus 18 from Gare Lille Flandres to Sacré Cœur, then rue Solférino to pl des Halles Centrales
Just another corner bistro with an accordionist leading a sing-along of Saturday night standards,

---

1 Dining on pavement terraces is one of the delights of eating out in Lille. 2 Many
restaurants offer a good-value daily set lunch. 3 *Moules-frîtes* is a staple dish of the city.
4 The distinctive sign for the Brasserie de la Cloche. ▶

LAURENT JAVOY/HELLO LILLE

ALARICO/S

PAGE FREDERIQUE/S

PAUL MAGUIRE/S

perhaps. Yet the atmosphere is second to none: simple local stews and platters hit the spot, beer and wine flow freely and the local crowd are some of the nicest people you could ever meet. Students passing through Lille for two or three years may choose newer addresses along the road, but those living in apartments in the streets between the boulevards drop in here to sup with friends and neighbours rather than cook for themselves. The menu is unashamedly Flemish, and local beers are pulled from the pump. After an arduous day recording our BBC feature *Allez Lille*, my colleagues and I chose this corner for an anonymous, off-duty collapse. Hearing our English conversation, a local birthday party at the next table sent us over a bottle of wine and invited us to join them for coffee. A coin or two in the ancient pianola, and the honky-tonk piano-roll music whirred into action. Thankfully, producer Jerome Weatherald had a spare recorder in his pocket and was able to capture a few moments of that magical mood on tape. We ended the programme with a hint of our wonderful evening at the Ducasse, and shared the true spirit of Lille in a way mere words might never have managed. Have a *hochepot* or *waterzooï*, a chunk of steak and a hefty slice of *tarte*, then pour a large drink and sing along to a *chanson* from the golden age to feel the glow for yourself. I returned a year later to celebrate the launch of the Beaujolais *nouveau* – a bottle of wine was left on our table to tempt us to try it. Only the dozen *escargots* among the starters break the €10 barrier and most classic mains (including rabbit with prunes) would now see change from a €20 note. €€€

LE FILS À MAMAN 41 rue de Gand ♀ 261 K2 ⊛ ☏ 03 20 21 02 33 w lesfilsamaman.com
🚋 Bus 9 to Lion d'Or, then cross pl Louise de Bettignies to rue de Gand
If traditional *estaminets* along the way hark back to the childhood of our grandparents, then this newcomer to the rue de Gand scene evokes more recent memories of the '70s and '80s. Think pink-spined *Famous Five* hardbacks (French author Claude Voilier continued to produce new stories decades after Enid Blyton stopped writing), *Star Wars* toys, early Gameboy consoles against red-brick walls and menus in scrapbooks. This particular Mummy's Boy (part of a new national chain) has a few clean-your-plate-and-eat-every-crumb bribes (spin a wheel for loyalty points) and menus reflect a parent's culinary efforts to persuade you to leave the computer games upstairs and join the family at the table. Proud provenance of meats and produce suggests a canny cook with an eye on nutrition; the actual dishes of Babybel croquettes and Snickers *gateau*, more realistic parental submission. This is food of the after-school comfort food variety. Pay under €20 a head for a set menu or a tad more *à la carte*. €€

LA HOUBLONNIÈRE 42 pl du Général de Gaulle ♀ 261 H5 ⊛ ☏ 03 20 74 54 34
w brasserie-lahoublonniere-lille.fr 🚋 Rihour; walk to Grand' Place
You may be forgiven for thinking Grand' Place is lined with restaurant tables to sip and sup the day away simply people-watching. In truth, most restaurants are to be found in the street that links the main square with place Rihour, place de Gaulle itself being given over to grand buildings and the goddess. However, Le Coq Hardi (page 94) and its neighbour La Houblonnière offer that rare treat: rows of tables out on the square with the view over Lille's favourite meeting place. Admittedly tables are rather close to gently paced traffic, but hey, you are eating and drinking in the heart of the city. Don't spend a fortune – €30 at a squeeze should see you all right for a full three courses. Basic menus start at around €16. Go for traditional foods such as *rillettes*, *andouillette*, a chunky *tartare* of smoked and raw salmon or

cheese dishes: *tarte au Maroilles* or *Welsh*. Not gastronomy, just hearty stomach-fillers halfway through a day's hardcore walking or before an evening's serious partying. Dine upstairs to enjoy witty artworks. €€

L'IMAGINAIRE   5 pl Louise de Bettignies ♀ 261 J3 ⊕ ☎ 03 20 78 13 81 🚌 Bus 9 to Lion d'Or
Between the better-known dining areas of the centre is a *bar à tapas* next door to the hotel De la Treille (page 70), overlooking the busiest junction of the old town. But it is what lies behind that makes this a dinner venue to consider. The terrace at the back of the restaurant has a surprisingly excellent view of the original gothic back-end of Notre Dame de la Treille on the crest of the castrum hill. Essentially it's a bar, but it's also an unexpectedly quiet and sunny spot for lunch or an early evening rendezvous. Classic lunch dishes, mostly under €18, include thyme-infused *souris d'agneau* (lamb shank), escaloped chicken (creamy Normandy-style), chicken wings (served in the local *façon*, smothered with melted Maroilles cheese), beef tartare or classic minced horsemeat with egg. A *plat du jour* is under €15, chips €4, and last time we checked there were generous salads for the not-quite carnivore. €€

M'EATING   179 av de Dunkerque ♀ 260 A3 ⊕ ☎ 03 20 22 89 49 🌐 meating-lille.fr 🕐 closed Sun & eves Mon–Wed 🚌 Canteleux
Ignore both pun and errant apostrophe, and rely instead on the effective subtitle 'Cantine du Quartier'. Turning up at this simple, off-the-beaten-track restaurant feels like having lunch at a friend's house, albeit beyond the ring road and twice across the canal. Don't let the map deter you though, since at not much longer than 10 minutes by *métro* from the centre, it is quicker to get here than many of the addresses in Vieux Lille. In a simple dining room, adorned with handwritten pages of family recipes, no-fuss French canteen standards are presented with a charmingly domestic reinterpretation of flourishes found at designer tables elsewhere. Expect the universal techniques of *les grands* (drizzling and edible flowers), but covering a lot more of the big round white plate than in more fashionable districts. Host Annie may suggest kitchen wizard Pierre's soup of the day, a plate of *escargots*, or a *cassoulet* of curried gambas and leeks to start, perhaps followed by a *carbonnade*, pasta or simple crusted cod on a watercress risotto main course, rounded off with a creamy *tarte au citron* or *chocolat*. Spend €20–30 a la carte or opt for a three-course dish of the day-based menu at €21. €€

P'TITE POUTINE   61 rue Basse ☎ 03 20 04 51 38 ♀ 261 G4 ⊕ 🚌 Rihour; from Grand' Place take rue Esquermoise to rue Basse
Canadian and Quebecois flags and moose antlers adorn the shop front, so no confusion here: this is not a contemporary Russian tea room, but an outlet for bowls of *poutine*, the ubiquitous Quebec import of chips in gravy with caramelised onion and authentic *couic-couic* cheddar curds. Lille lad Clément Hottin spent two years working in Montreal and claims to have been first to bring the authentic dish back to his home town, more than five years ago, when he opened this wood cabin on rue Basse. (Although these days you'll find plenty of other places around town serving the dish, whether sharing the bill with *Le Welsh* at bistros and brasseries or from food trucks ladling it into cardboard boxes.) House twists on the classic version include chicken or bacon *poutines*, even a Ch'ti edition with *carbonnade flamande*. In a flash of enlightenment, the short menu also offers an option with vegetarian gravy. However, since this is still charged with plenty of dairy,

true vegans have to hold out for the fully plant-based option at Annie's kitchen (page 136). There's a tiny dining room on the first floor, if no room on the pavement – there's hardly room to sit down downstairs here, with the space dominated by the take-away counter. €10 should assuage the appetite. They don't cook anything else here, but offer tarts and desserts prepared by their neighbour Elizabeth. The selection of Canadian Bull's Head root beer and soft drinks is a nice touch. €

LA PETITE COUR 17 rue du Curé Saint-Étienne ♀ 261 H4 ⊕ ℡ 03 20 51 52 81 w lapetitecour-lille.fr ⏱ closed Sun & Mon 🚇 Rihour; walk to Grand' Place & under Alcide arch to rue des Débris Saint-Étienne before turning left on to rue du Curé Saint-Étienne

Posher than before, yet remaining simple (if a tad more sophisticated in execution), this once merely very busy café with basic seating and tables is the great survivor in a quarter whose whims follow the winds. If proof was needed that the average age in Lille is 25 then this place, popular with families during the day and students at night, was textbook watertight evidence. Smartened up over the years, the days of a Sleeping Beauty forest of salad or basic *steak haché frites* have mellowed into a smarter dining room and courtyard serving classic bistro dishes with a more contemporary spice rack (try the *turban de poisson* topped with a truffled spinach and watercress sauce, if you don't believe me). Mains over €20, but a daily special around €15. Lunch menus from mid-€20s, à la carte closer to €40. €€€

LE POT BEAUJOLAIS 26 rue Pierre Mauroy ♀ 261 J5 ⊕ ℡ 03 20 57 38 38 w le-pot-beaujolais.fr ⏱ closed Sun & Mon eve 🚇 Gare Lille Flandres; rue Faidherbe, left on rue des Ponts de Comines to rue Pierre Mauroy

Le Beaujolais ancien est arrivé! Most restaurants in town remember Beaujolais only when the *nouveau* wine is released in autumn. In this tiny bistro, the spirit of the most traditional of regions is reflected year round in brown wood and check-cloth décor, and most of all in the menu. Outside traditional mealtimes a selection of terrines and tartines are available for those who fancy staving off hunger pangs with the taste of old Lyon. A modest outlay will buy an alternative to a conventional sandwich, this time layered with *chèvre* and smoked duck breast. But at lunchtime and evenings, tuck your napkin under your chin, take a deep breath, allow your waistline room to expand and get stuck in. This place is serious about its steaks, and meat is treated with as much respect as wine, even to the butcher's name listed on the menu. Expect quality with the *onglet* or *entrecôte*, but do not even think of ordering *côte de bœuf* if your vocabulary includes the French for 'well done' or even 'medium'. Classic comfort cooking means a steaming plate of *petit salé* with puy lentils or *andouillette* sausage in a *mâconnaise* sauce. Don't ignore the wine list. The Beaujolais classic crus are all there – and may be taken away too – so enjoy a Moulin à Vent or a Brouilly with the meal. Squeeze inside or sit on the pavement terrace and consider spending around €30 a head. Midweek lunchtimes see a menu at under €20 for two courses, and a dish of the day at €15. Keep an eye on this stretch of the rue Pierre Mauroy. For years it has been the least interesting of roads south of Grand' Place, but bars and restaurants are taking over from tired shops. Could be on the up. €€

LA RÉSERVE 47 rue du Marché ♀ 262 B4 ⊕ ℡ 03 62 28 51 02 ⏱ open daily 10am til quite late 🚇 Gambetta, then walk along rue Manuel to rue du Marché

You have heard of the concept of the *bar à vin*, but welcome to Lille's new *bar à manger*. Here, at this this little dining room with '60s throwback décor, eating is an art and you leave your pretensions outside. OK, plates are big (with an eye on Instagram), but the food on them will have more than enough flavour and texture to make up for the pretty colours nicely positioned. La Réserve is right in the heart of Wazemmes food market, so if you want to know the provenance of any of the ingredients, just point and raise an eyebrow – the restaurant buys fresh food every day from stalls across the road and makes up the menu accordingly. One day's tartare will be Angus beef, the next fine Charolais. Check the chalk board. The affordable dishes are mostly priced in the teens. Game and fowl is prepared to the sticky savoury max, fish fare floats off the fork into silky sauces, vegetables are crisp as the seasons and, in the age of the bake-off, there's no question about leaving room for dessert, since skills are honed to their finest here. Enjoy pavlovas, *mille-feuille* made with *beurre d'Isigny*, and pâtisserie to tease a tear and pop a shirt button or two, not to mention crusty organic home-baked loaves of bread that banish forever memories of floury white baguettes. It's also known as a *bar à concert* due to an excellent rolling programme of live music and punters' tendency to get up and dance. €€

SUZANNE   4 pl Philippe Lebon ♀ 262 E3 ⊕ ☎ 03 20 00 81 21 w suzannelille.fr ⏰ closed Wed lunch & Sun 🚋 République Beaux-Arts; take rue Nicolas Leblanc to pl Lebon
The menu really suggests this should be in the restaurant proper section, but the owners call it a bistro, so... Having stumbled across this bistro on a winter midday ramble in the museum quarter, I later received a rave tip-off from trusted local colleagues backing up my decision to declare this place 'one to watch'. Young chef Lucas Tricot may not have the high profile of his contemporaries across town, but was offering lunch menus at €27/34 with noon mains at €22. Bold colours on the plate do not eclipse well-foraged flavour, but having already been promised a full evening meal elsewhere, I opted for just a main course ravioli of spinach and jalapeño with strong savoyard cheese. While I wasn't up for a starter, curiosity was piqued at the prospect of a caramelised onion and herring pannacotta, which gave a me a hint as to the imagination that might be expected from the inevitable evening 5 or 7 small plate run (€54–72, with drinks €84–117). Some regulars, on the other hand, are lured by the talent of Lucas's partner Elisa Rodriguez, a remarkable pastry chef (and granddaughter of the titular Suzanne) whose dessert treats are known for letting natural tangs and textures flourish unsmothered by liberal use of the sugar shaker. Book nights at least 24 hours in advance and choose carnivore or vegetarian option – minds may not be changed on the day. €€€€

AU VIEUX DE LA VIEILLE   2 rue des Vieux Murs ♀ 261 H2 ⊕ ☎ 03 20 13 81 64 w estaminetlille.fr ⏰ 10.00–22.30 Mon–Sat 🚌 Bus 9 to Lion d'Or, then cross pl Louise de Bettignies to rue de la Monnaie & turn left on to rue Pétérinck
Once upon a time, *estaminets* belonged in old Flanders. Originally a bar in a corner of someone's front room, they were a place where neighbours might drop in for a beer for an hour or two before bedtime. Then Jean Luc Lacante, proprietor of the t'Kasteel Hof in Cassel's rural hinterland between the coast and Belgian border, became the unofficial *estaminet* ambassador, opening t'Rijsel in this corner of the old town. Next, with partners Raphaëlle, Franck and Hervé, came Chez la Vieille (page 94), followed by Vieux de la Vieille here and, both on rue de Gand, La Vieille France and L'Estaminet du Welsh (for Flemish rarebit in many incarnations from veggied to salmonated to burgerised). Such is the popularity of these simple bistros, while smarter premises

change hands like dancers in a reel, that there's even also a cabaret venue in nearby Lambersart. Such glimpses of Flanders past in the present are the perfect antidote to the trendiness that never quite takes over the city. No matter how close fingers come to the pulse of the present, hearts and souls are always closest to the past.

Since the Cassel crew first brought the simple, honest country-style café concept to the big city, a fresh generation of Lillois has been introduced to the simple pleasures known by their grandparents when this part of France was still ignored by sophisticated society and left to its own devices. This third *estaminet*-café sits at the point where the rue Pétérinck unbuckles its belts and expands into almost a square in that straggle of workshops, studios and quaint counters meandering from rue de la Monnaie to the cathedral. In keeping with the traditional café-bistro concept, it has old-style wooden games to play with while you linger over any of a couple of dozen artisan-brewed beers and the red-brick room itself is filled with drying hops and bric-a-brac from every granny's parlour. Papi and Memère's influence is to be found in homely *potjevleesch*-rich menus and the spirit of their guests. Hospitality spills over from the bowls of Flemish soups and stews into the friendliness of the clientele. If you can't find a table for two, certainly don't be surprised if a group of friends in a corner decide to squeeze closer together and invite you to sit with them. Try creamy chicory soup in a blue-and-white bowl as a winter warmer, or go full carnivore with black pudding and potato *tatin* prepared to order. The vegetarian options are mostly not vegan – expect lots of melted cheese and the occasional egg! Budget over €30 for three courses and the house craft beer. €€

BRASSERIES

L'ABBAYE   1–5 pl Rihour ♀ 261 H5 ❶ ☎ 03 20 54 67 37 w labbaye-brasseriepub.fr 🚇 Rihour
On the corner of Grand'Place and place Rihour, next to the theatre on the threshold of the pedestrianised shopping zone, this place was for years known as Café Leffe. Now, unshackled from the label of a national chain (though the brand still dominates the draught beer selection), these tables prove irresistible to the shopping-laden and the early. Meaty mains cost around €30 and include house speciality *les Chti'tes moules*, cooked in white wine and served with cheesy *flambé* in local *genièvre* gin and a massive side order of *frites*. Budget €16 for a classic omelette or share a large plate of cold cuts for under €20. Fast service keeps the beer flowing at the dithering point of the evening, as you debate whether to go to a show or a restaurant, stay and watch the match on the big screen, head out to a local club, or hop on a train to Belgium for more beer. €€€

ALCIDE   5 rue des Débris Saint-Étienne ♀ 261 H5 ❸ ☎ 03 20 40 80 00 w petitbouillonalcide. com 🚇 Rihour, then cross Grand'Place
In the last this edition of this guide, the future of this iconic dining room was once again in doubt. Having previously dropped the word '*brasserie*' in favour of the title '*restaurant*', its ill-advised contemporary décor threatened to smother the original Napoleon III style, and would-be fashionable food eclipsed the *saveurs* of the brewery and platters laced with the scent of the centuries. It temporarily closed and then reopened, but, as the company went into receivership, notices from bankers and lawyers replaced adverts for chefs in the windows. However, Alcide has been found under the arch at the main square since the 1870s, and has gone through many identities, reinventions and make-overs, and somehow always survived. At the time of writing,

while the 'Alcide' sign still dominates the square, the new name is officially Le Petit Bouillon Alcide. Early *bouillons* were *fin-de-siècle* budget brasseries where impoverished artists might order a bowl of broth or inexpensive cut of meat in plush velvet Art Nouveau settings – think *La Bohème*. The most famous and original *fin-de-siècle* bouillon, Chantier in Paris, is still going strong, as wealthy clubbers jostle with students in the queue. Here in Lille, the current Alcide offers a menu packed with predictable standards – braised leeks and *rillettes* among €4–7 starters and *tripes à la mode* or *petit salé* with lentils as €12 mains – in an approximate return to the original décor and appropriate price point. If service was a little hit and miss, and food pretty generic, well, that is not unexpected in a room that serves a hot meal anytime from midday onwards. It is an institution after all, saved this time by France's renewed love affair with soup kitchen kitsch! Leave your critical faculties behind and unleash your inner Rodolfo and Mimi. €€

BRASSERIE ANDRÉ 71 rue de Béthune ♀ 262 G1 ● ✆ 03 20 54 75 51 w brasserieandre.fr 🚋 République Beaux-Arts; cross pl Richebé to rue de Béthune
Opened by Belgians 100 years ago, and looking more at home in the back streets of Brussels than rue de Béthune's movies and shopping district, this true survivor of the golden age of brasserie is where good *moules* go when they die. Sumptuous traditional brasserie décor, with wonderful-panelled arches and dark wooden walls contrasting with white, starched napkins, tablecloths and aprons. Not cheap by brasserie standards – your meal could set you back €50 – but lunching neighbours will be businessmen, bankers and people who don't mind paying a tad over the odds for classic favourites in a classy setting. Non-mollusc munchers can indulge in beef, lamb and the like served in rich *bordelaise* fashion. Menus reek of tradition: starters featuring Burgundy *escargots*, house *foie gras*, or pigs ear confit and the northern treat of herring with warm potato salad; mains of Brittany lobster, *entrecôte*, *tournedos Rossini* and a pretty good line in roasted fish, be it cod, salmon or tuna. The pavement terrace fronts the main shopping area, and weekend service continues between mealtimes with a limited selection of dishes. The children's menu is not of a chicken-nugget standard, featuring instead fillet steak and roasted fish. Perfect for trainee gourmets. €€€

BRASSERIE DE LA CLOCHE 13 pl du Théâtre ♀ 261 J5 ● ✆ 03 20 55 35 34 w brasserie-la-cloche.hubside.fr 🚋 Rihour or Gare Lille Flandres
Having long had the square pretty much to itself, the Cloche has faced up to new competition with the emergence of a string of bars and bistros around the revived and revitalised cultural hub by the Opera House. The restaurant on the Rang de Beauregard is known for its distinctive sign on the wall, but even more so for its tables on the square itself, where informal and friendly waiting staff serve unpretentious fare to an undemanding public. Back in the day, the waiter's apron stains were a veritable menu for the illiterate. Now, smarter and with a more streamlined menu, all remains convivial, and portions are still the size that your most generous friends would serve you. The comfort dishes, including main *tartares* and *carbonades,* are priced in the teens. A midweek lunch of *plat du jour* and *café gourmande* is offered for well under €20, and a Saturday special of half a chicken with *maroilles* sauce and *frîtes* is just a few euros more. In the evening, the full *carte* is replaced by a choice of reasonably priced cheese and meat platters, tapas and dips to enjoy alongside the drinks list. As predicted, this is already a firm fave with the post- (and intermission) concert and opera crowd. €€

BRASSERIE LA PAIX 25 pl Rihour ♀ 261 H5 ⓦ ☏ 03 20 54 70 41 **w** brasserie-delapaix.fr
🕐 closed Sun 🚇 Rihour

Café society '20s- and '30s-style lives on here, with Art Deco walls and tiling and a welcome
and food straight from the heyday of the French brasserie. Past editions of the *Ch'ti* guide have
waxed almost Proustian on the subject. Main courses are mostly around €30; great platters of
seafood and roast *canette de Challans* cooked with fresh figs are among the attractions. The
period feel is strictly for diners inside the restaurant. Outside, enjoy the very modern spectacle of
shoppers trekking from boutique to boutique and commuters emerging from beneath the queasy
custard-coloured waters of the pyramid fountain at Rihour métro station. Menus from €25–30.
(Exceptionally, open Sunday lunchtimes during the Christmas market.) €€€

LA CHICORÉE 15 pl Rihour ♀ 261 H5 ☏ 03 20 54 81 52 **w** brasserie-lachicoree.fr 🕐 10.00–
05.00 Thu–Sat, 10.00–03.00 Sun–Wed 🚇 Rihour

We have all found ourselves here at some stage of a late-night session. This old reliable brasserie
on the corner is the perfect standby when an evening has just flown by at the bar, café or jazz
show and nobody is ready for bed yet. It's part of a stable of brasserie-style restaurants clustered
around the corner of place Rihour, the décor now Latin-block shades with strategically placed
artworks. Just when you start to feel that the place might have descended into a tourist spot,
you return to find the buzz remains young and happening, the youthful couple at the next table
finding time to hold hands between releasing their fingers to text updates of their dining to other
lands, and staff still lovely, happy and on top of their game. An all-day (until 22.30) midweek
menu of around €20 is a bit limited; the €30 version is more varied and full-blown; and the
discretely updated à la carte should nudge €40. However, a steaming bowl of onion soup topped
with a Gruyère-covered crouton should fill you up and leave the wallet relatively unscathed. Since
prices rise by around 20% after midnight, the waiters are perfectly happy to serve just a starter
or one-course refuelling option in the small hours. Summer sunrise, the place is busy with night-
shift workers, road sweepers and métro staff rounding off the night's work with a hefty steak and
refreshing beer, as the rest of us follow our noses to the bakery for breakfast *croissants* and hot
chocolate! €€€

ESTAMINET GANTOIS BRASSERIE FLAMANDE 232 rue Pierre Mauroy ♀ 262 H2 ⓦ
w hotelhermitagegantois.com ☏ 03 20 85 30 30 🚇 Mairie de Lille, then walk westward along av
du Président Kennedy & turn left on to rue de Paris

Noted and departed chef Sébastien Blanchet, later to be lionised in Biarritz, founded a
showcase fine-dining restaurant at the eponymous L'Hermitage Gantois hotel (page 72).
His flagship dining room off the lobby persuaded diners to part with €100 for a set menu
of mango-enlivened perch followed by a classically braised *jarret de veau* as lead-up to
traditional *tatin* and *clafoutis* comfort food. Next door, his Estaminet Gantois offered a bill
of fare to reflect the history of a once working-class quarter that inspired the revolutionary
anthem 'L'Internationale'. A set up of great *rillettes* and *terrines*, *hochepot* and the spoils of *la
chasse* worked for us when we came here for a dollop of proletarian fare before the evening's
performance of *Les Mis* at the Zenith. Today this is the only dining option on site – the high-end
gastronomy in the main dining room never stood the test of time, leaving what is not exactly
a true *estaminet*, but the more honestly subtitled Brasserie Flamande. Squeezing wealthy

hotel guests' expectations into this quaint corner of casual eating has not sat easily with the hotel price point market, and the concept was in throes of reinvention at the time of writing. Certainly, the humbler prices of this once second-string dining room have long gone. An interim menu features burgers or beef cheek *carbonnade* in the €25 bracket and roasted white fish on a honey and lemon risotto at €27, with a vegetarian Ch'ti salad starter at €21, meaning a budget of around €50 – neither blue collar stomach-filler, nor ideal of a five-star *bon vivant boulevardier* with a wallet open to innovation. €€€

MA REINE Hotel Arbre Voyageur, 45 bd Carnot ♀ 261 K4 ☎ 03 20 20 62 62 w hotelarbrevoyageur.com 🚊 Gare Lille Flandres, then bus 10, 14 or 50 to Lycée Pasteur
This brasserie at the hotel Arbre Voyageur (page 66), is, like sister dining room Jane, known for amazing pastries and desserts, and serves contemporary standards in a setting both stylish and informal. Good service and dietary issues responded to with discretion. €€€

MAMA SHELTER 97 pl Saint Hubert ♀ 259 H4 ☎ 03 59 82 72 72 w mamashelter.com/lille 🚊 Gare Lille Flandres; walk down av Le Corbusier and turn right into rue des Cannoniers
This dining room, with its tiny stage for live music and DJs and massively extended table football, feels like an American roadhouse. Yet alongside stateside features (such as homemade cookies and a glass of milk) are contemporary plays on brasserie regulars such as *oeuf mollet* with Maroilles cheese and gingerbread, and Franco-Italian fusion touches, such as parmesan on the *croque monsieur* and a beer-and-mushroom béchamel on local Saint Jacques. There's pork belly or seabream for meat eaters, and crunchy crisped cauliflower or focaccia with leek, stracciatella and basil for mere carnivoyeurs, who should avoid the house fries, cooked in beef fat. Lunch menus are well under €25; à la carte roams into the €40s. Spend €42 for weekend brunch (kids half price). Check the hotel listing on page 75 for more on the Mama concept. €€€

LE MEUNIER 15–17 rue de Tournai ♀ 259 G5 ⊜ ☎ 03 20 04 04 90 w restaurant-le-meunier.fr ⏰ 07.00–22.00 daily 🚊 Gare Lille Flandres
Once upon a time, every provincial French railway station had a stolid, reliable railway restaurant serving basic meat, fish and chicken – standard fare to while away the 2-hour delay between cross-country trains. At the side of the old Flandres station, amid *friteries* and burger bars, is to be found one such old-fashioned *buffet de la gare*-style dining room, fuelling weary passengers since 1946. Now open all day, it serves basic brasserie staples alongside burgers, pasta and *poutines* for younger tastes in a hurry. The *formule express* €15 quick lunch dovetails with train timetables and the dish of the day is posted online a week in advance. Don't expect fashionably pan-fried spring vegetables with steamed fruits in their *coulis* of pretension. Eat here to remember railway holidays chugging through a less sophisticated France in less demanding times. €€€

AUX MOULES DE LILLE 11 pl Rihour ♀ 261 H6 ⊕ ☎ 03 74 44 79 47 w auxmoulesdelille.fr 🚊 Rihour
Certainly not the original Aux Moules from rue de Béthune (page 106), but a post-pandemic makeover of the old stalwart Brasserie Flore, next door to the Chicorée (see opposite). It may brandish a famous name, but offers fish and chips on the set menu options and *gnocchi* à la carte for the less adventurous traveler. The sea is in charge of the menu, and of course there are loads of

mussels and other shellfish to choose from – shucked and plated in full view as expected. The choice also includes monkfish with marrowbone and a classic *sole meunière* with ratte potatoes – a reminder that Lille is not too far from Le Touquet. Most main courses priced well into the €20s. €€€

LE PALAIS DE LA BIÈRE See page 132.

TERRASSE DU PARC Resort Barrière, 777 Pont de Flandres ♀ 259 J5 ☎ 03 28 14 45 50
w hotelsbarriere.com ⏱ closed Sun–wed, open evenings only Thu–Sat 🚇 Gare Lille Flandres or Gare Lille Europe; take Parvis de Rotterdam exit from Lille Europe to Pont de Flandres
Less formal than upstairs at Les Hauts de Lille (page 114) in the Barrière casino hotel resort, the brasserie off the foyer offers players, guests and passers-by some distinctly local and regional flavours, and a value *plat du jour* without leaving the building. Dine garden-side overlooking the new business district's green pathways, or even sit out by the joggers' footpaths on red velour benches at wooden tables. Alternatively, you may prefer to stay indoors, in a bright and spacious room with a bold design by Pierre-Yves Rochon. Start with a visit to the €16 *hors d'oeuvre* buffet and round off the meal with the €13 dessert selection. You may even enjoy a double buffet for under €25 or spend €30 to have a brasserie main course in the middle. Otherwise, pay under €20 for a reliable fillet mignon, salad, burger or fish and chips, and slightly more for better steaks. I chose a lemony chunk of cod with a crispy herb crust alongside the usual trimmings. The restaurant also hosts a Sunday brunch, often with live jazz, spilling into the afternoon. Prices around €35. €€€

LES TROIS BRASSEURS 22 pl de la Gare ♀ 261 K6 ⊕ ☎ 03 20 06 46 25 w 3brasseurs.com
🚇 Gare Lille Flandres
Flanders is famed for its beers – whatever you do you must try at least one of the region's distinctive flavours. A new beer tourism industry has opened up (page 132) but the first microbrewery in town, and now a local institution and national chain, is Les Trois Brasseurs opposite the old Lille Flandres station. Once upon a time, Monsieur Bonduel, director of Pelforth – the commercial brewery behind the Pelican lagers favoured by Calais trippers – decided to get back to brewing basics, and put the brewery back into the brasserie. Now virtually every town in Europe seems to have its own brew-pub, but it was here, nearly three decades ago, that I found the genuine welcome that first drew me to Lille, and I will never cease giving thanks. The clientele ranges from solo business types at the bar to groups of friends, locals and visitors; bar staff are rarely less than convivial, but waiters never less than harassed. In this always-packed bar-restaurant, the only beers served are those brewed in copper vats on the premises. Choose a *palette* tasting tray of four small glasses of various home brews: *blonde*, *brune*, *ambrée* and *blanche de Lille*, a refreshing bitter-sweet thirst quencher ideally served with a slice of lemon. March and Christmas see seasonal specials added to the range. The menu is northern home cooking: rabbit stews, roasts and cholesterol-packed *Welsh* with a slice of bread and chips. And twists on the omnipresent *poutine* now abound, of course. If you are feeling really adventurous, try a beer tart or beer sorbet! The set-menu deals are the best value, starting well below €20, as is the house *flammekeuche*. Daily specials, such as marrowbone or a *carbonnade*, are also always reasonably priced. Find promotional combinations on noticeboards or in newspaper-style menus.

Otherwise, budget €30 and you won't go far wrong. House beers are available to take home by the bottle or *tonnelet* (mini-barrel). €€

RESTAURANTS

L'ADRESSE   See page 134 for full review of the gastronomic burger restaurant of the fine dining quarter.

L'ASSIETTE DU MARCHÉ   61 rue de la Monnaie ♀ 261 H2 ⊚ ☏ 03 20 06 83 61

w assiettedumarche.com ⏰ closed Sun 🚌 Bus 9 to Lion d'Or
Venture away from the cobbled streets around the Musée de l'Hospice Comtesse and into the sedate courtyard of a townhouse that was, once upon a time, Louis XIV's royal mint in the city and the building that gave the street its name. In our time, this *maison particulière* has a more modern tradition as a restaurant and this is the last dining room of the legendary Proye family who held court at the celebrated À l'Huîtrière (page 106). The cuisine *chez* Thomas Proye is something of an *assiette* from many *marchés* with talents and tricks culled from all six corners of France. If the regional or fashionable food terminology is too obscure, just ask your waiter to interpret. The *carte* wryly acknowledges the ephemeral nature of trendy menu-speak. There's nothing obscure about the ingredients, though: hearty halibut roasted with mustard and a Valenciennes *jarret* in beer were on the weekly menu when first we checked the place out. Flavours may not always have lived up to the excellent presentation on an initial visit, but on encouragement from some readers (mailbag has been evenly split on this one) we tried again and relished a starter of Camembert with black cherries and dessert of pan-fried pineapple and ginger *mille feuille*, the goal of fusion now comfortably attained. As for the wine list, it is a true *tour de France*. Pay €20 for a basic midweek lunch of main course and coffee or €24–30 for two or three courses on the weekly set menu, lunch and evening. Grazing free-range nudges the bill towards €50 a head before we even start on the wine. €€€

LE BARBIER QUI FUME   69 rue de la Monnaie ♀ 261 H2 ⊘ ☏ 03 20 06 99 35

w lebarbierquifume.fr ⏰ closed Sun eve 🚌 Bus 9 to Lion d'Or
Fear not, this *barbier qui fume* is not selling refills for vapes: smoking here is strictly culinary. Meats at this butcher's dining room are smoked over beechwood, giving them a subtle fragrance and flavour. And wood of a different type is used to similarly pleasing effect in the fine panelled décor of the elegant butcher's shop on the corner of rue de la Monnaie and the eclectic rue Pétérinck. Chandeliers hang above a grand Flemish dresser and a counter of prime cold cuts, each vacuum-packed to be taken home. The main attraction is the principal dining room (once trading as Le Barbier Lillois), with its ostentatious carpentry against smoke-blackened brick walls and an à la carte menu for the reduction of willpower and restraint. Might you opt for a coarsely chopped *tartare* with pistachio or *souris d'agneau* with rosemary and thyme, or perhaps your taste in lamb runs to a *carré d'agneau* with honey and cloves, ripened in the smoke house for 6 hours? Friends speak softly of a moist and vulnerably pink centre encased in the sweetest caramelised crust. No-one bats an eyelid at the price tag. The choice is slightly less steaky than before, with smokey twists on northern classics and even trout replacing beef in some dishes. Mains are served with optional salad, *gratin dauphinoise* or a chicory *tatin* as alternative to *frites*. If you believe that

For almost 100 years, seafood meant À l'Huîtrière, the Art Deco fish restaurant and oyster bar amid the chic boutiques of Vieux Lille. Alas, in 2015, after 80 years in the *Guide Michelin*, the icon of fine dining closed its doors for the last time. Then Aux Moules, too, tossed out its final empty shell, its well-worn banquettes and rickety tables – even the bar with its eight beer pumps was auctioned off – and the brasserie on the corner of rues de Béthune and des Molfonds was replaced by yet another brace of clothes shops.

There was always something special about arriving in the old quarter from the gorgeous bustling squares, hoicking heels from cobbles and entering À l'Huîtrière's Art Deco jewel box of a poissonerie on rue des Chats Bossus. It was the realm of a hunchbacked cat, where Neptune was king. Stunning mosaics shimmered above the glistening catch of the day: turbot and bream, baskets of oysters and wondrous confections bottled and *en gelée*, all bathed in a maritime twilight. Behind the shop, the restaurant was genteel discretion: light wood panels, wool tapestries and navy-and-white Limoges service on crisp white linens. The doors first opened in 1928, and for most of the next century, four generations of chefs, from Pierre Bailleul to his great-grandson Antoine Proye, wore a Michelin star with pride. Then, in 2012, as more fashionable new chefs from the TV and fusion generation seized the red guide laurels, the *macaron Michelin* was lost forever. Monsieur Proye added an oyster bar to complement his traditional dining room and *habitués* remained loyal to the end. At around 18.00, ladies who had spent an afternoon window-shopping would gather around two little pavement tables. In pashminas or sunglasses, according to *la saison*, they would order glasses of chilled chardonnay, designer handbags on tables giving way to dinky little plates of oysters for the *apéro* between life as one of *les girls* and evening role of good wife. But then, *la famille* Proye said its last adieu, and Lille lost the pearl in its culinary crown. For an almost biblical seven years, the iconic site stood dark, until in 2022 Bernard Arnhault, – CEO of LVMH, crown-prince of luxury goods and himself no stranger to the dining room – in unconscious homage to the accessories of *les apéro* girls, officially appointed the site the northern flagship of Louis Vuitton. Some 30 local craftsmen restored and recreated

meat is not meat unless it is scarlet and comes from a cow, then slices of 14-hour-cold-smoked beef with a roasted, unpasteurised Camembert and side dish of walnut salad might float your ark without upsetting your bank manager – in the €20s bracket for a main course. The restaurant serves robust red wines to accompany mains, and has a selection of sugary *cassonade*-type desserts to round off the meal. Since the Covid lockdown, the restaurant also now offers a click and collect option here and from satellite branches on place Rihour and Lille Europe. €€€€

the building's original marble, glassware, wrought iron, mosaics and marquetry, and now a posh handbag and luggage shop stands as a lasting monument to Lille's gastronomic heritage.

To lose one seafood legend might be regarded as a misfortune, however to lose two…. Just as TV news had been on hand to witness the end of an era of gastronomy in Vieux Lille, so cameras rolled on to rue de Béthune to report the demise of the original Aux Moules, an icon of simple *brasserie cuisine à la Lilloise*. A good, honest old-fashioned *luncherie*, this was where Jacques Chirac downed a beer for Dutch courage the day he announced his presidential bid, and where scores of workers would order the same platter five days every week. The Braderie will never be the same, wailed locals, bemoaning the loss of the annual front page *Voix du Nord* photo of the city's tallest pile of mussel shells every September. Rue de Béthune itself was no less altered for all time. Here, however, it was not perhaps the fickle favours of fashionable foodies that cast the sentence. It was simply a matter of time. After 40 years, Mme Michèle Courtois, owner since the 1970s, was ready for retirement. The restaurant had served much the same *moules-frites* menu since 1930, although back then the cost was 4 francs (a last supper in 2016 would have set you back €18). Home to symbols of Lille, from massive mural photographs of Braderie heaps to that gargantuan mussel shell suspended above the door, this landmark of the street is missed just as much for its desserts (*tarte à la rhubarbe* to end a meal and the biggest *éclair au chocolat* in town for a mid-shopping sugar rush) as its titular speciality.

While up-and-coming young chefs did not bite at the chance of taking over a classic brasserie – instead wanting to make their names with flash-fried belly of guinea-fowl in liquorice and beetroot foam with diced turnips and a lavender, squid and kidney *jus* (perhaps fashion did play a part in the demise after all) – there is consolation in the fact that there will always be honest brasserie cuisine in the heart of Lille. Just across the way, Brasserie André (page 101) keeps up the good work with classic mussel and brasserie standards for old-timers and businessfolk alike, and by place Rihour, an established restaurant has been rebranded with the iconic Aux Moules name (page 103).

LE BLOEMPOT   22 rue des Bouchers ♥ 261 G4 ⊕ w bloempot.fr 🚋 Rihour, pass the tourist office to rue de l'Hôpital Militaire, cross pl de l'Arsenal to rue des Bouchers; alternatively, take the Navette Vieux Lille almost full circle & step off on to rue des Bouchers
You don't phone to book a table here. You pray. Or, if your faith is not strong enough, you go to the website. Food lovers check online reservations and cancellation pages daily in hope of getting to dine at Lille's must-go address before the ageing process really starts to kick in. At first time

of typing, there were no weekend evening tables free for two months, and even now, a winter Saturday evening's waiting required at least one turned weekly page in the diary. Yes, it is still that popular. (Oh, if you do get a table, you must leave a non-refundable deposit of €20/person.) This is the restaurant that turned the dining map of Lille on its head and brought the world and its dinner date to rue des Bouchers. Just about the last street to qualify as Vieux Lille, rue des Bouchers has been home to an eclectic range of modestly fashionable eateries over the years I've been idling with intent in the quarter. Just a bit farther than you'd like to walk from the métro or nearest bus stop, the road has seen a succession of trendy dining rooms, each with smart brick walls, smart artworks and far smarter *habitués*; most stayed their two or three years before passing the tenancy on to the next cutting edge cook whose hairdresser's scissors were even sharper than the Sabatier knives in the kitchen. Then along came Florent Ladeyn, boy wonder of 21st-century cuisine (page 120). As every door in France was ready to open for this prodigious *jeune talent*, rather than set up another fine-dining *palais de gastronomie*, Ladeyn decided to follow his heart and open a simple kitchen-garden *cantine flamande* in the heart of the city. Now, 'wild and creative' *cuisine* is served against the industrial girder-and-brick backdrop of an old carpentry workshop behind the street, with outside space turned over to an essential potager for Ladeyn's young team to plunder. So, no massive terrace for the dining room overspill, just 40 covers that book up in the click of a mouse.

Lunch is €40, dinner €60 (add half as much again for the wine accompaniment); I can't call them menus because they are not. Come here for a culinary leap into the unknown. There's no advance warning of what will be set in front of you, no written menu, just a conspiratorial inclination of the waiter's head, until the dish is named with the integrity of a baptism as each *assiette* arrives *à table*. (Lone deviation from the norm is a vegetarian alternative that must be requested at the time of booking.) You only truly understand Ladeyn's concept of local when the first of many plates is wafted towards you. Ingredients may be sourced almost closer than your parking space, yet treatment and technique is borne of a wealth of global experience, with Latin American, Asian and Nordic traditions deployed in a corner of France where even the nation's Mediterranean diet is as alien as produce from a Pacific island. Told of a salt cod *brandade* that had emerged from the kitchen in claret hues of organic beetroot, we expected great things from what was not a *tartare*, but a Peruvian inspired *céviche* (raw, chopped, spiced and limed) of ginger-taunted sea bream with watermelon. Whatever the dish, sweetness will be taunted from local root vegetables, beets and nips midwinter or ripe, almost *vendange tardive* fruits at summer's end.

This is where the notorious small-plate tasting menu trend began, an innovation of Bloempot's inception. Nowadays, every other chef, from the corner caff to the casino's glistening tower, serves only a flight of mini-dishes on weekend evenings. If you cannot get this particular table on the rue des Bouchers, have no fear, you will not go hungry: this street now surpasses rue de Gand as a food destination in its own right. Dress code surprisingly informal, but not shabby. €€€€

IN BOCCA AL LUPO 1 rue des Vieux Murs 261 H3 34 03 20 06 39 98 w in-bocca-al-lupo.com closed Sun eve & Mon Bus 9 to Lion d'Or, then from rue de la Monnaie turn left on to rue Pétérinck

Opposite celebrated Italian deli-palace La Bottega (see opposite) stands its Latin sister. Where else would the trendy place aux Oignons crowd choose to lunch? It's seriously fashionable, with no linens, just shiny table tops, polished floors, comfy chairs and shelves of recipe books and peppermills. Somehow this contemporary city-centre look manages to straddle the very Flemish traditions of the quarter and the reassuringly conservative classic Italian flavours from *antipasti* to *dolci*. There are no anachronistic modern twists here, just *scaloppa alla Milanese* and *saltimbocca* to please the most critical *nonna* in the business. Produce comes from a family kitchen garden in nearby Bondues. No set menu, but budget close to €45 per healthy appetite. €€€

LA BONBONNIÈRE Lille's leading cabaret floorshow and dining room (page 141), hosted by award winning chef David Bève of N'Autre Monde (page 117).

LA BOTTEGA 7b rue Pétérinck ♀ 261 H2 ⊕ ☏ 03 20 74 33 12 **w** la-bottega.com ⏱ closed Mon 🚌 Bus 9 to Lion d'Or; from rue de la Monnaie turn left on to rue Pétérinck
For Italians, everything is about family, so no surprise that this memorable delicatessen and the restaurant In Bocca al Lupo across the way are both run by the ubiquitous Annunzio clan, whose menfolk famously got their kit off for a charity calendar 20-odd years ago. But here is the place where *la famiglia* makes the very best pizzas in Lille. It's no USA-style dough-fest; here, organic bases are spun and stretched to perfection and toppings have a provenance: ham *San Daniele*, *Gorgonzola Guffanti, salami di Napoli*. End the meal with a cherry *panna cotta* or a Flemish twist on *tiramisù* (ie: made with *spéculoos*). Budget in the late teens for pizza. €€

LE BRAQUE 69 rue de la Monnaie ♀ 261 H3 ⊕ ☏ 03 20 04 25 38 **w** le-braque.fr ⏱ closed Sun & Mon 🚌 Bus 9 to Lion d'Or
Next time, I'll book a table here. Damien Laforce is already the next-big-thing boy wonder, emerging from the shadow of Florent Ladeyn to open his own place in Vieux Lille. Every food critic in France is raving about it. Anecdotes about the best game pie since the end of the monarchy and fish from anglers not trawlermen mean I can't wait to give it a try. Meanwhile, expect evening multi-plate flights to soar upwards of €60 and the lunchtime *prix-fixe* close to €40. €€€€

LE CHANTECLER 22 rue Nicolas Leblanc ♀ 262 F3 ⊕ ☏ 03 20 57 48 19 **w** le-chantecler.fr ⏱ closed lunch Sat, all day Sun & Mon 🚌 République Beaux-Arts; cross pl de la République to rue Nicolas Leblanc
When this tiny shopfront bistro, across the road from the more famous Aux Ephérites (page 112), first opened, people queued outside its glorious Art Deco stained-glass window of a cock crowing at sunrise and they came back for the chips. The uneven chunky *frites maison* were the unlikely signature dish of original chef Philippe Nonet, who trained under the doyen of French cuisine, Paul Bocuse. House fries even made TV news when Nonet served them with saffron mussels for the 2012 Braderie. So new chef Théo Bardé had a big *toque* to fill when he took over. Already creating headlines across town, and unashamedly smashing tectonic plates with his instinct for fusion (*confit de canard* with curried hummus, anyone?), Bardé can nonetheless rein in his urge for culture clashes. Winter warmers include satay-glazed pork belly, and resolutely closer-to-home guinea fowl with brussels sprouts. Lunch mains cost €20-something, with starters that won't break the bank, for those who enjoy the choice. Evenings, however, follow the Bloempot (page 107) trend of a 'surprise' seasonal set menu. A comparatively modest €41 for 4 courses, with just

a €16 surcharge for 3 glasses of wine, make this is one of the more affordable blind flights of fancy. Who needs *frites*, after all? Flexibility for dietary and allergy requirements with advance notice. €€€€

CHEZ BRIGITTE 13 rue des Bouchers ♀ 261 G3 ⊕ ☎ 09 83 80 89 61 **w** chezbrigittelille. com ① closed Sun & Mon 🚇 Rihour, then pass the tourist office & turn right on to rue de l'Hôpital Militaire, then cross pl de l'Arsenal to rue des Bouchers; alternatively, take the Navette Vieux Lille almost full circle & step off at rue des Bouchers

Rue des Bouchers has become something of a pilgrim trail for food lovers ever since Le Bloempot (page 107) bloomed in what had previously been a mere side street of upmarket wine and burger bars. Turn up in search of Oui, the 18th-century vaulted cellar restaurant of Michelin chef Eric Delerue, however, and you will be met with a resounding '*non*'. Oui closed its doors a few years ago. Now, that cellar and the brighter ground floor main room with full height windows is Chez Brigitte. Eric's trailing houseplants on the rough brick walls have been replaced by portraits on plates, yet some traditions have survived the *regime* change. And there's been no fall in standards in the kitchen since **Clément Richevaux**, chef during Oui's final years, still wields his spoon and spice rack. He went into partnership with neighbouring bar owner **Guillaume Delbarre** to open this new restaurant named for his grandmother Brigitte. **Richevaux**'s '*fooding*'-style share plates of *acras*, sardines and anchovies remain as popular as ever. Set midweek lunch menus at €25–30 promote root vegetables in winter (carrot *velouté* with cheddar and garlic to start, turnips and parsnips instead of predictable Mediterranean veg with the main).

Mamie Brigitte's dishes on the *carte* (budget €50) include *escargots*; grandson **Clément**'s modern, lighter options include poached eggs with asparagus. Wild mushrooms garland main courses, whether risotto or joints of meat. Friday and Saturday evenings are inevitably given over to a blind small-plate menu (neighbour Le Bloempot has a great deal to answer for). Brigitte's version costs €50–106 for 4–6 courses, with or without the wines. I have not yet indulged in the full evening experience. The place only opened on the cusp of Covid and it is still on my to-dine list. €€€

CHEZ MON COUSIN 282 av de Dunkerque, Lambersart ♀ 261 G1 ⊕ ☎ 03 62 13 42 88 **w** nicolas-pourcheresse.fr ① closed lunch Sat, all day Sun & Mon 🚇 Métro Canteleux When Nicolas Pourcheresse (page 120) was in charge at La Table (page 122), you would not have seen much change from €100, nor would lunch at Méert have been a cheap date in his time. But drop in on his home turf and you'll find a midday menu in the €20s and genuine traditional fare. A pioneer of locally sourced dining, his current base in Lambersart is just across the Canal from Vieux Lille, (10 minutes by métro from the centre). Grazing à la carte, enjoy a range of variations on eggs Benedict or modestly priced entrees for around €8–14: sweetmeats, snails and even battered frogs legs *en cromesquis*. A *pâté en croute* of veal, heady with freshly crushed horseradish, comes in at under €10, or perhaps kick off the evening by ordering a €6 plate of chips with a spicy Spanish-style mayo dip as you browse the menu. Mains in the low €20s follow the locavore ethos: perhaps a freshly landed catch of the day, conventional *bavette* steak *à l'échalote* or pork caramelised with beer and garlic. There will always be new desserts, but regulars come back for almost Proustian rhum baba or Paris Brest pâtisserie in portions big enough to share. Set meals are €22–27 at midday or €37 for the menu du marché. A seasonal treat is La Serre (43 route de

Lambersart, Verlinghem) – a pop-up restaurant serving just 30 covers at Pourcheresse's kitchen garden greenhouse, only 2 miles up the road (page 120). Book via the main restaurant. €€€

CLAIR DE LUNE   50 rue de Gand ♀ 261 K2 📞 03 20 51 46 55 ① closed Wed 🚋 Bus 9 to Lion d'Or, then cross pl Louise de Bettignies to rue de Gand
Over the years, this place has opened the eyes and mouths of my friends to potential of *mignon* of pork in an arabica sauce, halibut in cider, and a somewhat scrummy *œuf cocotte* with smoked trout and leeks. My Normandy family appreciated quail indulged in Calvados. More recently, the playful imagination here has produced mango guacamole, while sundry receipts also recall classic standbys such as trout with almonds. Some may claim service to be brusque, but I have found nothing to complain about. The unpretentious staff did not bat an eyelid the Saturday evening I opted for a couple of starters instead of a 'proper' meal, having overindulged elsewhere at lunchtime, and paid me the same courtesies as others pigging out on the €30–40 nighttime menus. Lunch options half that price. €€€

CLUB MAROT   16 rue de Pas ♀ 261 H4 📞 03 20 57 01 10 w clubmarot.fr ① closed eves Sun & Mon 🚋 Rihour; take rue Roisin to rue de Pas
From the street, you would assume nothing had changed since you last walked past this discreet dining room by the Nouveau Siècle concert hall five, ten or 20 years ago. Only the sharpest eyes would notice the name above the window no longer reads 'Clément Marot'. It's always had the most understated frontage, reminiscent of the 'best' restaurant in every small provincial town, with no party fanfare, just a discreet notice by the window, and the end of lunch hour signalled by an afternoon queue for blood tests across the way at the Laboratoire d'analyses médicales. For years, this was the *royaume* of an old school *chef patron*, complete with post-war décor of heavy plate ice buckets and tureens on well-polished surfaces; certificates alongside framed paintings of favourite holiday spots; and a waitress in black skirt, white blouse and lace apron hovering by the champagne magnums and long-stemmed cut flowers

The very idea of rue de Pas without Clément Marot seemed unthinkable, but when *tempus fugit* met *plus ça change*, there was nonetheless a reassuring continuity provided by not one but two new young chefs: Clément's son Augustin and nephew Antoine. The cousins have certainly inherited the gastronomic gene, Augustin thriving at the more innovative bistros of Paris and Australia, Antoine earning his whites at a three-star Michelin establishment. These combined skills create their *restaurant bistronomique Lillois*, where they claim to offer a raffish, gently bad boy approach to the classics. Perhaps that *air cannaille* refers to a stylish contemporary plating of the dishes, but there is nothing too modish about reassuringly appetite-assuaging portions. Menus and inspiration change with the market, and early mealtimes in the new era saw reassuringly classic game and barnyard dishes on the bill (the route to the table as likely to be via the shotgun as the abattoir), yet with contemporary twists when it came to accompaniments and carbs. Venison and salsify pie, a *boudin blanc* and languistine ravioli. I really did not expect to witness the marriage of parsnips and grapefruit early on in the meal and felt just the slightest rocking of the boat when vanilla pods from the south seas brought an unexpectedly sweet kick to fish from France's north Atlantic coast. I have not yet tried the desserts, but if the Marot tradition at the end of the meal is carried through beyond the foothills and summit of the menu, I am willing to surrender. Some 20 years ago, I could not decide and just let the chef-patron choose for me. I may well never eat another *crème brûlée* as long as I live. It was pure cream, which still breathed the air of the dairy, and remains the best I have ever tasted this side of childhood. Set lunch menus are either side of €30, other menus range from €35–55, and the full-blown multi-course tasting experience is over €60 with a flight of wines on the side for €31–40 extra. *Plat du jour* mains are no more than €25. The wine list is impressive, though I forgot to ask if the original policy still stands. Under the Ancien Régime, rather than compromise with a half-bottle of a lesser vintage, we were encouraged to buy a full bottle with the assurance that, at the end of the meal, staff would wrap up the rest of the bottle to be enjoyed – as the wine list then had it – at your own table in the comfort of your own home. €€€

LE COMPTOIR VOLANT See page 135.

AUX ÉPHÉRITES 17 rue Nicolas Leblanc ♀ 262 F3 ⊕ m 09 81 31 55 24 w auxepherites.com ⏰ closed Sun & Mon 🚊 République Beaux-Arts; cross pl de la République to rue Nicolas Leblanc
Since the original Sébastopol closed down on the retirement of unmatchable genius Jean-Luc Germond, there had been a gastronomic void in the triangle between Beaux Arts and the places Sébastopol and Philippe le Bon. When nobody leapt in with the sort of plates that seduced Michelin and *Gault&Millau* inspectors, food lovers instead welcomed a simple little dining room in a seriously understated address (it could be taken for an insurance office), serving mainly lunches as an alternative to more flamboyant haute cuisine. This is *bistronomie*, the buzzword for classy inventive dishes to be enjoyed at simple tables, far from the starched linen and polished cruets of established venues. Here, original chef Alexandre Suergiu (now back where he belongs after a brief interregnum) wields a *menu du marché*: €30 for an *amuse-bouche* followed by three courses. Alternatively, select from a daily choice of two €8 starters, a brace of mains at €16 and a pair of €6 desserts. Those starters might include langoustine and smoked trout with a scoop of beetroot ice cream. Other menu options may feature tuna with kale and creamy cauliflower, pumpkin *crème brûlée*, even *foie gras* in hibiscus jelly. Desserts are quite conventional: crumbles, lemon meringue tart, chocolate mousse or (in strawberry season) a smackingly piquant *soupe des fraises*.
  Naturally, Suergiu now has his own inevitable blind tasting parade of eight plates – here at €62. The restaurant has smartened itself up since its early era. Now there's a more stylish look to the contemporary minimalism in the narrow dining room, with etched windows that deter unwary passing trade. Reservation nigh-on essential. €€

ESTAMINET GANTOIS BRASSERIE FLAMANDE See page 102.

LE FLAM'S 8 rue de Pas ♀ 261 H4 ☏ 03 20 54 18 38 w flams.fr 🚊 Rihour; take rue Roisin into rue de Pas
Welcome to the home of the *flammekeuche* – that not-quite-pizza, not-quite-*crêpe* adopted speciality of the city for a quarter century. We're talking about a large, thin dough base, spread with either savoury or sweet toppings; the former centred on cheeses, mushrooms and ham, the

1 Now an international chain, the Paul bakery began in Lille. 2, 3 & 4 If you are planning a picnic in the park or square, *boulangeries* and pâtisseries around town offer sweet and savoury treats alongside traditional baguettes. ▶

PAUL

La FLUTE PAUL

0,81 €

latter blending fruit, sweets and *eau de vie* toppings as found in any *crêperie*. Cut out a square of your '*flam*', roll it into a cigar shape and hold it with your fingers to munch over a chilled beer and a heated discussion about life, love and politics. No longer the fad of a decade ago, it's now quietly been dropped from many brasserie menus, but here it remains a budget treat, with lunchtimes bringing office workers and shoppers to take advantage of special deals (a savoury and a sweet *flammekeuche* with a 25cl glass of *bière blonde*). Come evening, this is a regular student hangout, 50m from Grand'Place, with groups of friends sharing a selection of *flams*, picnic-style. Snack deals from €10ish and all-you-can-eat options under €15. In good weather, step across the road to a summer terrace; in winter, stay cosy indoors by warm brickwork. €€

LE FOSSILE   60 rue Saint-Étienne ♀ 261 G5 ⊕ ✆ 03 20 54 29 82 w lefossile.com ⏰ closed Sun 🚇 Rihour; take rue Roisin to rue de Pas & left along rue Saint-Étienne
Many years ago, I knew a restaurant in Paris that never bothered with menus. They had only ever served one dish as long as anyone could recall and it was that or nothing! I was reminded of that place when we arrived at this fine old red-brick building between the Nouveau Siècle concert and car park building and the back entrance to the Novotel. Le Fossile arrived in Lille with a 35-year pedigree in Alsace, and my reminiscences were ignited by the house speciality, or perhaps that should read the house obsession: steak. Steak, steak or steak is the choice on the menu. Unlike my Parisian table of sepia-tinted memory, there is an option. Either go for *onglet* (the house cut) in any of three guises, or choose a *filet* steak (more of which follows). A friend with carnivore credentials to satisfy both Darwin and Tennyson salivated at a repast red in tooth and claw, and pronounced the signature *onglet à l'echalote* triumphant. Beef may also be served with mushrooms or on its own. A *filet* is presented in all the classic formats, *maître d'hôtel* or with Roquefort cheese, mushrooms, cognac, pepper and a choice of wild mushroom sauces. As you might expect, the wine list has practically adopted Bordeaux citizenship, and a first snuffling through the pages yielded a 2000 Château Beau Site *cru bourgeois exception* St Estèphe and a 2002 Margaux. Various steak main courses cross the €30 boundary (though the *onglet* incarnations are around €5 less), and the starters (very *escargot*, *très canard*, seriously *foie gras*) hover in the teens. Desserts are equally classical at around the €9 mark, but only a true trencherman will get that far. Still my wimpish *côterie* has not discovered the 'secret' pudding, the identity only revealed at the table. When pushing the boat out and loosening the belt buckle, do indulge in a glass of Armagnac. I only know one other eatery with anywhere near such a selection of *digestifs* and that is to be found over 1,000km south of Lille! Fossile's Armagnac archive ranges from 1888 to the turn of the millennium and features in the *Guinness Book of Records*. €€€

LES HAUTS DE LILLE   Resort Barrière, 777 Pont de Flandres ♀ 259 J5 ✆ 03 28 14 45 50 w hotelsbarriere.com ⏰ closed Sun–Wed, open eves only Thu–Sat 🚉 Gare Lille Flandres or Gare Lille Europe; take the parvis de Rotterdam exit from Lille Europe to Pont de Flandres
While time stands still in a world-class casino resort, fine dining at this flagship first-floor restaurant has nonetheless evolved. At first glance, it was a standard big-white-plate and tall-wine-glass institution, with menu prices tailored to fit expense accounts and just enough of a wink to the off-duty tastes of the local business community to woo corporate diners back in their own time. However, now lunch is permanently off the menu (sister dining room Terrasse

du Parc downstairs still serves brasserie meals both noon and night; page 104), this fine dining restaurant only opens evenings, three times a week, and brings a new approach. Yes, it's another be-surprised-by-our-chef flourish of three-, five- or seven-course options costing €50–70 (plus an extra €20–30 for a tailored chain of wine glasses with each dish). But Anthony Pichon has worked the international Michelin trail from London to Dubai, and displays a more global outlook for sourcing fine ingredients, so *wagyu* beef comfortably shares the kitchen with *côte d'opale* Dover sole. Naturally, both gastronomic reinventions and rediscovered working class standards (*riz de veau*) are served, plus the usual crab, lobster, *escargot*, *foie gras* suspects, through pigeon to turbot mains and complex desserts. €€€€

LE JARDIN DU CLOÎTRE 17 quai du Wault ♀ 260 E3 ⊕ ☏ 03 20 30 62 62 w alliance-lille. com 🚌 Bus L5 to Nationale, then rue Nationale to sq Foch & through the square to the pond; restaurant on the right bank
In the business-park perpendicular atrium of the hotel Couvent des Minimes (page 69) is this restaurant that boasts professional service, a fine *filet mignon* in the inevitable *blanche* and the ubiquitous piano player. This is where business people from TGV-Thalys business towns north, south and east of Lille meet up to discuss business policy over a jolly decent set-price business lunch around €25–45 (on expenses). Light touches include a filo-wrapped smoked salmon, fromage frais and cucumber starter or lamb wafted in coriander and thyme. Boats may be pushed out by á la carte indulgences such as the €65 caviar blini starter. €€€€

JOUR DE PÊCHE 2 rue de Pas ♀ 261 H5 ⊕ ☏ 03 20 57 60 59 w jour-de-peche.fr ⏰ closed Sun eve & Wed 🚌 Rihour; take rue Roisin to rue de Pas
Just over half a lifetime ago, my family treated me to a special birthday lunch. My first Michelin-starred restaurant meal at La Matelote, just along the seafront from the old port of Boulogne-sur-Mer, and it was everything I wanted it to be (delicious food, imaginatively and delicately presented by charming staff in a room that allowed for a relaxing family occasion to be celebrated in comfort). Chef Tony Lestienne understood his fish as well as he did his diners, and it was no surprise when he expanded his empire to the neighbouring Nausicaä sea centre and aquarium, and gradually built up his main restaurant business into a fine hotel as celebrated as that flagship restaurant. So when the lovely aroma of freshly roasted fish skin, luscious tomato and a waft of vanilla, combined with the-*apéro*-hour tones of Diana Krall, lured me in from the rue de Pas in Lille, I was not surprised to discover that the Lestienne family had arrived in the city. This time it was under the eye of the next generation of the Matelote lineage, Stellio Lestienne, who grew up in his father's kitchens and honed his trade on both sides of the Channel at the Waterside Inn and Lenôtre. In fact, the family connection to this site goes back half a century to when Lestienne *père* worked in these very kitchens when they belonged to a long-established Russian restaurant, Chez Koff.

All the cheering elements of that long-ago meal at the Matelote were echoed here in a room unencumbered by the impedimenta of an *étoile* or *macaron*. Forgoing *encornet* with red pepper, I opted for marine *rillettes*, served not on the usual 'bed' but here overcanopied with genuinely interesting leaves that tickled hitherto untapped flavours of a salmon, tantalisingly creamed with finely chopped shallots, chives and the deliciously unfashionable, but always appropriate, dill. I was still accepting the mute thanks of my lips and taste buds for such a wise choice when the main course arrived. I forgave the squarest plate I had ever known for the sheer quality of a midday masterclass on how to make a simple white fish noble enough to merit a public holiday. My plaice divested itself of its skin with the expert grace of a courtesan shedding a superfluous negligée. Within a ring of pert, cracking and perfectly pitched vegetables, lay three fillets on as excellent a risotto of *confit* tomatoes as I could dream on. This kitchen does more than merely respect its local produce, it flirts and flatters and dances attention on all its fish (from the rare to the everyday), until ripe for kissing, let alone serving on a plate. What would happen should the young master desert his ship? I need not have worried. Stellio had set up his team with an eye to passing on control, and very soon, he announced his departure for new challenges in Hong Kong before taking over his father's starred kitchen in the port. He very publicly handed over command in Lille to Maxime Deriot and since then, the Deriot family has entwined its own style and skills with the Lestienne legacy. When a startling flourish of inky purple in a local *bleue d'Artois* potato mash set off a *bavette d'Aloyau* laced with creamed shallots on a recent springtime menu, gasps were heard, lips smacked and appreciation hummed. Yet such beefy bravado did not eclipse the traditional supremacy of the seas. Roast sea bass and a monkfish ever so lightly poached in an eastern-inspired stock, and a substantial *choucoute de la mer* continued to respect the fishermen's credentials, as did seaweed butter for fresh bread before the first course arrived. While premium oysters come from the little Normandy port of Saint Vaast La Hougue, Boulonnais heritage is marked by seafood, not to mention cheeses by Maître Philippe Olivier as an alternative to the pavlova suffused with citrus fruit to subvert the sweetness of the meringue. The current front of house crew share the quiet professionalism of the original team; when, almost 45 minutes into my initial tarriance and well into my first course, the waiter confided the daily specials for the 20th time to a later arrival, it was with the same sense of enthusiasm and occasion he had shared with me. Lunch menus, at under €25 and just over €30, reflect catch of the day, and in the evenings diners may opt for a three-course menu *balade* for under €45. Otherwise, budget over €55. Since the sea lion's share of the year in my adult life has been lived in a French fishing port, my seduction threshold is quite high when it comes to inland fish restaurants. Jour de Pêche comfortably settled into the list of my favourite places in France, let alone Lille. Get here early or book. €€€€

LAKSØN 21 rue du Curé Saint-Étienne 261 H4 03 20 31 19 96 w lakson.fr closed Sun & Mon Rihour; then cross Grand' Place & walk under Alcide arch to Saint-Étienne into rue Lepelletier
On the cusp of the squares and Vieux Lille, and in the quarter of pricey *bijoutiers* and *antiquaries*, discover a Scandinavian delicatessen and dining room that has been feeding blinis, smoked fish and satisfying Danish pastries to the Lillois for more than 25 years. One of the best Scandi tables between Paris and the Baltic, it shares honours evenly between various Nordic nations from Denmark to Lapland. Menus are a veritable net-load of herrings, sprats, sundry smoked fish and crabs. With smoked salmon and gravad lax in pole position, a spicy Swedish salmon burger is pricey but appreciated and signature dishes include an *aumônière de crêpe au saumon fumé*, a distinctive Nordic wave of lobster tails, and eponymous (and salmonised) house poached eggs. Just leave room for one of the moreish Danish cheesecake or crumble desserts. Midweek set lunches are €25–30, platters from €25–40. If you are looking for an alternative approach to Lille's traditional comfort food, this makes a very tasty change. €€€

MÉERT 27 rue Esquermoise 📍 261 H4 ⊕ 📞 03 20 57 93 93 🌐 meert.fr 🕐 closed Mon & all eves 🚇 Rihour; cross the Grand' Place to rue Esquermoise

Best known as the pâtisserie to the great and the good, the grandest tea shop in the north of France (page 130) has a restaurant behind its exquisite shopfront and dainty *salon de thé*. Of course, as visitors to the Piscine museum in Roubaix (page 222) already knew, the house is no stranger to proper catering, so the arrival of a dining room around the courtyard at the back of the building was inevitable. A string of high-profile chefs from the kitchens of **Pourcheresse and Ladeyn** established headline-grabbing dishes in the early days. If you are returning for another rack of wild boar or suckling pig cooked in straw, however, maybe look elsewhere. Now Tom Truy-Courties serves variations on *les predictables du Nord* (*waterzooi, carbonnade*, sole *meunière* or veal *blanquette*) either side of €35 on the main course list, with starters at teens to twenties a tad more exotic (pumpkin and scallop soup or lobster Caesar salad). It's best to budget close to €70 for lunch midweek. The simpler set menu on Sunday only might offer a ham and cheese *croissant* followed by pasta or cod and dessert at the €40 price point. Dine inside or on the courtyard. €€€€€

N'AUTRE MONDE 1 rue du Curé Saint-Étienne 📍 261 H4 ⊕ 📞 03 20 15 01 31 🌐 nautremonde. fr 🕐 closed Mon 🚇 Rihour; walk through the squares to rue Esquermoise & take the first left

Had we but enough time on my last gastro dash around town before putting this latest edition of the book to bed, I would have come back to sample the latest look of N'Autre Monde. Alas, as ever, my diary was hijacked by the mushrooming of so many new restaurants replacing fallen stalwarts. Thankfully, I treasure previous memories of great lunchtimes at this otherworld of imaginative dining. Would-be culinary stars take note: a truly great chef does not have to be 'clever'. A *maestro* should be able to play his ingredients without too many theatrical flourishes. In this comfortable squeeze of a dining room between shopfronts, a stumble from Grand' Place into the old town, the weft and weave of nature is at the bidding of a virtuoso team for even the simplest dish on the menu. The piece of cod that passeth all understanding was sublime, divine and delicious: speared with a vanilla pod on a bed of the most basic garden produce. This stalwart of the greyer reaches of the Atlantic proved as exotic as a nobler catch. It also demonstrated that garden produce does not have to be red nor shiny nor drizzled with oils and vinegars to be worth a second glance. The root veg was a masterclass in steaming only to an awakening: each of a half-dozen winter varieties, privily spiced, attained perfection in texture and taste. North African and Indian Ocean spices fragrance the air, testament to a world food philosophy, always delightfully balanced so that the gentle scent of later arrivals' *tagine* in no way distracts from the playful mirabelle or pistachio lacings of your own final course. The option of a cheese plate is a no-brainer, given that next door is the counter of *maître fromager* Philippe Olivier – provenance impeccable. There were nine coffees to choose from, all arabica, and the counting of the teas required Homerian patience. Coffee is not exclusively shackled to the end of the meal. Exhibit one m'lud: a walnuted crumble of *sandre* served with *endive* braised in coffee. Since the menus change almost with each new moon, if you read it here, it will be too late to eat it there. (Though a friend once found the chef's recipe for rabbit thighs with sesame and *fourme d'ambert* cheese online, and will one day pluck up the courage to cook the dish!) In all likelihood, you'll never know the wild boar risotto or *sole en croûte* with a creamy cauliflower sauce ennobled with vanilla and almond. But the consolation is that you may discover something on your own visit that shall forever be hidden from me. I missed the *schawarma* of pollock with tahini and capers, but have seen great African influences now Renaud

Germonprez has taken over in the kitchen – a seamless handover that's kept punters and food writers sweet, while throwing eastern European, Caribbean and Asian cuisine into the fusion mix. Recent suggestions have included jerk pork hot dog flavoured with yuzu, cheddar and pineapple, while vegetarians have more to choose from, be it lentil and carrot dahl or grilled smoked leeks with hazelnuts in a Japanese-inspired citrus sauce.

You know the food is good when even business lunchers do the lovers' thing and pass forks across the table. This is not the exclusive province of expense account *divertissement*, however; on one visit, besides a smattering of *hommes d'affaires*, were a few true couples and plenty of ladies lunching *en fille*. A sharply coiffed man in black who knew the value of skincare lunched with a tousle-haired, bluff fellow in boots who knew the value of life. Expect to pay at least €40 for the first two courses. And budget over the €50 limit once dessert is factored in. There is usually a lighter-priced vegetarian plate for each course modestly couched amid the more exotic dishes on the menu. €€€€

L'ORANGE BLEUE 30 rue Lepelletier ♀ 261 H4 ⓫ ☏ 03 20 55 04 70 w restaurant-lorangebleue.fr ⏰ closed Sun 🚊 Rihour; cross the squares & walk under the Alcide arch to rue des Débris Saint-Étienne & continue to rue Lepelletier
I'm so glad that I took a short cut along rue Lepelletier on the eve of signing off a previous edition of this book, otherwise I might have missed out on the smart, efficient and welcome treat that is this popular eatery just a matter of yards from the Grand'Place. The large airy dining room has enough space 'twixt tables for plenty of bulky carrier bags – making it popular among the serious shopping set at lunchtime. Swift and friendly waiting staff whizz-glide through the room, managing the extraordinary feat of dashing from one end of the restaurant to another without anyone else feeling in the least bit hurried. Food-wise, expect to be assailed by heightened flavours, whether you take a menu priced in the €30s or graze à la carte. Mains range either side of a €20 note. One memorable treat *croquante* of haddock *à l'aneth* offered gossamer-fine leaves of filo, dill and smoked haddock that hit more culinary G-spots than you might expect. More recently, we dined in the teens on bream with quinoa and rhubarb vinaigrette. Pasta and salad options are served in huge quantities, as are all the main courses. Cheese does not wait for the end of the meal here, perhaps appearing (as Maroilles) inside gingerbread-tinged chicken, and (in *chèvre* guise) as stuffing to a saffron-teased salmon dish. Late risers looking for a kick-start to the remainder of their day might even forego the *plat principal* and opt for a starter and dessert in the name of a tardy brunch. Don't bother with the printed wine list – do as the locals and go for a seasonal suggestion chalked around the room. Sometimes it's around half the bottle price for a jug. There's no need to rush off after licking the platter clean: no matter how busy it is, staff encourage lingering with a good choice of *digestifs* from *fleur de bière* to *calvados*, to keep the feel-good factor nice and high. €€€

ORIGAN 58 bd Carnot ♀ 259 G3 ❹ ☏ 03 20 13 08 88 ⏰ closed Sun 🚊 Gare Lille Flandres; cross Parc Matisse to bd Carnot
This inexpensive *luncherie* is so painfully sharp that you'd cut yourself if you fell upon it by accident. At Origan, the fusion concept goes far beyond the plate. New York studio-style skylights burnish an endless row of shiny black tables with individual linen runners and, to keep the place exclusively packed with the young and fit, a painted grey doorstep is obviously inspired by the north face of the Eiger. You can guess just how New European the smart guys at the next table

will be merely by reading the menu: open sandwiches of *foie gras* with Granny Smith carpaccio, chopped hazelnut and a glass of white port (I kid ye not) have optional side orders of either a *légume du jour* crumble, tomato confit salad or gratin of penne with Grana Padano. Admit it, you can already picture their homes!

But don't mock, people this hip won't be fobbed off with anything but the best when it comes to actually eating. Food is prepared with flair and talent and served with style, and flavours certainly live up to the gilded frieze that runs the length of the restaurant, an enumeration of fine herbs scrawled across panels and mirrors alike. The monochrome of the décor serves to highlight the vibrant hues on the plates. Since this is already a hit with the busy and beautiful lunch crowd, most of the food is the sort of thing you might enjoy while keeping your finger on the pulse and your eye on the ball, and is itself a Euro-combo of mezze and tapas. The hyper-fusion theme continues through the proper main courses. Lunch menus and sandwich-based snacking at €18 and €21, weekly menu at €26 for three courses, à la carte budgets around €35. €€€

LE PICCOLO MONDO 2 Rue des Molfonds 261 H6 03 20 30 82 22
 lepiccolomondo.com closed Sun Rihour

A reliable local or holiday-style *trattoria* serving the usual aubergine and parmesan classics, Italian wine by the glass and a great range of yummy, generous and inexpensive pastas and pizzas. Eat well without running up a €30 bill. The unexpectedly smart low-key décor is offset by a lovely open fire on a wet autumn evening. It's tucked away in a side street between the shops of rue de Béthune and place Rihour métro. I've been dropping in for over 20 years. €€

RESTAURANT SÉBASTOPOL 1 place Sébastopol 262 E3 03 20 13 13 38
 restaurantsebastopol.com closed Sun République Beaux-Arts; cross pl de la République to rue Inkerman

Mea Culpa. Cards on the table. I forgot to take notes. It was a special day and I was reminiscing over memorable meals from the glory days of the Germond regime in this corner townhouse on the square, when we noticed the door was open once again. So we stepped inside, browsed the menu, had a delicious meal, and perhaps a little too much wine…and all I now recall is a gentle cloud of happiness in the moment, company, conversation and definite pleasure in the food. I have flashing images of roasted fish that caressed and curled around my fork, and echoes of the happiest of sighs that followed every mouthful of duck on the other side of the table. It was only later, and many miles away, that I learned the chef Antony Dorard was already being touted as one to watch. Instagram *aides-memoires* of other people's evenings show an artistic flair for presentation of vegetables that would not be out of place in a gallery. Impeccably sourced fish from the Côte d'Opale I can vouch for, despite amnesia over details, and the quality of pork and poultry has thumbs up from France's sternest critics. Dorard changes the menu at the end of every week, posting online before the weekend. The lunchtime *plat du jour* is priced at €16 (when I phoned to ask) and starters in the early teens, mains in the late twenties and desserts around a tenner. The late Empire-era dining room of the old days has now been replaced by a more streamlined, sleek, light-wood and shiny-tiled look, the age of traditional linens and heavy knives and forks long gone. If I promise to go back and write it all up properly next time will you forgive me? €€€

The heyday of hereditary Michelin stars is over. Throughout the last century, gastronomy had a long lineage of stars, *toques* and rosettes passed from *père* to *fils*. But then came reality television and a new cohort of young chefs whisked, sliced and flambéed their way into the spotlight. Generation Top Chef, named for a Masterchef-style TV show that tested France's kitchen talent to the limit, brought a new perspective to dining in Lille. The cream of the 21st-century crop hailed from the region and took their sudden *réclame* to the tables of the old quarter and beyond. To be fair, TV success was never an overnight phenomenon. Florent Ladeyn, the highest profile *nouvelle vague* surfer, had previously been hailed by *Gault&Millau* as the best young chef north of Paris. Growing up in his grandparents' simple country inn at Les Monts des Flandres, he had a dalliance with art school before his passion for cooking lured him back to the family Auberge du Vert Mont, where eventually he won a Michelin star. The restaurant, 30 minutes out of town, had France's leading food writers sitting up and begging for more. Ladeyn might have moved anywhere in the country, or beyond, to take his career to the next level. Instead, he spent two years planning **Bloempot** (page 107), his simple kitchen-garden canteen in Lille. Having achieved all this in his mid-20s, he then went on to train up a team even younger than himself for the day-to-day cooking, gathering both local talent and other *Top Chef* finalists. This included Damien Laforce, who became number two in the kitchen and is now fast becoming another name to watch himself at Le Braque (page 109). And as an antidote to the most in-demand address in Lille, Ladeyn

ROCOCO   Urban Hotel, 48b rue de Valenciennes ♀ 262 F5 ⊕ ☎ 03 20 92 50 57 🚇 Porte de Valenciennes; take bd Belfort to rue Trevisse, then pl Guy de Dampierre to rue de Valenciennes
A fabulously OTT dining room with enough Empire period gilded panels, mirrors and polished glass to make Versailles seem like an Ikea outlet. Originally established in the Cinderella quarter by a chef who earned his whites at the Why Dinette across town, the small but flamboyant Rococo restaurant swiftly developed as a destination in its own right, and is still always packed with weekday business lunchers on the €18 *plat du jour* and *café gourmand* menu. Evenings see guests from the Urban Hotel (page 78) and local cognoscenti more likely to opt for the three-course-under-€25 deal or graze à la carte closer to €40. New chef Antoine makes his mark with daily inspiration chalked on boards. Produce is mostly local, and the initially Asian-inspired fusion cuisine is now matched with the use of scents and spices from closer to home. Thus, as an alternative to predictably sweet-and-sour barely seared tuna, discover *gravlax* of pork (surely *carpaccio*?) bezinged with horseradish and mandarin. There's even an inspirational veggie option that eschews tofu in favour of roasted and blowtorched beetroot and cheese on a smoked garlic toast, served with mustard sprouts rather than predictable quinoa. €€€

opened the **Bierbuik** brewpub in Vieux Lille (page 128) for informal *frîtes* with *estaminet* fare.

Bloempot may have epitomised the locavore movement, but rival Top Chef Nicolas Pourcheresse went one step further with La Serre, a pop-up restaurant in the greenhouse where the legendary 'Red Chef' grows fruit, veg and aromatic herbs for his more orthodox addresses. Tables serve just 30 people, 4 miles out of town, a 20-minute bus ride and half-mile country walk away. The field is not just for show: herbs are snipped, fruit picked and root vegetables pulled from the soil all year. If you can't get a table, or turn up in the wrong season, fear not. **Chez Mon Cousin** (page 110) has a year-round, ever-evolving menu around similar criteria of 'local and fresh'. With his piratic Viking look, wild red hair, beard and tattoos, Pourcheresse launched Méert's dining room, then La Table at Hotel Clarance, before stepping down once Michelin-starred to set up solo around the city. His smallest, ultra-intimate restaurant offering close-up cooking to discerning diners in Vieux Lille was called Vagabond. But Pourcheresse rarely stays in the same place too long, and mere weeks into 2024, the Vagabond vanished from rue Saint André. The first many people knew of it was when the premises were reincarnated, with his blessing, as **Coup de Main** (page 124). To find out where he will be cooking and serving when you are next in town go to w nicolas-pourcheresse.fr. Meanwhile, more Top-Chef innovation can be found *chez* Steven Ramon at **Rouge Barre** just around the corner (see below).

ROUGE BARRE 50 rue de La Halle ♀ 261 H1 ⊕ ☏ 03 20 67 08 84 w rougebarre.fr ⏰ closed Sun & Wed 🚌 Bus 86 from Lille Europe to Lycée Pasteur, then bus 10 to Voltaire, walk rue St André to rue de La Halle
Lille has no shortage of 'up and coming' chefs and its 'one to watch' list is fast becoming a catalogue, since the city is home to a disproportionate number of TV cooking show finalists and winners, not to mention annual garlands for potential from leading food guides. However, the one really to watch was Steven Ramon, who shot to national fame as a semi-finalist in the 2014 *Top Chef* series (France's answer to *Masterchef*). Telegenic, curly haired and wearing his heart on the sleeves of his chef's whites, he was an instant hit with the public. No one could forget his tearful outpourings while strapped into a harness and sitting at a dining table suspended from a crane above a city street. This was reality TV, after all. He displayed an innate talent for working with fresh fish and vegetables, and spoke on television of his dream that one day he would open his own restaurant. This is that very restaurant, and it has been flying higher in Lille's gastronomic firmament than that notorious sky-hoisted table from his small-screen career. You will need to book to be sure of a chance of wading into his dining room on the quieter side of Vieux Lille.

Of course, *Top Chef* was not Ramon's first culinary rodeo. He had been studying food since his secondary school days at Lille's Michel Servet catering college, and had work experience placements at top addresses, even retaining Michelin garlands when eventually replacing his mentor as chef at La Laiterie in nearby Lambersart. Thus, a young lifetime of experience may be found on every plate. Lunchtimes may see mackerel tickled into unexpected perkiness with the anise-like forgotten flavour of lovage, to set up a €35 three-course menu where the main course of red mullet is given spicier treatment, served with piquant *charcuterie* and reliable market garden leek cabbage or cauliflower to beef up the dish on cold winter days, or more vibrant tomato and pepper when sultry summer veg is in season. Like-minded pastry chef Alexis Hubière shares the open relationship with the herb garden and spice rack to temper the sweet tooth of chocolate, caramel or creamy desserts, often with an unusual citrus tang. Similar dishes appear on the 5- and 7-course (€56 and €78) menus (served lunchtimes and evenings), with the added bonus of rather splendid mini sculptures of cheese, meats, piped creams and the inevitable *endive* as elegant *amuses-bouches*. Wine flights for these events are an extra €25/35. For me, the outstanding attraction of the place is chef Ramon's respect for the gastronomes of tomorrow. If there is an intelligent child in your life, come here to create one of their formative moments: for under tens, instead of nuggets or the *steak haché* panderings of so many restaurants, Rouge Barre will adapt the adults' menu to deliver a three-course meal, exploring textures and flavours tailored to the youngster's palate. All at €21. €€€€

LA TABLE Clarance Hotel, 32 rue de la Barre ♀ 261 F3 ☎ 03 59 36 35 59 w claracehotel.com 🚌 Bus L5 to Champ de Mars then bd Vauban to Square Daubanton to rue de la Barre
It was a chill November morning as I stood behind ranks of police cadets, serving soldiers, bemedalled veterans and flag bearers by the war memorial on place Rihour for the Armistice Day ceremony, when I bumped into an old acquaintance – recently elected to the city council. We decided to meet up for lunch in an hour or so, and I was delighted when invited to join him and a mutual friend at Hotel Clarance (page 69) after a frustrated week trying and failing to get a table at the then newly opened hottest address in town. Wafted from reception and waved through the paneled dining room to the library, an *escargot*-curved private niche, I wallowed in the not-what-you-know-but-who-ness of it all, as nary an eyebrow was raised at my joggers, scarf and denim-jacketed autumnal moochwear ensemble. Though with hindsight, perhaps it may have been my inappropriate attire rather than my companion's political influence that led us away from the expensive tailoring of the main room.

The chef then was Nicolas Pourcheresse, erstwhile creator of Méert's restaurant (page 117), who swiftly earned the restaurant its first Michelin star, just before backing out to launch his own string of established and pop-up spots around the city (page 120). Shortly thereafter, his successor Thibaut Gamba took the reins, retaining the star in his own right, and winning *Gault&Millau's* prize as France's most talented young chef. While it is tempting to wax lyrical with details of dishes savoured during his regime, it would be unfair, for at time of writing, Gamba himself has moved to fame in St Émilion, and his successor and erstwhile collaborator Alexandre Miquel has just taken over at the Clarance.

Still, the celebrated flourishes *à la* Nicolas *et* Thibaut certainly set the tone of the place, whether matching langoustine with *funghi* and borscht, creating trios of exotically flavoured and coloured butters, the master chef himself filleting a fish head at the table with a conjuror's *léger de main*, or the sheer Parisian brasserie theatricality of a whole roast cauliflower being wheeled through the dining room under a vast *cloche* dome, then being carved and side-plated by a brace of waiters with the *fin-de-siècle* solemnity that generally attends the presentation of a *chateaubriand*. The *bouche* is amused throughout the meal, with between-course cups or saucers of flavour and texture to set you up for the next big thing.

Miquel is a young lion, whose flair with desserts and chocolate had already drawn attention during several years working through the ranks at the Clarance. His exquisite *pâtissier* sugarwork and filigree artistry framing chocolate, fruit and even seafood is an Instagrammer's delight. The evening menu is another of those seven small-plate flights of chef's fancy that have descended upon the city; food alone comes to around €100 a person. Add the cheese board and the selection of wines and you may almost double that. The ultimate nine-plate version is €20 more (with added wines, cheese and an optional caviar appetiser, make that the best part of €500 for a couple). But the new chef's knack for teasing refreshing flavours from established ingredients shows in a winter selection that included barbecued Boulogne scallops with grapefruit and a pre-dessert mouthful of kiwi fruit tempered with wild honey & beer sorbet. Midday options now includes the €45 *l'Horloge* menu tailored for the modern business lunch hour, rather than a traditional French linger from pre-drink nibbles to dusk. Those who can afford to be late for their 2pm meeting may stretch to the longer *l'Idéale* at €60 – perhaps adding an optional glass of wine with each course for €35. With any menu, anytime, you may add a €25 cheese course – a curated selection from the trolley with almonds and a butternut squash *confit*. I recall the amazing combination of a similar artisanal chutney and exquisite fromage as being the highlight of my original lunch here. €€€€€

WHY DINETTE   7 sq Morisson ♀ 261 G6 ⊚ ✎ 03 20 50 30 30 w why-hotel.com 🚊 Rihour; walk past the tourist office & sq Morisson is on your left
From Place Rihour, ignore the Lorelei lures of the bustling restaurants on the main squares and shopping on rue Béthune, and make your way to the Why Hotel (page 78). At lunchtime, the hotel breakfast room becomes a lively hangout for local office workers and busy business types who nip out for a classy light lunch tailored to fit into an hour. A *plat du jour* (perhaps lamb, veal or a choice chunk of cod), served on a bed of fashionable beans and pulses of *MasterChef*-styled carbs, followed by the ubiquitous *café gourmand* espresso sharing a slate with a quartet of mini dessert treats, is a pretty good deal at around €21. I was particularly struck by the fact that the selections were not uniform. At our table, a different array of sweet things was presented to each diner: one had a teeny trifle, another a shot glass of lightly whipped mousse – even the *macarons* were not identikit. Service is professional and welcoming, and the large glazed terrace under the trees was perfect for lunch on the first day of spring. It's surprisingly close to anywhere you could want to be, with the brisk hum of other people networking while you are off-duty. Evening opening for drinks and €20–30 platters of serrano ham and cheeses. First Sunday of the month brings a three-hour brunch menu from 11.30 for €35. €€

WINE BARS

LES COMPAGNONS DE LA GRAPPE   26 rue Lepelletier ♀ 261 H4 ⊛ ✎ 03 20 21 02 79 🕐 closed Sun & Mon eve off season 🚊 Rihour; cross Grand' Place & walk under the Alcide arch to rue de Débris Saint-Étienne to rue Lepelletier
I stumbled across this summer terrace quite by chance: a gap in the alleyway opens out to reveal

a wine bar with a delightful courtyard. Families and friends sit and chat under sunshades, sipping wines from lesser-known French vineyards. Platters of *charcuterie* and farmhouse cheeses are colourful and plentiful, and the affordable *plat du jour* is around €12. The place positively hums with contentment, though beware that no reservations are taken, service can be a hit-and-miss affair and the opening hours of noon 'til midnight seem to vary with the weather. It's worth popping in to check on special theme evenings or culinary events. Budget €20 per person. €

COUP DE MAIN 112 rue Saint André ♀ 261 G1 ⊚ ⊙ restaurant closed Sun–Tue 🚌 Bus 10 from Gare Lille Flandres to Magasin
Confession time. I have never eaten here. I was fact-checking my never-to-be-read review of Nicolas Pourcheresse's Vagabond restaurant when I saw the news that the Red Chef had left the building and a brand-new establishment would be opening its doors on the site. Local lad Clément Delécluse, voted *meilleur jeune sommelier de France*, and Parisian chef Victor Berthe (with Plaza Athénée on his CV) had been working at acclaimed restaurant l'Empreinte, up the road from Pourcheresse's own Chez Mon Cousin (page 110), when they heard that chef Nicolas planned to leave rue St André. With his blessing, they set up Coup de Main as a destination for wine lovers – a restaurant/wine bar and retail wine cellar, with room for just 15–20 diners. Concept: choose your wine, then the kitchen will suggest the best dishes to go with the bottle. The plan was for all reservations to be done over the phone or in person, in order to get an idea of diners' tastes and requirements in advance. There would be a changing selection of one meat, one fish and one veggie dish each day, with meats and fish cooked in an open fire over vine stock. Set lunch around €20; six-plate flight menu in the evenings. Fine wines for sale in the cellar – with modest corkage charge to enjoy on site. €€€

CRÊPERIE SAINT GEORGES 19 rue Bartholomé Masurel ♀ 261 H3 ⊚ ✆ 03 28 05 36 50 w creperie-saintgeorges-lille.fr ⊙ noon–14.20 Tue–Sat, noon–13.45 Sun 🚌 Gare Lille Flandres; take rue Faidherbe to pl du Théâtre then rue Pelletier to rue Masurel
Enjoy the essential Breton accompaniment of cider rather than wine here. The seriously classy *crêpes* and *galettes* are basically a meal in a pancake – meats, fish, eggs, veg, and salads are wrapped up and presented on plates, slates and platters, before the expected sweet dessert options. Budget €20 up. €€

AU GRÉ DU VIN 20 rue Pétérinck ♀ 261 H3 ⊚ ✆ 03 20 55 42 51 ⊙ noon–14.20 Tue–Sat, noon–13.45 Sun 🚌 Bus 9 to Lion d'Or, & from rue de la Monnaie turn left on to rue Pétérinck: shop on your right
Go on, treat yourself to a nice glass of Languedoc wine at the first place in town to serve a tangy Picpoul de Pinet with a cold collation. Open lunchtimes only, this neat little wine shop – specialising in the once-overlooked but now ubiquitous full-flavoured delights of the former Languedoc-Roussillon region – serves a simple platter of food with which to sample Corbières,

---

1 Bars range from traditional locals to seriously fashionable spots. 2 Burgers at the city's annual street food festival. 3 Wine shops often double as wine bars. 4 Lille and the wider metropolitan area is awash with microbreweries, including Moulins d'Ascq. ▶

St Chinians, Fitous and Banyuls, or better-known bottles of the southwest. Since neighbouring *bar à fromage* Delassic Frères closed its doors, this is the last place in town where you may choose your cheese and ask the experts to find a matching wine. It's a good place to buy exotic specialities for picnics or presents: *aubergines à la Languedocienne* or jars of salt flavoured with spices and scents of the *garrigue* scrubland of the sultry south. Expect change from €20. €€

MONSIEUR JACQUES   30 rue de Gand ♀ 261 K2 ⊕ ☎ 03 20 74 85 59 ⏱ closed lunchtimes & all day Sun 🚌 Bus 50 to Lion d'Or

Besides a 300-label printed wine list, regulars check the blackboard here for the ever-changing selection of noteworthy Beaujolais and Languedocs by the glass. Choose *tartines*, *tapenades* or cold cuts to accompany the wine, in a peculiarly Gallic take on tapas. Interesting and not too pricey. Pay €20ish to keep the appetite at bay. €€

LE PRÉSENTOIR   24 rue Pierre Mauroy ♀ 261 J5 ⊕ w lepresentoirlille.fr ⏱ closed Mon & Tue 🚌 Gare Lille Flandres; take rue Faidherbe, then left on rue des Ponts de Comines to rue Pierre Mauroy

Next door to the long-established Le Pot Beaujolais (page 98) are labels from every other wine region and then some. This is a combined wine shop, wine bar and sort-of restaurant, though the menu is glorified tapas – olives and hummus, various meatballs, sardines etc, and some nice chocolaty desserts. Plates are small (starters and desserts under €10, mains in the teens), but well curated to go with the wine, whether fish for a crisp Loire or Alsace, something spicy with an earthy Corbières, a piece of duck to set off the Bordeaux or a gooey sweet pavlova when tastes run to Sauternes or Frontignan. The passion project of sommelier Ariane Laurent, this place is small, so consider booking in advance. Open evenings only and Saturday lunch. €€€

FOOD COURTS AND STREET FOOD

Food trucks have been the success story of the past several years, bringing world food and emerging chefs to new budget-conscious markets. A new street food festival has even joined the legendary annual soup celebrations on the gastro calendar (page 15). Recently, the trucks and trestles have started to move indoors with a crop of innovative food courts.

LE COMPTOIR HIRONDELLE   It started with a swallow and ended with a feast. As the food truck and street food movement gave Lille's dining scene a nudge, up popped this itinerant food court, a festival of street food that caused a big shake up in city-centre dining. The brainchild of Victor Lasch, Benjamin Frechet and Julien Hu, architects with a love of brewing their own beers, it first appeared in an abandoned garage between the university and Saint-Sauveur districts. There was a makeshift bar with babyfoot, mismatched tables, and food trucks and counters in any free corner. Friends of the trio, including an organic butcher and a market gardener, joined professional nomadic chefs to serve dishes ranging from Vietnamese vegan to hardcore carnivore. With some main courses under a tenner, it was a good excuse to explore a whole new cuisine. The Hirondelle closed at the end of the summer but, like its namesake the swallow, it flies back each spring to set up home in another abandoned or repurposed industrial

or public building. Since the 2023 Braderie, the founders have also established a full-time venue at Le Barge in the Solfé party district (page 153). Dubbed l'Hirondelle du poche, this is where they sell their beers – and they'll be first to let you know when and where the itinerant food court will be reborn each year.

GRAND SCÈNE 31 rue de Béthune ♀ 261 H6 ⊕ w grand-scene.com ⏲ 10.00–late Mon–Sat, 11.00–19.00 Sun 🚊 Rihour

Just around the corner from Kitchen Market (see below) is Le 31, the imaginative reincarnation of the Galeries Lafayette building (page 178). The street-facing entrance resembles a classic cinema lobby, reflecting its multiplex neighbours along rue de Béthune. Inside is a food court for start-up chefs. Here, young talent without the means to open a restaurant shares space as equals with established (even starred) culinary legends. So Nicolas and Grégoire who left business school to sell duck-based street food at Wazemmes market might set up alongside Syrian brothers Bassem and Reem's recreation of dishes from northern France's refugee communities – *le falafaluche* is their spin on a falafel sandwich.

With just ten counters, the cast of cooks is ever changing, so one visit you might enjoy a very French version of tacos, the next an authentic taste of Thailand. A great lure to keep punters coming is the roll-call of established restaurateurs dishing up treats next to the newbies. The Comptoir Valant guys (page 135) and pastry chefs from Tamper (page 134) have both served their party pieces. Even Michelin maestro Florent Ladeyn has dished out *estaminet* fare. Check out blind tasting events and music nights. There are two bars on site and the option of takeaway or delivery to your hotel.

KITCHEN MARKET Centre Commercial Les Tanneurs, 27 rue des Tanneurs ♀ 261 J6 ⏲ 11.00–23.00 Mon–Thu, 11.00–midnight Fri–Sat, noon–17.00 Sun w kitchenmarketlille.fr 🚊 Rihour; walk down rue de Béthune to rue des Tanneurs

Swap your lunch hour for a truncated gap year between C&A and Monoprix in a shopping mall straddling the pedestrian shopping quarter. Home to 1970s high-street stalwarts and a few smaller boutiques, this place has been revitalised with a food court that's always absolutely packed, seven days a week. As shoppers squeeze past to pick up milk and biscuits at the supermarket, grab a table amid an incongruous static zoo of lifesize model giraffes, elephants and zebras, then suss out the dozen or so food stands serving the world on a plate.

The stallholders' banter has an almost family buzz. Sisters Eloïse and Stéphanie host Ramen ton Bol, offering net-zero-waste Japanese specialities amid a raft of rival Asian options, including a sushi bar, Franco–Indian cheese naans at La Naanerie, and Bangkok flavours served by the legendary Ly at Thaï City Trip. Visit Madagascan, Lebanese and Argentine counters, or stay closer to home in Italy with Mama Buffalina's sourdough pizza or Papa Risotto's great *arancini*. Even France is represented by Ker Juliette's bréton *crêpes* and Sam'Regal, whose famous locavore burger truck will be found at every major festival either side of the Belgian border. Last time I went, the biggest queues were for *poutine* at Tata Jöelle. In the centre, Penny Lane Bar serves drinks no matter where your food comes from, and gets busy with an after-work crowd. Remote ordering is done via QR codes on the tables. Evenings are even more convivial with a monthly programme of events, from board games every first Tuesday to karaoke nights, concerts, and even glamorously hosted live streams of *Drag Race*!

BARS, CAFÉS AND TEA ROOMS

Nurse a coffee for an hour, have a beer with friends, a late-night light snack or mid-afternoon sugar rush. Traditional restaurants are not the answer: time to explore the infinite variety of bars, cafés and *salons de thé* that provide sustenance before, between and beyond mealtimes.

If, instead of a chunky espresso cup with wrapped sugar cube and square of chocolate, you prefer your coffee served in a large disposable cardboard container with a logo on it, then you may welcome the proliferation of American-style coffee chains offering frappé-fresco-latte-mochaccino-type concoctions. A number of these are emerging around Gare Flandres station, creeping across the Grand' Place and opening up in a former shop sometime soon next door to wherever you are staying!

L'ABBAYE See page 100.

AUX ARTISTES 1 pl du Concert ♀ 261 H2 ⊕ ☎ 03 20 21 13 22 🚌 Bus 9 from Gare Lille Flandres to Lion d'Or, then follow rue de la Monnaie
Sit on the strip of pavement terrace and watch the comings and goings of the Conservatoire opposite and the rue de la Monnaie to your right. Nothing special, just traditional cane chairs and smart blue awning to appreciate after an hour or so sightseeing. Fine for a quick beer and break after the Hospice Comtesse and Vieux Lille window-shopping.

BD + CAFÉ 5 rue Royale ♀ 261 G3 ⊕ ☎ 03 20 15 11 47 ⏱ 14.00–19.00 Mon, 10.30–19.00 Tue–Sat 🚇 Rihour; cross Grand' Place to rue Esquermoise into rue Royale
It had to happen. After the *café philo* and the *café littéraire*, here comes the *café* comic strip. Sadly, the more famous Café-Livres in an actual bookshop has closed down, but the French, like the Japanese, love their BD – *bandes dessinées*, comic-strip artwork and novellas – and vast sections of any self-respecting bookshop are devoted to the form. So now comes a café where aficionados may chat and browse over an espresso. Friendly welcome guaranteed in this bustling corner of the old town.

BERLINER 22 rue Royale ♀ 261 G3 ⊕ ☎ 03 20 39 38 54 🚇 Rihour; cross Grand' Place to rue Esquermoise into rue Royale
Previously better known as a Franco–German burger/bagel bar hangout, this is now very much the evening *rendezvous* for a lively, loud, youngish crowd with a penchant for Jägerbombing. Open past midnight.

BIERBUIK 19 Rue Royale ♀ 261 G3 ⊕ w bierbuik.fr 🚇 Rihour, then Navette Vieux Lille to Voltaire and walk south on rue Royale
Discover the affordable side of Bloempot (page 107) at chef-boss Ladeyn's ground-floor brew-pub serving bar food and legendary chips (double-fried in beef fat) with mayo on tin trays. Or step upstairs for an *estaminet* menu under €30. Beers never fail to surprise – your *demi* may be flavoured with locally sourced wisteria!

LE BIG LE MOI Café in a bookshop with readings and events. See page 159.

BISTROT DE ST SO See page 93.

CAFÉ DE FOY 6–8 pl Rihour 📍261 H5 📞03 20 54 22 91 🚇 Rihour
Squeezed between the thrusting elbows of many a visitor-packed bistro and ice cream parlour, Foy is a popular choice for budget-conscious *plat du jour* lunchers, rendezvous-shifting friends or mere people-watchers. Tourists know the packed terrace, but locals think of the first-floor room where Thursday night conversation goes beyond shopping stories and idle gossip. This is the *café philo* of the squares. If your French is up to it, take the plunge.

CAFÉ OZ 33 pl Louise de Bettignies 📍261 J2 📞03 20 55 15 15 **w** cafe-oz.com 🕐 14.00–03.00 daily 🚌 Bus 9 to Lion d'Or
Known to the locals as 'L'Australian', this is the Lille branch of a national chain of Aussie pubs. It serves nachos, burgers and *croque monsieur* bar snacks to mop up the Fosters, Monteiths, Tooheys and other brews from Down Under. Anglophone students, backpackers and sports fans come to watch the match on TV, others for a seemingly endless happy hour.

COFFEE MAKERS 151 rue Pierre Mauroy 📍261 J7 📞09 73 55 93 60 **w** coffeemakers.fr 🕐 until 18.00, closed Sun 🚇 Mairie de Lille
Step back from the tourist traps if you want a proper cappuccino or latte in Lille, and make a note of this address. On the southern slip of rue Mauroy below rue Molinel, a teeny-weeny narrow coffee shop crams in tables and chairs and is usually packed with locals who love a really good coffee (even tap water is purified before being pumped into the machine) and a range of cakes that verges on anglophile. The busy people of Lille swear by the coffee here, and the welcome is truly convivial. Light lunch for €8–12. Always a vegan option.

GASTAMA Officially this is the bar for backpackers dossing in comfort at the The People hostel upstairs. Like l'Australian, this is a great meeting point for travellers and locals alike. Mojitos and world beers fuel an international youthful buzz. See page 83.

KHEDIVE 7 pl Rihour 📍261 H5 📞03 20 54 37 82 🚇 Rihour
In these health-conscious times, when smokers are expected to rend their garments and carry a bell, and every unsuccessful retail outlet becomes a vape shack, this a socially incorrect *terrasse* for those who otherwise might be seen huddling on doorsteps and blocking the entrance to smoke-free railway stations and shopping malls (interestingly, the fug that garlands the portals of such breathe-right sanctuaries is like a triple espresso shot of nicotine that could flay and slay an asthmatic at 40 paces). On most café terraces, drinkers and diners may puff with impunity, but here, next door to l'Abbaye and in front of Foy, is a place where tobaccophiles may walk tall and strut. It's an address for those who still like a cigar and wheeze a sigh at the sight of a humidor. A sign in the window invites visitors to explore a 'Cave aux Cigares'. Snacks are served from 06.00 until midnight to satisfy munchies and refuel both those whose taste buds have been shattered by a life on the weed and tolerant non-smokers who fancy the jolt of a refreshing glass of beer and a rustled-up sandwich. The closed-in (in winter) terrace attracts a lively mix of students and musicians from

The dividing line between a bar and a café has blurred over the years. Generally, one does a lot more sitting down in the latter and standing around in the former, and bars stay open later – usually sometime between 23.00 and 02.00. You can enjoy a coffee in a bar or a beer in a café, so your choice really depends on where you feel most at home.

Cafés tend to be best for talking, and Lille has its regular venues for philosophising or swapping notes on this week's great read. Bars range from traditional locals to seriously fashionable spots where your clothes say more about you than your neighbour can tweet. For the hottest joints in town see page 152, and don't forget that the coolest hangouts may not be what you expect (Gastama bar at The People hostel – page 129 – is a great rendezvous). Who would imagine that for years the essential address in Vieux Lille would be Café Oz (a pub better known to locals as 'L'Australian')? Find it on place Louise de Bettignies, at the corner of rue de Gand and avenue du Peuple Belge. When televised sport is on the agenda, you will be amazed at the crowds at the English, Irish, Scottish and Welsh pubs across the city: the distinction between Celtic nations blurs somewhat. On the Solfé, there is a shamrock-daubed pub named O'Scotland. But this is, after all, a city with a Chinese restaurant called Amigos and an 'original French' Mexican fast-food outlet named O'Tacos.

The cooler the bar, the later it starts to get busy. Thus, *estaminets* and cafés might do a roaring daytime trade and wind down early evening,

nearby theatres and concert halls, shoppers and strangers, all squeezed around tables cluttered with ashtrays, beer glasses and army recruitment leaflets. Great for Christmas markets when a big €4.50 glass of mulled wine is better than any scarf for an early-evening warm-up.

MAISON DU MOULIN D'OR (MOREL ET FILS) 31–33 pl du Théâtre ♀ 261 H5 ⊛
☏ 03 20 55 00 10 w au-moulin-d-or.hubside.fr 🚊 Rihour; cross Grand' Place to pl du Théâtre
A pastel-blue legend of lingerie is reborn in arabica. In 1997, Morel et Fils, gentlemen purveyors of ribbons, laces and corsetry to ladies since 1831, reluctantly closed the doors of their Maison du Moulin d'Or, surely the prettiest shop in Lille (page 197). Now, with the familiar window displays, a terrace outside the Opéra, stripped floors, a grand staircase and much original décor within, it is a welcome and welcoming café-bar, still under the care of a seventh-generation *fils* of the original Monsieur Morel. Great photographic exhibitions.

MÉERT 27 rue Esquermoise ♀ 261 H4 ⊛ ☏ 03 20 57 07 44 w meert.fr 🚊 Rihour; cross Grand' Place to rue Esquermoise
Charles de Gaulle himself would never have dreamt of saying 'Non' to the celebrated *gaufrette* – or filled waffle – that has graced many a palace and presidential biscuit barrel since this shop started

while party places often unbolt the front door any time from 17.00 to 20.00. Early doors at truly trendy establishments are not before 22.00.

Sometimes, you'll find two sets of prices on display. In most cases, the lower price applies to drinks served to those standing at, or leaning against, the bar, and the higher for waiter service at a table. In some livelier establishments, the second figure indicates a 10–20% price hike after 22.00 or midnight. At a neighbourhood bar, one orders a drink, enjoys it and pays on leaving. Busier, hipper hangouts may expect payment at time of ordering. If all this sounds stressful and complicated, don't worry. Settle down, have a drink and forget about it. There is never any pressure to move on once you have ordered your first tipple. A modest *espresso* may last an afternoon, if you've a mind to settle down on a comfortable terrace, and a glass of beer caressed as long as you like as the evening dissolves past the witching hour. Beers come in bottles or draught (*à la pression*), served usually as a *demi* (25cl) in a tall glass. Each bar seems to have its own name for a larger half-litre measure, but if you fancy something close enough to a pint, ask for a generic *grande*. Beer is best-value, wine often surprisingly expensive by the glass, and spirits decidedly shocking considering how cheap they are in supermarkets. Soft drinks, or *sodas*, include Coca Light (Diet Coke), Orangina and occasionally the local fizzy violet-flavoured lemonade. Perhaps order a *diabolo,* flavoured with *sirop de cassis* or *menthe*. And don't forget the mineral waters. A refreshing compromise is a lager shandy, known locally as a *panaché*.

trading in the 1760s. This unassuming house speciality of the chocolate-box quaint pâtisserie is a tiny miracle: a light, feathery, crispy wafer packed with a sugared explosion of flavour. The town's most famous son continued his regular order for the *gaufrettes* all his life, and ate them, so he wrote, 'with great pleasure'. The Belgian royal family gave their warrant to Monsieur Méert in 1849. The pretty cake shop, decorated in 1839 with mirrors, balconies and Arabian Nights exotica, is a feast for the eyes. The tea room behind the shop serves sumptuous afternoon teas, and a selection of cakes and pot of tea should prove a memorable indulgence. Lemon meringue tarts are creamy delights; the *safari* a surprisingly heavy dose of fluffiness for hardcore chocolate addicts only. Robust wallets may be needed at the lunchtime restaurant; see page 117.

LE PAIN QUOTIDIEN 22bis rue Basse ♀ 261 H6 ● ☎ 03 20 42 88 70 **w** lepainquotidien. com ⏱ 08.30–18.00 Mon–Fri, 08.30–19.00 Sat–Sun 🚇 Rihour
Travellers who usually take the Eurostar on to its final destination should recognise the name and décor of this café from its Brussels incarnations. Regular visitors to Lille will expect to find it on place Rihour, where it held court for decades. But now you'll need to cross the squares to the old town to find the current address. A cheerful clone of the ideal *bruncherie* pushes the same indulgence buttons as the original. Imagine turning up mid-morning at a country farmhouse,

7

just as the farmer's wife is removing the day's baking from the oven. OK, so no-one wipes floury hands on an apron, but the welcome smells and tastes are the same, whether you want a generous *tartine* of freshly baked bread, butter and apricot jam or a slice of lemon tart. Yummy hot chocolate and coffee take the chill off a December mooch around the antiques shops. Salads and sandwiches are served at hefty family-sized tables in a wide, airy room dominated by a massive dresser sporting numberless jars of tempting preserves.

LE PALAIS DE LA BIÈRE 11 pl Gare ♀ 261 K6 ⊕ ☏ 03 20 06 38 94 🚉 Gare Lille Flandres
A smart, modern, airy and bright bar in contrast to the greasy chips and soggy beermat norm of station 'caffs'. Nice place for coffee and *croissant* between stepping off the Eurostar and walking into town. Good brasserie menu for grilled steaks should you arrive with an appetite.

LA PÂTE BRISÉE 65 rue de la Monnaie ♀ 261 H2 ⊕ ☏ 03 20 74 29 00 w restaurant-lapatebriseelille.fr ◷ Closed Sun eve 🚌 Bus 9 to Lion d'Or
Once a popular pâtisserie across from the Hospice Comtesse, now this cosy red-brick dining room is an equally cheery restaurant, serving sweet and savoury pastries to eat indoors on marble-slab tables, or outside on a pavement terrace. I love a cheesy tart, but traditional *quiche*-lovers will

find plenty of variations on the theme to relish, usually around €15 or a couple of euros more for a trio of mini versions. I followed the indulgences of the lady at the next table whose eyes were watering with the effort of not talking with her mouth full, as she dabbed at the lightest pastry crumbs at the corner of her lips in her eagerness to advise me on my first journey though the menu. Nowadays, that *carte* includes big salads and robust *grandmère* lunch stews as found round the corner on rue du Gand (all under €20 with just steak options crossing the rubicon). An inexpensive fruit flan for dessert was so lipsmackingly yummy I clean forgot to make notes, but it blended sharpness and sweetness of late plums with a texture that melted off my fork. Now under new management.

PAUL 8–12 Pierre Mauroy ♀ 261 J5 ⊕ ☏ 03 20 8 20 78 w paul.fr 🚊 Rihour; cross Grand' Place to the Vieille Bourse
Don't bother with breakfast in your hotel: come to Paul for the best breakfast in town. Not the biggest, nor the most varied, but certainly the best. This corner-site bakery opposite the Vieille Bourse is the place to go for fresh *croissants*, just-baked bread and creamy, piping-hot chocolate first thing in the morning. A breakfast tray served on solid wooden tables against the blue-and-white tiled walls and heavy tapestries of a bread and cake shop is the perfect way to start the

Celestin 20 rue Esquermoise ♀ 261 G3 ⊕ ☏ 09 81 21 67 21 w celestinlille.fr ⏲ 11.00–14.00 & 15.00–19.00 Tue–Fri, 10.00–19.00 Sat 🚊 Rihour; cross squares to rue Esquermoise. Microbrewery in Vieux Lille. Sat guided tours on the half hour from 11.30.

Hein Brique House 13 pl Saint-Hubert ♀ 259 H4 ⊘ ☏ 03 20 47 53 83 w briquehouse.com ⏲ noon–23.00 Mon–Wed, noon–midnight Thu, noon–01.00 Fri–Sat, noon–22.30 Sun 🚊 Gare Lille Flandres; av Le Corbusier, then right into rue des Cannoniers. Baptiste & Joseph's micro-chain of microbreweries serves their craft beers & appropriate meaty, veggie or cheesy burgers, salads & sandwiches with carby sides.

Moulins d'Ascq 47 rue de la Distillerie, Villeneuve-d'Ascq ♀ 259 K3 ⊕ ☏ 03 20 41 58 48 w moulinsdascq.fr ⏲ 17.00–21.00 Mon, 17.00–23.00 Tue–Wed, 17.00–midnight Thu–Fri 🚊 Line 1 to 4 Cantons Stade, then bus 66 to Harrison. Tours of organic brewery & tap-room tastings.

Tandem Brasserie 382 rue de Bondues, Wambrechies ♀ 261 G1 ⊕ ☏ 03 20 31 78 57 w brasserie-tandem.com ⏲ noon–14.30 Mon–Tue, noon–14.30 & 18.00–23.30 Wed–Fri, from noon Sat 🚊 Bus L1 to Wambrechies Mairie then walk. Aymeric and Pierre-André's brewery taproom & restaurant has been so popular in the 5 years since they started brewing that they have crossed the canal to larger premises. Chef Michel still serves Eastern Med mezze (hummus, falafel, kefta, halloumi etc). Sat afternoon brewery tours at 14.15.

Les Trois Brasseurs See page 104.

day. Find inspiration in the words of wisdom painted on old wooden beams, or concentrate on the scrumptious homemade jams and crunchy, crusty baguettes. There are a range of breakfast options at around €3–6. Paul has now spawned scores of satellite bakeries, *viennoiserie* counters and dining rooms across Lille, throughout Paris and beyond, but this old corner shop between the Opéra and the main square remains something special. For those who like their *pain rustique* served with a healthy dollop of irony: now that Paul has a counter in London's Eurostar terminus St Pancras, the takeaway outlet at Gare Lille Flandres around the corner is a Marks & Spencer food hall selling British sandwiches!

TAMPER ESPRESSO BAR 10 rue des Vieux Murs ♀ 261 H2 ⊕ ☎ 03 20 39 28 21 w tamperlille.com ⏱ until 18.00 Mon & Wed–Sat, until 15.00 Sun 🚌 Bus 9 to Lion d'Or, then walk up rue de la Monnaie & turn left on to rue Pétérinck
In a city where *crème pâtissière* is practically a lifestyle, who would have expected a modest North-American carrot cake to become a tea-time best seller? Yet the moist and lightly luscious slice *chez* Marie-Sophie and Germain was already making newspaper headlines in Lille within a month of the espresso bar opening its doors. Now it woos the hipster late-breakfast brigade with avocado on toast, egg-in-a-hole (aka egg on toast with attitude) or global vegetarian (not vegan) specialities such as *shakshuka* and *huevos rachcheros*. Dishes in the early teens before budgeting for the chai latte.

LES TROIS BRASSEURS See page 104.

AU VIEUX DE LA VIEILLE See page 99.

BURGERS

A few years ago, burgers were all the rage: food trucks, even fine dining addresses set up to put *haute cuisine* or even merely hot *cuisine* between a couple of baps, *brioches* or bagels. Naturally, many did not survive the test of time, but the passion for a non-American reinvention of the beef-in-a-bun concept means you are still spoilt for choice and there are still some memorable addresses to discover. And you never know where you'll find the next big thing. For two days in 2024, Michelin legend Florent Ladeyn (page 120) stepped behind a pop-up burger counter in Wazemmes to deploy a new recipe. Check out the listings for bistros (page 93), brasseries (page 100) and restaurants (page 105) for some top-end options, as well as the Food Court and Street Food selection (page 126).

L'ADRESSE 34 rue des Bouchers ♀ 261 G4 ⊘ ☎ 03 59 89 66 33 w ladresselille.fr ⏱ closed Sun eve & Mon 🚌 Rihour; pass the tourist office then go right on to rue de l'Hôpital Militaire & cross pl de l'Arsenal to rue des Bouchers; alternatively, take the Navette Vieux Lille almost full circle & step off at rue des Bouchers
It stands to reason that if a burger bar were to open on rue des Bouchers, there would be no polystyrene packaging within a hundred paces. And so it is here, where a simple beef patty with

a lettuce leaf, gherkin and slice of processed cheese simply would not *coupe le moutarde* when punters are going to shell out €15–25 for a burger made with quality breads. My first sandwich here had cod topped with Munster cheese, asparagus, spinach and hollandaise sauce. Seasonal concepts may blend dairy toppings with soft fruits and roasted Mediterranean vegetables. Lunchtime sees the 'BBC' deal (this stands for Burger, Boisson, Café) with one of six burgers, a cold drink and an espresso for €20. Popular à la carte is La Basque, a *pain boulanger* stuffed with both beef and prosciutto, creamed chorizo, root veg, crushed tomato and baby spinach leaves with a chutney of the day. The Catalan option is built around roasted cod with spicy salami, lentil *purée* and creamed chorizo. Do not expect an automatic 'fries with that' accompaniment. The kitchen chooses a default 'side' according to style of the burger. Thus, a *choucroute*-based winter warmer was served with simple steamed potatoes; a *parmentier* came with mash. Since *patron* Frédéric Parois used to run a wine bar, there is an excellent selection of wine by the glass.

BERLINER   These days more of a bar with burgers and beers. See page 128.

BIOBURGER   19 pl de Béthune 262 G1 09 77 97 96 26 w bioburger.fr
 République Beaux-Arts
Stop here for burger grazing with a conscience after the Beaux Arts museum, on movie night and before hitting the clubs. Opposite McDonald's, here everything is organic (or *bieau* in local *patois*), the potatoes for the chips are local, toppings are imaginative (guacamole, hummus, caramelised onions) and prices range around the €9–13 mark (meal deal +€4). There are three seriously impressive non-meat options: choose between a burger made of chopped mushrooms or minced beetroot with cumin, or even the dairy-rich Rustique (baked Camembert with fig and honey chutney). The soft drinks are a cut above, including mint tea and lashings (well, 37cl) of ginger beer.

LE COMPTOIR VOLANT   22 pl des Patiniers 261 J3 w comptoirvolant.fr closed Sun lunch Gare Lille Flandres; walk along rue Faidherbe to pl du Théâtre then take rue de la Grande Chaussée to turn right on rue des Chats Bossus
Ten years ago, when Lille was at peak gourmet burger, this guide tipped a rosy future for a modest food truck serving takeaways in suburban supermarket and bike shop car parks. Manned by seemingly all-American boys, the burger van always promised to be a cut above. For a start, the French guys behind the diner-check shirts, aprons and preppy demeanour were César Toulemonde and Greg Chaignaud, local schoolboy chums intent on serving up classic know-how and meat preparation skills *à la française*. Both burgers and steaks *tartares* delivered with what they called 'Beef & Love' at their peripatetic pop-up. Now they have a more sedentary full-time address thanks to shopfront premises in the heart of Vieux Lille. Just as with the food truck, cheeseburgers feature proper Swiss AOC Emmental cheese with bacon and seasonal baby spinach leaves topping minced steak marinated in a port, veal and shallot stock. Even house chicken nuggets are made from prized organic poultry from nearby Licques. You may choose to top your *frites* with mature English cheddar, or forgo the fried stuff for a bowl of red cabbage coleslaw. A veggie burger is built around portobello mushrooms. The original van still follows its well-run circuit – itinerary online. Minced beef patties, whether cooked or raw, are priced around €8–13; add another €2–3 if you want posh fries with that. Call m 06 44 32 20 92 or click and collect from wherever the van is parked on the day.

FACTORY & CO Gare Lille Europe ♀ 259 J3 ✎ 03 20 21 03 41 **w** restaurants.factoryandco.
com/lille-europe ⏲ breakfast–19.15 daily 🚊 Lille Europe
From a past life as a faux-Irish bar to a New York deli, here, next door to the station waiting room,
is the place for a last supper before catching an early-evening Eurostar home (or a serious carb
fix anytime). Slap bang in the middle of Lille Europe station, choose burgers from €10 upwards
(or around €20 if you want fries, a drink and a thick slice of cheesecake with that), hot dogs or a
packed and stacked smoked salmon bagel. Breads are baked on site, pastrami is the real stateside
deal and there are loads of cheesecakes to choose from.

VEGETARIAN AND VEGAN

What a difference a decade makes. There has never been a better time for
non-meat eaters, with no fear of inappropriate metaphors, to dine with the
rest of the herd. For years I was constantly amazed at the European concept
of vegetarian. Researching a millennium Paris guide for the meatless
and fancy free, I regularly encountered bacon served as standard on the
vegetarian special and, on one occasion, a respected airline served all its
passengers broccoli quiche – except for the single soul who had requested
the vegetarian alternative, which turned out to be roast chicken! For a while,
Lille's enviable range of ethnic restaurants were the go-to, since cuisine from
eastern Mediterranean, Hindu or Muslim cultures is often far more likely to
include interesting vegetarian options.

Now, the fusion generation welcomes these influences into the
mainstream. And a new age of enlightenment means that plant-based,
officially vegetarian and even some vegan dishes are now appearing on most
bistro and brasserie menus. Even traditional restaurants will run to a plant-
based starter and main. In many café and restaurant listings earlier in this
chapter, you will find somewhere to suit the most diverse group. At Rococo,
for example, the chef turns his back on the easy tofu option by roasting and
blowtorching local root vegetables, and even ultra-carnivorous gourmet-
burger-meisters come up with more than mashed beans for their veggie
option. And don't forget food courts (page 126), where several counters
reflect the new culture of meat-free cuisine. That said, in the past few years,
a number of exclusively vegetarian and vegan restaurants have come into the
mainstream – my favourites are listed here.

ANNIE'S KITCHEN 222 rue Léon Gambetta ♀ 262 B2 ❶ ✎ 03 20 37 32 88
w annieskitchen.fr ⏲ closed Mon–Tue, Sun eve 🚊 Gambetta; walk rue de Flandres to
rue Gambetta
This is the vegan bistro that even carnivores cannot resist. Just what truly meat-free should be like.
With no compromise on taste or tradition, here classic French and global bistro fare is reinvented
with a mission to create authentic comfort food that tastes as good as it did before the modern age
of enlightenment. Possibly the best vegan address between Paris and Brighton, it's a true modern
estaminet. There's no clever plating on bizarre props, just goodly portions served on proper crockery.

Perhaps start off with a *tapas* sharing platter for well under €10. The very small menu has only a handful of dishes (mains around €16 on my visit), including a *bourgignon* that simmers portobello mushrooms instead of beef in a just-as-wished-for, rich red-wine sauce. And burgers are legendary, to convert the heartiest trencherman. You may even request a gluten-free version. When Annie's delivered its own vegan take on the ubiquitous *poutine* (page 97), with chips drenched in gravy and topped with grated cheese and fried onions, everything on the plate was plant-based – and, unlike the usual artery clanger of the Canadian original, no near-death cholesterol hit. €€

BIOBURGER   See page 135 for this organic burger bar with a surprising range of meat-free options.

CIRQUE   139 rue des Postes ♀ 262 B5 ⊕ ☎ 03 62 10 76 86 w lecirquelille.fr 🚉 Wazemmes; walk east along rue léna to rue des Postes
Admittedly this is not a dedicated vegetarian restaurant, but there's a pretty fair chance of a tasty meat-free option on the menu here. It offers Fairtrade and locally sourced organic lunches in the market quarter of Wazemmes. Good soups and quiches. €

LA CLAIRIÉRE   75 bd de la Liberté ♀ 261 F6 ⊕ ☎ 03 20 11 23 16 w laclairiere-restaurant.com ⏱ closed Mon, Sun–Wed eve 🚉 République Beaux-Arts or bus L5 to Nationale
A couple of Parisian high-fliers moved to Lille and decided to open this vegan bruncherie in a bright and airy café. They are keen followers of the locavore movement, sourcing ingredients as close to home as possible – just like at Bloempot (page 107). Here, nothing pretends to be a meat-free version of regular fare; instead you will find simple but good, honest plant-based food that looks traditionally healthy with lots of pulses and leaves and brightly coloured veg. An instant hit with the student market, its Paris provenance also caught the attention of the stylish set, with *Elle* magazine reviewing it on the same page as La Table at Hotel Clarance (page 122). However here, midday set-menu options hover either side of €20. Mains under €15 will be seasonal stews, bakes and well-filled plates. Starters and desserts are around €6. You really should call ahead to be sure of a table, and in good weather you may choose to sit outside to watch the boulevard *flâneurs*. Not only are dogs welcome here, but Haron, the *chien maison,* is a virtual *maître d'*, now with young pup Savie as apprentice pooch *d'acceuil.* €€

LAYALINA   14 rue d'Arras ♀ 262 F5 ⊕ ☎ 03 20 42 85 58 w layalina-lille.com 🚉 Grand Palais, then bus 14 to Douai-Arras
Not a hand-on-heart meat-free zone, this Mediterranean hideaway serves massive mezze spreads with lots of falafel and hummusy stuff, even actual vegan and gluten-free options. €€

Eating and Drinking   VEGETARIAN AND VEGAN

7

8

Nightlife and Entertainment

Lille famously boasts that Saturday night always offers a choice of a hundred diversions – and it is no bragging exaggeration. This is a city that knows how to fill the hours of darkness. Quite apart from the diversity of bars and restaurants, from the *intime* and quirky rues de Gand and Bouchers to the city of singles that is rue Solférino, the variety of performances would not disgrace a national capital city. Look out for the free listings magazine *Sortir*, which is published on Wednesday and can be picked up from your hotel or the tourist office. Local paper *La Voix du Nord* also has comprehensive arts and entertainment news and reviews.

THEATRE

When it comes to the stage, **Théâtre du Nord** on Grand' Place is a very good place to start. For 15 years, from 1998 to 2014, the American actor and director Stuart Seide's artistic direction put this venue on the national cultural agenda. His challenging, fresh approach to world classics led to ground-breaking productions of Beckett, Molière and of course Shakespeare – a *Romeo and Juliet* twisted the central schism by 90 degrees, presenting the divide as less between Montague and Capulet than between two generations. In a city with almost half the population under 25, that certainly created more than a murmur.

Seide's successor, Christophe Rauck, took the theatre in new directions, adding a second playhouse and performing arts school. His inaugural season featured a programme of classics (Racine to Beckett) alongside new works, and a shift towards community theatre, using three performance spaces: a smaller space in Lille alongside the main auditorium, and a partnership with the **Idéal Theatre** in Tourcoing. The theatre's newest director, David Bobée, has a background in both circus and opera, and is a champion of diversity who channels Lille's traditional revolutionary spirit by challenging casting concepts.

Young theatre has its own voice at **Le Grand Bleu**, where programmes are essentially geared to the hip-hop rather than hip-replacement set. Other alternative venues include **Théâtre de la Verrière**, **Le Massenet** in the Fives quarter and semi-itinerant **Théâtre des Nuits Blanches**. Conventional and comfortable family fare is served at **Théâtre Sébastopol**, where you'll find the types of light comedies that would run on Shaftesbury Avenue, Broadway or Grands Boulevards. A weekend bill may feature old favourites like *Le Dîner des Cons* ('The Dinner Game'), traditional farce or concerts by TV crooners. A few doors along, the smaller **Comédie de Lille** playhouse is home to stand-up comedy and touring productions of plays and children's theatre, and joins larger playhouses in hosting the annual Lillarious comedy festival (page 14). International acts and tours perform at **Le Prato** and Villeneuve d'Ascq's **La Rose des Vents**. During festivals, scores of other spaces, great and small, are called into service. Playhouses in other towns in the conurbation are also worth checking out since most venues are within half an hour of Grand' Place – remember, public transport across the Métropole continues until midnight. Do not dismiss Maisons Folies, Gare Saint-Sauveur or other recently established venues (page 206). These exciting and vibrant performance spaces have already been bagged by dance companies, musicians and experimental theatre groups. There's more fringe theatre and comedy at other alternative venues.

Theatres often close Monday, but several offer Sunday matinées. Tickets for many productions may be bought from FNAC (w fnac.fr), either online or in person from their Grand' Place box office (page 172). In more traditional theatres, it is still customary to tip no more than €1 when being shown to your seat.

Comédie de Lille 204 rue Solférino 262 D2 03 20 53 54 94 w comediedelille.fr République Beaux-Arts; rue Inkerman to rue Solférino

Le Grand Bleu 36 av Marx Dormoy 260 A6 03 20 09 88 44 w legrandbleu.com Bois Blancs

Idéal 19 rue des Champs, Tourcoing 03 20 17 93 30 Free bus from Lille Opera House 1hr before performances

Le Massenet rue Massenet 259 K6 03 20 04 81 65 w theatre-massenet.com Fives

Le Prato 6 allée de la Filature 262 F5 03 20 52 71 24 w leprato.fr Porte de Douai; turn left into allée de la Filature

La Rose des Vents Scène Nationale bd Van Gogh, Villeneuve d'Ascq 03 20 61 96 96 w larose.fr Pont de Bois; walk along rue Vétérans to bd Van Gogh

Théâtre de la Verrière 28 rue Alphonse Mercier 262 C2 03 20 54 96 75 w verriere. org République Beaux-Arts

Théâtre du Nord 4 pl du Général de Gaulle 261 H5 03 20 14 24 24 w theatredunord. fr Rihour or bus 12 from Gare Lille Flandres to Théâtre

Théâtre Sébastopol Pl Sébastopol 262 D3 03 20 54 44 50 w theatre-sebastopol. fr République Beaux-Arts; rue Inkerman leads to the theatre

8

CABARET AND CASINO

For years, showbiz glamour and comedy were an essential part of Lille nightlife, as served with a flourish and a flounce at the late lamented Folies de Paris. Here, *La Cage Aux Folles* met Hollywood with the biggest cross-dressing

floor show north of the capital – a pancake-pasted flurry of feathers, sequins and star lookalikes. Customers would be entertained, mocked and teased in camp patois by the revue's outrageous director Claude Thomas, then be transported to a world where every Celine, Marlene or Liza was a boy, and a stripping Michael Jackson was revealed as a Y-chromosome-free zone. While no self-respecting Parisian is likely to admit to visiting the Paris cabarets, you would always find locals at the Folies. When the Folies went dark, it seemed Flanders had shed its plumage. Now, however, the *royaume* of the showgirl is set for a revival with La Bonbonnière by the Beaux Arts quarter and the advent, across town, of occasional floor shows at the casino.

LA BONBONNIÈRE 57 Rue du Molinel ♀ 262 G1 ☏ 03 28 53 09 14 w cabaretlabonbonniere. com ⏱ 19.45 Tue–Sat, 13.00 Sun 🚇 République Beaux-Arts
The back story is almost as outrageous as the frocks. As the legendary Folies de Paris nightspot closed its doors in Vieux Lille and its successor was already limping towards oblivion, the stars aligned in the most unlikely of places. David Bève had just been crowned one of France's most promising young restaurateurs by the prestigious *Gault&Millau* guide, and, with the gastronomic world queuing for a table at his N'Autre Monde restaurant (page 117), his future was mapped out with another bistro about to open its doors. Then he met Christopher, aka Chris Candy, drag artiste extraordinaire. Two years of planning later, with Christopher directing shows and David's alter ego Sweet Mama acting as front of house and MC, they launched the cabaret venue La Bonbonnière.

To a generation reared on *Drag Race*, this new venue still evokes hints of the 65-year-old Paris institution Michou, where A-listers from Madonna and Liza to Bardot and Mireille Matthieu would go to watch themselves being parodied in drag. Chris Candy's own Britney and Barbie are joined by scores of other celebrity evocations *en travestie* from a team of showgirls in feathers and heels. Of course, with David Bève running the place, your meal is a cut above the identikit rubber chicken and predictable desserts of most cabaret venues. This talent who was expected to rule the world of Michelin-starched linens creates the menus, and head chef Henri prepares the dishes every night. They're served at your table by Sweet Mama herself, along with the rest of the cast. Think traditional *escargot* vol au vents or gravlax blinis with blueberry chutney and bison grass vodka to start, followed by filet mignon of pork and creamed chorizo, with inventive and original approaches extending to other diets – vegans may be offered walnut and seasonal vegetable-stuffed courgettes. The emphasis is on locally sourced produce tickled with a fusion of global techniques. Dinner, drinks and show from €89, show only €59.

AU BONHEUR DES DAMES 61 rue Achille Pinteaux, Wavrin ☏ 03 20 58 55 53 w aubonheurdesdames.fr 🚆 Train from Gare Lille Flandres to Wavrin & it's a 20min walk from the station; alternatively, drive/taxi for 20km journey from Lille
The Full Monty with a side order of foie gras and Sauternes – this is a French twist on Chippendale-

◀ 1 Théâtre Sébastopol is one of several performing arts venues in the city. 2 The elegant décor of the Opéra de Lille can match the stage for theatricality. 3 Le TriPostal hosts regular late-night parties during festival season. 4 Lille's large student population means the city has a thriving music scene.

style entertainment, for those who like their hen nights scented with squeals and baby oil. Provided by Au Bonheur des Dames, some way out of town, it's a celebration of depilated masculinity, from the sunbed to the stage, and is a hit with office-party crowds who admire men still able to walk the walk after waxing the boxer line. It is more popular apparently than its predecessor in Lille itself, where the hunks lost a certain credibility by doubling as drag queens and dressing as Madonna before getting their more manly kit off for the girls. The most common complaint was that the boys' glittery eyeliner detracted from the full effect of the thongs, but how things have changed. An ad recruiting exhibitionists for the venue once read: 'Nous recrutons pour les weekends deux strip teasers, profil 18/25 ans, corps sportif et gueule d'ange. Envoyez votre candidature avec plusieurs photos...', roughly translated as 'We are recruiting weekend strippers aged 18–25. If you have a fit body and the face of an angel, apply with lots of pics...' However, real angels don't wear mascara, not on this side of the '80s. Menus range from €40–50 (for those who like their chicken on a plate) to more than €60 (for girls with a champagne lifestyle who prefer their beef hot and peppery). Those who prefer to keep their beefcake at a distance can opt for gluten free or vegetarian menus.

CASINO BARRIÈRE DE LILLE 777 bis Pont de Flandres ♀ 259 J5 ☏ 03 28 14 45 00 w lucienbarriere.com ⌂ Gare Lille Europe; take Parvis de Rotterdam exit to Pont de Flandres The casino-hotel has a purpose-built showroom theatre for 1,200 diners, a range of theme bars and a snack bar, as well as its principal restaurant. The casino spreads itself across 40,000m^2 of the city, which may not sound much, but works out at 4ha for living high on the hog in smart suits while betting the farm on evens. The showroom has no regular year-round cabaret, but seasonal musical shows feature a few days each month (jukebox '80s show and occasional standup), there's a strong run of concerts by French recording artists, and occasional touring plays visit for one-night stands. The Barrière website and tourist office have the current listings. If the very notion of a casino conjures promises of full James Bond role-play, you may be only slightly disappointed, since while ties are appreciated on gentlemanly necks, they are no longer de rigueur. Full evening dress may be out, but smart and stylish is still essential to get you through the door, thus trainers and T-shirts have no place even in a modern casino. If the old Folies punters make it through the door, we may yet see the dry martini being replaced by a chuche mourette, shaken not stirred! Even poker fantasies are PC: no smoking is allowed in the gaming rooms or show rooms, although stressed-out gamblers may adjourn to a dedicated fug-filled room for a wheeze, cough and ciggie break before returning to the tables. And not all casino employees work as croupiers or bouncers – the venue has its own resident addiction counsellor.

CINEMA

Le 7ème art thrives in and around Lille, with at least one international independent film festival each year. Kinépolis, the out-of-town multiplex at Lomme, boasts 23 screens, but there's no need to leave the city centre, since cinema flourishes along the pedestrianised rue de Béthune. Most new hits are shown at the 14-screen Ciné Cité UGC, while just along the pavement, the six salles of the Majestic specialise in original-language versions of international flicks, with subtitles rather than the dubbed versions screened elsewhere. Artier yet are the preferences at the Métropole nearer the station. For a truly art-house experience, head to the cultural quarter beyond the boulevard de la Liberté, where the Gare Saint-Sauveur complex has its own 208-seat cinema.

However, the coolest place to go to the flicks has to be l'Hybride, an old garage down by the Parc Lebas, where you may flop with friends on old comfy sofas and enjoy an eclectic programme as likely to feature obscure eastern European offerings as an early Buster Keaton or late technicolor Hitchcock. On your first visit, you'll need to pay an extra euro for membership of the cinema, which, after a shaky financial gestation, is now run as a members' club. The venue also hosts annual animation and short film festivals. Another must for *cinéastes* is Le Fresnoy in Tourcoing, easily reached by métro.

In addition to the press listings and reviews in *Sortir*, a free guide produced by the mainstream picture palaces of Lille may be found at the tourist office. Budget tip: midweek morning screenings, at 11.00, are often half price.

Ciné Cité UGC 40 rue de Béthune ♀ 261 H6 w ugc.fr 🚊 Rihour

Le Fresnoy Studio National des Arts Contemporains 22 rue du Fresnoy, Tourcoing ☎ 03 20 28 38 00 w lefresnoy.net 🚊 Alsace; take bd d'Armentières then rue Capitaine Aubert

Gare Saint-Sauveur See page 200.

L'Hybride 18 rue Gosselet ♀ 262 G5 ☎ 03 20 53 24 84 w lhybride.org 🚊 Mairie de Lille, then bus 14 to Jeanne d'Arc

Le Majestic 54–56 rue de Béthune ♀ 261 H7 ☎ 03 20 54 08 96 w ugc.fr 🚊 Rihour

Le Métropole 26 rue des Ponts de Comines ♀ 261 J6 w ugc.fr 🚊 Gare Lille Flandres; take av le Corbusier, the rue Faidherbe & left on rue des Ponts de Comines

MUSIC AND DANCE

For me, nothing comes close to the experience of the Sunday evening tango in the courtyard of the Vieille Bourse (page 202), but for those who like their music interpreted by professionals, the city is home to some world-class venues.

LIVE MUSIC The **Orchestre National de Lille** (ONL) is housed in the big, round Nouveau Siècle building to the side of Grand' Place. Surrounded by restaurants, the building might easily be dismissed by diners as just another office block and multistorey car park. But nothing is ever quite what it seems in Lille, as I realised on my first visit to the car park when I noticed signs for motorists disconcertingly, albeit politically correctly, translated into Braille. Full orchestral programmes alternate with chamber concerts, and the all-too-rare, occasional Sunday-morning recitals are ever a firm favourite with locals. Open rehearsals are fascinating and free to watch – check the ONL website for details – and there is a superb season of pre-concert talks. The orchestra's founding director, Jean-Claude Casadesus, wooed international soloists to his concerts over 30 years with lunch at local fish restaurants. At the time of writing, his successor Alexandre Block was poised to hand over the baton to American violinist and conductor Joshua Weilerstein in late 2024. Concerts by the ONL are not limited to the Nouveau Siècle hall. The musicians play at the opera house and many other venues around the region, as well as numerous prestigious international events. Programme details are posted on the ONL website, and occasionally include unexpected treats – recently, they played live for a screening of arguably the greatest musical ever filmed, *Singin' In The Rain*.

A few streets away is the **Conservatoire**, behind place du Concerts market in the old town. More than a music school, it's a lovely little concert venue for morning or afternoon Brahms or Mozart and unexpected concerts of new and classic works.

For a harder edge, rock or contemporary indie sounds can easily be found in a district of more than 100,000 youngsters. Some 6,000 people a night can raise the roof at the **Zenith Arena** or shake the stars in the open air at the **Stade Pierre Mauroy** football stadium; smaller crowds pack **Le Splendid** (a former cinema) and **La Malterie**. Tickets for major events may be obtained through FNAC (page 172). Bars like **Le Bel Ouvrage** by the church of St Michel have more intimate spaces for gigs on the fringe of the Solfé district. The **Aeronef** venue, high above Euralille, is a typical Lille curiosity. Originally an underground organisation for disaffected youth, the club moved to its new high-rise home among banks and financial institutions when offered the venue by the city. Multinational corporations pitched in with generous grants, and the kids were left to organise their own fun. So much so that when a band offended public morals with sexually explicit antics on stage, organisers, expecting a mass withdrawal of funding or legal action, were merely sent a stern memo from the authorities.

Elsewhere, even hotels and restaurants act as venues: Mama Shelter (page 75) has a full programme of DJs and concerts at the hotel brasserie, with 'best of' highlights from recent performances screened in hotel bedrooms. Regular concerts and recitals are also held at various churches in central Lille and all venues open during the year's many music festivals. Programmes for all events are available from the tourist office; look out in particular for the **Lille Piano Festival**, and the ten-day **accordion festival** in Wazemmes (page 14).

Tourcoing hosts its own jazz festival, with fringe events spilling over the Belgian border. Despite no longer having a full-time dedicated jazz venue, good jazz may be enjoyed in Lille for much of the year. The **Jazz en Nord** and **Blues en Nord** festivals (w jazzenord.com) run across the wider metropolitan area for several months at a time, staged in halls as varied as the Conservatoire and the Casino.

Lille 3000 is always full of memorable events, which have had a lasting impact on the city's nightlife. ▶

Whatever your musical taste, whatever the year, cancel sleep on 21 June. **National Music Day**, created by former culture minister Jack Lang (later *député* for Boulogne), is an amazing occasion. Free concerts are held everywhere – villages, towns and cities – and Lille manages to upstage most of the country with performances in public spaces, matched by live entertainment inside and outside almost every restaurant, café and bar in town. If you can get a table anywhere, keep ordering food and drink as the performances continue through the evening and into the night. If not, just move from street to street as swing blends into rap and baroque into rock.

Lille3000 seasons always bring exciting music events to unexpected venues, reflecting countries and cultures honoured in the biennial themes – from K-Pop to Latin street dance, Bollywood to Kletzmer – and, like the repurposed buildings, stay in the city's repertoire for years to come. Remember, too, that Gare Saint-Sauveur (page 200), not far from the club district, adapts to festivals and has a thriving music venue in its bistro. The Maisons Folies also echo to a range of sounds (page 210), as does the modular **Grand Sud** concert venue.

Aeronef Euralille ♀ 259 H5 ☎ 03 28 38 50 50 w aeronef.fr 🚊 Gare Lille Europe or Gare Lille Flandres; take av le Corbusier to av Willy Brandt, look for the signs, then scale the outside of the tower block

Le Bel Ouvrage 4 parvis Saint Michel ♀ 262 E4 ☎ 03 20 35 37 95 ⏰ 17.30–02.00 Mon–Sat, closed Aug 🚊 République Beaux-Arts; take rue Nicolas LeBlanc to rue Solférino to parvis Saint Michel. Arrive after 23.00 to get the feel of the place. Very friendly bar, interesting exhibitions & live music.

Conservatoire de Lille rue Alphonse Colas ♀ 261 J2 ☎ 03 28 38 77 50 w conservatoire. lille.fr 🚊 Bus L90 to Lycée Pasteur, then bus 10 to Pont Neuf, av Peuple Belgye to rue Alphonse Colas

Le Grand Sud 50 rue de l'Europe ♀ 262 F5 ☎ 03 20 88 89 90 w lille.fr/Le-Grand-Sud 🚊 Porte des Postes

La Malterie 42 rue Kuhlmann ♀ 262 B5 ☎ 03 20 15 13 21 w lamalterie.com 🚊 Porte des Postes; take bd Victor Hugo to rue Kuhlmann

Orchestre National de Lille Nouveau Siècle, 30 pl Mendès France ♀ 261 G5 ☎ 03 20 12 82 40 w onlille.com 🚊 Rihour; take rue Jean Roisin to rue de Pas

Le Splendid 1 pl du Mont de Terre ♀ 259 K8 ☎ 03 20 33 17 34 w le-splendid.com 🚊 Hellemmes or Lille Grand Palais, then bus 18 to pl du Mont de Terre

Stade Pierre Mauroy 261 bd de Tournai, Villeneuve d'Ascq ☎ 03 20 59 40 00 w stade-pierre-mauroy.com 🚊 4 Cantons; follow signposts to stadium. The sports stadium doubles as a major concert venue.

Zenith Lille Grand Palais, 1 bd des Cités Unies ♀ 259 J7 ☎ 03 20 14 15 16 w zenithdelille.com 🚊 Lille Grand Palais; then follow signs

BALLET Another nationally acclaimed company is the **Ballet du Nord**, now under the direction of Sylvain Groud. Performing all over Europe, the company is based in Roubaix, with three principal performance spaces: their Grand Studio, **Le Colisée** next door, a large theatre equally as

Set up the mood for the evening at Hall U Need (page 55). During the day, the place is geared towards the family market, but in the evenings this virtual and real-life gaming venue, with distractions ranging from a bowling alley, table football and pinball to escape games and a VR arcade, is the ideal rendezvous with friends before hitting the nightlife scene. Local beers and snacks are served at the bar or on a summer terrace. Open until midnight weekdays and even later on Friday and Saturday.

popular with the world of rock as of dance (where Jacques Brel gave one of his final performances) and **La Condition Publique** (page 224). Ballet also features on the programme of the Opéra de Lille (see below) and touring companies bring popular productions of *The Nutcracker* and *Swan Lake* to the Théâtre Sébastopol (page 139).

Ballet du Nord Grand Studio, 33 rue de l'Epeule, Roubaix ◊ 03 20 24 66 66 w balletdunord.fr ☒ Gare Jean Lebas
Le Colisée 31 rue de l'Epeule, Roubaix ◊ 03 20 24 07 07 w coliseeroubaix.com ☒ Gare Jean Lebas

La Condition Publique 14 pl du Général Faidherbe, Roubaix ◊ 03 28 33 48 33 w laconditionpublique.com ☒ Eurotéléport

OPERA Inspired by the Paris opera house, the elegant bars and salons of the **Opéra de Lille** can match the stage for opulence and theatricality. And with soloists and choirs mixed and matched from the leading companies of Europe, the season here is among the Continent's best bargains. Even following it's early 21st-century renovation, top-tier seats still only cost between €30 and €75 depending on the production, and there are always plenty of tickets offered at €5–20, even for the highest profile performances. Daring seasons present little-known works and lesser-known composers such as Jean-Philippe Rameau alongside intelligent and original stagings of well-known classics, bringing together emerging young performers on stage with exciting mentors in the pit and rehearsal rooms. A triumphant co-production (with Brussels opera) of *Rigoletto*, with a witty beach-hut design, showcased some of the most exciting new musical talent around and sold out almost instantly. A delicious new staging of Mozart's rarely performed *La Finta Giardiniera* won word-of-mouth acclaim to make it as popular as a *Don Giovanni*, which shared the bill at the time of typing with *Tristan and Isolde* and *Die Fledermaus*. A stunning foyer, glittering with opulence and sheer dazzling style, hosts weekly recitals and €10 performances on Wednesday evenings at 18.00. Balconies and vast

Nightlife and Entertainment   MUSIC AND DANCE   8

windows offer breathtaking views over the city, and the extraordinary rehearsal spaces in the attics have access to amazing terraces looking out over the new and the old towns. The opera house is also home to dance, with premieres of new works and visits by ballet legends including Bill T Jones and William Forsythe and the Frankfurt Ballet company.

As if that were not enough, the district has a second opera venue: the **Atelier Lyrique** in Tourcoing produces studio versions of contemporary and classic works. A cycle of all the Mozart–Da Ponte comic operas once shared the honours between the main house in Lille and the intimate space at Tourcoing.

Atelier Lyrique 82 bd Gambetta, Tourcoing ↘ 03 20 70 66 66 w atelierliriquedetourcoing.fr 🚊 Carliers

Opéra de Lille Pl du Théâtre ♀ 261 J5 ↘ 03 20 38 40 40 w opera-lille.fr 🚊 Rihour; cross the squares

CLUBS

Traditionally there have been only two rules to remember when setting out for a night's clubbing in Lille. First, stay in the bars until late, since no-one, but nobody, is seen in a club before well past midnight, however early the doors officially swing open. Secondly, if you really want to party on down, you go to Belgium. Move directly to Belgium, do not pass Go (page 154).

Although hardened merrymakers continue to make the cross-border trip to Brussels and other Belgian towns, and London's latest venues will always be a siren for the continental Eurostar set, the second tenet is perhaps a little unfair these days. Lille's smaller clubs are pretty cool and great for letting evening spill into night and flow towards the dawn. With new local venues on the student word-of-mouth trail, the days of forcing a designated driver to Brussels, Pecq and Tournai are numbered. The night scene in Lille is pretty much an attitude-free zone of tolerance with fewer of the rigid barriers between crowds that one finds in Paris and London, yet still manages to avoid the sorry air of piteous compromise found in many French provincial cities.

A legacy of Lille3000 (page 208) has been the emergence of semi-permanent and even pop-up venues. Le TriPostal (page 207) in particular hosts regular late parties during Lille3000 festival season, and the St So (page 93) is as much a social as a cultural hub these days.

Of course, it pays to choose a nightspot best suited to your age, musical tastes or sexual comfort zone. So do check out the *Ch'ti* guide at your hotel reception or online at w lechti.com for views from the student community on which are the current clubs and bars to bless with your company. Listen to

◀ 1 The Nouveau Siècle is the home of the Orchestre National de Lille. 2 Gare Saint-Sauveur has its own cinema as well as a thriving music venue.

I AM SAM, SAM I AM If a bartender or a bouncer asks you *'C'est qui, Sam?'* ('Who is Sam?'), they simply want to know which of you is the designated driver – who will remain sober when the rest of the party hits the bottle! Sam is the star of a TV and film cartoon campaign to promote sensible drinking when out on the town. The mini-films show Sam getting the girl, not having a hangover and generally being everyone's respected best mate (watch on YouTube, searching for 'ckisam'). So, if you are not drinking alcohol with your meal, in the bar or at the club, the answer to the question 'C'est qui, Sam?' is 'C'est moi!'

AND WHERE IS ANGELA? Another question, *'Où est Angela?'* ('Where is Angela?'), is your password to safety, should you feel threatened, harassed or simply uneasy on a night out. The Ask For Angela campaign launched in Lille in 2023, with Privilege and Queen Victoria bars and Aeronef and Box clubs first to sign up. Whether female or male, straight or LGBTQIA+, if you're worried about a stranger or afraid someone might spike your drinks, ask any member of staff for Angela and someone will look after you until you are safe. Look for the *Ici Demandez Angela* sticker by the front door or on a mirror in the toilets. The scheme also runs in many shops and on Ilévia public transport.

the word on the streets around Les Halles (page 152), or find a stylish bar in Vieux Lille or student dive anywhere and pick up flyers for clubs. Up-to-date listings and a diary can also be found online at w lillelanuit.com.

Admission is often free midweek; where door charges are made, this may include the first drink. Drinks usually cost around double or treble the prices charged in bars.

The Box 3 rue Saint-Étienne ♀ 261 H3 ☏ 06 12 42 42 51 🕐 23.00–07.00 Mon–Sat 🚇 Rihour; cross Grand' Place. Closest club to Grand' Place & home to House. An easy trot across the square to an early morning onion soup at La Chicorée (page 102) when the head has banged quite enough thank you.

Dukes Club 6 rue Gosselet ♀ 262 G5 ☏ 20 88 30 00 🕐 23.00–07.00 Fri–Sat 🚇 République Beaux-Arts; take rue Gaulthier de Châtillon to rue Jeanne d'Arc to rue Gosselet. This long-established haunt of the post-student crowd has grabbed back its

original name, after an identity crisis 10 years ago. This is where men with unforgivable eyes break their promises & girls whose lips are wishes pretend to believe, & a riper crowd orders shorts from the bar & sips, talks & dances 'til late with younger punters. Promoted as the venue for mid-20s to mid-40s, the looks & labels door policy feels more big city than laid-back Lille. Not for the casual moocher who never worries about changing shoes.

Les Folies 52 av du Peuple Belge ♀ 261 J2 🕐 23.30–06.00 Thu–Sat 🚌 Bus 9 to Lion d'Or. The former *Cage aux Folles*-style cabaret venue previously known as Les Folies de Paris is now an old-fashioned bop until you drop place in the heart of Vieux Lille and a popular rendezvous for friends.

The Hive 51 rue Puebla ♀ 260 E7 ⬚ 06 98 09 18 19 ⏱ 23.00–05.00 Wed–Thu, 22.00–06.00 Fri–Sat 🚆 République Beaux-Arts; walk rue Gambetta to rue Solférino to rue Masséna. Right by Les Halles and the party bars, this venue offers no hint of its former identity as a medieval-style tavern. An electro soundtrack provides an appreciative buzz that welcomes you to a street-level bar, where regulars knock back a verre or few at bee-themed tables & honeycomb-shaped stools before heading downstairs to the dance floor.

Joy Club 3 rue Ernest Deconynck ♀ 262 D1 ⬚ 03 20 57 04 16 w joyclublille.fr ⏱ 23.30–07.00 Mon–Sat 🚆 République Beaux-Arts; take rue Gambetta to Solférino, then bear right to rue Deconynck. One of the biggest venues in central Lille, this is almost an institution, whatever the latest name change. Enjoying a very loyal following with college crowds, it becomes a virtual HQ for scores of new arrivals each freshers' season. It's still a venue that has never been too cool for Kylie. You are as likely to hear chart pop as more conventional club sounds. Perhaps this is the reason you'll find a wider range of clubbers here, with locals & tourists mixing in a genuinely friendly, non-judgmental atmosphere. No worries if you did not pack your smartest influencer outfit, unlike at Dukes half a mile down the road.

Le Network 15 rue Faisan ♀ 260 D6 ⬚ 06 70 23 06 41 w le-network.fr ⏱ 23.00–07.00 Tue–Sun 🚆 République Beaux-Arts; follow bd de la Liberté to rue Puebla to rue Faisan. From early days as student venue Network Café, Le Network is now a major venue, with a global roster of DJs luring serious party crowds from across northern Europe each weekend. Still hosts student nights Tue–Thu. Electro-themed Fri & Sat & a more chilled pace on Sun.

Nox 7 rue des Arts ♀ 261 K5 ⏱ 23.30–06.00 Thu–Sat 🚆 Gare Lille Flandres. Going to press, I heard great things about this central club welcoming a truly mixed crowd.

The Room 53 rue Gambetta ♀ 262 E1 ⬚ 06 14 22 85 06 w theroom-lille.fr ⏱ 23.00–06.00 Thu–Sat 🚆 République Beaux-Arts. The address is what France calls *l'incontournable*. Previously Gotha VIP, Le Flib & Le Théatro, this venue is known by a new name to every fresh wave of students. Hit the floor or suss the crowd from the mezzanine. Contemporary R&B, hip-hop & rap sounds. Arrive after midnight, leave at dawn, crash at a friend's place then go for a healthy brunch.

Le Stairway 18 rue de la Halle ♀ 261 G1 ⏱ 23.00–05.00 Wed–Thu, 22.00–06.00 Fri–Sat 🚌 Bus 50. It's neither the hottest nor coolest venue, & opens unfashionably early at weekends, but is still a hit with the Les Halles set – at least those who still fancy a bop at the cocktail hour to '80s & '90s sounds at levels that won't drown out conviviality.

LGBTQIA+ VENUES

Lille's LGBTQIA+ community is far less ghettoised than in other cities. Old-style gay bars stock a free map-guide listing other gay and gay-friendly establishments across northern France. It's a sign of the open times that many formerly LGBTQIA+ addresses that closed during the Covid pandemic are now mainstream local bars and clubs, still retaining some of the old clientele but now truly integrated into the wider community, and the most

Pl des Halles Centrales, rue Solférino 📍 260 D7 🚊 République Beaux-Arts; take rue Gambetta to rue Solférino to pl des Halles Centrales

Wazemmes may be the daytime weekend capital, but another marketplace, the former **Les Halles** wholesale district straddling rues Solférino and Masséna, is the centre of nightlife. Part student hangout, part city of singles and part party-animal safari park, its restaurants, bars and pavements are an electrifying life-force on Friday and Saturday nights. The old covered market itself houses a run-down supermarket that still manages to catch both party buzz and cheery chaos as people stock up on last-minute supplies for rendezvous with friends in a student bedsit before hitting the bars. Like any city's party zone, bars and restaurants open and close with the regularity of a revolving door, but firm favourites survive each new influx of undergraduate revellers.

La Boucherie, an institution since the social dark ages, is a veritable meat-rack – lively dance floors, cruisy cocktail bar and the benchmark of the social scene – and first point of contact for freshers making new friends. Gen Z Insta-kids on the floor tonight may well be the progeny of Millennial and Gen X hook-ups in this very room. Those who care about looking cool may or may not still hang out at **Café La Plage**, where the original pavement tables were upcycled surf boards. Before dusk, the classic taste for is *faux*-British-pub style places, such as **Atomic**. Still going strong, it's where former, as well as current, students, feel young or old enough to get a nostalgia kick from the noise level of the classic rock soundtrack. For the *vrai* Brit experience, there's the pub quiz and big screen ruggerness of **The Queen Victoria**, whose beer is brewed in Bedfordshire. It's accompanied by live music on Fridays and DJs on Saturdays. Alternatively, go for Brit-*ish* style, *à la française*, at **The Fridge**. Here, happy hour kicks off as early as 17.00 with Le Triple Dragon trio of shots to be downed in rapid-fire succession. Further fusillades of shots, within a student budget at €2 a tot, are served at **Shooter's Bar**, a true *troquet du coin* where young crowds gather twixt threshold and kerb. The pavement is just as much a *rendezvous* outside the open doors of **Le Solférino**, a traditional *bar-tabac* on the corner of rue Masséna where card-carrying *étudiants* should ask for a discount. This is a great central point for diverse groups of friends to meet up before hitting

popular venues (such as the new NOX nightclub; page 151) are promoted as LGBTQIA+ or Queer friendly.

Le Privilège 2 rue Royale 📍 261 G3 📞 03 20 21 12 19 🕐 17.00–01.00 daily 🚊 Rihour; cross Grand' Place to rue Esquermoise & on to rue Royale. A handful of small rooms for chilling out with friends. Welcoming bar staff & manageable prices for a late-night last the clubs. If beer is more your thing, the newest arrival (for all generations) is **Le Barge**, aka l'Hirondelle du Poche, the long-awaited mini spin-off bar from the architect-brewers behind the Comptoir Hirondelle pop-up food court phenomenon (page 126). Elsewhere, sporty types make noisy alpha-male sounds during Six Nations or Euros seasons at sundry Celtic bars. Year round, try **O'Scotland** or the neighbouring **l'Irlandais** (open well into the small hours). Cocktails are served everywhere, but drop by **Le Farafina** for tequila, punch and the finest range of rums, served amid a fabulous cellar and terrace covered in African jungle décor (owner Barou hails from Burkina Faso).

Local restaurants, on the other hand, are strictly for old acquaintances who like to hear each other's voices. The season's newest crop of dining rooms provides a perfect hideaway for couples. Trends change fast here, so it really does pay to walk slow and watch where locals go. There are more than a few bars, cafés and restaurants well worth a detour along rues Gambetta and Puebla. This is one quarter where you should never rely on the printed word to be on trend. Oh, and don't pronounce the full word when referring to Solférino. That is the mark of a stranger or wrinkly. It is the Solfé!

Atomic 138 rue Solférino ♀ 260 D7 ☏ 03 20 40 18 39

Le Barge 151 rue Solférino ♀ 262 D2 w barge.bar

La Boucherie 32 rue Masséna ♀ 260 E6 ☏ 03 20 30 66 06

Café La Plage 122b rue Solférino ♀ 260 D6 ☏ 03 20 13 98 04

Le Farafina 165 rue Solférino ♀ 262 E3 ☏ 03 20 54 72 24 w lefarafina.fr

The Fridge 166 rue Solférino ♀ 262 C1 m 06 63 40 18 88 w thefridge.fr

L'Irlandais 162 rue Solférino ♀ 262 D1 ☏ 03 20 54 92 15

O'Scotland 168 rue Solférino ♀ 262 D1 ☏ 03 20 57 90 67

The Queen Victoria 161 rue Solférino ♀ 262 E3 ☏ 03 20 53 33 51 w queenvictoria.fr

Shooter's Bar 23 rue Masséna ♀ 260 E6 ☏ 03 20 57 01 66

Le Solférino 156 rue Solférino ♀ 260 D7 ☏ 03 20 57 03 43

drink within an easy walk of Grand' Place. A dinky dance floor gets the boys on their feet when the varying music policy veers towards the anthemic. Predominantly gay. Pioneered 'soirée messaging' for texting fellow barflies to break the ice before starting a conversation.

Silom Bar 138 Rue Nationale ♀ 260 E6 ☏ 07 65 78 44 40 ⏱ 17.00–02.00 Thu–Sat, 17.00–01.00 Sun & Tue–Wed 🚇 Grand Palais then

If you are really lucky or truly blessed, then, fortified with a sturdy breakfast at Paul (page 133), you might cross Grand' Place in time for a second cup of coffee at the Nouveau Siècle concert hall (page 143). Occasional Sunday morning chamber concerts at the concert hall offer an ideal programme of music to face the world by. The only tough challenge for those who have made the most of their Saturday night is finding the correct doorway in a 360° building when they are pie-eyed! You may also find a mid-morning performance at the Conservatoire (page 146). Otherwise, check in advance with the tourist office for other concerts around town and budget your hangover accordingly. If you need more than a spiritual detox, then the Turkish bath spa at the Maison Folie Wazemmes (page 210) could well prove your salvation.

bus 18 to Nationale. The newest arrival on the scene is a friendly, inclusive & cheerful bar where the tats & muscle brigade settle down with drag queens, doe-eyed ingenues & run-of-the-mill wage slaves, & where feather boas accessorize with suit trousers and work shirts or chinos & T-shirts to nary a sideways glance. Tinsel & retro sounds from peak-Madonna to perennial Abba; you're as likely to see a drag show as an ironic beefcake parade. What a 21st-century gay bar should be like.

LEAVE THE COUNTRY

When bars in old Lille wind down, punters break for the border and fun *sans frontières*. The Belgian city of Tournai is within the MEL Lille Métropole district and home to the eye-wateringly expensive but still definitive night spot the **Zoo Club**. And nearby Pecq is a party animal's natural habitat with **Ikona Club** – the current successor to Pulse and Le Bush, which traditionally wooed the Lille post-bar crowd in the small hours. Friday welcomes the hardcore rap, hip-hop and R&B set, and Saturday has theme nights. For many years, Le Disco Bus collected Lille's serious *transfrontière* boppers, with crowds waiting outside Gare Flandres for all points Belgian. Now, designated drivers earn the gratitude of as many as can squeeze into the rental Renault Megane.

Fun is not just for motorists. Just as Lille provides entertainment for millions who live within an hour of the city, locals board high-speed trains in both directions. Once upon a time the weekend was an excuse for local youth to hop aboard the party trains to Amsterdam, then the early Eurostar years saw the last train to London packed with bright-eyed clubbers heading for cool Britannia to hit the floor before returning bleary-eyed back to the station for the first train back to Lille. Eurostar even had a special nightlife fare for party animals ricocheting between London, Lille, Paris and Brussels. Alas, new border controls mean London is now off the spontaneous *transmanche* whim menu. These days, the speedily mobile social set use fast trains to party in their continental capital city of choice. Brussels is the most popular cross-border break and for the past 30 years most clubbing travellers have headed for **Fuse**, within walking distance of the Eurostar terminal, as well as countless other bars and clubs. Allow around 35 minutes by TGV/Eurostar from Lille Europe.

France provides other lures. Paris is packed with clubbing, theatrical and gastronomic excuses for spending the evening away from home. In summer, the Ouigo rail link (page 62) to Disneyland Paris from €10 is an unlikely choice for the otherwise too-cool-for-the-magic young, free and childless in search of the American dream during late-night opening season. Since Marne La Vallée after midnight has little to offer, these superannuated *mousquetaires* tend to hit the nightclubs of Pigalle and the Bastille post whirling on the tea-cups and screaming on the rollercoasters, having checked Parisian listings on w timeout.com/paris. They then chill out at the after-parties in the capital before taking a return train home after lunch on Sunday.

To be truly daring, take a TGV to Marseille, Montpellier, Lyon, Nice, Nantes or Bordeaux. You could even watch the sunrise over the Med, but you might not get home in time for breakfast!

Fuse 208 rue Blaes, Brussels w fuse.be
① 23.00–07.00 Fri–Sat
Ikona Club Rue de Tournai 180,
Pecq, Belgium ☏ + 32 465 55 04 00
① 23.00–06.00 Fri–Sat

Zoo Club Grand'Route 666, Tournai, Belgium
☏ + 32 456 02 39 27 ① 23.00–06.00 Fri–Sat

9

Shopping

Lille has four main shopping areas, each to be explored and exploited to the max. For sheer chic, absolute style and total magic, **Vieux Lille** has to be visited. Even without money, it is worth pressing your nose against a window and inhaling the wealth. The second you step away from the squares of the town centre and take to the cobbles of the old town, the shops shriek class. And they drop names the way a starlet drips diamonds. Kenzo and co come into sharp focus within the first 50m, and Louis Vuitton has taken over one of the most loved frontages in northern France (page 106). If you are an old hand at Lille shopping, you'll know antique dealers cluster around the roads just north of **Grand' Place**, but you might not have spotted the latest trends. Tableware is still huge and Villeroy & Boch has its own *vitrine* in town (try rues de la Bourse and Esquermoise for that sort of thing). **Rue Basse**, long-time poor relation to the other streets looping around Notre Dame de la Treille, has been colonised by stylish new shopkeepers. Décor and furnishings are well worth the browsing, and the fun is in finding ever more antique dealers with tiny shops groaning under the weight of chandeliers and hiding Drouot bronze *animaliers*, intricate marquetry and lovely Lalique glassware. The **place aux Oignons** and its tributaries, **rue aux Vieux Murs** and the variously spelled **rue Pétérinck** (sometimes Pétérynck), are a hive of good taste and creativity. Find wedding dresses made with antique fabrics, artists' studios, delicious specialist food shops and some amazing tableware in galleries and *ateliers* tucked away behind the cathedral.

Wherever a shop closes down, the chances are that within weeks yet another vape shop will pop up in its place. E-cigs are huge in Lille, and on almost every corner you'll find somewhere offering strawberry- or coffee-flavoured refills for your sonic screwdriver mouthpiece. Some boutiques on the edge of the classy districts have designer carved pipes that look to have been inspired by Sidney Paget's illustrations of Sherlock Holmes. **Vaporama** (♀ 261 J3) on place des Patiniers evokes the age of tabacs, humidors, *fumoirs* and snuff shops – I saw a rosewood e-pipe on sale for €119!

From **Grand' Place** (♀ 261 H5), shopping possibilities fan out in all directions. Where Vieux Lille meets the squares are rows of extravagant footwear boutiques, while the budget shoe shops along the rue Faidherbe

THE CH'TIPPENDALES

If proof were needed that Lille has the heart and passion of the Mediterranean, it may have been found in a simple calendar that illustrated the early years of the millennium. To launch the century, and to raise money for charity, the male shopkeepers of Vieux Lille presented themselves to their patrons (albeit via the camera lens) in all their rugged nakedness. No coy hiding behind flower arrangements à la WI: here, proud masculinity of rippling commerce was draped around historic buildings, noble statuary and the grandeur of the opera house. Making headlines when they first posed shirtless for the millennium, within a few years the boys' flaunting had become more flagrant and they were dubbed by the press the Ch'tippendales! In our more enlightened times, this may explain the beefcake photos behind the tills in some establishments, and allow you to view the now grey-haired chap behind the counter in his natural colours.

have been kicked out by ever larger pharmacies. Rue Nationale has its banks and Printemps department store (home to Parisian and international designer labels), while the pedestrian zone sprawling out towards place République is shoppers' city. Rues Béthune, Neuve, Pierre Mauroy and Tanneurs, with all their tributaries and back-doubles, boast most major high-street names, and plenty more besides. Even though Galeries Lafayette has now left the building, its former home is a showcase complex for contemporary brands. Meanwhile, new and traditional outlets bring shoppers out into the sunlight, while C&A and Monoprix provide the initial attraction to the **Tanneurs** mall (page 179). Once home to H&M (before it swapped allegiance and decamped to the larger malls) it is now one of the most popular lunch venues in town. A major rainy-day option featuring some of the same shops and more is the fabulous **Euralille** complex (page 179), its new Westfield logo dominating the landscape between the two railway stations and a draw in its own right. And a new mall, Lillennium, has opened across town.

In a district best known for the Sunday market at Wazemmes, **rue Gambetta** is worth being aware of, even if only for its Sunday opening hours. It is also the cheapest side of town, where you'll find the kitschest of budget retro clothing (page 163) – though this is now more of a Saturday than a Sunday thing – and loads of bazaars selling everything under the sun. There are literally hundreds of shops, boutiques, stores and stalls to discover in Lille. Follow your nose, your eyes, and trust your willpower over your wallet!

True bargain hunters should take the tram or métro out to Roubaix, home of serious savings. Twin giants of factory-outlet shopping have long wooed visitors here away from Lille, charmed by the prospect of designer labels at

Shopping

9

30–70% off high-street prices. And Les Aubanes, a former Sunday morning stalwart of rue Gambetta, has opened a far bigger store here, where you will find clothes, saucepans, household goods, toys and games from last year's mail-order catalogues: La Redoute uses this store to offload surplus stock, making it great for a budget Christmas list. If you plan to go to Roubaix, don't just visit the shops – as a cultural centre in its own right, it's worth making a day of it (page 221).

Don't forget, for all the categories below, in addition to our suggestions in the listings, you'll find many more of each type of shop in the big malls (page 178).

OPENING HOURS

Unless otherwise stated, shops usually open 14.00–19.00 on Monday and 10.00–19.00 Tuesday to Saturday. Those in Vieux Lille and the city centre close all day Sunday, with smaller shops often closing all day Monday and for lunch between noon and 14.00 the rest of the week. Sunday hours on rue Gambetta are usually 09.00–13.00. Many French supermarkets also now offer Sunday morning opening year round. For shopping malls, check individual listings (page 178).

ACCESSORIES

BENJAMIN 45 rue de Béthune ♀ 261 H7 ☏ 03 20 54 69 67 🚇 Rihour; rue de la Vieille Comédie leads to rue de Béthune
Benjamin has been accessorising Lille's best-dressed set since 1926. Here you'll discover hats, gloves, brollies and finishing touches for any outfit – perhaps honour the era of the architecture with a '20s-style cloche, treat yourself to a post war trilby or pick up a Russian-style fur affair for the full mysterious stranger schtick.

SHERILEY 94 rue Saint-André ♀ 261 G1 ☏ 03 20 14 00 37 🚇 Gare Lille Flandres, then bus 10 to Conservatoire
This is the place to come for discounts on big-name handbags and luggage. It's worth a couple of hundred metres of cobbles in your second-best Louboutin heels.

BOOKS

In addition to the listings below, the nationwide station news and book chain Relay sells bestsellers and local maps.

LE BATEAU LIVRE 154 rue Gambetta ♀ 262 C2 ☏ 03 20 78 16 30 w lebateaulivre.fr
🕐 10.00–13.00 & 14.00–19.00 Tue–Sat, closed Sun & Mon 🚇 République Beaux-Arts; cross the square & walk along rue Gambetta; the shop is on your right, shortly after passing rue Masséna
Even if your own French is rusty, your kids could become proficient if you take home a children's

book in the local language. Most bookshops in town have a junior section, but this *librairie* is strictly for under-16s and is a temple to the joy of reading. Ask the staff what they would recommend – maybe an original *Babar* story, or even a translation of *Harry Potter*. Think how cool your kids would be considered if they could drop the French for muggles and Hogwarts into the playground conversation (*moldus* and *Poudlard*, in case you were wondering).

LE BIG LE MOI 124 rue Pierre Legrand ♀ 262 F5 ☏ 09 81 64 56 85 w librairielebiglemoi.fr ⏱ 10.00–19.00 Mon–Sat 🚇 Fives
Since central Lille lost its much-loved Café Livres, where to go for a cuppa, slice of cake and a reading, talk or workshop? A short distance from the touristy centre, literally two métro stops from the squares, lies the answer: this community bookshop with over 7,000 books in stock and an online catalogue to browse before you get here. The website also features customer book reviews and recommendations, and details of upcoming events covering everything from political activism to philosophy to children's story sessions.

BOUQUINERIE SOLIDAIRE OXFAM 9 rue de l'Hôpital Militaire ♀ 261 G7 ☏ 03 20 67 63 48 ⏱ noon–19.00 Mon–Fri, 11.00–19.00 Sat 🚇 Rihour; take rue du Palais Rihour to rue de l'Hôpital Militaire
This is a proper Parisian *bouquiniste*-style secondhand bookshop on the fringe of the Rihour-Béthune district, complete with genuine old-fashioned store front and trays of bargain paperbacks in the street and tempting shelves within. Since the cherished VO bookshop on rue Molinel is long past its epilogue, this is where you might read books in an author's native tongue, be that English, German or Russian. You'll also find classics with those uniquely French, faded beige, pictureless covers – whereby a professorial thesis looks like a romantic novel looks like a revolutionary treatise, in a bibliophile tradition unchanged over centuries. There are reliable bins of Agatha Christies and Patricia Highsmiths too, plus yards of old travelogues and some green- and pink-spined classic kids' books. Nearby, another Oxfam outlet sells secondhand clothes.

CROCKBOOK 28 rue des Ponts de Comines ♀ 261 H5 ☏ 03 20 51 49 05 ⏱ 10.00–19.30 Mon–Sat 🚇 Rihour
Great value art books and exhibition catalogues can be found at this discount and remainder book shop. Save a fortune on museum shop prices. It also has good recipe books, lavishly illustrated for browsing, and perhaps a dictionary, too, to help you find the English word for *maizena*.

FNAC See page 172.

LE FURET DU NORD Pl du Général de Gaulle ♀ 261 H5 ☏ 03 20 78 43 43 w www.furet.com ⏱ 09.30–19.30 Mon–Sat 🚇 Rihour
It took a teacher, a dairymaid and a butcher's boy with a passion for reading to turn a small shop serving local rabbit hunters into the biggest bookshop in France. Originally, Le Furet du Nord had a modest home on a street behind place Rihour and was the local rendezvous and general store for poachers and gamekepers. Then in the 1930s, local schoolmaster Georges Poulard bought the shop and opened his first bookstore, retaining the shopfront with the

LES VINS GOURMANDS

LES VINS GOURMANDS

LES VINS GOURMANDS

original 'Northern Ferret' name. After the war, Paul Callens, son of a butcher from Tourcoing, decided against joining the family business and started work as a salesman at Le Furet. He had grand ideas for creating the biggest bookshop in France, and when his dairymaid girlfriend Florence gave him her life savings, he bought the shop. In 1959, when a national department store on the Grand' Place closed down, the former butcher's boy went into battle with car giant Renault to buy the premises from the Parisian owners. The business expanded, as did Callens' imagination. It became the first bookshop in France to allow browsing and self-service, welcomed the arrival of budget paperbacks to promote literature for all, and is now an institution on the square and a symbol of Lille itself. With a network of gantries, staircases and lifts, the many must-see departments include 'English Books by Furet' and an enviable travel selection.

An essential stop for bibliophiles with 135,000 titles in stock across 4,500m^2, and a dedicated reading area on the first floor, where readers may meet authors to discuss their works. If you are still interested in northern ferrets, then try the nature and natural history department on the 5th floor.

GODON 16 rue Masurel ♀ 261 F3 ☎ 03 20 31 56 19 **w** www.librairiegodon.com ⏱ 14.00– 18.30 Wed–Sat 🚍 Bus 50 to Lion d'Or, & follow rue Chats Bossus to rue Basse, then 2nd right on to rue Masurel
The leader among the classic *bouquinistes* and old-school booksellers of Vieux Lille, and recognised as one of France's leading experts on old books and engravings, Godon has been around the old town for around 140 years at various addresses, and in its current home since the late 1990s. Regularly found at the Paris and Lille book fairs, this antiquarian bookseller is the perfect place for that Flaubert first edition you always dreamed of owning. The collectors' catalogue may be downloaded from the website.

VIEILLE BOURSE See page 200.

CLOTHES

FASHION Chanel and many other designer labels have swapped individual boutiques in Vieux Lille for outlets within Printemps department store (page 178) or moved indoors at the larger malls (page 178).

La 7ème Compagnie 11 rue Jean Sans Peur ♀ 261 G6 ☎ 03 20 54 39 63 ⏱ 10.00– noon & 14.00–19.00 Tue–Sat 🚍 République Beaux-Arts; take bd de la Liberté to rue Jean Sans Peur
Epaulettes, camouflage and good strong fabric. Here you'll find outfits with a military look, from practical combats and standard army-surplus clubwear to costume items such as British Guardsman's uniforms.

◀ 1 Browsing for books and art at Vieille Bourse. 2 The famous waffles at Pâtisserie Méert. 3 True cheese lovers go to a specialist *fromagerie*. 4 Les Vins Gourmands has a wine for any occasion.

La Botte Chantilly
12 rue Lepelletier ♀ 261 H4 ☎ 03 20 55 46 41 w la-botte.com
🚇 Rihour; cross Grand' Place & walk through the Alcide arch towards rue Lepelletier
For over a century, Lille's most famous shoe shop lived on rue de la Grande Chausée, in the former home of d'Artagnan (page 182), where the Deparis family first set up in the 1890s to create the famous Chantilly cavalry boots worn in the Lille garrison. However, the threat of structural collapse hanging over the site, aggravated by the need to shut down the business for a year or longer if they wanted to stay put, nudged an eventual move to even larger premises in a former print works on rue Lepelletier, just around the corner. It's not the company's first encounter with change: after World War II, and the diminution of a military presence in town, *la famille Daparis* decided to design and sell civilian – albeit couture – footwear for men and women. Now in a new light and airy 3-storey showroom, with glass atelier-style roofs, France's largest collection of handmade shoes outside Paris may be seen and snapped up. All leading French and international brands can be seen here, even British Cockett & Jones shoes as created for *James Bond*.

Caroll
10–12 rue de Béthune ♀ 261 H6 ☎ 03 20 12 04 44 w caroll.com 🚇 Rihour; cross pl Rihour to rue de Béthune
Comfort is the keynote at Caroll – all silks and cashmeres, cotton and light linen. Even dedicated followers of fashion have been won over by this high street line for those who like to lounge while power dressing. Smart, ready-to-wear women's jackets, trench coats, skirts and pantsuits blur the line between boardroom and cocktail lounge. There's another branch on Grand' Place, a counter at Printemps department store and an outlet in Roubaix selling last season's look at a discount.

Danie Hoo
10 pl des Patiniers ♀ 261 J3 m 06 80 32 11 32 w daniehoo.com
🚇 bus 9 to Lion d'Or
Deliciously retro, Danie Hoo offers surprisingly affordable women's fashion. Expect chic mini lines and prints that would have turned heads in the heyday of Chelsea, floaty midis evoking the soft focus of the *Teach The World to Sing Coca Cola* era, lace sleeves on a classic LBD, and prices comfortably within the €20–50 range. Good knitwear. Bags and bangles, too.

Loding
13 rue Lepelletier ♀ 261 H4 ☎ 03 20 40 08 47 🚇 Rihour; cross Grand' Place & walk through the Alcide arch towards rue Lepelletier
Happy Father's Day, or just welcome to your new moneyed lifestyle. This is the place for classy menswear – shoes, shirts, cufflinks and cashmere sweaters, plus classic gentlemen's club colours and décor. It reeks of tradition, but dates back to the late 1990s.

Louis Vuitton
3 rue des Chats Bossus w 261 J3 ☎ 09 77 40 40 77 🚇 Gare Lille Flandres or bus 9 to Lion d'Or
How did France's premier luxury brand find itself setting up home in an Art Deco fish shop? See page 106.

La Mesure au Masculin
49 rue de la Monnaie Lille ♀ 261 H2 ☎ 03 20 06 95 71
🕐 regular hours Tue–Sat, appointment only Sun–Mon 🚇 Rihour or bus 9 to Lion d'Or
Eric Sagniez has the measure of a man and was one of the first shopkeepers in Vieux Lille to reopen his boutique after the lockdowns of 2020. His argument was that, with society returning

to near normal after Covid, there would be more weddings, and so Lille would need more bespoke suits. Those in the market can choose from a range of 3,000 fabrics that evokes Roubaix's textile heyday, from cashmere to flannel, and marvel at the skills of a master tailor at every stage in the creative process. Should your budget not extend to the full three-piece suit, how about a made-to-measure shirt? Reservation recommended.

VINTAGE BARGAINS The shopfronts of Old Lille seem never to change, but there have been seismic tremors under the cobbles since the start of the 2020s, when many boutiques showcasing haute couture and the next generation of designers simply failed to re-open after pandemic lockdowns. Sometimes, moving business online proved a more sensible direction. In other cases, French labels were snapped up by international brands and incorporated within larger outlets. Nathalie Chaise and Constance le Gonidec have been among recent casualties, and another loss was the irrepressible Miss Sixty, where a Bardot pout would always trump a Cyrus twerk. But that old-school style, where street smarts could be fun without being outrageous, and faded jeans and printed T-shirts looked as though they had been cut to be worn with Gallic insouciance, has returned to the cobbles. And returned in the most unlikely guise. Charity shop chic (see Oxfam on rue de l'Hopital Militaire) has always been a standby for the transient student population, and the *friperies* of Wazemmes and Gambetta provided outfits for entire families struggling to make ends meet, but the passion for vintage fashion today is driven as much by environmental conscience as Proustian *recherche des looks perdus*. Thus, racks of pre-loved, previously worn and reclaimed frocks, suits, tops and trews are finding their way across the elegant portals of Vieux Lille.

Bon Chic Bonne Fripe 234 rue Léon Gambetta ♀ 262 B2 **w** bonchicbonnefripe.fr ⏰ 13.00–10.00 Tue & Thu, 14.00–19.00 Wed, 11.00–19.00 Fri–Sat 🚊 Gambetta
Leather jackets, trainers and streetwear are the top finds at this latest vintage shop in the original bargain quarter. Messaoud and Sophie started their business in Paris's legendary Clignancourt flea market in the 1990s before taking it online with an eBay shop. They opened their latest shop in Lille in 2023.

Ding Fring 8 rue Saint-Pierre Saint-Paul ♀ 262 A3 ✆ 03 28 07 32 81 ⏰ 10.00–19.00 Mon–Sat, 09.30–13.00 Sun 🚊 Gambetta
Ding Fring has branches all over northern France, from Boulogne to Armentières. This is one of the few *friperies* open at the same time as Wazemmes Sunday morning flea market.

Faubourg des Marques 98 rue du Faubourg-de-Roubaix ♀ 259 K3 ✆ 03 20 55 00 60 ⏰ 10.00–13.00 &15.30–18.30 Tue–Fri, 10.30–noon & 15.00–18.00 Sat 🚊 St Maurice Pellevoisin
The name is a nod to the former Faubourg des Modes alternative fashion district, launched in 2007 by designer Agnès b and Mayor Aubrey. It comprised more than a dozen workshops from which a

new generation of designers could sell direct to the public, cutting out middlemen, catwalks and fashion shows. Alas, pandemic fallout and a spat between the mayors of Lille and Roubaix ended the project's public funding. While the big gesture hothouse is no longer, its name lends a touch of legacy to another outlet, actually a 15-minute walk from the Eurostar station, where top-end vintage and more recent wares are displayed by size rather than label. If you've a couple of hours before the train home, it's a good alternative to Westfield Euralille on the other side of the station for a final spree.

Funny Vintage 124 rue Léon Gambetta ♥ 262 D2 ☎ 03 62 65 79 67
w funnyvintage.wixsite.com/lille ⏱ 14.00–19.00 Tue–Thu, 11.00–19.00 Fri–Sat
🚊 République Beaux-Arts
Louis and Valerie, long-time lovers of 20th-century fabrics and design, took their passion for '50s–'90s clothing from pop-ups and collectors fairs to an actual shop in Wazemmes. Find period décor and accessories, alongside classic American and Japanese clothing.

Kilo Shop 14 pl des Patiniers ♥ 261 J3 ☎ 03 74 09 10 33 w kilo-shop.com ⏱ 14.00–19.30
Mon, 11.00–19.30 Tue–Sat 🚌 bus 9 to Lion d'Or
Where once you might have dithered over designer prêt à porter and one-off creations, here you buy fashion by the kilo. Just check the coloured tags and tip your haul on to old-fashioned greengrocer's scales: perhaps €20 for all reds, €30 for greens, €60 for orange etc. This was the Kilo Shop deal back in its original branch at Wazemmes; now beautiful people in the more fashionable centre can appreciate the same budget strategy. Genuine Levi 501s from the 1980s, a Primark gilet or a backless Prada midnight frock : if the clothes are blue, then its €40 and you may add some socks and a scarf to make up the weight.

MAD Vintage 56B rue de Béthune ♥ 261 G7 ☎ 03 20 22 09 10 w madvintage.fr
🚊 République Beaux-Arts
This peripatetic outlet for classic clothing with an international edge has now settled in a prime retail space in the pedestrian quarter.

Tilt Vintage 33 rue de la Clef ♥ 261 J4 ☎ 03 20 55 55 86 w tilt-vintage.com ⏱ 14.00–
19.30 Mon, 10.30–19.00 Tue–Sat 🚌 bus 9 to Lion d'Or
This national chain of upmarket vintage wear has shops from Bordeaux to Paris. As well as Lille's old town address, Tilt now has a new outlet within the Citadium in Le 31 on rue Béthune (page 178). Buy gift vouchers online to give to friends travelling to Lille.

FACTORY OUTLETS
McArthurGlen Mail de Lannoy, Roubaix ☎ 03 28 33 36 00 w mcarthurglen.fr ⏱ 10.00–
19.00 Mon–Sat, 10.00–18.00 Sun 🚊 Eurotéléport
Confirming Roubaix's status as the home of bargain designer shopping, this open-air mall above the main métro station is an avenue of dozens of outlet stores. Mostly they're French high-street names; international firms offering permanent discounts of 30–70% include Boss, Calvin Klein, Blanc Bleu, Lacoste, Pierre Cardin and Puma. And there are non-wearable treats *chez* Haribo, Villeroy & Bosch and Le Creuset.

L'Usine 228 av Alfred Motte, Roubaix ☎ 03 20 83 16 20 w usineroubaix.fr ⏱ 10.00–19.00 Mon–Sat 🚇 Eurotéléport, then bus L4 to Les Hauts Champs

This is where it all began 40 years ago, and where 4 million French and Belgian shoppers each year choose to eke out their euros. It was the very first outlet shop in France: three storeys of the former Motte-Bossut cotton mill, stuffed with linens, clothes and shoes at ludicrously low prices. Since Roubaix was the capital of France's mail-order industry, with Les Trois Suisses and La Redoute both based here, whenever new catalogues were published, old stock needed to be sold off as swiftly as possible.

Today this includes end-of-range goods, factory seconds, and everything from footwear to table linen at prices to raise the most plucked eyebrow. The minimum year-round discount on high street branches is 30%, but savings can top 70% in sales season. These days, the old makeshift sales space has been converted into a purpose-built shopping mall with a choice of restaurants and even a hairdressing salon on the premises for those planning to make a day of it. Stock up on Adidas, Etam, Lacoste, Nike and Damart, or even more exclusive labels at the new Galeries Lafayette outlet store within the complex.

XXL

Le Petit Monde des Rondes 341 rue Gambetta 📍 258 A7 ☎ 03 20 54 50 82 🚇 Gambetta; take rue de Flandre to rue de la Paix d'Utrecht, then rue Gambetta

Big girls don't cry, they dress up in pretty things, from frilly undies to wafty, summery picnicky outfits. There's a new splash of colour every couple of weeks, when Frédérique unveils her latest themed window display. This shop offers more than traditionally 'flattering' vertical lines and muted shades – instead you'll find bold patterns, fun knitwear and the brightest of hues.

COSMETICS AND PERFUME

SEPHORA 7 pl du Général de Gaulle 📍 261 H5 ☎ 20 67 41 20 w sephora.fr 🚇 Rihour

The national cosmetic chain retailer now has a branch on Grand' Place, which stays open until 19.00. A second shop, in the Euralille complex (page 179) remains open an hour later.

CRAFTS

LA DROGUERIE 50 rue Basse 📍 261 G4 ☎ 03 20 55 36 80 w ladroguerie.com 🚇 Rihour; cross the squares, rue Esquermoise & turn right to rue Basse

If you're looking to accessorize or to tart up an old frock found in a flea market, then come here, where fabrics, silks, wools and jars of buttons and beads are stacked along the walls in a Bohemian dressmaker's delight.

ROUGIER & PLÉ 80 rue Pierre Mauroy, Centre Commercial Les Tanneurs w 261 J6 ☎ 03 20 74 44 99 w rougier-ple-lille.fr 🚇 Gare Lille Flandres; go left into rue de Priez, then at the foot of rue Faidherbe walk around church to rue Mauroy

Now that the craft shop in Euralille has been replaced by yet another homeware outlet, come here for good art supplies.

FLORISTS

Vieux Lille is decorated with unexpected and unlisted stylish artisanal florists, whose teeny *échoppes* are garlanded with blossom and leaves, hidden behind climbers and foliage and fronted with trestles containing miniature pewter pots and pails with hyacinths and micro-topiary. They're ideal for those whose grasp of the language of flowers is ungrammatical and whose fashion sense does not quite have the cutting edge of secateurs.

INSTANT CANDIDE 12 rue de la Barre ♀ 261 G3 w instant-candide.com 🚊 Rihour, then Navette Vieux Lille to Citadelle
This old-town florist deals exclusively in bouquets of dried flowers – perfect should you wish to unleash your inner Miss Haversham and bring the flowers home as a keepsake.

OH LES FLEURS 21 bd Louis XIV ♀ 259 G7 ☎ 03 20 88 03 40 ⏰ 08.30–20.00 Mon–Sat, 08.30–13.30 Sun w ohlesfleurs.com 🚊 Grand Palais
Useful to know if you need to surprise someone special with a last-minute gesture, this corner shop promises to deliver flowers within 4 hours. So if your wedding anniversary comes as news to you over the hotel breakfast buffet, then a loving look, wry smile and shifty phone skills should save the day.

FOOD AND WINE

THE DAILY BREAD
Le Colibri See page 66.

Au Pain Levé 2 bd Belfort ♀ 259 H8 ☎ 06 14 13 84 96 w painleve.fr ⏰ 07.00–19.00 Mon–Sat, 07.00–13.30 Sun 🚊 Rihour
It shares a name with the bus stop at the top of the road, but people from across town come here for the delicious breads (including a multi-seed loaf) to counter the effects of a weekend of doughy white baguettes. Delectable pastries both sweet and savoury.

Le Pain Quotidien See page 131.

Paul See page 133.

THE FOOD
L'Abbaye des Saveurs 13 rue des Vieux Murs ♀ 261 H2 m 06 66 33 54 65 ⏰ 10.00–19.30 Tue–Sat, 10.00–14.30 Sun 🚊 Bus 9 to Lion d'Or, rue de la Monnaie then turn on to rue Pétérinck
Franck and Anthony, faces of L'Abbaye des Saveurs, are both passionate about local produce and this is reflected in the range of meats, sweets and local delicacies, from jars of *potjevleesch* to rounds of cheeses. Most items are supplied directly from the farmers, and shop staff will advise on which producers open their farms to visitors, should you fancy a day in the country. For true

beer lovers, this is the place to find artisanal beers from across Flanders, *bières sans frontières*, with superb ranges of the best of Belgium to complement around two dozen local breweries represented on the shelves, available by the bottle or the barrel. If you are planning a party in Lille, then rent a beer pump from the shop.

L'Arrière Pays
47 rue Basse ♀ 261 H4 ☏ 03 20 13 80 07 w arrierepayslille.fr 🚊 Rihour; cross squares to Esquermoise to rue Basse
Old town grocery shop selling incredible and wonderful preserves, oils and pâtés in little bottles and jars. The place doubles as a restaurant and *salon de thé* (page 93).

Bio c'Bon
1 bd JB Lebas ♀ 261 J3 ☏ 03 20 63 02 35 w bio-c-bon.eu ⏱ 09.30–20.00 Mon– Sat, 10.30–13.00 Sun 🚊 Lille Grand Palais or bus L5 to Liberté
This organic supermarket, formerly based in the heart of Vieux Lille, now enjoys a new location on the city centre edge of the Saint-Sauveur district. Buy weigh-and-pay nuts, dried fruits and pulses – as well as vegan food.

La Bottega
7b rue Pétérinck ♀ 261 H2 ☏ 03 20 21 16 85 w la-bottega.com 🚊 Bus 9 to Lion d'Or, then rue de la Monnaie to rue Pétérinck
Everything Italian, from espresso machines to beautifully crafted Venetian carnival masks, pasta, pesto, coffee and Tuscan olive oil celebrate *la dolce vita* at La Bottega in the heart of Vieux Lille. This is the deli to find ingredients used by the very best Italian restaurants in the city (page 109). If the Latin smile behind the counter looks familiar but you cannot quite place it, perhaps you do not recognise its wearer with his clothes on. Gilberto Annunzio had been known to display his Latin credentials on the celebrated Vieux Lille calendar (page 157).

La Comtesse du Barry
21 rue Esquermoise ♀ 261 H4 ☏ 03 20 54 00 43 w boutiques. comtessedubarry.com 🚊 Rihour; cross Grand'Place to rue Esquermoise
Pâtés in jars and tins of preserved delicacies from across France, but mostly southwestern farmyards, line the shelves here. Pick up *foie gras*, smoked salmon, terrines and platters for lunch, or get them gift-wrapped as savoury presents.

Maison Benoit
77 rue de la Monnaie ♀ 261 H2 ☏ 03 20 31 69 03 w maison-benoit.com ⏱ 09.30–19.30 Tue–Sat, 09.00–13.30 Sun 🚊 Bus 9 to Lion d'Or
Belgium's Neuhaus and Leonidas both have high-profile counters in Lille, but forsake them in favour of a taste of the domestic product. Benoit is Lille's most famous chocolate shop, with over 50 varieties of chocolates and truffles to tempt the sweet and bittersweet tooth.

Pâtisserie Méert
See page 130. When closed on a Monday, find the famous waffles at Printemps department store (page 178).

Philippe Olivier
3 rue du Curé Saint-Étienne ♀ 261 G4 ☏ 03 21 31 94 74 w philippeolivier.fr 🚊 Rihour; cross squares, go under the Alcide arch & turn left
Maître Olivier is one of the country's grand masters of cheese. His main store in Boulogne supplies the Elysée Palace, Vatican and White House. Buy a Camembert marinated in calvados or try a local

Flanders speciality such as a Mont des Cats. There are more branches on rues Gambetta and Basse and another shop in Lens, if you are heading out of town to visit the new Louvre.

THE WINES AND BEERS
L'Abbaye des Saveurs See page 166.

La Cave du Parvis St Maurice 98 rue Pierre Mauroy ♀ 261 J7 w lacaveduparvis.fr
📞 03 20 13 76 68 🚇 Gare Lille Flandres; take rue de Priez, then at the foot of rue Faidherbe, walk around the church to rue de Paris
This treasure stands in the shade of the St Maurice church. Come for wines, wine accessories and lots of wine wisdom. Knowledge and insight are dispensed in drops to even the most casual of browsers, but by the figurative magnum to those who book special *soirée découverte et dégustation* tutored tasting sessions. Buy a place at one of these evenings as a gift. It was on this very street, a generation ago, that I bought the treasured coffret of scent bottles, Le Nez du Vin, to help train a young sommelier in his craft. Don't be misled by the modest shopfront. As the sign in the window explains, 'Our window may be small, but our cellar is huge', and there are around 17,000 labels to be discovered here.

Celestin See page 133.

Au Gré du Vin See page 124.

Le Présentoir See page 126.

Les Vins d'Aurélien 5 rue Jean Sans Peur ♀ 261 G6 📞 03 20 64 36 63
w lesvinsdaurelien.fr 🚇 Rihour; take rue du Palais Rihour to rue de l'Hôpital Militaire to rue Jean Sans Peur
Around 1,000 wines collected over eight years are held in what might become the Lille wine-lover's Diagon Alley. Aurélien himself, *caviste* and infectious enthusiast, has the air of a bearded Harry Potter as he shares his total love and appreciation of the wines from France and beyond. He knows the people and stories behind each bottle, from great traditional houses to the *chais* of exciting new *vignerons*. Shell out €80 for one of his themed tasting events (rums of the world, discover the Rhône, Bordeaux versus Burgundy, etc) or just chat about *la bouteille juste* for your next dinner party.

Les Vins Gourmands 33 rue Esquermoise ♀ 261 H4 📞 03 20 30 12 20
w lesvinsgourmands.fr 🚇 Rihour; cross the square to rue Esquermoise
Since Annie-Paule gave up her fabulous boutique around the corner and across the way, I've been seeking another shop where one's every purchase is a lesson. This will do nicely. Well-read and open-minded staff know not only their French *cépages* and vintages, but have a good knowledge of the wider world. So when talking of the picnic or dinner party you have in mind, do not be

◀ 1 Euralille is one of France's biggest shopping centres. 2 The pretty streets of Vieux Lille make a delightful place to go window shopping.

surprised to be offered a New Zealand white or South African red as well as a Burgundy and a Côtes du Rhône.

GIFTS

ARTISANAT MONASTIQUE
Parvis Notre Dame de la Treille, pl Gilleson ♀ 261 H3 ☎ 09 70 35 21 41 w artisanat-monastique-lille.fr 🚌 bus 9 to Lion d'Or then walk from rue de la Monnaie to the cathedral

Religious and liturgical gifts, from monastic-themed accessories to devotional items. The range of gifts also includes food and drink created by monks and nuns from monasteries, convents and abbeys across France and stamped with the Monastique logo. This was introduced throughout France as a type of 'AOC' label by a canny Cistercian abbott, as proof of religious origin after many supermarket own-label and factory-produced foods were marketed with fake brands and saintly images of abbeys and monks.

NATURE ET DÉCOUVERTES
Euralille ♀ 259 H4 ☎ 03 20 78 01 00 w natureetdecouvertes. com 🚌 Lille Europe; cross parvis Mitterrand to Centre Euralille

A fabulous calming oasis in any shopping centre, where ecologically responsible shoppers may browse in a state of relaxation occasioned by cups of freshly infused herbal tea and headphones playing sounds of whales and rainwater. Wooden toys, ramblers' accessories, books, gifts and a range of eclectic wonders. I love the store's suggestion of the perfect present to mark the birth of a child: an acorn and planter so that a tree grows with the new life.

THE WIZARD'S SHOP
35 rue Neuve ♀ 261 H6 ☎ 01 85 09 74 50 w the-wizards-shop.com ⏰ 11.00–19.00 Mon–Fri, 10.00–19.00 Sat 🚌 Rihour; take rue de Béthune to rue Neuve

You can't actually get to Hogwarts *à grand vitesse* from Lille, but rue Neuve boasts a pretty nifty rival to Mr Ollivander's wand shop. This is a charming little emporium with plenty of shelves and boxes for wands, *bijoux* and house accessories whether your own wizard is in Gryffindor or Hufflepuff. Skip the throng at the official branded Harry Potter shop on platform 9¾ at Kings Cross before taking the Eurostar – this is a far less stressful option for mere muggles.

HOME

ARNAUD PEREIRA
156 rue du Molinel ♀ 262 G1 ☎ 06 11 61 60 15 w arnaud-pereira.fr 🚌 République Beaux-Arts

Each generation brings a new rediscovery of a traditional art form. Some 25 years ago, the first Bradt guide introduced us to M Moisson's work as a copyist (see opposite). This time, I was peering through a workshop window at the Beaux Arts end of rue Molinel when M Pereira opened the door for a chat. Another of those skilled creatives who silently step in whenever a national monument is in need of repair, he blends artisan work in classic restoration with an artist's eye to create striking pieces of his own for home and garden. Since he is often on call to help out with France's heritage around the hexagon, it is best to ring ahead to check the shopfront studio is open to visitors.

CAMILLE STOPIN 14 pl Louise de Bettignies 📍 261 J3 📞 03 20 55 39 02 🕐 09.00–noon & 14.30–19.00 Mon–Fri (appointments are preferred) 🚌 bus 9 to Lion d'Or

For something rather special, this family of cabinet-makers has served Lille's stylish householders since 1860. Father-and-son craftsmen work on restoring and creating some choice pieces of furniture. The family has been called upon by France's museums to restore some of the nation's premier furnishings. Should you find a battered *escritoire* or *armoire* at the Braderie or the flea market, this is the place to take your antiques. If you've brought the car, push the boat out.

GUILLAUME MOISSON 3 rue Pétérinck 📍 261 H2 📞 06 12 79 42 22 w guillaumemoisson. com 🚌 bus 9 to Lion d'Or, then rue de la Monnaie to rue Pétérinck

When I first discovered this gallery, it was known as the Atelier Un Vrai Semblance, the go-to place for a Rembrandt on a budget. In those days, people in the know would drop in to Guillaume Moisson's studio to see if he could run them up a quick Rubens or come up with a nice Cézanne for the spare bedroom. Moisson earned his living making copies of immortal artworks from the world's leading galleries. After a successful first career recreating greatness as a scenic artist for the theatre, he set up this little studio, between the rue de la Monnaie and the cathedral, where he produced copies of Caravaggios on demand for a four-figure sum (reproduction Monets from perhaps a little less). Of course, he is a talented artist in his own right and his once-secret private gallery is now the main event. Forget the past, and pop round to consider a Moisson original for your home, without a trace of faux-vism or impression of Impressionism.

HOME ENTERTAINMENT/MUSIC

For musical instruments, go to place Vieux Marché au Chevaux off place Béthune (🚌 République Beaux-Arts) where several small shops (especially RoyezMusik) sell keyboards, accordions, woodwind and brass instruments. For something to play in the park with friends on a Sunday, head down to the flea market at Wazemmes (page 176) and pick up an accordion for €60 or guitar for €25. Serious guitar collectors should visit Cosmik Guitare across the way in the Beaux Arts district.

BESIDES RECORDS 47 Rue d'Amiens 📍 262 G1 📞 03 20 95 43 55 w besides-records. tumblr.com 🕐 11.00–18.00 Tue–Fri, 11.00–19.00 Sat 🚌 Rihour; take rue Béthune to rue d'Amiens

Old-style record shop for lovers of vinyl, a clientele that now includes new-generation students who were not even born when the albums were first released, as well as a reassuringly familiar crowd in faded heavy metal t-shirts.

CARREFOUR Euralille 📍 259 H4 📞 03 20 15 56 00 🕐 09.00–22.00 Mon–Sat 🚌 Gare Lille Europe

The hypermarket at Euralille has a good department selling electrical goods, CDs and computer accessories. Their own-brand products often come with a two-year warranty. See also page 177.

COSMIK GUITARE 42 rue Caumartin ♀ 262 C2 ✆ 06 21 29 83 32 **w** cosmikguitare.com
⏱ 13.30–19.00 Mon–Fri 🚊 Gambetta; walk rue Littré to rue Brûle Maison
Qualified *luthier* Frank Bolaers makes guitars. His shop and workshop are a veritable gallery of handmade instruments he has created, from exquisite woodwork to extraordinary artworks. Prices are way, way north of €2,000, but he will tune and repair almost any workaday or classic guitar within the budget of mere mortals.

FNAC 20 rue Saint-Nicolas ♀ 261 H6 ⏱ 10.00–19.30 Mon–Sat **w** fnac.com 🚊 Rihour; on Grand' Place, walk through La Voix du Nord building
Hi-fi and photographic equipment and accessories, plus books, and assorted discs, are all available at the nation's favourite chain store and concert box office. A self-service gift-wrapping desk is located near the cashiers.

O'CD 21 rue des Tanneurs ♀ 261 H6 ✆ 03 20 40 04 62 **w** ocd.net ⏱ 14.00–19.30 Mon, 10.30–19.30 Tue–Sat, 14.45–19.30 Sun 🚊 Rihour; rue de la Vieille Comédie leads to rue des Tanneurs
This is a long-established swap shop for pre-downloadable media. Secondhand vinyl CDs and DVDs are bought and sold daily. All discs may be heard before you buy.

URBAN MUSIC Galerie Grand' Place – La Voix du Nord, 8 pl du Général de Gaulle ♀ 261 H6 ✆ 03 20 63 90 83 🚊 Rihour
On the ground floor of the Voix du Nord building, this is a proper record shop for those whose ears are strictly analogue. Everything is on vinyl, be it Motown, soul, funk, jazz, French rap or classic reggae – in fact any music of black origin. It's cheekily (or cannily) located close by mainstream music shop FNAC.

JEWELLERY

LES GEORGETTES 90 rue Esquermoise ♀ 261 G4 ✆ 03 20 12 98 14 **w** lesgeorgettes.com
🚊 Rihour; cross squares to rue Esquermoise
Les Georgettes is the new resident of the former Vieux Lille home of Brit-chic doyenne Poppy Milton. Here, leather settings for pearls, coral or precious stones and writhing wrought metalwork are combined to make truly original bracelets and earrings, with every piece available for customising to your personal style (they call it 'demandware').

LE PAGE 6–10 rue de la Bourse ♀ 261 H5 ✆ 03 20 12 04 04 **w** lepage.fr 🚊 Rihour; walk past the opera house to rue de la Bourse
A jewel box of a shop, Le Page's ornate façade is always one of the treats of the town when Christmas lights are switched on. Upstaging even the building are the watches and trinkets from Gucci, Chanel and Rolex.

1 Besides Sunday's flea market, Wazemmes' glass market hall is a midweek magnet for shoppers. 2, 3, 4 & 5 Almost anything you might want can be found at the city's markets, be it antique books, fresh produce or home décor. ▶

MARKETS

BRADERIE See below.

PLACE DU CONCERT Pl du Concert ♀ 261 H1 ⏲ 07.00–14.00 Wed, Fri & Sun 🚌 bus 50 to Lion d'Or then follow rue de la Monnaie to the marketplace

Officially known as the Marché du Vieux Lille, the food market on place du Concert is a treat in the centre of the old town. Chic and low-key, it may have none of the bustle of Wazemmes, but it's the go-to place for produce from farmers' stalls, organic specialities and some Asian spices, as well as the staples of good cuisine. It's useful for finding fabrics too. Within walking distance

CHIPS WITH EVERYTHING: THE BRADERIE, EUROPE'S BIGGEST FLEA MARKET

An institution since the dawn of the 12th century, the Braderie de Lille, an annual citywide flea market cum garage sale, is one of the highlights of the French calendar. It regularly attracts more than 2½ million visitors – ten times the local population – to mooch over 100km of pavements and browse the stalls of Europe's biggest antique and junk fair. And of course it's an excuse for a party, too.

In the early years, this was the Foire de Lille, a market for itinerant international traders to set up stall on what is now Grand' Place for two weeks in summer. But it was in the early 16th century, when a local law permitted servants to sell their employers' cast-off clothing for one night only between dusk and dawn, that centuries of flea market tradition were launched. To this day, *les lillois* still pitch tables and groundsheets outside their homes, as Parisian dealers wander from street to street in the small hours hunting for antiques and collectables.

For years, the Braderie has been held on the first weekend of September, the annual *rentrée* as France goes back to work after the long summer holidays. Over 48 hours the city buzzes as *chineurs* and *flâneurs* mooch and dither between stalls and doorsteps, while restaurants serve the single menu of *moules-frites* around the clock. An estimated 500 tonnes of seafood will be consumed over the weekend, with restaurateurs competing to build the tallest stack of mussel shells – a contest won for decades by the much-missed Aux Moules on rue Béthune (page 106).

An earlier fast-food phenomenon was launched in 1446, when Godin Maille and Pierre Tremart, two merchants from Flanders, hit upon the idea of selling freshly roasted chicken and herrings in the centre of the market square at the Foire. The Flemish word for 'roast' is *braden*, and so, they say, the word Braderie was born.

The Braderie has long reflected contemporary life, with youthful protestors during France's political upheaval in 1968; a mussels-free event from some fine restaurants, most of which are not averse to sourcing the dish of the day from these very stalls.

SEBASTOPOL Pl Sébastopol 📍 262 D2 🕐 07.00–14.00 Wed & Sat 🚇 République Beaux-Arts; rue Inkerman to market square
In the shadow of the extravagantly overdesigned theatre come cheery local traders with mainly a food market. Look out here for chicory (known in France as *endive*), the pepperiest and crunchiest accompaniment to any picnic. Dubbed *les perles du Nord*, these are the stars of the fruit and veg stalls. I have also found some stylish jewellery here on occasions and friends swear by the bag stalls as excellent value.

in 1945 when a freshly liberated nation was subject to rationing; and in the 1880s, traders dressed up in period costume to recreate the scene after the Austrian siege of the city as featured in Francois Watteau's famous painting *La Braderie de Lille en 1800*. The original work may be seen at the Musée de l'Hospice Comtesse (page 186).

Over the past two centuries, Lille's modern Braderie had only been cancelled during wartime occupation. Then, on Bastille Day 2016, a lorry drove into festive crowds in Nice, killing 86 people, and so Lille's Braderie was cancelled as France came to terms with a new wave of terrorism. The following year, Mayor Martine Aubrey and Prefect Michel Lalande worked with police and intelligence services to find a solution. It was business as usual in the heart of Lille, while the perimeter of the Braderie was far more strictly controlled than in previous years, when bric-a-brac had spilled out into residential areas far beyond the centre. With 1,000 tonnes of concrete barriers and 30 police checkpoints, the street sale returned, this time contained within the original boundaries of Vieux Lille and the city centre. The pill was sweetened with a free concert by multi-million-selling Glasgow band Texas, to bring back the festival spirit.

From the confines of Vieux Lille and the squares, the market now carries over into the Wazemmes district, rue Gambetta and the rues Douai and Arras. While shops may now offer their bargains indoors, rather than in the streets, locals from Wazemmes and Moulins have the run of the Parc Jean Lebas, and professional antique dealers pay for pitches on boulevard de la Liberté and by the Esplanande of the Champs de Mars.

Newer, specialist Braderies have been set up as well. The Palais des Beaux-Arts has hosted a comic book market and the Gare Saint-Sauveur was handed over to local children, for stallholders under the age of 14 to sell their old books and toys.

Hotels in and around the city book up well in advance (although cars are banned in the centre of town) and public transport runs all night.

VIEILLE BOURSE Secondhand books and prints; see page 200.

WAZEMMES MARKET Pl de la Nouvelle Aventure ♀ 262 A3 ⓘ flea market Sun morning; covered produce market 06.00 until late afternoon Tue–Sun 🚊 Gambetta; cross rue du Marché & walk around the church to pl de la Nouvelle Aventure

Emerge from Gambetta métro station and prepare for all your senses to be ravaged. Surrender to the pulse of the city and simply follow the crowds past puppies and chickens, rabbits and budgerigars. Around the church of St Pierre and St Paul swims a tide of humanity, past antiques, bric-a-brac and junk, and piles of clothing. On place de la Nouvelle Aventure, the adventure continues, around mounds of gloriously plump fresh chicory, rose-red radishes and tear-blushed artichokes from the market gardens of Artois and Flanders, and past puppets and playthings, smart coats and swimwear. Shop doorways are flung open on a Sunday, and cries of 'Special prices just for you Monsieur, Madame, only today from my cousin in Africa' ring out. It goes on into the red-brick market hall itself: past fresh North Sea fish on the slab and crates of seafood; past cheeses from the region and beyond; past exotic sausages and pristine plucked poultry. Through the hall is the flower market, laden with carnations and lilies, and spring blooms or Christmas wreaths.

From café doorways hear the sound of the accordion playing. An old man on a bicycle offers bunches of herbs from his panniers to passers-by and a younger biker steps off his Harley to try on a new-old leather jacket for €70. Backs are slapped, hands are shaken, noses are tapped and deals are struck. As church bells toll for mass, traders' cries mingle with the sound of a barrel organ. At the back of a lorry blocking rue des Sarrazins, gleaming saucepans are offered at never-to-be repeated prices, and in the midst of the whirlpool of the market square a salesman demonstrates his miracle wonder-broom or incredible, magical vegetable-slicing machine.

On street corners, enormous rotisseries drip juices from turning chickens on to trays of roast potatoes and vegetables, the scent of a traditional Sunday lunch competing with more exotic aromas from enormous drums of couscous and paella as a French market merges into a multi-ethnic North African souk. Follow your nose and keep your hand on your wallet. All in all, Wazemmes on a Sunday morning is an unforgettable experience for bargain hunters and browsers alike.

PHARMACIES/CHEMISTS

See page 27.

SUPERMARKETS/DEPARTMENT STORES

The big names in retail continue their gobal domination. Shopping malls all have their own hypermarkets: there's **Carrefour** in Westfield Euralille, **E.Leclerc** in the new Lillennium complex and even Les Tanneurs has a **Monoprix**. Corner shop-style, 7-days-a-week mini versions of the big store brands – including **Monop'** and the most prolific **Carrefour Extra** or **Carrefour City** – now fill the city and you are rarely more than 5 minutes from a grocery shop for essentials. Until recently, Leader Price and Franprix (essentially Leader Price with posher lighting) were French domestic discounters to rival Lidl and Aldi, but corporate gulping mean they have now virtually gone as more and more sites have beem taken over by Monop', Carrefour Extra or **G20** (which reads like a global summit, but sounds like '*j'ai vin*', or 'I have wine', which better grabs your attention).

CARREFOUR Euralille ♀ 259 H4 ☎ 03 28 52 99 79 ⏱ 09.00–22.00 Mon–Sat, 09.00–12.30 Sun 🚉 Gare Lille Europe
This massive hypermarket is the place for stocking up before catching the train home. In fact the branch is so big that staff are able to use roller skates to whizz between the checkouts and aisles. A logo featuring a belfry and a heart denotes local produce, and the store sells a good selection of ales and prepared foods from the region, plus a large range of fresh halal meats. For free parking in Euralille car park, get your ticket stamped at the checkout.

E.LECLERC In Lillenium; see page 178.

MATCH Halles Centrales, 97 rue Solférino ♀ 260 D7 ☎ 03 20 57 71 45 w supermarchesmatch. fr ⏱ 08.00–20.00 Mon–Sat, 08.30–12.45 Sun 🚉 République Beaux-Arts; rue Gambetta to rue Solférino
Match has the best ever setting for a supermarket: the old iron-and-glass structure of Lille's former wholesale food market in the heart of the party district (page 152). An in-store bakery produces decent breads all day long (loaves hot from the oven, or cooler and sliced to order), and there's a fair range of general groceries – including a surprising variety of gluten- and sugar-free options. Students can sign up for a 10% discount on their shopping.

MONOPRIX Les Tanneurs shopping centre, 80 rue Piere Mauroy ♀ 261 H7 ☎ 03 28 82 92 20 ⏱ 08.30–20.30 Mon–Sat 🚉 Gare Lille Flandres or bus L5 to Tanneurs
Since moving from its larger home on rue Molinel, this modest supermarket has provided some solace to the town-centre workers who still mourn the passing of the Marks & Spencer food hall up

the road. There's a good grocery section on the lower level, even a mini kosher counter. Upstairs, find a limited range of clothes and household wares. If the little lift from street level is out of order, mobility-restricted shoppers should use the entrance on rue des Tanneurs, and get staff to call the in-store lift back down to grocery level.

PRINTEMPS   41–45 rue Nationale ♀ 261 H5 ☏ 03 20 63 62 00 ⏱ 09.30–19.30 Tue–Thu & Sat, 09.30–20.00 Fri ☗ Rihour; the rear entrance to the store is behind Palais Rihour
This branch of the famous Parisian department store is the place to come for fashion, classy luggage and decent tableware, with many high-end global labels from across Lille all under one roof. Most hotels give out a free city map published by the store, often featuring a voucher for up to 15% off your first big shop. If buying big, consider the tax rebate scheme (page 50) offered at the customer service desk. Car park beneath the store.

UNDER ONE ROOF

LE 31   31 rue de Béthune ♀ 261 H6 w Le31Lille.fr ☗ Rihour or République Beaux-Arts
What can replace a flagship department store? When Galeries Lafayette left the centre of town, no single business could have filled all those empty shopping floors. So welcome Le 31. The top storeys have been taken over by the Okko Hotel (page 77) complete with its own business centre and club. Climb yet higher and you'll get to another co-working space, WoJo, boasting a networking roof terrace. Back down at street level, work off stress at the Fitness Park gym, the Climb Up climbing wall or one of Team Break's immersive game experiences, from escape rooms to virtual TV quiz shows. Other exercise is catered for with a branch of Decathlon sportswear, while Le 31's main shopfront targets GenZ (and some borderline Millennials), who have their own retail space known as Citadium. This either speaks to you directly or it makes you feel very old indeed. On-trend labels, yoof accessories and lots of trainers are served amid street art, a nail bar and gaming diversions. Next door, looking like a classic cinema foyer, is Grand Scène (page 127), the food court for chef startups. The centre also has its own subscriber car park, with an entrance at 6 Rue de la Rivierette (w indigoneo.fr).

LILLENIUM   2 rue du Faubourg des Postes ♀ 262 B5 ☏ 03 20 54 10 12
w lillenium-lille.com ⏱ 10.00–20.00 Mon–Sat; Leclerc 08.30–20.30 Mon–Sat, 08.30–12.30 Sun; restaurants from 09.00 Mon–Sun ☗ Porte des Postes; follow pedestrian signs to avoid the traffic!
If it wasn't on the inside of the motorway ring road loop that surrounds the city, you'd call this the 'out-of-town mall'. It still has the air of a shopping centre that prefers its punters to drive rather than take public transport – 90 minutes of free parking is offered by the shops, yet it is less than 20 minutes away by métro. Lillenium has the usual lures of Wi-Fi, phone charging and loyalty cards, plus a big, bright and airy gym too. There's also enough space for a good programme of pop-up attractions. In early 2024, an immersive wizarding experience blended the worlds of *Harry Potter*, *Game of Thrones* and *Lord of the Rings* for the Instagram-canny set, and ice hockey classes filled the void when the magic vanished. High-street names include Darty, H&M, Diechmann, Yves Rocher and New Yorker, but the main attraction is an E.Leclerc hypermarket.

LES TANNEURS 14 rue Pierre Mauroy, 17 rue du Sec Arembault 📞 03 20 54 10 12 📍 261 J6 w lestanneurs.com ⏱ 10.00–19.30 Mon–Sat; Kitchen Market 10.00–22.00 Mon–Sat, 10.00–15.00 Sun 🚊 Rihour; rue de Béthune to rue des Tanneurs

This modest shopping mall in the heart of the outdoor pedestrian zone has proved a good duck-in-and-escape option whenever the heavens open. As shopping centres go, it's a manageable and undaunting size; its initial attraction for me was the clusters of very comfy armchairs for much needed mid-spree recuperation. And even now, the smartphone charging station remains an afternoon lifesaver. There is something remarkably decadent and exhibitionist about relaxing in soft furnishings in a public thoroughfare. The car park entrance is on rue Molinel, or you can walk in from the three shopping streets. There are some homeware stores and toyshops, with goods ranging from Barbie Lego and Playmobil plastics to handmade wooden delights, though the principal sirens remain C&A and Monoprix (page 177). These days, however, it's less about the shopping: the main attraction is the fantastic Kitchen Market food court (page 127).

WESTFIELD EURALILLE Av le Corbusier 📍 259 H4 📞 03 20 14 52 20 (Euralille), 03 20 13 50 00 (Aeronef) w westfield.com ⏱ 09.30–20.00 Mon–Sat 🚊 Gare Lille Europe or Gare Lille Flandres; cross the parvis François Mitterrand

Between the two railway stations (and still called Euralille) is one of France's biggest shopping centres. With new floors, lighting and a general make-over in the run up to joining the Westfield stable, the mall of malls remains a key player in Lille. Hardcore consumers may squeak with excitement at a massive Carrefour hypermarket (page 177) and specialist shops such as the temple to new-age consumerism, Nature et Découvertes (page 170). There's also the best of the high street, with clothing and homeware brands, a brace of hairdressing salons, and lots of eating options between the street and the supermarket. Personally, I mourn the sheer audacity of the pet superstore that once advertised the special offer '15 caged birds for the price of 12', either the zenith or nadir of promotional hype.

Exhibitions and displays in the centre have ranged from taxidermy tableaux of zebra and rhino on loan from the Natural History Museum, through the throne from *Game of Thrones* (during a SeriesMania convention) to a free circus with high wires and trapeze acts above the heads of bemused shoppers. Ask at the reception desk for a loyalty card for access to the otherwise expensive posh loos and discounted deals at many stores. There are plenty of opportunities to sit down, charge your phone, plug in the laptop and check your socials between bouts of spending. But the building is more than merely 140 shops spread over two storeys of consumerism, with dining or refuelling options at parvis level. Beyond Westfield are office units, hotel rooms and serviced short-stay apartments hidden behind smoked glass. Even the originally underground nightclub L'Aeronef is now an establishment venue several levels above ground, with a programme of cutting-edge rock music and bad-taste film festivals. Together with Christian de Portzampac's 'ski-boot' Tour Crédit Lyonnais balanced over Lille Europe station and Rem Koolhaas's own Grand Palais exhibition centre and concert venue, Euralille is testament to Koolhaas's concept of 21st-century living, Lille's remarkable civic optimism and Mayor Mauroy's belief in the Eurostar dream. Arguably it's paid off. Outside, the parvis François Mitterrand has been colonised by the e-scooter and rollerblade fraternity. A statue of President Mitterrand waves passengers on their high-speed way, a gigantic bunch of tulips is a cheery legacy of Lille2004 and the recently ripened Parc Matisse offers a comfortable walk towards Vieux Lille.

Shopping   **UNDER ONE ROOF**

9

10

Walking Tour

This favourite walk takes in the 'best of…' and is the perfect appetiser to an indulgent weekend. Straight from the Eurostar station, it meanders through the three central squares, along the cobbles of the historic old town, and finishes in the wide open space of the largest park and woodlands in the city.

It also brings you within a lip's smack of the most delicious little food stores in town, so bring a basket and shop for a picnic (following our suggestions on page 21) to round off the hike and build up your strength for the return walk to your hotel. Another gastronomic subtext of my preferred saunter is that it takes you past many of the best restaurants in town, so you may always whip out your phone and photograph the menu for later!

Although the circuit is perfectly manageable within an hour for those who prefer a brisk constitutional, I recommend allowing 2–3 hours and taking your time. Every other shop window is a digression in waiting and so many old buildings deserve a more leisurely appreciation.

Note: If you would rather not start at the station, you could always pick up the trail at Grand' Place or place du Théâtre.

THE WALK *Map, page 258*

From Gare Lille Europe, step down to parvis François Mitterrand, with its giant tulips. To your right is **Parc Matisse** (page 218) and the **Porte de Roubaix** (page 199); to your left **Euralille** (page 179). Head towards the Gare Lille Flandres and perhaps check out an exhibition at **Le TriPostal** (page 207). At the place de la Gare, bear right along the rue Faidherbe towards the place du Théâtre, the belfry and the opera house (page 197).

Step inside the **Vieille Bourse** (page 200) and savour the timeless atmosphere of this unique enclave, then come out on to place du Général de Gaulle, or Grand' Place (page 195). The central square of Lille, its many façades reflect the city's varied and dazzling history. Spot gilded suns atop

1 Place aux Oignons was once the keep of the city's original fortress. 2 The pont de la Citadelle leads to the bucolic Bois de Boulogne. ▶

public buildings, symbol of Louis XIV, and admire the central fountain and **La Déesse** (page 195).

Pass the archway inscribed with the name of Brasserie Alcide, and instead follow rue de la Bourse, with its 17th-century houses adorned with images of innocence and corruption, to rue de la Grande Chaussée. Follow the pointing arm above the first shopfront to direct you along the cobbled street now lined with designer names, but once where d'Artagnan lived (page 191) in the house that spans numbers 22 and 24. Pause at the spectacular Art Deco mosaic shopfront of À l'Huîtrière, former seafood restaurant and current Louis Vuitton flagship (page 106), and step inside just to admire the 1928 décor. Next, follow rue des Chats Bossus to place du Lion d'Or and walk down to 29 place Louise de Bettignies to admire the Baroque façade of the Demeure Gilles de la Boë. (You won't find any trace of Louise here, that is another trail entirely; page 216.) You may always trot down towards rue de Gand for some menu fantasising, but there's still plenty to see back in the oldest street in town.

So, turn back to place du Lion d'Or and walk along Lille's first commercial centre, rue de la Monnaie, with original shop signs above doors denoting early merchants' trades. Stop at the **Musée de l'Hospice Comtesse** (page 186) then turn left into rue Pétérinck, where 18th-century weavers' houses have now become very fashionable artists' studios, boutiques and eateries. This road leads to place aux Oignons, which may seem an appropriate name in light of the many small delicatessens in the area but is actually a corrupt spelling of the word *donjon* (dungeon). For here was the keep of the original fortress on marshland that was the city's cradle.

Having explored all the treats on offer in place aux Oignons and its tributaries, take the little alleyway that leads to place Gilleson, and climb the steps to the side entrance of **Notre Dame de la Treille** (page 206). Walk through the magnificent church and leave by its brand new doors. Turn left into rue du Cirque, stopping at any little art or antique shop that takes your fancy. Turn right on to rue Basse and take a sharp left into rue Lepelletier, at a tiny little bakery with leaded-glass windows reading '*A Notre Dame de* *la Treille'*. This is now a branch of the ubiquitous Paul (page 133), and if you have not already succumbed to the gastronomic temptations on the walk thus far, grab a pastry or bread to sustain you for the rest of the trek!

By now you may have got hopelessly lost thanks to the sirens of so many boutiques and antique shops nudging into your peripheral vision, and the fact that none of these streets follow any geometric rules. But if you are sticking closely to the map, you should be able to take the first turning on the right, rue du Curé Saint-Étienne, to lead you to rue Esquermoise (and further enticements of Méert's tea rooms and Celestin microbrewery!).

Just across rue Esquermoise is rue Saint-Étienne, a narrow street that takes you past the town's major Renaissance façade, encased behind a plate glass wall at number 4 and a former staging post on the Santiago de Compostela pilgrim's route from the Low Countries to Spain.

At place Mendès France, with the undistinguished circular Nouveau Siècle building (page 143), turn a sharp left into rue de Pas, crossing the bustling rue Nationale into rue J Roisin. This leads you to place Rihour (page 196) and the tourist office and remains of the Burgundian ducal **Palais Rihour** (page 194). It's worth a dawdle if brasserie-menu browsing or enjoying stalls at the Christmas market; otherwise, continue past the palace along rue du Palais Rihour and turn right on rue de l'Hôpital Militaire.

Cross rue Nationale once more to turn left along the thoroughfare until you come to square Foch with its statue of **P'tit Quinquin** (page 199). Walk through well-maintained gardens, where you may appreciate other statues including a bust of Maréchal Foch or the saucier Suzanne at her bath. Keep on through the leafy squares (the next garden is called square du Tilleul) until the road opens up to a canal basin, and stroll along quai du Wault, admiring swans before emerging on to square Daubenton. Look across at the charming and elegant **Jardin Vauban** (page 215), with its puppet theatre and manicured pathways. Opposite you, across the pont de la Citadelle, is the **Bois de Boulogne** (page 215), a perfect place to relax with a picnic. Afterwards, decide whether to stay in the park, walk around the fortifications or perhaps drop by the zoo (page 215). Then hop on the L1 or L5 bus or stroll back to the centre.

Museums and Sightseeing

PRICES AND OPENING HOURS

Most museums charge admission. Prices listed below are the full adult rate. You will usually find discounted rates for children, seniors, students, visitors with disabilities etc. Holders of the Lille City Pass (page 60) get free entry at many museums and sites, together with unlimited public transport in the metropolitan area. Several places do not charge for admission on the first Sunday of the month (check museum or tourist office websites). Prices are usually for the permanent collection; a supplement is often charged for special temporary exhibitions (check online). National museums close on Tuesdays and local museums on Mondays. Most places close on December 25, January 1 and May 1. See *Chapter 12* for details of excellent collections mostly located just a bus, métro, train or tram ride out of town. In May, some museums stay open until midnight or beyond on the Nuit des Musées (page 14).

Double check **opening hours**. Since no hours are set in stone, before setting out on a dedicated mission to any one specific museum, always phone ahead or go online just to be sure.

THE UNMISSABLES

PALAIS DES BEAUX-ARTS Fine Arts Museum; pl de la République ♀ 262 F2 ╲ 03 20 06 78 28 w pba-lille.fr ⏲ 14.00–18.00 Mon, 10.00–18.00 Wed–Sun, closed Tue & pub hols 🚊 République Beaux-Arts 🥏 €7 (free admission 1st Sun of the month; always free access to atrium & the town models)

For years, in a modest office tucked away behind the magnificent splendour of the museum, the original curator Arnaud Brejon de Lavergnée (now retired) pondered over the Palais des Beaux-Arts's many treasures. France's second museum after the Louvre has Goyas, Rubens, Picassos, Lautrecs and Monets, but the greatest treasure of them all was Brejon de Lavergnée himself, self-effacing overlord of the museum's reinvention. The passions of this modest and unassuming art lover are as much a part of this fabulous palace as the rich red walls, the floppy chairs, and the catalogue of some of the world's greatest artworks. During the building's renovation, Monsieur Brejon de Lavergnée could be seen at the station platform, clutching bubble-wrapped masterpieces to his chest as he personally escorted the Palais's jewels to be restored at the National Gallery in London. Until the day in 1997 that President Chirac inaugurated the new museum, every picture, every frame and every detail came under his exacting scrutiny. Monsieur Brejon has since handed over the reins to Alain Tapié, who in turn passed on the responsibility to current curator Bruno Girveau, but he long continued leading privileged visitors around the museum. On the eve of a legendary Rubens exhibition, I left my allotted tour group to tag along behind the master as Monsieur Brejon laid bare the genius of the artist to a privileged party including Prince Jean of France aka the Duke of Orléans, banker, philosopher, MBA, erstwhile footballer and Dauphin and pretender to the throne of France.

The breathtaking art collection was brought to Lille on the orders of Napoleon, who stripped the walls of palaces and private galleries throughout his European empire, from Italy to the Low Countries. The plan paid off: what had been a pleasure for the cultured few is now a cherished symbol of civic pride, and was the triumph that awoke the world to the news that Lille had achieved greatness.

Today's visitors take one of the twin grand staircases adorned with leaded windows heralding the *arts et métiers* of Lille to the first floor, where room after room offers French, Flemish and European masterpieces from the 17th to the 19th centuries. Highlights include Rubens's *Descente de la Croix*, an entire room devoted to Jordaens, and a succession of high-ceilinged galleries housing the works of Van Dyck, Corot and Delacroix with Watteau, *père et fils*, the collection's first curators. Best of all is the celebrated pair of Goyas, *Les Jeunes* and *Les Vieilles*, the former a timeless portrayal of a teenage crush, as relevant to the TikTok generation as to its own time, and the latter a cruelly satirical dissection of old age: crones at one with their malevolence. With so many riches, it is easy to skip past a corridor devoted to the Impressionists. Make time for Monet, Van Gogh, Renoir and Sisley, not to mention Lautrec and Rodin's *Burghers of Calais*.

Back on the ground floor, the sculpture gallery includes the best of 19th-century classical statuary, some imperial, some disturbing. From here, the collection leads to the rear courtyard and a remarkable modern prism comprising the glass-fronted administration block and a sheet of water that turns the grey skies of the north into pure natural light to illuminate the basement galleries – a good halfway refreshment point for your visit.

The underground rooms should not be missed. A Renaissance room includes Donatello's bas-relief *Festin d'Herod*, and many sketches by Raphaël. It also houses 19 of Vauban's detailed models of his fortified towns – among them Lille and Calais – frozen in time and space between sheets of glass in an otherwise blacked-out exhibition of the landscape of 18th-century France and Flanders.

The catalogue of treasures on every floor could never leave anybody feeling short-changed. In his day, anyone lucky enough to come across Monsieur Brejon de Lavergnée escorting his guests around the gallery, his infectious enthusiasm drawing total strangers to his enlightening discourse on a favourite painting, well, that was a bonus beyond price. Happily, there are still some genuine enthusiasts entertaining groups in corners and galleries. The bright and airy foyer is open to the public as a meeting place or coffee stop – admission free.

LOUVRE-LENS See page 238. It's well worth the train journey to visit the only Louvre outside Paris, an amazing 21st-century museum in its own right.

MUSÉE DE L'HOSPICE COMTESSE Art and History Museum; 32 rue de la Monnaie
📍 261 J2 📞 03 28 36 84 00 w mhc.lille.fr ⏱ 14.00–18.00 Mon, 10.00–18.00 Wed–Sun, closed hols 🚌 bus 9 to Lion d'Or 💶 €3.70; joint tickets also available with Palais des Beaux-Arts

I love the stillness of the old hospital ward, with its boatbuilder-vaulted ceiling. This most tranquil of sanctuaries is a season apart, even from the rest of the historic quarter. Tucked away behind the shops and archways of the oldest street in town, the former 13th-century hospital captures the life and talents of another Lille in another time. The city's benefactress Jeanne de Constantinople, Countess of Flanders, built the hospice for the needy in 1237, a charitable gesture that has echoed down the centuries in a city that nurtures the ideals of civic responsibilities. After all, the celebrated annual Braderie (page 174) was born of a sense of *noblesse oblige*, with servants granted the right to sell their masters' clothes in these very streets. Once both hospital and convent, the site has been restored as a museum of local arts and crafts. Outside is a medicinal herb garden; within, find an eclectic collection of carved furniture, rare musical instruments, domestic tableaux and wooden panels adorned with paintings of local children. The art collection includes paintings by Flemish and northern French masters, among them Louis and François Watteau, as well as tapestries by Lille's famous weaver Guillaume Werniers. The kitchen is typically decorated with the traditional blue-and-white tiles of the Low Countries, and vestiges of original murals may be seen in the 17th-century convent chapel. The chapel, 15th-century ward and other buildings around the central courtyard are favourite locations for informal concerts and intimate musical recitals. Guided tours are available at no extra charge most afternoons.

LA PISCINE See page 222. A truly remarkable building that very nearly upstages Roubaix's remarkable art collection.

LAM See page 229. This modern art museum features works by Picasso, Braque, Modigliani and much, much more – you won't regret the métro ride out of town.

MUSEUMS AND GALLERIES

CENTRE DE L'ART SACRÉ Within the Cathédrale Notre Dame de la Treille (page 206).

INSTITUT DU MONDE ARABE See page 227. The celebrated Paris Museum has set up home in neighbouring Tourcoing.

MUSÉE DES CANONNIERS SEDENTAIRES DE LILLE Army Museum; 44 rue des Canonniers ♀ 259 H3 ☎ 03 20 55 58 90 ⏰ 14.00–17.00 Mon–Sat, closed hols (1st 3 weeks of Aug & 15 Dec–2 Feb) 🚉 Gare Lille Flandres; cross Parc Matisse & pass through Porte de Roubaix to rue de Roubaix, then right into rue des Canonniers & 2nd right into rue des Urbanistes 💶 €5

It's fitting that a garrison town should have a museum of military hardware, and over 3,000 weapons, documents and maps from 1777 to 1945 are on display in the former Urbanistes convent. The stars of the show are the magnificent cannons, most notably the Gribeauval – the Big Bertha of its day. Despite the postal address, the public entrance is on rue des Urbanistes.

MUSÉE D'HISTOIRE NATURELLE Natural History Museum; 23 rue Gosselet ♀ 262 G5 🌐 mhn.lille.fr ⏰ check tourist office for opening date, times & updated address 🚉 République Beaux-Arts or bus 14 from Gare Lille Flandres to Jeanne d'Arc

This was always my favourite time warp, even if sometimes more for the rooms than the collections. I felt as though I had entered a Victorian draper's shop with a nice line in sabre-toothed tigers. A typical 19th-century museum, with glass cases, iron walkways and spiral staircases, this very old-fashioned throwback to the days of hands-off musty scholarship was an anachronism in a city that prided itself on cutting-edge exhibitions. There is something comfortingly nostalgic about whale skeletons suspended from the ceiling, irresistibly camp tableaux of stuffed birds and animals and studiously catalogued trays of geological specimens and fossils. Having long remained a temple to incongruity, the site is now undergoing a seven-year rebuilding project that's swallowed up all the other public buildings on the block. The pandemic era saw the creation of a new wing to give the museum a main entrance on a main road (it had previously been a back-street affair in the heart of academia); once university administrative offices, the new space has amazing murals showing the region's geological history along the main staircase. A splendid courtyard garden with glazed walkways filling the museum with light is planned to unite old and new, and an innovative museum for the under-threes, where play is education, is on the to-do list. The great news is that even when several years of renovation and reinvention

11

are completed (within the lifespan of this guide), the main Victorian gallery will be preserved as it was. Even if the front door has moved around the block.

MUSÉE DE L'HOSPICE COMTESSE See page 186.

MUSÉE DE L'INSTITUT PASTEUR Pasteur Institute Museum; 8 bd Louis XIV ♀ 259 H8
☎ 03 20 87 72 42 w pasteur-lille.fr/fondation/musee ⏱ 10.00–noon & 14.00–17.00 Sat–Sun
🚇 Lille Grand Palais; take bd Vaillant to bd Louis XIV 🎟 €6
Previously only open by appointment, and now a few doors along the street, this museum celebrates the life and work of Louis Pasteur and his successors. Probably not on the unmissable list of Covid deniers, antivaxxers and conspiracy theorists, this museum is more than homage to Pasteur, pioneer of pasteurisation and also the first dean of Lille University's faculty of sciences. It celebrates other great scientists and researchers whose pioneering work transformed modern medicine. This includes Pasteur's own successor at the Institute, immunisation professor Albert Calmette, who, together with veterinarian Camille Guérin, saved lives and bruised the shoulders of millions with the creation of the BCG vaccine against tuberculosis. It is in his apartment that the collection is now housed. While early displays are fascinating, the museum is more than just a Victorian cabinet of curiosities – it also looks at today's technology and the continuing work of the Institute through the eras of AIDS and Covid.

MAISON DE L'ARCHITECTURE ET DE LA VILLE Urban Architecture Centre; pl François
Mitterrand ♀ 259 H4 ☎ 03 20 14 61 15 w waao.fr ⏱ 10.00–12.30 & 14.00–17.30 Tue–Fri
(exhibition & festival dates vary) 🚇 Gare Lille Europe; cross the piazza below the station, entrance
is under the viaduct 🎟 free
A legacy of 2004 Capital of Culture festivities, this gallery devoted to urban architecture is slap bang in the heart of the Euralille district, underneath – almost propping up – the concrete viaduct avenue le Corbusier. Not merely a showcase for town planning, the venue plays a key role in city festivals and hosts workshops and talks on architecture past and present across the region. Slightly more offbeat are special dinners when chefs and architects work together to illustrate design concepts on a plate.

MAISON NATALE DU GÉNÉRAL DE GAULLE Général de Gaulle's birthplace; 9 rue
Princesse ♀ 261 G1 ☎ 03 59 73 00 30 w maisondegaulle.fr ⏱ 10.00–18.00 Wed–Sun 🚇 bus 5 to
Les Bataliers, then av Peuple Belge to rue Jemmapes & cour Boisseau to rue Princesse 🎟 €6
War hero, statesman and Europe's most celebrated Anglo-sceptic, Charles de Gaulle was born here, in his grandmother's house, on 22 November 1890,

Museums and Sightseeing MUSEUMS AND GALLERIES

◀ 1 The Palais des Beaux-Arts is filled with artistic masterpieces. 2 Original murals adorn the 17th-century convent chapel of the Musée de l'Hospice Comtesse. 3 Charles de Gaulle's birthplace is now a fascinating museum dedicated to the statesman.

opposite Église St André where the once and future president was baptised (see his christening robes in the museum). The exhibition tells the story of the first president of the Fifth Republic with lesser-known tales from his early life, and documents his refusal to accept Marshal Pétain's 1940 truce with Nazi Germany, rallying the Free French army with his historic broadcast from London that same year. Dramatic episodes are well illustrated, and exhibitions have included the very Citroën DS in which the president was travelling outside Paris when he survived an assassin's bullet. Last admission is 1 hour before the museum closes. The Navette Vieux Lille passes close by, otherwise it's a long walk on the cobbles to the far side of the quarter. To make the walk more productive, you can follow two itineraries in the footsteps of the great man, marked with embossed bronzes in the pavement; maps are available from the museum. It's an old house, so wheelchair users are advised to call in advance to see how much of the museum would be accessible. The usual high-security measures at all French public buildings and museums are even higher here. Expect bag searches.

PALAIS DES BEAUX-ARTS See page 184.

MUSÉE DES ÉCOLES Old School Museum; 2 rue Frédéric Mottez 259 G7 06 64 44 53 02 Lille Grand Palais €4

Step back in time to schooldays between the wars. Housed in the former 19th-century école Ruault-Récamier, Lille's museum of school life is a fascinating taste of the past. Historians and scholars may appreciate thousands of original books, maps posters and impedimenta of discipline, but most visitors will simply want to sit at the old wooden desks. On the first Saturday afternoon of the month (and first Tuesday of half term), from 14.00, a costumed schoolmaster gives a dictation class, and volunteer pupils must scratch away with quill and ink – strictly for those whose French is up to it. Class is followed by a traditional *goûter* snack!

MUSÉE DE L'ILLUSION Museum of Illusions; 101 av le Corbusier 259 K6 03 28 82 04 63 w museedelillusion.fr Gare Lille Europe; between the two stations, opposite Euralille €19 (children/family discounts available)

A fairground hall of mirrors for the digital age. From traditional geometric optical illusions to virtual reality, tease and taunt perception and perspective in the ultimate participative experience.

SITES AND MONUMENTS

CITADELLE Av du 43ème Régiment d'Infanterie 260 B1 bus L5 to Champ de Mars €7 (advance reservation essential, guided tours only on selected dates in summer)

A town in its own right, France's Queen of Citadels was the greatest fortress of the reign of Louis XIV. When the Sun King commissioned the great military architect Sébastien Le Prestre de Vauban to protect his kingdom with a ring of 100 fortified towns, this imposing and impenetrable, pentagonal, star-shaped Citadelle was hailed as the masterpiece of the world's finest military engineer. Built by 400 men in just three years using 16 million newly baked bricks, the garrison opened in 1670 as home to 1,200 soldiers. Some 350 years on, it is base to 450 allied NATO soldiers from the French army's most powerful deployable operational unit, the Corps de Réaction Rapide-France.

In April, 14 of the 28 northern fortresses hold an open day; otherwise, the public are permitted to tour the site only on summer Sunday guided tours organised by the tourist office. Visitors are expected to behave themselves. When a couple of schoolchildren sat on the parade-ground rostrum, the young soldier of the 43ème Régiment accompanying our group was confined to barracks, a sharp reminder that this is no museum, but a working garrison. Its five-sided design is as effective a security measure today as it was in the 17th century – and is said to have inspired the US Pentagon. Soil banks the ramparts to absorb artillery shells, and the main walls are 4m thick. The principal entrance, Porte Royale, was built at an angle to the drawbridge to avoid direct hits. This gateway, facing the old quarter of Lille, was a major strategic and symbolic feature with regal motifs and Latin mottos representing the king himself. In the centre of the pentagonal parade ground is a ship's mast, a reminder that the fortress was built along the banks of a river and was originally protected by the navy. Soldiers stationed here today still wear naval badges. Around the parade ground are renovated barracks, an arsenal, chapel and officers' quarters. Check the walls within and outside for memorial plaques. The king, a regular visitor, appointed Vauban as the first governor of the Citadelle. His successor, Charles, Comte d'Artagnan (best known as hero of Dumas's *Three Musketeers*), died in 1673. The original governor's residence is no more, but traces of the gubernatorial doorway may still be found in the chapel. Vauban's original models for the fortified towns of the north are displayed at the Palais des Beaux-Arts (page 184). The rest of the Vauban collection is housed at Les Invalides in Paris.

LA DÉESSE See page 195.

L'HERMITAGE GANTOIS See page 72.

BELFRY OF THE HÔTEL DE VILLE Town Hall; pl Roger Salengro ♀ 259 G7
📞 03 20 49 50 00 🕐 11.00–13.00 & 14.00–17.30 Tue–Sun 💰 €7.50 (free 1st Wed of the month) 🚇 Mairie de Lille

Although the Christmas Ferris wheel on Grand' Place offers the best view in town, there is a summer alternative. From April to September (check with the tourist office first), take a detour from the historic and shopping quarters and climb to the top of the 104m belfry of the town hall (after the first 109 steps a lift may take you the rest of the way). Like a fairy tale suitor, you will need to ring the bell at the large wooden door at the foot of the tower on place Simon Vollant. Completed in 1932, the UNESCO-listed tower crowned Emile Dubuisson's striking Hôtel de Ville, which replaced the original Gothic Palais Rihour building with a ferro-concrete tribute to the gabled houses of Flanders. It's more than merely a nice place to enjoy a pleasant view: in 1950 the top of the tower became Télé-Lille, the first regional television studio. Holding up the tower are the figures of giants Lydéric and Phinaert, the Romulus and Remus or Sirius Black and Voldemort of Lille. Lydéric was raised by wild deer and a hermit after his family was killed by the tyrant Phinaert. On 15 June 605, the two fought; Lydéric was victorious and founded the town. The history of Lille is told in a huge comic-strip fresco inside the building, painted by the Icelandic artist Erro. The building was constructed over the ruins of the original working-class quarter of Saint-Sauveur where, in the long-demolished bar La Liberté, local wood-turner Pierre Degeyter composed and played the music for Eugène Pottier's socialist anthem *L'Internationale* for the very first time in 1888. The address is named for Roger Salengro, another of Lille's native socialist mayors and government minister between the wars. He had been taken prisoner of war in 1915 after being captured attempting to rescue a colleague's body from no man's land. However, his war record and patriotism were called into question during a malicious slur campaign by his political enemies on the far right, and he was eventually hounded and consequently committed suicide in 1936. Before the Théâtre du Nord opened on Grand' Place, the building had been known as the Salle Salengro.

MAISON COILLIOT 14 rue de Fleurus ♀ 262 E4 🚇 République Beaux-Arts; take rue Nicolas Leblanc to pl Lebon on to rue de Fleurus
All the houses around the Church of St Michel are identical. All but one, that is. If 14 rue Fleurus looks more like a Paris métro station than a private home, then thanks are due to its original owner, Monsieur Coilliot, a ceramics maker who commissioned Hector Guimard to redesign his house. Guimard's celebrated Art Nouveau flourishes – dark green swirls and horticultural sweeps – are the hallmark of the capital's subway system. His reinvention of the domestic townhouse is no less flamboyant, using Coilliot's own ceramics alongside cast iron and volcanic rock. These remarkable windows, balconies, gables and even a suggestion of a pagoda on the roof are worth a modest detour when trekking between local museums, for although still a private address, the house was so designed that the interiors appear open to the street.

1 Built in the 17th century, Lille's Citadelle is still a working garrison. 2 Rarely open to the public, the grand hall of the Chambre de Commerce et d'Industrie on place du Théâtre. ▶

MÉMORIAL DE LA RÉSISTANCE DE NOBLE TOUR Resistance Memorial; rue des
déportés ♀ 259 H7 ⏰ Apr–Nov 15.00–17.00 Sun 🚇 Lille Grand Palais

The least-known memorial to the unsung martyrs of the Resistance, the Noble Tower hides an urn containing ashes of prisoners deported and cremated in concentration camps. The names of the camps are inscribed on the urn's bronze cover. The 14m-wide circular tower was built in 1402 in the Burgundy reign of Philippe le Bon, and its 3m-thick walls were restored by Vauban after Louis XIV's siege destroyed most of the building. All that remains is the crypt. Check with tourist office for open days.

MONUMENT AUX VICTIMES DES 18 PONTS Monument to the Victims of the 18
Ponts Explosion; rue de Maubeuge ♀ 262 F5 🚇 Porte de Douai, then bus L1 to rue Valenciennes

One of the most dramatic wartime memorials in Lille does not commemorate military action, but a tragic wartime accident at 03.00 on 11 January 1916, killing 134 (mostly civilians) and destroying 21 factories and 738 houses. It was no air raid, but an explosion in a munitions factory that lit up the night sky between Lille and Holland. Pause here awhile between the métro and your hotel or restaurant.

PALAIS RIHOUR Pl Rihour ♀ 261 G6 ⏰ by appointment with tourist office 🚇 Rihour

To many, this old building behind the monumental war memorial is merely a rather quaint tourist office. I've even heard some visitors dismiss the Gothic arches and mullioned windows as a Victorian folly. Heresy. Cross the threshold and you are standing in the remains of a ducal palace, seat of power in Lille for over 450 years and boasting an A-list guest list that has included England's Henry VIII and France's Louis XV. The original Palais Rihour was built by Philippe le Bon, Duke of Burgundy, when he moved the court to the city in 1453. His son Charles le Téméraire completed the palace 20 years later. It was through the Burgundian line that Lille passed to the Hapsburgs when Marie de Bourgogne married Maximilien of Austria in 1474. When Philip IV of Spain sold the palace to the city in the 17th century, it began a new life as the town hall and continued to serve the community until ravaged by fire in 1916. The stairwell and chapels, among the finest surviving examples of flamboyant Gothic architecture in town, could hardly house a city's local government, so a new Hôtel de Ville was built in Saint-Sauveur (page 191). The ground-floor guards' chapel serves as the city's main tourist office. Climb winding stairs to an upper chapel to admire trefoil windows and a vaulted ceiling. Burgundian coats of arms adorn the walls, and a real sense of the original palace remains. Exhibitions, events and concerts are sometimes held here, including the international media launch for Bradt's very first guide to Lille, providing the perfect opportunity to sneak a peek at an oft-overlooked monument. Do take time to admire the beautifully restored glass of the sacristy.

Named after Lille's most famous son, but still known to everyone simply as Grand' Place, the main square is the very heartbeat of the city. Almost pedestrianised, with a serpentine trail of traffic that slithers slowly and safely along two sides, this is a veritable forum where shoppers break their day, friends plot an evening and revellers celebrate the night.

The essential rendezvous is the central fountain around the column of **La Déesse**, the goddess and symbol of the spirit of the city. The statue commemorates the bravery of the townsfolk who withstood the siege of Lille by 35,000 Austrian soldiers in 1792. The original idea, mooted the day after the victory, was to build a monument by melting down all royal statues (the Revolution was at its height and Marie Antoinette had not yet been executed). Enthusiasm waned, but eventually the Déesse was cast by Théophile Bra, with the intention of placing her atop his Arc de Triomphe in Paris. That plan too was abandoned, and the goddess returned to Lille, standing for three years in place Rihour before moving to Charles Benvignat's column on Grand' Place in 1845. Her crown represents Lille's ramparts, her right hand is ever ready to fire another cannon, and her left points to a plaque inscribed with the brave words of Mayor André's rebuttal of Austria's demands. Tongues soon began to wag, however, since from upper windows locals noted the goddess's uncanny resemblance to Mme Bigodanel, the 54-year-old wife of the then mayor. It seems her fuller figure had not gone unnoticed by the artist.

Under her watchful gaze, students hold protest rallies, bands play on Pride Weekend and the city's tame giants parade during the Fêtes de Lille. Grand' Place has a habit of dressing for every occasion: most famously as a Christmas grotto in December and January when, surrounded by Cinderella candelabra, a huge Ferris wheel swings sensation seekers into the skies to take in the panorama of gables and belfries from a swaying cradle high above the cobblestones. The wheel turns from mid-morning until well past midnight. Sometimes the cobbles are covered with plants, lawns and box hedges as city gardeners decide to transform the square into a park. Perhaps one day the whole area will become a farmyard, with rows of market-garden cabbages in front of the theatre, and a herd of cows grazing contentedly outside McDonald's. On one memorable visit, thousands of screaming fans turned out for a free concert on a sultry summer's night, and obliging students on rooftops sprayed the crowd from water bottles.

Around the square, look out for carved and gilded images of the sun, symbol of King Louis XIV, whose royal bodyguard lived in the Grande Garde, a splendid galleried building that today houses the Théâtre du Nord. Alongside the theatre is the striking frontage of the home of *La Voix du Nord*, once a wartime Resistance news-sheet and now the regional daily newspaper. Dominating the square, its tiered roof is topped out

Museums and Sightseeing SITES AND MONUMENTS

11

by three golden Graces, symbolising the regional provinces of Artois, Flanders and Hainaut. Nearby, Continental Europe's biggest bookshop, Le Furet du Nord (page 159), boasts half a million volumes in stock, and is spread over eight storeys on different levels served by a complicated arrangement of lifts, staircases and walkways. Across the square, linking Grand' Place with place du Théâtre, is the stunning Vieille Bourse, while at the corner, the archway bearing the name of the Brasserie Alcide is the gateway to Vieux Lille. Brasseries, bars and cafés abound, the square and its arteries liberally sprinkled with tables for alfresco dining and people-watching.

PLACE PHILIPPE LEBON ♀ 262 E4 🚊 République Beaux-Arts; take rue Nicolas Leblanc to pl Lebon

This intersection of rue Solférino boasts the kitschest statue in town. On the edge of the original university district stands a lavish homage to Louis Pasteur, first dean of the science faculty (page 189). As the microbiologist who first discovered that germs cause disease and the pioneer of pasteurisation, the great man is shown surrounded by grateful mothers offering their babies aloft. And you thought science could not be camp. This is a cult classic. Totally fab. The original faculty building around the corner is now the Moxy hotel (page 76). Across the square is the Romanesque-Byzantine church of St Michel surrounded by identikit townhouses; the mould-breaking Maison Coilliot (page 192) is on rue Fleurus. Walking south, Solférino leads to an equestrian statue of Joan of Arc. To the north is Théâtre Sébastopol (page 139) and Les Halles (page 152).

PLACE RIHOUR ♀ 261 H5 🚊 Rihour

Place de Gaulle trickles into place Rihour, home of the Palais Rihour (page 194) and tourist office, by way of a row of restaurants, cafés and bars where late-night revellers adjourn for an onion-soup breakfast in the small hours. A massive war memorial dominates the square, and is the scene of civic remembrance services on Armistice Days on 8 May and 11 November. Some rather disturbing coloured lighting illuminates the fountain that rinses the glass pyramid above the métro station; the result varies from fairground garish to an effect not unlike spilt hospital custard. In winter, a Christmas market of wooden chalets sells hot mulled wine and handmade gifts.

Arrive at the end of the morning to see a monochrome line of committed smokers in front of the métro pyramid. Waiters and *maîtres d'hôtel* in black (whether T-shirts or formal wear), chefs in whites, all stand with both hands fully occupied in service industry multitasking: texting and smoking at the same time. As the body clock strikes a quarter to the hour, the *confrérie de la clope* disperses to the bistros and brasseries of the quarter and all are ready for the first punters when the belfry chimes midday.

PLACE DU THÉÂTRE ♀ 261 J5 🚊 Rihour; walk along the rue des Mannaliers past the Vieille Bourse

Behind the Vieille Bourse, and looking down towards the old station, is the place du Théâtre. Pedestrianised as part of the city's millennium renovations, this is the **crossroads** of Lille ancient and modern. (Spot the iron arm hanging above the junction of rue de la Bourse and rue de la Grande Chaussée pointing visitors to Vieux Lille.) The two most striking buildings on the square are surprisingly new, dating from the 20th century: the Neoclassical opera house, with its monumental sculptures of Apollo and the Muses, and the splendid 76m neo-Flemish belfry of the imposing Chambre de Commerce et d'Industrie – both built by Louis Cordonnier.

The Chamber of Commerce building is home to a magnificent hall, used for civic and corporate events, but rarely seen by the public (except during heritage weekend – see page 15). Rumours have long whispered that, with the business and administrative affairs of the city now managed in the shiny new southeastern quarters of Lille, Cordonnier's masterpiece may become the latest grand building to be reborn as a cultural venue open to one and all. But realisation of the dream seems to follow geological time.

The Opéra's lavish restored interiors are even more dazzling than ever. Inspired by the Palais Garnier in Paris, the Opéra de Lille has always been a place to be seen, and its programme usually features both classics and new works with an international cast of principals (page 149). Opposite is the Rang de Beauregard, an extraordinarily ornate terrace of 14 three-storey houses and shops constructed in 1687 to complement the Vieille Bourse, and lovingly restored. Look closely at the elegant shopfronts: still embedded in the walls are cannonballs from the siege of 1792. The favourite façade and interior is found *chez* Morel et Fils, purveyors of legendary lingerie from days of yore until the millennium. Today, the vintage mannequins welcome guests to the emporium's reincarnation as a charming café, the Maison du Moulin d'Or (page 130).

PORTE DE GAND ♀ 259 H1 🚊 Rue de Gand

The last remaining fortified entrance to Vieux Lille stands astride the rue de Gand, looking down over the cobbles and menus of this fashionable dining area. Until recently, the windows at the top belonged to a restaurant. From the old town, admire the coloured patterns in the brickwork above the archways. From the other side, Porte de Gand can be seen as part of some serious defensive walls. The original perimeter was strengthened twice in the 17th century, with the porte and ramparts built in 1621 by the Spanish authorities against the French, and an extra line of defence added by Vauban against everybody else. Between the two walls are hidden gardens.

11

PORTE DE PARIS Pl Simon Volant ♀ 262 H3 🚊 Lille Grand Palais; take rue des Déportés past the Hôtel de Ville

On the traffic roundabout named after the monument's architect stands the greatest of the three remaining city gates. Unlike the portes des Roubaix and Gand, this is an unashamed piece of monumental triumphalism, a lavish declaration of the might and majesty of Louis XIV and a celebration of Lille's embrace into the Kingdom of France. Unveiled in 1692, this *arc de triomphe* has an image of the king himself surrounded by angels and cherubim. Columns frame niches holding classical images of war and power, with Hercules and Mars paying tribute to France's own Sun King. Originally the gateway rose above the town's fortifications. However, walls were torn down in 1858 to make way for boulevards, and the rest of the district of Saint-Sauveur was demolished in the slum-clearance programmes of the 1920s. A small landscaped garden replaces the moat, once spanned by a drawbridge, and the Baroque arch itself is as imposing as ever. Impress your new friends with the trivial nugget that the gateway was not dubbed the Porte de Paris until the Revolution. Despite its regal statuary, it was originally called the Porte des Malades ('Sick People's Gate') because it led to the hospital. And though Porte de Paris once shared its name with the street leading to the main squares, the road has now been rebaptised in honour of former mayor Pierre Mauroy.

PORTE DE ROUBAIX Parc Matisse or rue de Roubaix ♀ 259 H3 🚊 Gare Lille Europe; from the station enter the park & follow the footpath to the city walls

From rue de Roubaix, this nearly neglected old gateway long presented a rather sorry and run-down appearance, and most passers-by do simply just that. Yet this is the door that saved a city. The Parc Matisse offers a far more appropriate perspective from which to view this remnant of the old fortifications. Here, its crenellations and drawbridge channels may be seen to best advantage, and you may imagine the moment in 1792 when the door was slammed in the face of the Austrian duke of Saxe-Teschen and his army of 35,000 men. If the two smaller archways seem to give the gate an air of a triumphal arch, blame it on the commuters. The side walls were opened up in the 19th century for a long-forgotten tramway to the suburbs. The gateway took a belated bow with architectural Botox and celebratory illumination in the inaugural City of Culture celebrations.

P'TIT QUINQUIN Sq Foch, rue Nationale ♀ 261 F5 🚊 Lille Grand Palais, then bus L5 to Nationale

This is the statue to a lullaby that won the heart of a town (page x): the sentimental patois melodrama of a poor lacemaker whose child would not

Museums and Sightseeing SITES AND MONUMENTS

◀ 1 Built in 1692, the Porte de Paris is the most lavish of Lille's three remaining city gates. 2 The Maison Coilliot is a wonder of Art Nouveau architecture. 3 P'tit Quinquin commemorates a lullaby that won the city's heart.

11

stop crying. *Le P'tit Quinquin* was composed in 1852 by town-hall clerk Alexandre Desrousseaux, and was soon adopted as a bedtime ballad by every mother in town. When the composer died in 1892 it was adapted as his funeral march, and the town commissioned Eugène Deplechin to build a memorial to the songwriter. The statue of Desrousseaux's working-class *Madonna and Child* is as unashamed a manipulator of the heartstrings as the song itself. If you would like to hear the tune, make your way to the place du Théâtre at noon, when the bells of the clocktower chime the lullaby every day.

VIEILLE BOURSE Pl du Général de Gaulle ♀ 261 H5 ⏱ Tue–Sun 🚇 Rihour
The greatest legacy of the Spanish occupation of the city was this jewel box of a Bourse de Commerce merchants' exchange between the two main squares. Exquisite and unmissable, it's the most beautiful building in town and has been restored to its original Flemish-Renaissance brilliance. In fact, the Bourse comprises 24 individual 17th-century houses arranged around a cloistered courtyard. Although at first glance the houses, with

GARE SAINT-SAUVEUR

Bd Jean-Baptiste Lebas ♀ 259 G8 ☎ 03 28 52 30 00 w garesaintsauveur.lille3000.eu 🚇 Lille Grand Palais 🎫 free
The main legacy of Lille3000's Europe XXL season is beyond question the reinvention of an old railway station and goods yard between the city centre and residential Moulins quarter. Instead of demolishing a site once known as the Faubourg des Malades and imposing yet another office block or sports stadium on the landscape, Lille opted to inspire a new community straddling the 19th and 21st centuries. More than merely another arts centre, Gare Saint-Sauveur, opposite Parc Lebas (page 218), at the foot of the great thoroughfares of Liberté and Solférino, is a grand space designed for living. With the original railway tracks still embedded in the ground and distinctive thick, red walls of the industrial revolution, some 21ha of land cordoned off from the people of Lille for generations was handed over, parcelled and portioned by architects Franklin Azzi. The two striking station buildings are linked by a south-facing terrace for lazy summer days and nights. One hall is now a cinema and brasserie, the exposed timbers and revitalised brickwork framing more modern concepts of interior design. The other space was left empty, a blank canvas for a grand exhibition centre, performance area, theatre or concert hall that is ripe and ready for constant reinvention. At one point, there was even an 'hotel' called the Europa where subterranean-themed rooms (with industrial art) could be rented for 30 or 60 minutes at a time. The bistro at the St So, as the site is known to the locals (pronounced

their ground-floor shops, may seem identical, the intricate carvings and mouldings on each façade are unique, thanks to the skills of builder Julien Destrée who worked on the project from 1652 to 1653. Destrée had already won a distinguished reputation as a carpenter and sculptor, and he dressed his masterpiece with ornate flourishes of masks and garlands on the outer walls. Lions of Flanders adorn the four doorways into the courtyard, which is itself decked with floral and fruit motifs. Today, above the symbols of the original guilds that once traded here, is a discreet row of contemporary logos representing the private enterprises sponsoring the restoration. As the sun rises over Lille, it catches the gilded belltower on the roof and radiates golden beams across the Grand' Place. Step inside the contemplative cloister to find a charming weekday market selling antiquarian books under the gaze of busts of local pioneers of science and literature. It's a sanctuary from summer sun and winter winds alike, and people come here to sit and read or play chess from mid-morning until early evening. Sunday evening in summer finds the old walls echoing to the sound of the tango (page 202).

'sunso'), is an essential venue for chilling out with friends or catching live music during the afternoon or evening. Reservations are advised for performances.

Social anarchy of festival fever allowed the inaugural seasons a free-flow feel. A visitor might set up a table or pitch a tent on the site, or hang out at the book exchange café, where paperbacks were dropped and picked up by strangers. A huge wall was erected one summer for visitors to scrawl their thoughts and, across the site, the Braderie tradition of anarchic free trade was celebrated as anyone who wished might set up stall to sell their attic trove or rummage through a neighbour's unwanted treasure. You could nip out for a coffee and a mooch and end up invited to an alfresco dinner party with strangers. A communal kitchen garden is the ultimate allotment project.

Today, the site has become an essential part of the community. In spring, the entire population might be invited to the station to pick up a planter box, compost and bulbs to cultivate at home in gardens or on balconies. A few months later, the boxes are returned in full bloom and laid out in intricate patterns to cover the Grand' Place in a carpet of flowers: a massive garden project for the city landscaped by the people.

At this long-forgotten railway station at the far end of the boulevard of respectability and best behaviour, Lille's twin passions of art and hospitality are consummated over coffee, a beer, a good book, a song and a bargain.

11

It was a Sunday evening, summer had already surrendered to the anticlimactic half-season prologue to autumn and Lille lay between excuses. A rare weekend with no festival, no season, no theatre. To cap it all, as I glided upwards from the métro to a subdued place Rihour, it was raining. Not heavily, just the lightest drizzle of a mild evening on the cusp of equinox. Yet, I was contemplating a sulk. Just when I thought that Lille held no more teasing for me, I looked up and stared across the empty squares.

Those yellow, syrupy pools of light that slipped from glistening gables to bright washed cobbles lured me across the place du Général de Gaulle towards the inexcusably beautiful Vieille Bourse. The sounds of music filtered through: echoing cracked shellac tones of a long-forgotten afternoon crooner at 78rpm, and from Renaissance arched doorways escaped the unmistakable Latin sound of the tango.

Long shadows sliced the glow from the cloisters and I prowled around the building, looking for an open door. From the place du Théâtre I stepped up and through the entrance to the Vieille Bourse, Lille's timeless Rialto for bibliophiles and chess players, where usually the most physical effort comes from the holding to the light of the slightly foxed uncut pages of a 19th-century novella, or the flourished taking of a queen's bishop by a cannily primed pawn.

Before me was movement, the seductive synchronicity of backs arching in tandem, toes pointing forward then sliding up close-pressed calves, waists pulled, shoulders shrugged, and eyes locked in concentrated complicity. But this was no geriatric *thé-dansant*, nor a choreographed show dance. This was Lille taking its weekend rites as a right to the last second of liberty. In a city defined by youth this was, in fact, a genteel coup of measured effusion, *sagesse* and experience over unrefined *jeunesse* and exuberance.

In the squares outside, the weather dictated the sprit. Within, the soul triumphed over the elements. Generations swept across the courtyard, defying the rain and convention. The will was for a Latin night and, enclosed by red brick, white stone and a garland of gables framing the evening sky, a Latin night triumphed.

All along the cloisters around the dance floor stood students with bicycles and as yet uninitiated couples, soon to learn from a generation who knew (from the tango) the potent supremacy of prized promise over instant gratification.

As the gramophone played, so the ages merged. Just as a record from over half a century ago was boosted through digital speakers, so groomed grey heads led where tight designer-encased buttocks and thighs followed. Age and social status played second fiddle to the imperative pulse of the accordion. Where dinner jacket took to the floor with a yellow cardie, and a classic little black dress and the partiest, stripiest cocktail stilettos followed the lead of a jumper and jeans.

A great bearded bear of a working man in a heavy, plaid woodsman's shirt lumbered rhythmically and steadily through each stride and turn of the dance, while his whisper-waisted partner, hair a pre-Raphaelite tumble of curls, neatly picked her way around his strides, turning his bulk into gallantry. Behind them banker-brown brogues stepped from caution to promise, lured into seductive swirls by sharp white Vogues.

A well-upholstered Juno clasped a tiny lad to her embonpoint, as they danced, cheek to breast, his eyes peering through the shade of her formidable protection to follow her feet, defining determined arcs through shiny puddles. And on the far side of the Bourse, sharp, bright tailor's eyes peered expertly through wire-rimmed spectacles as a veteran of the dance floor continued nimbly to foot it across the courtyard, his younger companion knees bent, raised, swept and strutted in coy assertion of confident complicity in this ritual courtship.

Shoddy trainers kicked off and toes treading rainwater, the most timid of onlookers would allow himself to be lead across the flagstones floor by a lady of means, experience and purpose. Other discarded pumps and boots lay safely dry behind pillars as barefoot bohemia joined the measured maelstrom, delicately turning and tripping through the puddles.

Ahead and among these shifting couplings, a sweeper picked his way through the swirl with his broom pushing the rainwater away from the participants, every thrust of his brush an unconscious echo of the discipline of the dance all around.

Of course, the city had been dancing long before the rain shower beckoned me across the squares to discover yet another of its secrets. And the modest ball continued until the lights in the Bourse were switched off at bedtime, to a genteel round of applause, an announcement of the following week's rendezvous, the promise of dance classes for novices and the *bonbon* reward of one last dance under the stars of a freshly rinsed clean indigo sky before bedtime.

And I headed back to the métro having learnt the happy lesson never to take this city for granted.

Tango at the Vieille Bourse is held between 19.30 and 23.00 on Sunday evenings in summer (Jul–Sep) except during the Braderie. Enter from rue des Manneliers.

11

CHURCHES

ÉGLISE STE CATHERINE Terrasse Ste Catherine ♀ 261 F3 ☏ 03 20 55 45 92 ⏱ 13.00–17.30 Sat (& Wed–Fri in school hols) 🚊 Rihour, then Navette Vieux Lille to Voltaire & walk rue Royale 🎟 free

Out-of-towners rarely discover this 13th-century church. Yet until work started on Notre Dame de la Treille (page 206), this was home to the town's precious statue of the Virgin Mary. Rubens' *Martyrdom of Sainte Cathérine*, now in the Palais des Beaux-Arts (page 184), hung here for years, and many striking works by lesser-known artists may still be seen in the spacious and bright interior. The altar is graced by some excellent artworks including adoration of the shepherds and images inspired by Leonardo's *Last Supper*. Over the centuries this parish church of the rural suburb of Faubourg de Weppes expanded to become a traditional Flemish *hallekerque* (page 206). Its three spacious naves were probably saved from demolition during the Revolution when the building was called into service as a barn, before returning to the Catholic Church in 1797. By then it had lost the ornate iron partition grilles and other elaborate furnishings. Other splendid items remain, however, from carved choir stalls to beautifully painted pillars, and Ste Cathérine has at last won historic monument listing status.

ÉGLISE STE MARIE MADELEINE Rue du Pont Neuf ♀ 261 J1 ☏ 20 49 52 🚊 Rihour, then Navette Vieux Lille to Pont Neuf

Two decades ago, some of the world's leading cinematographers united to illuminate and interpret the interior of this deconsecrated church. Peter Greenaway, Miwa Yanagi, Chiharu Shiota, Emir Kusturica and Erwin Redl each designed a two-month reinterpretation of the building, to reintroduce Lille to one of its forgotten treasures. The unassuming flat frontage belies the magnificence within, notably the dome, so painstakingly restored in the 18th century. It's now reclaimed as an exhibition venue, so it's always worth checking listings mags and sites to see what's on.

ÉGLISE ST MAURICE Parvis St Maurice, rue de Paris ♀ 261 J6 ☏ 03 20 06 07 21 ⏱ 13.15–18.00 Mon, 10.15–12.15 & 13.15–18.00 Tue–Sat, 15.30–20.00 Sun (guided visits, in French 15.00–17.00 Sun; telephone for English & signed tours) 🚊 Gare Lille Flandres; turn left on to rue de Priez at the foot of rue Faidherbe

This is one of the sudden surprises that make Lille so special. Unless you decide to take a short cut from the station to the pedestrian shopping streets, you might never see this magnificent 15th-century church, its gleaming white stone façades restored to pristine condition – at the cost of many a

---

1 The beautiful Vieille Bourse was built in the 17th century as a merchants' exchange.
2 & 3 Église St Maurice is built in the Hallekerque Flamande, or 'Flemish Market Church', style.
4 Notre Dame de la Treille, the city's cathedral, took over 150 years to build. ▶

summer night's sleep to neighbours within earshot of the sandblasting. Built on marshland, it has five high naves to distribute its weight equally across a wide area, in a style known as Hallekerque Flamande – literally 'Flemish Market Church' – after the airy market hall-style interior. Yet another unsung art collection may be viewed here, even if many original treasures have since found their way into the Palais des Beaux-Arts. The dramatic stained-glass windows of *The Passion* were inspired by the heroic 19th-century style of Ingres. Summer Sunday organ recitals are worth catching, as are occasional Saturday night concerts by local musicians.

NOTRE DAME DE LA TREILLE Pl Gilleson ♀ 261 J3 ✎ 03 20 31 59 12 00 w cathedralelille. fr ⏱ 10.00–noon & 14.00–18.30 Mon–Wed & Fri–Sat, 10.00–18.30 Thu & Sun: respect service times; remains open 1 hour later May–Sep 🚍 bus 9 to Lion d'Or, then take rue de la Monnaie & it's the 1st left to pl Gilleson

For most of the last century, Lille was a city with three-quarters of a cathedral. Notre Dame de la Treille had not only a fine Gothic chapel and apse, but also the largest expanse of corrugated iron in northern Europe. For, although the foundation stone had been laid in 1854 and the bulk of the edifice completed by the end of the 19th century, work during the 20th century finally ground to a halt when the money ran out in 1947. What might have been the great front entrance was hastily boarded up. By 1999, in the golden age of accountancy, funding was finally found and Lille eventually unveiled its cathedral in 2008. From the outside, architect P L Carlier's designs are very much of the age of the out-of-town shopping mall. But from inside the church, it is quite a different story: imposing yet welcoming, a delicate blend of light and shade. Ladislas Kinjo's rose window produces a powerful effect within, and the remarkable doors created by sculptor and Holocaust survivor George Jeanclos, representing a barbed-wire vine of human suffering and dignity, are quite magnificent. The cathedral stands on the Îlot Comtesse, site of the former château of the counts of Flanders, and the surrounding streets follow the line of the old fortifications, with traces of a moat still visible. A Museum of Sacred Art in the crypt opens on weekend afternoons from 14.30 to 19.00, housing 200 works of art and historic objects, including the original statue of Notre Dame de la Treille, dating from 1270. Regular free guided visits.

OTHER ARTS AND CULTURAL VENUES

A tradition of reclamation and reinvention, renaissance and revival with a dash of pure *chutzpah*, has led to an exciting programme that has seen old and abandoned buildings being called into service as arts and cultural venues. Inspired by the original Maisons Folies concept (page 210) during Lille2004, it is largely sponsored, nurtured and mentored by the Lille3000 team.

Besides the original Maisons Folies, Lille2004 opened up numerous overlooked or forgotten buildings to the public. Many have since have been taken very much to the hearts of the Lillois and their visitors. The Église Ste Marie Madeleïne (page 204) continues to stage occasional exhibitions after its stunning debut. A remarkable floral hall, **Palais Rameau** on boulevard Vauban (page 217), has had a habit of stepping out of retirement time and again, should occasion demand it. Years of neglect were finally countered with a major renovation project unveiled in late 2024. Even at its lowest ebb it was always an essential diversion for anyone with a soul, one of northern France's most delightful buildings.

LE GRAND SUD
Rue de l'Europe ♀ 262 F5 ✎ 03 20 88 89 90 🚊 Porte des Postes, then bus L7 to Prévoyance; take rue Romain Rolland to rue de l'Europe

Between the existing green spaces of the Jardin des Plantes, the Cimetière du Sud and the Parc de l'Aventure, this is a venue that could be staging an international rock concert one night and your best friend's 35th birthday the next. Less an arts/exhibition centre than other new addresses, this modular and versatile building is essentially a community space and locals may book the site for family functions.

LA MALTERIE
42 rue Kuhlmann ♀ 262 B5 ✎ 03 20 15 13 21 w lamalterie.com 🚊 Lomme Lambersart, then bus 10 to Croix du Temple; walk along rue de l'Egalité

Like Chez Rita in Roubaix (page 224), this vast, multi-storey industrial building on the edge of the city has been colonised by a community of artists in residence. Much of the building is given over to individual studios, where artists working in all media are commissioned to work on Lille3000 projects or follow private passions. The ground floor includes a concert venue with an eclectic programme of events throughout the year, as well as a versatile exhibition space. Upstairs you'll find an artists' canteen, top-floor dance studios and even darkrooms for traditional photography.

LE TRIPOSTAL
Av Willy Brandt ♀ 259 H4 ✎ 03 20 14 47 60 🚊 Gare Lille Flandres

The enduring legacy of 2004 was the renaissance of a tired postal sorting office at the side of the Gare Lille Flandres. Its harsh, state-owned railway and postal service architecture lent anonymity, allowing the site to be reinvented with each phase of every festival. The potential of an industrial warehouse-style shell with mail cages and three 2,000m² galleries was irresistible, attracting around a quarter of a million visitors in its first season. Martine Aubry, charismatic mayor and all-round superwoman, wrested Le TriPostal from its landlords to allow it to remain open for five more years. It is still going strong two decades later. Past shows have included futuristic robots, Buckingham Palace reinvented as a council estate, and a sensual tickling machine. It has highlighted gems from private collections, and even held a Saatchi retrospective. A key venue (and box office) for Lille3000 festivals,

11

It may be two tropics up and several time zones across, but for one magical night on the cusp of an Indian summer and autumn in Flanders, Lille became Rio. A wise woman once told me that Lille, hugging France's most northerly border with Belgium, was *la ville la plus méridionale*, the most southerly city in France: nothing to do with the climate, but rather the warmth of its people and welcome. And so, despite a distinct late-September chilly nip in the air, hundreds of thousands of locals and visitors took to the streets to launch the latest incarnation of Lille3000.

Lille's inaugural reign as European Capital of Culture began with a party and an avalanche of invention, imagination and creativity. When it was time to hand the baton to the Irish and Greeks, the city decided that the fun was not going to stop and immediately created Lille3000, a promise to reinvent the city and region with a world-class arts fest every couple of years. Thus, in 2006, the city became a Bollywood fantasy, with Gare Flandres railway station illuminated as the Taj Mahal, and the main street lined with elephants. The following decade dressed that same rue Faidherbe with a dozen of artist Fabio Ricardo's towering totems shipped over from Brazil's own Mardi Gras. That launch night saw the city dance, strut and swagger in celebration of Rio, one of the five 21st-century Renaissance cities feted by Lille for three dazzling months of memorable weekends.

Dress code for opening night was clear: '*À poil ou aux plumes!*' (feathers or birthday suit). Modesty forbids me from going into too much detail as to my own costume for the evening. Suffice to say that it involved a last-minute foray to pound shops and garden centres, judicious and hitherto unexplored use of gaffer tape, pipe cleaners and twine, and that more than one Disney princess north of Marne la Vallée had lost her sparking crown before I hit the city centre at 20.00 on Saturday night, a couple of *bières blanches* and a hearty *estaminet* supper to the good. As ever, the parade began by Gare Flandres, reached the Opera, then snaked round Grand' Place where we waited. Cheers from crowds in the previous squares and a seismic rumble of drums shook the cobbles, and the lights of a thousand smartphones from the multi-tiered crowds created a microscreen wall heralding each new arrival. Street lights had been dimmed and silhouetted on every balcony and in each window of the familiar buildings of the squares were privileged spectators, themselves forming a backdrop to an anticipatory son et lumière as images of Brazilliant beaches, faces, parties and personalities were projected on to the gabled façades, outshining the gilded symbols of France's own sun king in a kaleidoscope of colour as the samba rhythm got ever closer.

Rio may have provided the illuminated backdrop and monumental totemic taut-buttocked statues, but the samba rhythm came from 2,000 local drummers, musicians and dancers in homemade headdresses and costumes. The parade was headed by France's very own Giants of the North, those Brobdingnagian figures of domesticity, emblems of every town from Lille to Dunkerque. Towering fathers with tankards, mothers with babies; quintessentially French, yet totally appropriate to welcome the great giant heads of extravagant Latin floats to follow. Hovering above, a vast inflatable Godzilla loomed and swerved across the crowds, and three motorised farthingale dresses topped by a trio of opera singers belted out arias and choruses from *Carmen* and *La Traviata*.

Eventually, the crowds scattered, many to find paths through the ruelles and backstreets of Vieux Lille for fireworks, at Louis XIV's citadel. Others spilled along the squares or explored hitherto ignored corners of the centre in search of more music, served through the night whether on official stages or makeshift arenas. There was a traditional *bal musette guinguette* accordion ambiance at square Foch, around a monument to a lullaby, DJs outside the theatres and opera houses, and even Zumba on Grand' Place. Sounds of music spread from the Bois de Boulogne all the way to the Gare Saint-Sauveur and the party beat at the Maison Folie Moulins.

The night may eventually have ended, but traces of its spirit remain. Every season of Lille3000 brings its celebrated metamorphoses – delicious installation art to gladden the heart and quicken the step and turn back the body clock just enough to make your day, including the iconic tulips that greet arrivals on the Eurostar. Not only that, but the team have kept hold of such commandeered buildings as **Le TriPostal** (page 207) and **Maisons Folies** (page 210) for further events, and breathed new life into **Saint-Sauveur** (page 200). You may have had to turn more than a hundred pages before reading this, but in so many of the previous and following chapters, the legacy of those Lille3000 seasons lives on in public spaces and parks, and new galleries and performance venues whose working lives continue far beyond the original time-stamped programme. Between official festivals – each attracting over a million visitors to programmes of art exhibitions, performances, parades and deliciously overblown public gestures, such as massive soup banquets to feed a city or teeny restaurants hidden inside giant art installations – the Lille3000 brand attaches itself to some fantastic mini cultural seasons. As their slogan says, '*Le voyage continue*' ('The journey goes on').

Lille3000 \ 03 28 52 30 00 w lille3000.eu. *As ever, news and programme information for the next festival will trickle from the festival's website and from the Lille Tourist Office. Le TriPostal will serve as box office and rendezvous.*

it hosts special events during non-festival months and years, and is often a venue for clubbing and social events.

MAISONS FOLIES

'Folly' is too frivolous a word. In reviving abandoned or forgotten buildings, this audacious project has breathed new life into many a community: creating exciting spaces able to adapt to the imagination of each quarter. It is the longest-lasting legacy of the original Capital of Culture, a fabulous scheme that created a dozen permanent arts centres in Lille and across the region into Belgium. Transforming abandoned buildings and creating entire new community spaces, the Maisons Folies are at once a celebration of the past, an indulgence for the present and a magnificent gift to future generations. Former industrial, military and religious buildings become galleries, theatres, nightclubs, party venues and recording studios, with artists in residence, gardens in the sky and libraries. Named for the architectural follies that were the bricks-and-mortar whims of both wealthy aristocrats of the Ancien Régime and industrial *nouveaux riches*, these projects should revive and inspire local communities and entertain their visitors for years, even decades, to come. Unlike Marie Antoinette's model farm and other mini-châteaux and fairy-tale boathouses, Maisons Folies belong to the people: kitchens and dining rooms, where locals may prepare and serve their own meals; gardens for those who want to get their hands dirty; libraries with books in many languages; not to mention the opportunity for local children to meet and work with resident artists. Folies came of age as a focus for the diverse communities of the 21st century. The project has evolved comfortably over its first two decades. Sites, once forbidden to their communities, have become so much a part of everyday life that their involvement in all activities and occasions is a given. Lille3000 sets out its diary across these venues with ease, so festival time is not contained within strict city limits, but carried across into the wider community, generating a previously unimaginable sense of involvement.

LILLE
Maison Folie Wazemmes Usine Leclercq, 70 rue des Sarrazins ♀ 262 A4 ✎ 03 20 78 20 23 w mfwazemmes.lille.fr ▦ Gambetta

A 19th-century textile factory which finally closed its doors in 1990 has been reinvented with a stunning yet sympathetic building alongside the original structure, a brand new, undulating, red-brick road and public square in the vibrant Wazemmes district. Indoor and outdoor spaces, conceived by architect Lars Spuybroek, are thrilling, eye-catching and versatile. Alongside studios, an exhibition hall and an urban orchard is a well-judged theatre space, and the Folie is home to many local arts and performance groups. However, to the locals its allure is far more practical. They wanted a

Paris may have hosted the 2024 Olympics, but Lille gets to open the 2025 Tour de France. And before that the city hosted international rugby and proudly celebrated the Euro football championships. In Lille, however, mere sport is no bar to an arty party. And nowhere is that more true than Maison Folie Wazemmes, where a deliciously inventive and challenging free exhibition 'Footorama' gave us the gloriously dubbed *BarbieFoot* – a broad-grin-inducing joyous treat, neatly inverting the concept of France's favourite boys' toy. This was half a generation before the women's game broke into global consciousness and years before Hollywood gave us Margot Robbie.

Table football, known as *babyfoot*, has been a staple fixture in French bars for the best part of a century, since local firm Stella started manufacturing in nearby Tourcoing in 1928. The 'Pimp Your Baby' gallery of the exhibition was filled with customised *babyfoot* tables reinterpreted for today. Among some fabulous gender stereotype challenges was Chloe Ruchon's flamingo-pink table, where the football players had been replaced by big-haired, nipped-waisted, flashy-lashed Barbie dolls. Other exhibits continued the theme, including *Stud XI*, London-based Columbian artist Freddy Contreras's tableau of high-fashion high-heeled shoes, complete with soccer studs, hanging on locker room hooks – a vaguely disturbing mixture confronting not only sporting sexism, but an oppressive attitude to women in lads vs WAGs culture. And that's not to mention a hand-stitched football by Costa Rican Pricilla Monge that upon closer inspection appeared to have been made from women's sanitary products.

The feminist slant was not the only angle to the show. A superb interactive alternative version of football, played sitting down, provided original family fun, and a dark room with speakers belting out sounds of the crowd at a local match let the game play out in your imagination in a wave of camaraderie. Yet another installation featured witty and inventive knitted creations based on insults to referees and opposing fans. Check out the programmes at Maisons Folies and other alternative venues whenever the world of sport comes to town.

Turkish bath, so the architect created a luxurious sauna and steam complex incorporating the warm red-brick vaulting with some beautiful tiling and interior design. Zeïn Oriental Spa (w wazemmes.zeinorientalspa.fr) has separate women's and men's days and times during the week and mixed sessions weekend evenings and all day Sunday.

Maison Folie des Moulins 47–49 rue d'Arras 📍 262 G5 📞 03 20 95 02 82
w mfmoulins.lille.fr 🚇 Porte d'Arras

This former brewery, an abandoned site of brick and copper, is now the very heart of the Moulins district, which already had a thriving arts scene (the Prato Theatre and Univers Cinema are both within a short walk). An imposing 140m² exhibition hall doubles as theatrical rehearsal space, and recording studios open out into a weekend nightclub dedicated to contemporary sounds. Two interior courtyards host open-air performances and the building's original function is reflected in a new bar-brasserie on site.

Maison Folie Beaulieu Pl Beaulieu, quartier de la Délivrance, Lomme 📍 260 A6 📞 03 20 22 93 66 🚇 Maison des Enfants

This late addition to Lille's Maisons Folies opened its doors five years after its siblings. The Maison Folie Beaulieu enjoys a close association with local theatre companies and the Centre Régional des Arts du Cirque.

Maison Folie Lambersart Le Colysée, av du Colysée, Lambersart 📞 03 20 00 60 06
w lambersart.fr/le-colysee 🕐 13.00–18.00 Wed–Sun 🚇 Bois Blancs; follow signposts through the park

Technically this Folie belongs to the commune of Lambersart but, since it is just across the river from Lille proper, it counts as a city venue. Originally known as Maison de la Plaine, it is an open-space Folie by the waterside, where Vauban once built a fortress and where locals would dance at a guinguette by the banks of the Deûle. Inspired by the latter, the architects conceived a house of the future and set it in a meadow, where once again people may come to take in the air. The project soon evolved into Le Colysée, with an art gallery and two 40-cover restaurants on site. There's free parking here, too: a rarity in Lille.

ARRAS
Hôtel de Guines Rue des Jongleurs 📞 03 21 51 26 95

Next to the Musée des Beaux Arts in the St Vaast Abbey, a grand 18th-century private house has two wings embracing an enclosed courtyard. Its grand façade was already listed as a national monument before the Maisons Folies project was launched. The stylish rooms are perfect artists' salons for many a cultural rendezvous, and experts from a nearby theatre help create performance areas for concerts and cabarets. It's also home to a summer song festival.

MAUBEUGE
Les Cantuaines La Porte de Mons, pl Vauban 📞 03 27 62 11 93

Here, an artists' retreat sits within a former convent on the site of a 16th-century hospice at La Porte de Mons, the last great town gate to be constructed for Louis XIV by Vauban. Seven cells near the chapel have been converted into studios for artists in residence. The gardens host exhibitions and performances, and the grand gateway itself, long-time home of the local tourist office, is now a brasserie and art gallery.

MONS-BAROEUL
Fort de Mons Rue de Normandie 03 28 77 44 35 Fort de Mons
This place thrills me as a performance space: brick and sky crying out for open-air theatre and screaming with potential. An elegant 19th-century moated fortress with three paved courtyards, rather than the traditional central parade ground, now houses a cinema, restaurant and library, with exhibition halls and music and dance venues within fortified walls.

ROUBAIX
La Condition Publique See page 224.

TOURCOING
L'Hospice d'Havré See page 228.

VILLENEUVE D'ASCQ
La Ferme d'en Haut See page 232.

BELGIUM
Courtrai
Lille sur l'Isle L'Isle Buda, 9 Budastraat (+32) 056 27 78 40
On an island on the River Lys, warehouses and cloisters become theatres and museums. The Limelight Centre for Contemporary Arts boasts a cinema, restaurant and galleries, and even the river itself becomes an exhibition space with floating billboards presenting art on the waters.

Mons
Les Arbalestriers 8 rue des Arbalestriers (+32) 065 33 55 80
Outside, an open-air summer theatre; within, a café-concert, *médiathèque*, exhibition hall and auditorium. Thus a former school in the heart of town becomes the cultural crossroads of Mons, working with theatre companies across the French border in Maubeuge.

Tournai
Seminaire de Choiseul 11 rue des Soeurs de Charité
Tournai's original 13th-century church of Ste Marguerite was mostly destroyed by fire and rebuilt in 1760 in the style of a Neoclassical temple. An earlier 16th-century tower remains, however, and is a landmark in the centre of the Belgian town. As a Maison Folie, the church hosted visiting exhibitions, staged concerts and creative workshops and was at the heart of local fairs, markets and carnivals.

PARKS AND GARDENS

Lille boasts 350ha (and counting) of green spaces within the city limits, and the wider region stretches out into open country (see page 229 for the lakes and hilly walks of Villeneuve d'Ascq nature reserve). Even if you have no time to head to the sand dunes by Dunkerque or the farmland beyond the city, enjoy a breath of fresh air within a few minutes of your next urban adventure.

BOIS DE BOULOGNE Av Mathias Delobel ♀ 260 B3 🚌 bus 12 to Champ de Mars
Countryside comes to town where panthers prowl, joggers run and families take the air. Neatly tied up in a loop of the River Deûle's canals are 50ha of greenery, picturesque towpaths and an island filled with monkeys. The woodland is civilised by the Parc de la Citadelle, home to the famous fortress (page 190), but elsewhere within the Bois de Boulogne is where the city loosens its tie on weekends and holidays. Children love the zoo (✆03 28 52 07 00 w lille.fr/Zoo-de-Lille 🍃 €6), with its Île des Singes ('Monkey Island') and contented rhinos and zebras. There is also a playground for rides, side-shows and candyfloss moments (page 55). Outside the zoo is a cobbled pathway that forms part of the arduous Paris–Roubaix cycle race, known colloquially as 'The Hell of the North'. Fitness fanatics pace themselves running around the former moat, following the signposted route between the ramparts and the willow trees. You can always spot soldiers and foreign legionnaires by their blue tracksuits. Lovers wander into the woods, while more decorous strollers prefer the esplanade, landscaped in 1675 by Vauban himself, or even the Champ de Mars where funfairs pitch their tents during school holidays. If all seems carefree and inconsequential, take a moment to pause by the Monument aux Fusillées on square Daubenton at the edge of the Bois. Félix Desruelle's memorial pays tribute to those Lillois members of the French Resistance shot by the Nazis against the walls of the Citadelle. On avenue Delobel, discover the most unusual of war memorials: the Monument aux Pigeons Voyageurs. It pays homage to the 20,000 pigeons who died for *la patrie*, carrying messages to and from the frontlines in World War I, saving thousands of allied lives. A female figure of peace is depicted releasing a cloud of birds. After the war, shooting pigeons was made a crime.

JARDIN VAUBAN Bd Vauban ♀ 260 C4 🚌 bus L5 to Champ de Mars
A delightful 19th-century park, often overshadowed by the large lush expanses of the Bois de Boulogne across the River Deûle, this is a pretty

◀ 1 The Jardin des Géants mixes art and nature to delightful effect. 2 The Maison Folie Wazemmes is a lively arts and leisure space in a converted textile factory. 3 The greenhouse at the Jardin des Plantes is full of tropical species. 4 The Île des Singes ('Monkey Island') in the Bois de Boulogne is a favourite with children.

I was searching the streets of Lille for an Alice band. Or, to be precise, a memento of the Alice network. A statue of one of Britain's greatest heroines, a woman who saved hundreds of lives during the Great War. A woman who never existed.

Alice Dubois was British Intelligence's Queen of Spies. This quiet, unassuming woman ran the largest network of secret agents in occupied France, recruiting informers and undercover agents under the noses of the occupying German forces. In fact, Alice was the code name of a governess from Lille. Louise de Bettignies' high-born family had fallen on hard times before the war, but, since she spoke fluent English, German and Italian, and could also converse in Spanish and Russian, she was able to earn a living as a tutor to children in influential households across Europe.

When the Germans marched into Lille in October 1914, Louise fled to St Omer where she tended to wounded soldiers. In February 1915, she offered her services to British Intelligence. With her perfect language skills, this poised aristocratic woman was well placed to set up a network of spies to infiltrate the German command and logistics HQ in Lille.

From a new base across the border in Belgium, she passed on to London details of enemy troop movements and munitions bases. As her network expanded to Valenciennes, Cambrai and beyond, she and her assistant, Marie-Léonie Vanhoutte from Roubaix, also established an underground escape route to smuggle wounded British and Allied soldiers through enemy lines into neutral Holland.

This Alice Network was a huge success, with more 80 agents in and around Lille, but the two women could not stay invisible for long. By September, Marie-Léonie had been captured, and Louise herself was taken prisoner a few weeks later. In eight short months, Louise de Bettignies had proved herself one of Britain's greatest wartime heroines. Her death sentence in 1916 was commuted to a life of hard labour.

Yet her spirit was undimmed, and she rallied fellow prisoners in Cologne to rebellion and protest. So when she contracted pneumonia, her captors refused medical attention and Louise died in gaol on 27 September 1918, just weeks before the Armistice. She was only 38 years old. Her body was returned to France and the family vault in Saint-Amand-les-Eaux. But she

confection of dainty flowerbeds, waterfalls, lawns and grottos, landscaped in 1865 by Paris's chief gardener, the aptly named Barillet Deschamps. Poets' Corner contains memorials to writers and musicians, and a monument to Charles de Gaulle stands at the square Daubenton entrance. Locals visit an immaculate miniature orchard to meet the present-day gardeners who are always willing to give advice and tips on growing fruit and vegetables at is remembered in her adopted city of Lille with a street named after her in the centre of Vieux Lille.

Reading her story during the centenary celebrations, I decided on my next visit to Lille to find the memorial and pay my own tribute. So, when changing trains shortly after Armistice Day, I set off to place Louise de Bettignies at the start of rue de Gand. There, by avenue du Peuple Belge, I saw the statue of an heroic woman.

On closer inspection, despite the defiant pose – arm raised aloft like Delacroix's *Liberty Leading the People* – this was not Louise but Jeanne Maillotte, an earlier heroine. Lille has never been short of strong women: the Countess of Constantinople, whose Hospice Comtesse next door was the forerunner of universal healthcare; Grand Place's La Déesse statue; P'tit Quinquin, embodiment of motherhood and inspiration of bells and lullaby.

This Jeanne was landlady or barmaid at a beer cellar on nearby place aux Bluets back in 1582. Popular with garrison soldiers, she raised the alarm when she spied enemy forces hiding among Sunday market shoppers. Grabbing an axe from the bar, she led a battalion of archers into action. Yet another heroine, but not Louise.

On my next visit, the tourist office told me to try boulevard Carnot. But where? The long, wide thoroughfare runs from the Opèra to the city limits. Perhaps place Carnot garden, that small patch of green, where rue des Arts meets the boulevard? The monument is probably there, I was told. Stopping only to buy a scarf and gloves (it was a cold winter's morning), I set off to cross the three squares, finally to meet my heroine. A monument there marked the site of a 13th-century convent, then a school that eventually became Louis Pasteur's science faculty, later moved to the arts quarter by a statue of another Jeanne, Joan of Arc. Not our Louise.

I followed the boulevard to its natural conclusion, towards the ring-road flyover, and there, in the shade of dusty trees, I found her monument – noble head turned aside as a grateful wartime Tommy kisses her hand. Bring flowers and pause awhile.

Memorial Louise de Bettignies *Bd Carnot* ♀ *259 H2* 🚊 *from Parc Matisse (by the station) follow Pharaon de Winter to bd Carnot*

home. The most famous corner of the park is the puppet theatre in Monsieur Rameau's Goat House, where every Sunday and Wednesday Jacques le Lillois performs for local children (page 55). This Chalet aux Chèvres was one of Charles Rameau's many eccentric legacies to the town. He was a noted horticulturist who gave Lille the splendid Palais Rameau (♀ 260 C5) at the junction of rue Solférino and boulevard Vauban, a vast floral hall that doubled as a circus and performing arts venue. These munificent bequests were given freely on the condition that his grave at the Cimetière du Sud ($\heartsuit$ 262 F5) is ever marked by a bed of potatoes, tomato plants, strawberries, a vine, a rosebush and dahlias.

JARDIN DES PLANTES Rue du Jardin des Plantes $\heartsuit$ 262 G5 📞 03 62 26 08 28 ⏰ park Apr–Sep 07.30–21.00 daily & Oct–Mar 08.30–18.30 daily, greenhouses 09.00–noon & 13.30–17.00 daily 🚇 Porte de Douai or Porte d'Arras

Just a little too far south for most visitors to bother with is one of the most romantic escapes in the city, where many a troth has been plighted at the top level of the conservatory, or in the cooling summer shade of the *orangerie*. For here, just below the ring-road, lie waterfalls and tropical greenhouses, alongside rare plants and trees from many lands. Botanists are not the only visitors to feel their pulses quickening when they wander through the lovingly maintained gardens. Sense the sultry south in the most unlikely corner of northern France.

PARC JEAN-BAPTISTE LEBAS Bd Jean-Baptiste Lebas $\heartsuit$ 262 H5 🚉 Gare Lille Flandres then bus L5 to Liberté

Some 20 years ago, this conversion of a car park into a haven of greenery was gifted from the city to its residents and guests, opening midway through the year. Where Porte de Paris and boulevard de la Liberté come to their natural conclusions, tarmac was laid to lawns and century-old chestnut trees augmented by more than 12 dozen new lindens in 3ha of unexpected city-centre garden. Naturally, there are nice chairs and lamps, with of course a *boulodrome* for the grown-ups and a children's play area too. All wrapped in high railings with monumental gateways to the various boulevards back into town, and to the Gare Saint-Sauveur (page 200) by the railway tracks.

PARC MATISSE Euralille $\heartsuit$ 259 H3 🚉 Gare Lille Europe

Part of another grand project within a grand project (the wish to create a green belt around the old city walls), the Parc Matisse was chosen to be one of the installation-art sites of Lille2004. Happily, this newest of city parks has ripened and weathered itself to sit well in the urban landscape. Spindly saplings have now emerged as vibrant adult trees, lawns have mellowed to meadow, wild flowers sitting comfortably against centuries-old walls as a foreground to the futuristic glass empire of Lille Europe that rises from the gardens. Popular with picnickers as much as with those looking for a short cut through the Porte de Roubaix (page 199), the park has come of age and proven itself as a treasured haven. You can tell it works – even office workers hold hands as they stroll through its eight green hectares.

PARC BARBIEUX See page 226.

JARDIN DES GÉANTS Rue du Ballon ♀ 259 J2 ✆ 03 20 21 22 23 ⏰ 09.00–sunset (latest 21.00) 🚊 Gare Lille Europe; behind the Hilton hotel above the station turn left to rue du Faubourg de Roubaix then right on rue du Ballon & follow signs

By the Cimetière de l'Est between the Eurostar station and the Madeleine district, the Jardin des Géants is really more of a conceptual art installation than a stroll through nature to be honest. Leafy lanes, bamboo and water features are threaded with eccentric modern sculptures of giant chairs and faces in metal and willow.

12

Beyond the City

Parc Barbieux's pretty gardens and Disney-quaint houses line the roads on the half-hour tram route to the two major satellite towns of **Tourcoing** and **Roubaix**. For those in a hurry, the métro cuts journey times in half, blurring boundaries between the city of Lille and other towns of Lille Métropole. The metropolitan population is over 1 million, and the conurbation's cultural honours are now shared fairly around Lille's immediate neighbours. So Ballet du Nord performs at the huge Colisée theatre in Roubaix, and Tourcoing's Atelier Lyrique stages intimate productions of favourites from Mozart to Bernstein. Tourcoing has its annual jazz festival and hosts a branch of a national museum, while Roubaix holds an open-air art market and rooftop picnics. **Villeneuve d'Ascq** may now be a university centre with one of the leading modern art collections in northern Europe, but was once known for windmills and watermills. Lille's tourist office has information on events surrounding towns within the metropolitan area and offers plenty of seasonal alternatives to conventional public transport – canal boats and vintage trams among them.

The elephant in the room is the neighbouring town of **Lens**, home to a spectacular Louvre Museum. Should you wonder why there are no high-profile transport and PR links to one of the region's most important attractions, you need to understand micro politics. While Lille is capital of the Nord *département*, Lens is just across the county line, in the neighbouring *département* of Pas-de-Calais, and in France, anywhere beyond a local political border may as well be in another time zone. So, while Lens is close enough to be a virtual suburb of Lille, it is not on the local transport map, meaning you'll have to find your own way there (page 235).

For more information on any towns, villages and sites away from Lille itself, visit the tourist office on place Rihour (page 49), where the *département* du Nord, Métropole Européenne de Lille (MEL; European metropolitan area) and wider region provide information and brochures.

Advice on museum opening hours and free or discounted admission can be found on page 184.

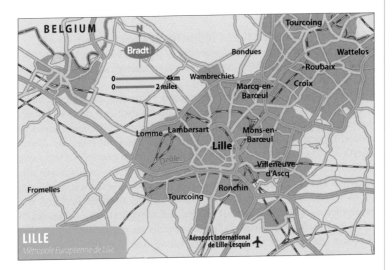

ROUBAIX

The town of a thousand chimneys evolved from the 15th to 19th century, as Roubaix developed its textile industry. Originally a useful winter sideline for farmers, making fabric and clothes created a boom town during the Industrial Revolution, with wealth matched only by social conscience. A succession of enlightened civic and business leaders saw Roubaix pioneer childcare, social housing, family allowance benefits, allotments and hospitals for workers. Meanwhile, town fathers accumulated an incredible collection of sample books, fabrics, fashion designs and ephemera: a comprehensive catalogue of styles from the ancient Egyptians to the 20th century.

This archive is now displayed to best effect at La Piscine (page 222), alongside private art collections of entrepreneurs who owned the original mills. The only Ingres in town (even Lille's Palais des Beaux-Arts cannot claim one of these), Picassos and works of local artists Cogghe and Weerts are to be seen there. The exhibits' original home was destroyed in World War II; however, architect Jean-Paul Philippon reinvented one of the great buildings of Roubaix's heyday to provide a worthy successor, within the one building in town where citizens of all classes had mingled as equals.

For years before the Maisons Folies project breathed new life into abandoned factories and sites, Roubaix was reinventing its architecture to serve future generations. It is not all about preserving the past. As Banksy is to Bristol so New York subway artist JonOne is to Roubaix. Since 2017's Street Generations exhibition, the town has been a mecca for street artists and its murals and installations inspire an annual walking trail and map. Pick up a copy from the tourist office (3 bis rue du Chemin de Fer ℡ 03 20 65 31 90 w roubaixtourisme.com ⏰ 09.30–noon & 13.00–18.00 Mon–Sat).

WHAT TO SEE AND DO

La Piscine – Musée d'Art et d'Industrie Art & Industry Museum; 23 rue de l'Espérance 📞 03 20 69 23 60 w roubaix-lapiscine.com 🕐 11.00–18.00 Tue–Thu, 11.00–20.00 Fri, 13.00–18.00 Sat–Sun 🚊 Gare Jean Lebas; take av Jean Lebas, turn right on rue des Champs & left to rue de l'Espérance 💶 €9 (audio guide from €1)

The sun also rises at the former municipal swimming pool. A dramatic stained-glass window radiates stylised sunbeams over this most ambitious project: an exciting, eclectic and always stimulating collection housed in a building that is itself the town's greatest art treasure of them all. Albert Baert's Art Deco swimming pool is listed as the finest example of the genre in the land. Even when I was picking my way through the construction site, ten years after the pool had been abandoned and as work was beginning on its renaissance, the building still had the power to thrill. Restored and reinvented as a combination art gallery and sensual archive of textiles, it takes the breath away. Original floors and walls are impressive enough, but the form and shape of the place is a ravishing assault on the senses. Along with the Palais des Beaux-Arts in Lille, this is one of the musts of the area.

It is built in the fashion of a Cistercian abbey, around a central courtyard that was once a rose garden, now a *jardin des plantes* reflecting the textile industry (flax, mulberry and the like having played their roles in Roubaix's past). To one side sits the magnificent vaulted swimming pool, to the other a municipal bathhouse, where some tiled bathrooms remain. Other wings house the art collection.

And what a collection it is, with Bonnard, Dufy and Gallé among the big-name draws. Most artworks date from the end of the 19th and the first half of the 20th century, providing a forensic examination of the lives and people of Roubaix. Originally housed in a college across the way, the museum grew from a collection of fabrics from the factories to include works of art accumulated and acquired by the town's industrialist families. Some works reveal remarkable insights into the lives of the town's working men and women.

CROIX

The small town of Croix, just beyond Parc Barbieux, on the tram route between Lille and Roubaix, has a very different trail celebrating the impressive bourgeois architecture – a style travel writer Michael Leech termed 'Snow White Perpendicular'. Here, the mill owners who created 19th and early 20th century Roubaix built charming family homes, and the British Holden family, pioneering philanthropic industrialists, donated a charming bandstand to the park behind the town's Mairie. But Croix's main claim to fame is the remarkable Villa Cavrois (page 226), a 20th-century château that shares national heritage status with Versailles and Fontainebleau.

Others are deliciously camp: Shaw's middle-class morality, with allegorical images of high ideals. I love the harlot rising above her surroundings, the rose symbol of her baser trade being replaced by the lily of purity as she rejects sin in favour of redemption. Some offer a more perceptive grasp of reality: an initially enchanting idyll of children playing in a field takes on a grimmer aspect when you see the eldest little girl burying her dolls, as factory chimneys beckon her beyond ambrosia to an adult life of toil. Social politics merge with artistic merit in a gallery devoted to the emancipation of women through art. A wry evocation of the *Mona Lisa* shows a modern woman of learning; Camille Claudel's evocative bust of a child was a challenge to her mentor and former lover Rodin, to acknowledge paternity of their daughter.

As you wander through the galleries, occasional sounds of splashing and shrieking within the unmistakable acoustic of swimming baths leads you to the heart of the museum, the pool itself. The witty sound effect is even more effective in situ. A sheet of water still runs almost the length of the Olympic baths, fed by the fountain head of Neptune at the end of the dazzling mosaic basin. This continues to reflect the brilliant-coloured glass sunrise and sunset windows at each end of the building. Catch your breath, then walk along boardwalks lined with 19th- and 20th-century sculpture. These, like Cogghe and Weerts' paintings in earlier galleries, reflect the social history of the town. Some are worthy religious icons, others starkly socialist interpretations of the dignity of the working man. Cogghe's *Madame Recoit* (staff spying on their mistress's liaison) is simply delicious. A massive Moorish arch in Sèvres porcelain dominates the room, and along each side of the pool are ranged tiers of original shower and changing cubicles. Glazed to protect their exhibits, these are now treasure houses, including a remarkable range of ceramics by Picasso. On upper levels the textile collection reveals gowns and underwear, accessories and shoes of bygone ages. The *tissuthèque* is an archive of thousands of years of material patterns, from ancient Egypt to the present day. Around the museum, filing-cabinet drawers of fabrics allow visitors to plunge hands into a sensory wonderland of the soft and silky, matted and furred. If you have the opportunity to attend special events around temporary exhibitions, do not miss out. I shall never forget a classical concert under the sculpture gallery's stained glass window – Ravel's *Kaddish* in tribute to a remarkable exhibition of Chagall.

Take time to reflect on the day with a cool drink in the restaurant or on its terrace, run by Méert of Lille (page 130), flicking through an art book from the excellent museum shop.

La Manufacture Jacquard Museum; 29 av Julien Lagache ℡ 03 20 65 31 90
w lamanufacture-roubaix.com ⏲ 14.00–18.00 Tue–Sun, guided visits 14.30 & 16.00
🚃 Eurotéléport, then bus L3 to Manufacture Fraternité 🎫 €6
A loom with a view on the history of the weaving industry, this working museum explains the story of the mass production of textiles. See the

evolution of looms, from original hand-operated contraptions, through the growth of Jacquard machines, to contemporary computer-operated systems. The museum is a great place to shop for faux-medieval wall hangings, arts and crafts tableware and contemporary scatter cushions.

Maison Folie – La Condition Publique Pl Faidherbe ✆ 03 28 33 48 33

w laconditionpublique.com ⏱ 13.30–18.00 Wed, Sat & 1st Sun of the month, plus certain Fri eves 🚇 Roubaix–Eurotéléport, then bus 35 to Condition Publique 🥬 free

I've loved this Maison Folie (page 210) ever since visiting its construction site as a work in progress. A magnificent building, reminiscent of a Victorian railway station without the trains, it's the place where wool, and occasionally silks, would come to be treated and packed. In recent years it has hosted many festivals, concerts, sports clubs and events, the cobbled driveway between its two vast warehouses delivering an air of a town within a town. One quirky aspect of the original building is an eccentric sloping lawn on the glass roofs. To provide a constant year-round temperature, the glazed roof was turfed over and workers would often lie down in their lunch hours to doze in this incidental meadow in the sky. Indoors, discover the exhibition halls, arts space and facilities of Maisons Folies, a grand *estaminet* and local heritage centre. Visit in December for the traditional Braderie de l'Art, hybrid make-over and flea market. People sell old junk and artists use the bric-a-brac to make original works which they then sell on for anything between €1 and €300. The rest of the year, there's a regular pop-up repair café for restoration and upcycling.

Chez Rita 49 rue Daubenton ✆ 06 41 08 40 95 w chezrita.fr ⏱ phone for opening times

🚇 Gare Jean Lebas, then bus Cit5 to Flandre

Is it a biscuit or is it art? Once upon a time, a generation ago, the Rita waffle factory closed down. The family who ran the business wanted to leave something to the local community that had served the company so well for so many years, so they handed over the factory building to a community of artists, who now work, rest and play in its nooks and crannies, workshops and loading bays. Each corner has been converted into an individual's creative space, with easels, divans, installation art and canvases personalising each artist's studio. With superb Art Deco etched glass, wide industrial doorways and a romantic roof where invited guests might sit to watch a sunset, the building has a personality to rival any of the artworks on display and on sale. Some lunchtimes, the artists open their *estaminet* bar and café, where modestly priced pâté, salads and locally brewed ale are always on the menu. A weekly *soirée librairie* is a co-operative affair shop selling books, artworks, etc.

1 The modernist Villa Cavrois was designed to perfection by Robert Mallet Stevens.
2 Roubaix's La Piscine, a former swimming pool turned art gallery, is as beautiful as the works it houses. ▶

Parc Barbieux Av Jean Jaurès 🚊 Parc Barbieux

Trams from Lille to Tourcoing and Roubaix run alongside this prettiest of gardens where, for generations, middle-class families pushed prams and strolled away the hours of sunny Sunday afternoons. Delightful flowerbeds, rare trees and hidden statuary punctuate the manicured lawns. You may be forgiven for imagining such long narrow strips of colour might have been laid out to complement the tramway. In fact, they were created in the 18th century by Georges Aumont, a Parisian landscape gardener, on a site originally earmarked for development as a canal.

Villa Cavrois 60 av John Fitzgerald Kennedy, Croix ✆ 03 20 73 47 12 w villa-cavrois. fr ⏱ 10.00–18.00 Tue–Sun 🚊 Tram R to Villa Cavrois, then 900m walk rue along Hem & av JF Kennedy 🎫 €11 (free some Suns – see website)

This modernist château is worth half a day out of anyone's life. Quite rightly declared a national monument, it's a full-scale manifesto of design. Unlike their fellow industrialists, whose early 20th-century fairy-tale homes overlook the public parks of Croix and Roubaix, Paul and Lucie Cavrois, dreaming of a forever home, decided to hand the entire project to architect Robert Mallet Stevens. Designed in 1929 and realised within three years, every inch of the house – from the geometric yellow-brick and glass exterior to the light fittings and furniture within – is one man's vision and the result is perfectly stunning. To step inside the gleaming hall and reception rooms, you might expect to find Fred Astaire and Ginger Rogers gliding across the shiny floors as in an RKO cinematic fantasy of sheer style. Outside, immaculate lawns, paths and cubed topiary border the slice of water that is a mirror lake, reflecting the whole project in an interwar reimagining of Le Notre's Versailles landscaping. The breathtaking perfection of the home belies the hard work of restoration. When the Cavrois family left the villa in the 1980s, the building fell into neglect, and was the haunt of vandals and social outcasts for more than a decade. Acquired by the state in 2001 and listed on the heritage register to secure funding, the house finally returned to its original glory and opened to the public in 2015.

McArthurGlen See page 164.

L'Usine See page 165.

TOURCOING

In a region famous for belltowers, Tourcoing, renowned as a centre of the arts ancient and modern, makes space for a museum of bell-ringing, as well as some excellent art exhibitions. From towers to cellar, and open only on selected dates is **Musée du 5 juin** (✆ 03 20 24 25 00 w museedu5juin1944. asso.fr), housed in the Nazi bunker and command centre which tracked progress of both the Résistance and the Allies on D-Day. The Tourist Office is at 9 rue de Tournai (☏ 03 20 26 89 03 w tourcoing-tourisme.com ⏰ 09.30–12.30 & 14.00–18.00 Mon–Fri, 09.30–12.30 & 14.00–17.30 Sat).

WHAT TO SEE AND DO

Intitut du Monde Arabe Institute of the Arab World; 9 Rue Gabriel Péri ☏ 03 28 35 04 00 w ima-tourcoing.fr ⏰ 13.00–17.45 Tue–Sun, guided tours 15.30 Sat–Sun 🚋 Colbert; rue du Gand to rue de la Bienfaisance 🎫 €5

Just as Roubaix's Piscine turned an extraordinary Art Deco swimming baths into a destination museum, now another of France's heritage pools is reborn as a cultural icon. The École de Natation's galleried swimming pool, home to Les Enfants de Neptune school, produced champion swimmers, divers and water polo teams for 95 years until it its last whistle was blown in 1999. It remained just another listed building until re-opening in 2016 as France's second Institut du Monde Arabe – the Classical architecture here offering a sharp contrast to the sheer glass modernism of the original Paris museum. As with Louvre-Lens (page 238), this is a regional triumph. Galleries and temporary exhibitions display celebrated art and crafts of the wider Arab world, from early religious creations to a show focusing on Picasso's relationship with the Arab avant garde and an exploration of contemporary Moroccan creativity. It's very much a community centre, too, and locals may attend classes for speaking, reading and writing Arabic or learning Middle-Eastern cooking skills. There's also a rolling schedule of performance and music.

Le.Fresnoy Studio National des Arts Contemporains National
Contemporary Art Studio; 22 rue du Fresnoy ☏ 03 20 28 38 00 w lefresnoy.net 🚋 Alsace 🎫 cinema €6, exhibitions €4 (exhibition hours vary)

This arts centre and college sits on the site of an old bowling alley, dance hall and fleapit cinema and hosts lively programmes of exhibitions and film screenings. However, any event is easily upstaged by the building itself, the vision of architect Bernard Tschumi. Le Fresnoy is perhaps the only building for miles to have been designed to pander to human nature. Its charm lies in a magical hinterland between two roofs: Tschumi decided to retain the original shells of the 1905 movie theatre and hall, and create a footpath between the old tiles and the futuristic canopy of the modern centre. And so it is that students, locals and visitors alike may wander arms entwined around chimney-stacks on a network of suspended metal gantries and steps. One path leads to a dead end behind a sloping roof. 'Why?' I asked. The answer was simple: 'The architect said that young people need somewhere to, you know, to kiss!' On summer nights they may hold hands as well, since the design also incorporates a mini-grandstand for watching old movies projected on to the tiles. Films are also screened in the art centre's two small cinemas. One season, Le Fresnoy twinned itself with the home and studio of film-making legend Jean-Luc

Godard and ran live feeds of the master's works in progress. As a college concentrating on audio-visual arts, it was ahead of its time, being one of the first establishments for students of techniques that now dominate the crossover between museums and the internet.

MUba Eugène Leroy
Fine Arts Museum; 2 rue Paul Doumer ☎ 03 20 28 91 60 w muba-tourcoing.fr ⏲ 13.00–18.00 Wed–Mon; exhibition hours vary 🚊 Tourcoing Centre; walk rue Leclerc to rue Paul Doumer 🚻 €9

It was inevitable. No museum worth its place in the modern world can live without an acronym. Just as the Musée d'Art Moderne (see opposite) is now the LaM, so the Musée des Beaux Arts has become the MUba. Of course, another reason for the rechristening was a mega donation in 2009 of the works and archives of local artist Eugène Leroy. In order to keep the artist's complete *œuvre* intact, his sons presented the town with around 200 paintings, drawings and sculptures by Leroy as well as a vast collection of works by other artists. Besides this bonus collection, there's plenty to enjoy from the original museum. Eclectic, imaginative and never less than stimulating, Tourcoing's own collection has long spanned the artistic spectrum from Brueghelesque Flemish works to Cubists, and the archives are regularly ransacked by curators to keep exhibitions fresh and nicely incongruous. Find a Rembrandt next to some local's portrait of a much-loved grandmother or discover a Picasso between a couple of mundane still lives. My favourite painting remains the deliciously grand portrait of *Mlle Croisette en Costume d'Amazon*, a prim and proper bourgeois equestrian pose with more than a hint of passion beneath unseen corsetry. Pictures are housed in elegant galleries dating from the 1930s. If the museum's pick-and-mix nature appeals, cast your eye over the frontage of nearby **Maison du Collectionneur** (3 sq Winston Churchill), an architectural buffet of a house whose original owner wanted to combine as many styles as possible on one façade.

Maison Folie – L'Hospice d'Havré
100 rue de Tournai ☎ 03 59 63 43 53 ⏲ 13.30–18.00 Wed–Mon 🚊 Tourcoing Centre; rue de Tournai to rue Havré

Known locally as Notre Dame des Anges, this former monastery and poorhouse has retained all its original buildings, and the various wings and cloister are a living record of styles from Lille Baroque to Louis XIV's 18th-century influences. The chapel, gardens, hospice and baths now house an exhibition hall, artists' workshops, concert hall, restaurant and comic-strip centre in novel incarnation as Tourcoing's Maison Folie (page 210). The blend of historical monument and free-for-all accessibility is rather exciting and, like so many Maisons Folies, lends a supercharge to the most modest occasion. The chapel gives chamber music a deserved home in a town known for jazz. Guided tours take place on the first Sunday of each month (except August) at 11.00.

Musée du Carillon Bell-ringing Museum; 11 rue de Tournai ☏ 03 59 63 43 43 ⏱ May–Oct 15.00–18.00 Sun 🚇 Tourcoing Centre; cross pl République

Not only does this bell-ringing museum include some 62 bells weighing more than six tonnes, but the bell-ringer's cabin offers the best view of the town! Housed in the 16th-century tower of the St Christophe Church, the original mechanism for the clock can be viewed in a first floor gallery. The 17th- and 18th-century carillon of bells was destroyed in the French Revolution, while a second 19th-century ring of bells, cast in Amiens, sounded until 1870 and was later looted during World War I. The third generation of bells was set up in 1961. Other galleries explain the manufacture and use of church and secular bells through the ages.

VILLENEUVE D'ASCQ

Villeneuve d'Ascq is renowned as the home of Lille's university campus and also boasts a vast shopping mall, making it easy to forget that there is a strong rural heritage to be explored in this bustling satellite. Just outside the centre is a museum of windmills, a fascinating and unexpected little treat, as is the farming Musée du Terroir. Get outdoors at the Parc Urbain and use your field glasses at the Héron nature reserve, where a lake and forested artificial hillside welcome 200, mostly migratory, types of bird. Walking maps to some 30km of country footpaths, over 155,000ha of open spaces and six lakes can be found at the tourist office (Château-de-Flers, Chemin du Chat Botté ☏ 03 20 43 55 75 w villeneuvedascq-tourisme.eu).

WHAT TO SEE AND DO

LaM Musée d'Art Moderne Modern Art Museum; 1 allée du Musée ☏ 03 20 19 68 88 w musee-lam.fr ⏱ 10.00–18.00 Tue–Sun 🚇 Fort de Mons then bus L6 to LaM, & follow the footpath into the park 🎫 €7

Discover the greatest artists of the 20th century in the galleries and gardens of this unexpected cultural park in Villeneuve d'Ascq, Lille's university campus suburb. Renamed the 'LaM' following its first major expansion programme, the light and unassuming brick building that was once known merely as the Modern Art Museum makes no attempt to upstage the top-notch collection that it houses. A comprehensive tour through the most influential painters of each key artistic movement of the past 100 years includes half a dozen Picassos, Braque's *Maisons et Arbres*, works by Rouault, Klee, Miró and Masson, and some renowned canvases by Modigliani, including his *Nu Assis à la Chemise*. A powerful, almost pulsating tableaux by Fernand Léger provides a thrilling evocation of the region's dual heritage of socialism and industry – the bulk of the museum's wealth comes from generous bequests to the community from the private collections of Roger Dutilleul, and Jean and Geneviève Masurel. The Fauvist and Cubist rooms are most popular, but post-war artists are equally well represented through

more recent acquisitions. Temporary exhibitions vary in style and quality. If you are lucky, you may spot an engaging new genius. Of course, you may have to wade through more than a few luminaries of the post-talent movement to find it. Step between eras, and look through huge plate-glass windows at lawns where locals walk their dogs, ride their e-scooters and kick footballs between sculptures, including Picasso's *Femme aux Bras Ecartés* and Alexander Calder's *Southern Cross*. The park opens an hour earlier and closes an hour later than the museum. Jewellery and other objects by local artists are sold in the museum shop, and a café and restaurant on site provide plenty of opportunity to continue the 'Yes, but is it art?' debates. Download a free app from the App Store or GooglePlay to carry your own guide to the museum on your smartphone or tablet.

Forum des Sciences Centre François Mitterrand Science Museum & Planetarium; 1 pl Hôtel de Ville ↳ 03 59 73 96 00 w forumdepartementaldessciences.fr ⏱ school term 14.00–18.00 Wed & Fri–Sun, school hols 11.00–18.00 Tue–Fri & 14.00–18.00 Sat–Sun; call to check 🚇 Hôtel de Ville 🎟 €8 depending on which attractions you visit (free admission 1st Sun of the month)

Experience Lille's night sky by day at the planetarium. You may not want to take the trip to Villeneuve d'Ascq simply for the planetarium but, if travelling with children, this science centre makes an enjoyable diversion and a good bargaining chip for buying your own time at the modern art museum. Entertaining and informative shows (some in English) range from

◀ 1 An impressive collection of 20th-century works is housed in LaM Musée d'Art Moderne in Villeneuve d'Ascq. 2 The Institut du Monde Arabe in Tourcoing displays art and crafts from the Arab world. 3 Distillerie Claeyssens in Wambrechies has been making *genièvre* gin for 200 years. 4 Tourcoing's MUba Eugène Leroy contains many artworks by the museum's namesake.

speculation as to life on Mars to the history of time itself. All presentations begin with a simulation of the Lille sky at dusk. A splashy, hands-on activity centre appeals to little ones, and adults will enjoy thought-provoking temporary exhibitions, such as a walk through the life, art and science of Leonardo da Vinci.

Maison Folie – La Ferme d'en Haut 268 rue Jules Guesde, Flers Bourg ☏ 03 20 61 01 46 w lafermedenhaut.villeneuvedascq.fr 🚇 Pont de Bois, then bus L6 to Château

The Upper Farm of the former Château de Flers (which is itself home of the tourist office and archaeological museum) is a typical red-brick and white-stone building of the region. In its Maison Folie incarnation (page 210), farming heritage may be explored in an experimental kitchen, and many dance, drama or cabaret shows could well be accompanied by a meal in the performance space. I found an exhibition of circuses on my earliest visit. The town has a long love affair with the big top and involves acrobats and performers in its work with children with disabilities and learning difficulties. As I was browsing fascinating displays, and discovering a charming and unsung aspect of the local community, I could hear jazz musicians preparing for a performance later the same day.

Musée de Plein Air Open-Air Museum; 143 rue Colbert ☏ 03 20 63 11 25 w enm. lillemetropole.fr/parcs/musee-de-plein-air 🚇 Pont de Bois, then bus 36 to Mairie de Croix; 25min walk is signposted

This open-air museum is in fact a preserved rural hamlet with architectural exhibits and traditional skills on display. Staff dress up in traditional costumes, visitors can meet the animals, and on the first Saturday of the month children may enjoy pony rides around the site. Family workshops are held at 15.00 every Saturday.

Musée du Souvenir Museum of Remembrance; 77 rue Mangain ☏ 03 20 91 87 57 w villeneuvedascq.fr/memorial-ascq-1944-2 ⏱ 13.30 Wed (other days, please check) 🚇 Pont de Bois, then bus 13 to Masséna & 10min walk is signposted

If you come to Villeneuve d'Ascq on a Wednesday, find time to pay respects to the memory of the victims of the Ascq Massacre on Palm Sunday 1944. When local members of the Résistance blew up a train on the Tournai–Lille railway line, though no-one was injured, an SS convoy from the Russian front rounded up every man in the little community of Ascq. Some were shot in their homes, others taken to this site to be executed. In total, 86 died in the massacre, some as young as 15 years old. This simple museum has the usual wartime posters, but far more poignant are the clusters of personal effects of the victims that make the tragedy horribly personal. In the 1960s, when the area was swallowed up by the expanding city of Lille, it was decided to rename the district Villeneuve d'Ascq in tribute to those who died.

WAMBRECHIES

Wambrechies is one of nine towns making up the Val de Deûle that follows the serpentine river out of the city centre. Indeed, most people come to Wambrechies for hiking routes along the riverbanks. For more information on these, visit the Office de Tourisme Val de Deûle et Lys (Fondation Ledoux, 21 pl du Général de Gaulle ✎ 03 59 50 74 49 w valdedeule-tourisme. fr ⏲ 09.30–12.30 & 14.00–17.30 Tue–Fri, 10.00–12.30 Sat, mid-Apr–mid-Oct 14.30–18.30 Sun).

WHAT TO SEE AND DO
Distillerie Claeyssens 1 rue de la Distillerie ✎ 03 20 67 89 44
w distilleriedewambrechies.com ⏲ tours 09.30–12.30 & 13.30–17.30, closed hols 🚃 bus L1 to Wambrechies Mairie; rue 11 Nov 1918 to rue Leclerc to rue de la Distillerie
There is nothing high-tech about this distillery that has been making *genièvre* gin from junipers for the past 200 years. Original wooden equipment still sifts seeds, mills flour and heats, cools and distils the spirit, just as it did in Napoleonic times, when the waterways of the Deûle brought grain from Belgium after an edict banned the use of French crops. The hour-long tour is an anecdote-filled meander through a past that can hold its own in the present. An opportunity to taste the robust tipple follows the tour and a shop sells not only the *genièvre* itself, but two rather special by-products: beer made during the fermenting process, and a single malt of Highland quality.

Musée de la Poupée et du Jouet Ancien Doll & Antique Toy Museum; Château
de Robersart ✎ 03 20 39 69 28 w musee-du-jouet-ancien.com ⏲ 14.00–18.00 Sun, Wed & school hols 🚃 bus L1 to Wambrechies Mairie 🎫 €4
At last, they tie the knot. The wedding of Barbie and Ken is a glittering occasion, the guest list itself reads like a who's who of Barbie. There's Beach Barbie, Beautician Barbie, Flight Attendant Barbie and, for all I know, Feng Shui Consultant Dietician Barbie, in the biggest gathering of big hair on plastic heads since *Dynasty* slipped off the TV listings pages. The nuptial tableau featuring scores of versions of the doll from each year of her long

---

SCENIC TRAM RIDE

A 1906 vintage tram (w amitram.asso.fr) runs every 15 minutes along the canal bank from Wambrechies to Marquette on Sundays, Wednesdays and public holidays between April and September, 14.30–19.00. Passengers may join the tram at Vent de Bise in Wambrechies or rue de la Deûle in Marquette. Pay €6.50 return and sit on authentic wooden benches, as refurbished in 1926.

career is staged in a model of a Gothic cathedral, and is typical of the imaginative displays at this charming museum of childhood. The setting of the museum itself is something of a happy ever after, housed in the family château of Juliette, the last countess of Robersart. Two galleries feature dolls and toys from every era. Among the most interesting items in the permanent display are miniature fashion outfits made to patterns printed in the leading women's magazines of the last century.

BONDUES

Résistance Museum; see Marcq-en-Baroeul, below.

MARCQ-EN-BAROEUL

For generations, Lille's Seurat-style Sunday in the country was spent in Marcq-en-Baroeul, with the racecourse a magnet for a working man planning a flutter on the horses on his day off. Today's attractions include the **Septentrion Gallery** (Chemin des Coulons ⋏ 03 20 46 35 80 w galerieseptentrion.com ⏱ closed Mon), a contemporary art space sharing its name with a local gastronomic restaurant, housed in a magnificent building in a 24ha park. The park is also home to the 16th-century **Château du Vert Bois** (Chemin des Coulons ⋏ 03 20 46 26 37 w fondationseptentrion. fr), which has charming grounds and a museum of telecommunications. The château estate actually straddles the border with the neighbouring commune of **Bondues** and its museum devoted to the **French Résistance** (2 Chemin Saint-Georges ⋏ 03 20 28 88 32 ⏱ 14.00–16.30 Tue–Fri), which, although small, is important in the homeland of Charles de Gaulle. In little over a year from spring 1943, some 68 *résistants* were executed at the Fort de Bondues. The museum, founded by volunteers, is housed in the remains of the fort. Marcq-en-Baroeul's tourist office is at 5 place du Général de Gaulle (⋏ 03 20 72 60 87).

WATTRELOS

This is where the northern passion for good times beats its heart. March has the annual Salon des Artistes, April brings a great parade of giants and September boasts Les Berlouffes, France's second biggest flea market on the weekend after the Braderie of Lille (page 174). The art of fun is explored in the **Musée des Arts Populaires et Traditions** (96 rue François-Mériaux ⋏ 03 20 81 59 50 w ville-wattrelos.fr/le-musee ⏱ 09.00–noon & 14.00–18.00 Tue–Sat, 15.00–18.00 3rd Sun), a museum of daily life and traditions housed in a former farm building. Among these traditions are the local throwing sport of *bourl* (*pétanque* or *boules* are here regarded as games for wimps) – you may even be tempted to give it a go yourself, now that the modern courts are no longer made from cow dung and beer. The tourist office is located at 189 rue Carnot (☏ 03 20 75 85 86 w wattrelos-tourisme.com).

BEYOND THE MÉTROPOLE

The Maisons Folies network stretches far beyond Lille Métropole, even across the border into Belgium. So if you have a day to spare for exploring, check out the list on page 210. This is a land rich in shared history, with Henry V's Agincourt around 100km away, Henry VIII's Field of the Cloth of Gold at Balinghem on the D231 between Ardres and Guines, and a muster point outside Boulogne for Napoleon's putative invasion of Britain. And, of course, Flanders fields lie all around you. Since the last edition of this guide and the creation of Hauts-de-France (page 6), the region has extended to embrace the homes of various royalty and Impressionists, so we have included several places to break your journey on a trip to Paris and beyond. Check with the regional tourist office (page 13) for more information.

LENS For half a century, the town of Lens was known for just two things: sports and unemployment, with an internationally known stadium, Stade de la Licorne, home to the Racing Club de Lens football team (better known as Sang et Or – Blood and Gold – after their red and gold colours) and a legacy of abandoned coal mines and slag-heaps. Today, this is a happy town with pride in its newest acquisition and its role as an essential stop on any cultural tour of northern Europe. Just a half-hour drive or 40-minute train ride from Lille, Lens is home to fresh galleries of the world's most famous museum, the Louvre, and the town basks in glory, with restaurants and shops to greet day trippers. Market stalls pop up every Tuesday and Thursday morning on place du Cantin, Philippe Olivier (page 167) has a cheese shop at 39 rue René Lanoy and master *chocolatier* Jean-Claude Jeanson sells some of his signature sweets at the museum (notably lavender-flavoured chocolate pyramids), but the main counter for *bonbons* and cakes is at 42 place Jean Jaurès. Of course, football and rugby fans still come to Lens on match days. Those whose partners don't share their sporting passion and wish to keep their relationships intact may still soak up the atmosphere in the streets, yet watch the match on three TV screens while chomping on traditional local cuisine at the restaurant l'Ardoise on route de Béthune. The Tourist Office is at 16 pl Jean Jaurès (☏ 03 21 67 66 66 w tourisme-lenslievin.fr).

Getting there and away Several trains depart Gare Lille Flandres for Lens every hour. The quickest direct trains do the journey in 39 minutes; slower services take around 50 minutes. Fares are around €9 each way, and a bus links the station to the museum. Travellers with mobility issues should contact Assist'en Gare (page 34) for assistance; many trains are wheelchair accessible, as is the bus.

12

Strait of Dover

Calais

Dunkerque

Balinghem

Boulogne-sur-Mer

Le Touquet

Étaples-sur-Mer

St-Omer

Cassel

Nord

Pas-de-Calais

Azincourt

Loisinard

Ablain St-Nazaire French Military Cemetery

Vimy

Arras

Ayette

Thiepval

Authie

Baie de la Somme

Somme

FRANCE

Lens

Essex Farm

Ypres (Ieper)

Tyne Cot

Comines-Warneton

West-Vlaanderen

Roubaix

Lille

Pecq

Tournai

Kortrijk (Courtrai)

Lewarde

Nord

Le Cateau Cambresis

Ors

Maubeuge

Mons

Hainaut

BELGIUM

Oost-Vlaanderen

Brussels

Aa

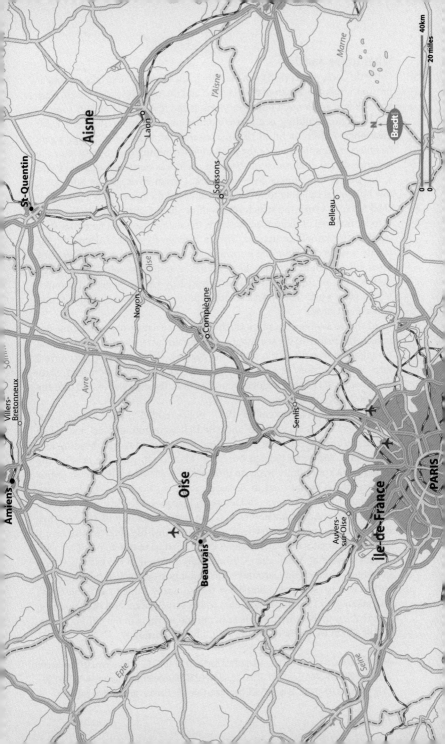

What to see and do

Gare de Lens Don't rush from the train to the bus stop. First, take a moment or two to walk the length of the platform and discover the station itself. Here you will find art to reach out to your senses and history to chill your soul.

The station building is a listed monument, a stunning 1926 Art Deco creation by railway architect Urbain Cassan, commissioned to design a *gare* to reflect the importance of the *bassin minier* mining community after the original station, and much of the town itself, was destroyed in World War I. Inspired by the miners' lives and work, Cassan envisaged an 80m-long, low horizontal building to reflect the tunnels of the mines, and a 23m-high clocktower to evoke the structure of a mine shaft. Constructed in the new-wonder material of reinforced concrete, the station has worn far better than many better-known structures. Simple lozenge-style frieze décor for the façade is echoed in stunning ironwork on windows designed and forged by artist Edgar Brandt. Step into the ticket hall to admire mosaics, also inspired by the work of the miners of Lens, created by Cubist Auguste Labouret, whose glass works and mosaics adorn some of Paris's finest churches and department stores.

As well as a subterranean motif, the serpentine nature of the building also reflects the reality of the seemingly infinite railway trucks that shuttled coal through goods yards to the rest of the country. However, these rails have a more sinister history as a modest plaque on the platform wall reveals. Sixty years before 9/11 entered global consciousness, the date was etched into the lives of the people of Lens.

At 04.00 on 11 September 1942, police raided homes across Lens. Altogether, 317 men, women and children were rounded up and taken to the platform at the Gare de Lens and loaded on to trucks, heading to a Nazi camp across the Belgian border in Malines. In vain, the head of the local Jewish community wrote to the *préfet départemental* (the most senior French official in the area) in Arras, pleading for the life of children born in France, such as six-year-old Denise and Jacques, aged five, as well as for those parents and grandparents who had fled persecution in 19th-century Poland and found sanctuary in Lens. By the time his letter was received, 700 fellow inmates from the Malines camp, victims of the *rafle de Lens*, had already arrived at Auschwitz. All the children named in the letter perished in the gas chambers and, around a week after posting the letter to Arras, the author was arrested at his home (on the ironically named rue Émile Zola) and taken with 15 of his neighbours to the same station and the same fate. Before the war, there were 991 Jews living and working in the mining towns, 467 of whom were sent to the camps. Only 18 returned.

Musée du Louvre-Lens 99 rue Paul Bert ☎ 03 21 18 62 62 w louvrelens.fr ⏲ museum 10.00–18.00 Wed–Mon (Sep–Jun 10.00–22.00 1st Fri of the month); park summer 07.00–21.00 daily, winter 08.00–19.00 daily 🚆 SNCF train from Gare Lille Flandres to Lens, then bus 41 to museum (every 30mins); if driving, follow signs for car parks & walk through park to museum (guests with disabilities may use the designated drop-off point by the entrance) 💿 €11; free audio guide connects to smartphones

Just as Lille must thank François Mitterrand for wooing Eurostar to the city, so Lens owes President Chirac a drink for sending it one of the world's most renowned museums. It was Chirac's final campaign against France's Paris-centric approach to the arts (although this had not been a problem for him when he was mayor of the capital). He decided that the Paris museums needed to reach out to the regions, so the Centre Pompidou went to Metz in the east and the Louvre was thrown to the north, the region later the recipient of the Institut du Monde Arabe (page 227) as well. The leading cities of the former region of Nord-Pas-de-Calais fought for the prize, but the outside candidate won, since Lens was the only major town in a region with almost 50 major museums that had no decent gallery of its own.

Since the location of the museum is a major part of the nation's industrial heritage, the building's Japanese architects created a park from a former coal mine with a meandering line of low-level glass and aluminium buildings, their walls reflecting northern skies and a landscape where pit-heads once dominated the horizon. The brief was to showcase, not upstage, both art and landscape, rather than to create an architectural statement. While the original industrial buildings are but a memory, two slag-heaps remain and there are plans to include a model of the original mine within the museum.

What has been created at Lens is a virtual time machine of art. This unique museum for our time has unrivalled access to the stores and archives of the parent museum in Paris, where just a tiny fraction of the national collection would ever see the light of day. Now, in a versatile new space, the art of the whole world may be seen in a timeline that takes us from the marvels of the ancient world to living memory; from anonymous heroic statuary to framed and signed dignity of the likes of Raphael and Ingres.

The principal wing is a vast 120m walk through the centuries, stepping around sculptures, canvases, artefacts and legacies from every generation. About to undergo a redesign at the time of writing, the Galerie du Temps (Time Gallery) previously had a timeline on the walls to provide visitors with a global view of cultures through the ages, providing parallel reflections

INDUSTRIAL TRANSFORMATIONS

The Lovre-Lens is the region's most subtle reinvention of its mining heritage. Pit buildings at nearby **Lewarde** are now a heritage centre and museum of mining, while **Noeux-les-Mines** converted its slag-heaps into artificial ski slopes and launched the year-round winter-sports resort **Loisinord**.

with the art of the East and Arab worlds to the left and Western creativity on the right. Similarities, rather than differences, struck the visitor, as an oriental portrait of a prince hung but a glance away from a European portrait of power, painted within the space of a generation at a distance of many thousands of miles. Timelines also reveal the gentle evolution of familiar art, from vessels and icons of ancient civilisations to souvenirs of more recent centuries as painters left their studio for the great outdoors, then swapped the sharp eye of the recorder for the misty spirit of Impressionism. Rather than divide collections into movements and styles, this 3,000m²-experience is designed as an opportunity to wander among the exhibits, and the massive hall allows visitors the space to enjoy and appreciate art and creativity around them. In busy periods, admission may occasionally be postponed in order not to crowd the gallery. The collection evolves, with its most famous initial exhibit (Delacroix's *Liberty Leading the People*) now safely home in Paris, making way for other treasures to travel north. Later distinguished visitors from the capital have included Vermeer's lacemaker.

Occasionally, the artworks become a backdrop for performing arts, so check online for details of concerts and other events in the exhibition halls, as well as a purpose-built theatre. One temporary exhibition on the animals of the ancient Egyptians opened in the galleries with a ballet of Camille Saint-Saëns' *Carnival of the Animals* simultaneously staged in the building.

A variety of alternative spaces emerge through the free-flow experience. Since the project's aim was to bring treasures of the Louvre to fresh audiences, even the 'stacks' are no dusty archives. Underground is a mezzanine gallery with virtual lecture booths for studying specific works and a glass wall looks down on the art stores. There's also a restoration studio so visitors may observe experts reviving paintings and statues. Another bubble in the *médiathèque* stages thrice-weekly lectures with curators and experts inviting the public to explore just one item from the collection in great detail.

Picnic in the grounds, snack on a €12 lunch at the cafeteria or sip a drink outside on the terrace. You might even cross the gardens to the museum's own restaurant, **l'Atelier du Cerisier** (w lecerisier.com). Just as Nausicaä in Boulogne chose Michelin-starred chef Tony Lestienne to run the food side of things, here Marc Meurin, bearer of two Michelin stars (and patron of the now departed Monsieur Jean in Lille) first took the helm of the original eponymous Atelier. His successor, Elie Beghin, who swiftly won the site a fresh Michelin star, now offers €35–65 set menus.

AMIENS Until Lille worked the miracle that led to its own renaisssance, Amiens was the place everyone expected to get the Eurostar station. It was,

---

1 The Musée du Louvre-Lens brings the treasures of the Louvre to a former mining town. 2 Pretty Amiens is home to the largest Gothic cathedral in the world. 3 The Canadian memorial at Vimy Ridge is a moving testament to the horrors of World War I. ▶

JORDAN TAN/S

ZJTMATH/S

KEV GREGORY/S

In Northern France, you are never more than a heartbeat away from memory. Across the region known to history as Flanders Fields, World War I graves and monuments mark the countryside from Paris to the coast, many close to Lille itself. Take a tram ride from the city to the **Musée de la Bataille de Fromelles** (rue de la Basse Ville, Fromelles 📞 03 59 61 15 14 w musee-bataille-fromelles.fr ⏱ 09.30–17.30 Wed–Mon 🚇 Métro 2 to St Philibert then bus 62R to Mairie Fromelles, walk 450m 🎫 €5), to learn the story of the first major battle fought by Australian troops on the Western Front. Recent DNA techniques have helped to identify the bodies of 250 Australian and British soldiers discovered here, and each man has now been given a named grave.

For the Great War centenary, coaches left Lille for **Ypres** in Belgium, home to the vast **Tyne Cot Cemetery** and **Essex Farm**, inspiration of John McCrae's immortal poem *In Flanders Fields*. There are no more buses, but it's an easy drive from Lille. In the opposite direction, the chic resort of Le Touquet is a mere stone's throw from the large Commonwealth cemetery at **Étaples**. Designed, like so many memorials and cenotaphs, by English architect Sir Edwin Lutyens, this necropolis is the final resting place of nearly 11,400 victims of both World Wars on the site of a camp once home to 100,000 soldiers.

Back near the Belgian border, you can cycle or hike the **Wilfred Owen trail** (w tourisme-cambresis.fr/following-owen). The *Anthem for Doomed Youth* poet died crossing the Sambre-Oise canal a week before Armistice and is buried in the village churchyard of **Ors**.

Owen's most famous words, '*Dulce et decorum est pro patria mori*', hang in the air at the poignant Ring of Remembrance at the **Ablain St-Nazaire French Military Cemetery**, also known as Notre Dame de Lorette, near Arras. The 360° memorial is inscribed with the names of all 579,606 soldiers who died in the Nord and Pas-de-Calais *départements*. American, British, French, German, South African…they're listed not by nationality, but alphabetically by name. Beneath **Arras** (page 244) itself lie the **Wellington Tunnels** that hid 24,000 Allied troops. Nearby, Canada's national memorial stands at **Vimy Ridge**, where you can walk through preserved trenches.

Each Allied nation has its own physical epitaph as you trace the route of the bloodiest of all battles, the Somme. Some 11,000 Australian soldiers are honoured at **Villers-Bretonneux**, while the **Longueval Monument** commemorates New Zealand soldiers who died on 15 September 1916.

after all, the only major city on the direct line between Calais and Paris. But this was a rare missed opportunity for Picardy's historic capital. The city still has plenty else to boast of, not least the largest Gothic cathedral in the

On the base of its white column is a Maori sculpture and an engraving reading 'From the uttermost ends of the earth'. At nearby **Delville Wood**, also in Longueval, the 1st South African Infantry Brigade is respected, and in Bellau, Native American soldiers are remembered at the **Musée de la Mémoire de Belleau** (pl du Général Pershing, Belleau \ 03 23 82 03 63 w museedebelleau.com ⏱ 8 May–11 Nov 10.00–12.30 & 13.30–17.30 Thu–Mon 🍽 €2). A red Welsh Dragon with barbed wire in its claws honours eight days of fighting by the 38th Welsh Division at **Mametz Wood** and 5,000 soldiers from Northern Ireland are recalled at the **Ulster Memorial Tower** in Thiepval.

The **Thiepval Memorial** (8 rue de l'Ancre, Thiepval \ 03 22 74 60 47 w historial.fr ⏱ 09.30–18.00, to 17.00 Nov–Feb, closed mid-Dec–mid-Jan), dedicated to 72,194 British and South African soldiers who went missing on the Somme between 1915 and 1918, stands by the largest British war cemetery. An interactive display of letters, photos and personal effects provides a poignant reminder of the human cost. The memorial's sister **Péronne Museum** (Château de Péronne, pl André Audinot, Péronne \ 03 22 83 14 18 w historial.fr ⏱ Apr–Sep 09.30–18.00 daily, Oct–mid-Dec & mid-Jan–Mar 09.30–17.30 Thu–Tue) provides further history on World War I.

Around 2,000 Chinese and 1,500 Indian labourers, employed by Britain to recover these bodies, themselves died serving on the Western Front. Most are buried at the **Ayette Indian and Chinese Cemetery,** down a rough farm track in the village of Ayette, 14km south of Arras. Only 64 were ever identified.

Continuing south, **Compiègne** makes a fitting final stop a tour of the region's World War I sites: it was here that the Armistice ending the conflict was signed on 11 November 1918 (page 247).

Both **Hauts-de-France Tourisme** (w hautsdefrancetourism.com) and **Somme Tourisme** (w somme14-18.com) have a variety of helpful planning resources, with suggested routes and itineraries and further information about these monuments and other sites on the memorial trail. With hundreds of thousands of names carved along the route, you may wish to dedicate your travels to the hero of your own family history. The **Commonwealth War Graves Commission** (w cwgc.org) has advice on finding records, or you can have a tailor-made itinerary designed for you by **Tommy Atkins Tours** (w tommyatkinstours.com).

world: **Notre Dame d'Amiens** (w cathedrale-amiens.fr) dwarfs its Parisian namesake, with a 42m-high nave and 112m spire, and was built in a single lifespan. It even has a record in stone of the names of the builders who started

12

work in 1220, clocking off 68 years later. There are great views from towers, which, like the gargoyles, were restored by 19th-century architect Viollet le Duc, the man who renovated Carcassonne's turrets and ramparts. See it at its best on a summer night, awash with colour during the *Chroma* digital light show, or enjoy the winter encore during the Christmas market (which also features a skating rink). It makes the ideal starting point for visiting all seven cathedrals of Picardy: Notre-Dame de Laon (blueprint for Chartres), Noyon, where Charlemagne was crowned, Senlis, St Quentin, Beauvais and Soissons. The perfectly preserved medieval streets around the cathedral host sundry **Jules Verne** tours, either by tourist train or self-guided with hidden QR codes to uncover gems from the life and works of one of the world's best loved authors. Verne's beautiful house is also open to visitors, as is the **Musée de Picardie** (w amiens.fr/Vivre-a-Amiens/Culture-Patrimoine/Etablissements-culturels) – France's first purpose-built art gallery, template for the nation's great museums. The other *incontournable* is below the town, on the water: **Les Hortillonages**, a wetland of floating floral and market gardens, with countless cultivated islands accessible only by boat. Explore the network of waterways on a traditional *rieux* farmers' boat, modern electric vessels or even during a dinner cruise. Details are available at the Tourist Office (23 pl Notre Dame ☎ 03 22 71 60 50 w visit-amiens.com).

ARRAS When you visit the Maison Folie (page 210), explore the rest of this stunning town. Incredibly, those 17th- and 18th-century squares are not the real thing, but recreated faithfully from the original architects' plans rescued from the rubble when Arras was razed in two wars. Climb the belfry for views, then descend into the bowels of the town to visit a remarkable network of underground passages linking the cellars of the old houses and commandeered by the Allies in World War I as a command post. Railways ran under the city to the front line. Discover the **Wellington Tunnels** (w carrierewellington.com), linking chalk quarries dug 20m below ground by New Zealand soldiers to keep 24,000 Allied troops hidden before a surprise attack in 1916, and don't miss the unforgettable Canadian memorial and trenches at **Vimy Ridge**. Elsewhere in town, the **Beaux Arts Museum** offers free admission to its collection of masterly Flemish and Dutch works, including Rubens' *Saint Francis Receiving the Stigmata*. Other treats include a UNESCO-listed Vauban **citadel** and the **Cité Nature Museum and gardens** (25 bd Schuman ☎ 03 21 21 59 59 w citenature.com). The tourist office is in the Hôtel de Ville (Pl des Héroes ☎ 03 21 51 26 95 w arraspaysdartois.com).

AUVERS-SUR-OISE You may never have visited Auvers-sur-Oise, but you will recognise almost every twist in the road and river bank. Almost as far south as you can go without leaving the region, Auvers is where Vincent Van Gogh spent his final months, frantically painting scores of canvasses. Church, wheatfield, even the attic bedroom familiar from a million prints and tea-towels: all form part of the **Chemin des Peintres Impressionist trail**, an open-air museum bidding for UNESCO heritage status. Indoor sites include the Maison du Docteur Gachet (ⓒ year-round), as immortalised by Paul Cézanne (its windswept garden captured by Van Gogh himself), and the very room in the Auberge Ravoux where Vincent lodged the last three months of his life (ⓒ March–Nov). Details and a choice of circuits – a 1-hour walk around the town and banks of the Oise or a longer 2½-hour route taking in other sites linked to Daubigny, Corot, Morisot, Pearce, Renoir, Douanier, Rousseau and Pissarro – are available from the tourist office (Parc Van Gogh, 38 rue du Général de Gaulle ☏ 01 30 36 71 81 w tourisme-auverssuroise.fr ⓒ closed Mon).

AZINCOURT For most of the past 600 years, nobody bothered making the journey, now 90 minutes' drive west of Lille or 45 minutes south of Calais, to Azincourt. Better known to you, me and William Shakespeare as Agincourt, this is where English bowmen gave Henry V his historic victory in battle and the Bard an excuse for the classic St Crispin's Day speech. Unsurprisingly, the French school curriculum does not dwell on the story of the country's greatest humiliation, let alone the Shakespeare play – which only received its French premier in 1999. Incredibly, the landscape has hardly changed, and standing on the field of Azincourt, seeing almost the same contours as did the young king in 1415, you may understand his improbable victory. Over 30 years ago, when first I declaimed that speech and played out the aftermath in my mind, I saw rows of leeks, just as Henry and Fluellen recalled the Welsh did good service in a garden where the leeks did grow. Then, there was just a small amateur exhibition in a village room down the lane, and a bar serving instant coffee at the corner of the field where I walked out to let imaginary forces work. My own passion for the Bard and this scene led to an invitation to sit on France's committee for choosing a design for a memorial, and today you may stiffen the sinews, summon up the blood and follow your spirit to **Azincourt 1415** (24 rue Charles VI ☏ 03 74 63 00 24 w azincourt1415.com ⓒ 10.00–17.30 Wed–Mon; closed Mon Oct–Jan 🍽 €9). This combined battle museum and visitor centre has been built to resemble a flank of archers, for a little touch of Harry within the girdle of its walls.

BOULOGNE-SUR-MER This delightful port, with its old town perched on the hill, is as charming as ever. Visit the **Château Museum** (Château Comtal, rue de Bernet ☏ 03 21 10 02 20 w musee.ville-boulogne-sur-mer.fr ⓒ closed Tue) and walk the ramparts. By the port, **Nausicaä** (Centre National de la Mer, bd Sainte Beuve ☏ 03 21 30 99 99 w nausicaa.fr) – an interactive museum of the sea with sharks, sea lions and exposition of green issues – makes a fascinating day out (free summer shuttle bus to/from the town). The tourist office is at 30 rue de la Lampe (☏ 03 21 10 88 10 w boulonnaisautop.com ⓒ closed Sun Nov–Mar).

CALAIS The Channel port once known for booze cruisers may not be as quaint as its neighbours, but take time to explore arts and fashion at the **Musée des Beaux-Arts et de la Dentelle** (25 rue Richelieu ⬩ 03 21 46 48 40 w mba.calais.fr ⏰ closed Tue). There's also a war museum in a bunker, a lighthouse and many fine restaurants. Other innovations include a street art trail – maps are available from the tourist office at 12 boulevard Georges Clemenceau (⬩ 03 21 96 62 40 w calais-cotedopale.com ⏰ Sep–Apr 10.00–18.00 Mon–Fri, 10.00–17.00 Sat; May–Aug 10.00–18.00 Mon–Sat, 10.00–17.00 Sun).

CASSEL Come to Cassel for the true spirit of Flanders, with windmills and *estaminets* (and inspiration for half the menus in Lille). There are delightful gardens to explore, as well as artworks in the **Musée de Flandre** (w museedeflandre.fr). The tourist office is at 20 Grand Place (⬩ 03 74 54 00 77 w coeurdeflandre.fr ⏰ closed Mon (except peak summer) & Sun Nov–Mar).

LE CATEAU-CAMBRÉSIS Le Cateau-Cambrésis is notable as the birthplace of Henri Matisse. Visit the restored **Musée Matisse** (Palais Fénelon ⬩ 03 59 73 38 00 w museematisse.fr ⏰ closed Tue) devoted to the artist and his works. The local tourist office is located at 9 place Commandant Richez (⬩ 03 27 84 10 94 w tourisme-lecateau.fr ⏰ closed Tue & Sun).

COMPIÈGNE Officially, you visit Compiègne for the grand royal and imperial **château** (⬩ 03 44 38 47 10 w chateaudecompiegne.fr ⏰ 10.00–18.00 Wed–Mon), designed for Louis XV and home to the Napoleons. With requisite chandeliers, salons and ballroom, France's largest neo-classical palace is home to three museums. One is devoted to Second Empire art and court life; another to Empress Eugénie, from her Spanish origins through her imperial heyday as mistress of taste (even her five weeks as head of state) to her 50-year exile in England; and France's national Motor Museum is also housed here. It's not cars nor imperial *carrosses* that most merit a detour on the winding journey to Paris, however, but a plush green-and-gold railway carriage previously used by Napoleon and Eugénie that sits in the middle of the forest. Maréchal Foch, who had commandeered the train's dining car as his mobile office, had it brought here to a peaceful clearing as a discreet rendezvous for signing the Armistice with Germany on 11 November 1918. And here, on 22 June 1940, the Nazis returned to force a French surrender before setting fire to the carriage on Hitler's orders. A replica *wagon lit* stands in the **Mémorial de l'Armistice** (Route de Soissons, Compiègne ⬩ 03

◀ 1 Boulogne-sur-Mer's old town is charmingly picturesque. 2 Van Gogh's final months are commemorated with a statue and a walking trail at Auvers-sur-Oise. 3 The field of Azincourt still looks much as it did during the battle there in 1415.

Lille and its region has as many stories to tell of World War II as it does of World War I (page 242). Explore tales of battles, occupation and resistance at the Résistance museum at **Bondues** (page 234), the Nazi bunker at **Tourcoing** (page 226), the **Calais** defences, the V2 rocket base at **La Coupole** (see below) and Lille's **Noble Tour** (page 194). See where heroes faced firing squads at Lille's **Monument aux Fusillées** (page 215) and **Villeneuve d'Ascq** (page 232), or where families and children were rounded up to be deported to death camps from the station at **Lens** (page 238). At **Dunkerque**, visit the evacuation beaches (see below). And back in Lille, remember France's leader in exile, **Général de Gaulle** (page 189).

44 85 14 18 w armistice-museum.com ⏱ 10.00–18.00 daily, closes 17.30 Dec) museum about the wars.

DUNKERQUE The port of privateers and adventure has museums of fine arts, maritime heritage and piracy. Since Christopher Nolan's 2017 film, tours have been organised featuring sites from the big screen as well as locations around town and the **Dune Marchand** nature reserve. The tourist office can be found on rue de l'Amiral Ronarch (📞 03 28 26 27 28 w dunkerque-tourisme.fr).

SAINT-OMER Come to Saint-Omer for the **Musée Sandelin** (Rue Carnot 📞 03 21 38 00 94 w musees-saint-omer.fr ⏱ closed Mon & Tue) to see how a table should be laid; for **Arc International** (132 av du Général de Gaulle 📞 03 21 12 74 74 w arc-intl.com), better known as Crystal d'Arques, Europe's largest glass-making empire, to buy your own tableware (photos and selfies banned during the tour); and for the fabulous Marais Audemarois's hidden world of floating gardens, chicory and kingfishers, best explored by canoe or tour boat from café-restaurant **Le Bon Accueil** (w bonaccueil-marais. fr) at Salperwick. Also visit Saint-Omer for **La Coupole** (rue Clabaux 📞 03 21 12 27 27 w lacoupole-france.com), a Nazi V2 bunker just out of town, housing twin museums of life in occupied France and the space race, alongside a planetarium. Take time out, too, to visit the **aerodrome**, where RAF predecessor the Royal Flying Corps was based during the Great War, and where you will find a rarity – an RAF memorial away from British soil.

---

1 Dunkerque's maritime heritage is an important part of the city. 2 A different side of Calais can be seen on the city's street art trail. 3 The Marais Audemarois in Saint-Omer is an idyllic area of floating gardens and wildlife. 4 The grand château at Compiègne is a Versailles for the imperial era. ▶

Tourist information can be found at 4 rue Lion d'Or (℡ 03 21 98 08 51 w tourisme-saintomer.com ⏰ summer 09.00–18.00 Mon–Sat, 10.00–13.00 Sun; winter 09.00–12.30 & 14.00–17.30 Mon–Sat).

HIKING AND BIKING

If you've a yen for the great outdoors, rather than simply site-hopping on four wheels, leave the city behind and explore the countryside of the Nord *département*. The **Nord Évasion** website (w evasion.lenord.fr) publishes imaginative hiking, biking and even horseback itineraries for exploring trails of buccaneers, bandits and garlic smokers. Walk the Flanders Opal Coast in the wake of legendary corsair and buccaneer Jean Bart; ride the frontiers where smugglers once toted contraband between Belgium and France; enjoy intimate and welcoming country *estaminet* bars in front rooms of village houses and *cafés randos* in the countryside; or simply head out into the natural and regional parks within reasonable reach of Lille. You will also find rural cousins of those **Greeters en Nord** (page 63) who offer personalised walks, rides and tours of places they love. For a cycling tour of village breweries, see page 132.

If the annual Paris–Roubaix challenge was not enough, the first stage of the 2025 Tour de France (which starts in Lille) will doubtless inspire thousands to discover the area on two wheels, with events across the region. The rest of the time, help for planning a cycle trip is available from **France Vélo Tourisme** (w en.francevelotourisme.com), with advice on itineraries and taking cycles on public transport, as well as listings of bike-friendly hotels and restaurants. Route options range from half-day excursions to week-long adventures or longer, covering both official cycle paths and off-piste options, and come with GPX links for downloading maps. There are also addresses and contacts for bike hire (useful since Ilévia's urban city bikes by the hour won't hack the wider countryside). Other helpful maps, brochures and tips can be obtained from the main tourist office in Lille (page 49) and Hauts-de-France Tourisme (w hautsdefrancetourism.com).

Appendix 1

LANGUAGE

The principal language of Lille is, of course, French, but, with its historical and geographical history, the Flemish side of the city is comfortable speaking Dutch. After all, until Eurostar awakened Britain to this gem on its doorstep, virtually every visitor came from Belgium. The Flemish for Lille is Rijsel, by the way.

The locals have their own patois, Ch'ti, a variation of Picard argot spoken across northern France. You will rarely come across an entire conversation in the northern tongue; however, local cabarets aimed at domestic rather than visiting audiences will feature a smattering of phrases, and should you hang around a genuine *estaminet* you may well pick up some words that would baffle a Parisian! If you fancy trying your hand at a few words, do so in the comfort of your own home online (w freelang.com/dictionnaire/chti.html). But don't worry if you don't get it. Local variants on language the world over, from rhyming slang to Yiddish, are designed for local communities. Outsiders are meant to be baffled! And you will probably have to let playground and street slang pass you by. Even vintage vernacular Verlan (from *l'envers*) is popular 'back slang' (try *beur* for *arabe*), and still commonly spoken.

Around Wazemmes you may well hear Arabic, so a few choice words and phrases from your wider travels may stand you in good stead.

FRENCH The French are in general better mannered than their anglophone friends and neighbours, and simple courtesies are a way of life, with the lack of them making a negative impression.

The simple greetings '*Bonjour*' ('Good day') or '*Bonsoir*' ('Good evening') are essentials. Use these as much as possible. Even in a doctor's waiting room, a general 'Bonjour' to the assembled company is expected.

When a shopkeeper says '*Bonne journée*' or '*Bonne soirée*', that is the equivalent of the American salutation 'Have a nice day!'

Traditionally, one should use the courtesy titles *Monsieur* (Sir) or *Madame* (Madam) when speaking to strangers. Nowadays one should always refer to an adult woman as *Madame*, whether or not she sports a wedding ring. 'Ms' does not exist in France. In fact, in 2013, *Mademoiselle* was formally dropped as a title on official forms. Oh, and courtesy applies to waiters as well: it is considered plain rude to snap the fingers and yell '*garçon*'. Restaurant staff in France are considered professionals: many will have studied for years from the age of 14 in order to perfect their art.

Physical greetings, both handshakes and kisses – long an essential part of life – are less ubiquitous since the Covid pandemic. Nods and smiles, once considered rude, are now an acceptable alternative in many cases. Take your cue from the locals, but don't be afraid to decline palms and cheeks

Nonetheless, many people continue to shake hands whenever humanly possible. The French love doing it. The kissing on both cheeks business has its own rules that remain practically Masonic. Between older men in the north, it is rarely done except 'twixt father and son or heads of state who hate each other (though the taboo applies less to the student generation), but if a woman is being introduced or encountered on a social basis (at a dinner party perhaps), the brushing of proffered cheeks is the thing to do. Usually twice in Lille, although between friends this may become three pecks, and within families four times is not unknown. (I have finally worked out the rules for cheek air-kissing: once = rude, twice = polite, thrice = friendly, four times = familial, five times = foreplay.)

Shake hands on entering a room, meeting someone for the first time in the day and on ending a conversation. The only exception would be at a urinal or during an autopsy. I've even found hands extended my way in an abattoir. To refuse would have gone down as well as a discussion on the many uses of tofu.

Then comes the heady question of pronouns, the second person in particular. In school we learn that *tu* and *toi* are the familiar version of 'you', with *vous* being the more formal usage. Of course there are no hard and fast rules, but I strongly recommend using vous to start any conversation and be guided by the local as to how you should continue.

There are, of course exceptions. These days, young people – and Lille is a student town – tend towards *tutoyer* (ie: use *toi*) as a matter of course, and in trendy or gay bars the informal form is the norm, rather as the words 'love', 'darling' or 'mate' might be bandied in a British pub. Rule of thumb: always use *vous* when talking to someone of a different generation.

Remember your p's and q's. *S'il vous plaît* and *merci* cost nothing and should be used at every opportunity.

Note: During UK sporting fixtures, I adopt Australian or Canadian nationality and accent if outnumbered on public transport.

Useful phrases In Lille, English is pretty widely spoken. A huge percentage of the population is involved in further education. The international business community and canny shopkeepers may handle most conversations in your native tongue. However, it is always appreciated when visitors make at least a modest attempt to speak the local language. So the following words should be used – even if you bashfully return to English after the initial contact:

Bonjour/bonsoir	Good day/good evening
Au revoir	Goodbye
Bonne nuit	Good night
Bonne journée/soirée	Have a nice day/evening
Merci	Thank you
S'il vous plaît	Please
Oui	Yes
Non	No
Comment allez-vous?/Ça va?	How are you?
Très bien, merci	Very well, thank you
Au secours!	Help!
Aidez-moi!	Help me!

Only once you have memorised thus far may you learn the following phrase:

Parlez-vous anglais?	Do you speak English?

However, if you can remember that, then surely the following nuggets cannot be too difficult to deliver (* examples given are in the masculine; women should add an 'e', or 'ne', to each national adjective):

Je ne comprends pas	I don't understand
Parlez moins vite, s'il vous plaît	Speak a little slower, please
Je ne sais pas	I don't know
Je suis anglais/écossais/gallois/ irlandais/américain/canadien/ australien*	I am English/Scottish/Welsh/ Irish/American/Canadian/ Australian
Avez vous une chambre avec deux lits/ avec un grand lit?	Have you a twin/double room?
Avec baignoire/douche	With bath/shower
Où est…?	Where is…?
Où?	Where?
Comment?	How?
Quand?	When?
Pourquoi?	Why?
Je voudrais…	I would like…
Combien?	How much?
Bon marché	Cheap
Cher/chère	Expensive

L'addition, s'il vous plaît	The bill, please
Je suis végétarien(ne)	I am vegetarian
Je suis malade	I am ill

If you are still reading this chapter, the chances are your French grammar is pretty rusty and you want to know which words are masculine (using *le* or *un*) and which feminine (*la* or *une*). Well, I hate to break it to you, but you are hardly going to squeeze in a decent education between the top of this page and the index, so allow me, in my unorthodox way, to suggest an extremely useful compromise: learn essential nouns, use gestures, smile and remember to say *merci* (that sound you just heard was Mrs Stockton, my third-form French mistress…fainting).

Useful nouns

beer	*une bière* (page 90)	money	*l'argent*
		motorway	*l'autoroute*
bread	*le pain*	park	*un parc*
breakfast	*le petit déjeuner*	passport	*un passeport*
bus	*un car*	petrol	*l'essence (gazole*
bus station	*la gare routière*		is diesel)
car	*une voiture*	postcard	*une carte postale*
chemist	*la pharmacie*	railway station	*la gare* (train)
condom	*le préservatif*	soup	*potage, consommé,*
credit card	*la carte de crédit*		*soupe, bouillon*
dinner	*le dîner*	stamp	*un timbre*
doctor	*le médecin*	telephone	*le téléphone*
fish	*le poisson*	ticket	*le billet/ticket*
hospital	*l'hôpital*	toilet	*les toilettes/WC*
letter	*une lettre*		(pronounced
luggage	*les bagages*		doob-levay-say)
lunch	*le déjeuner*	town	*la ville*
meat	*la viande*	train	*le train*
menu	*la carte*	water (mineral)	*l'eau (minérale)*
métro station		wine	*le vin*
(but NOT			
railway station)	*la station*		

Days and months

Monday	*lundi*	Sunday	*dimanche*
Tuesday	*mardi*	January	*janvier*
Wednesday	*mercredi*	February	*février*
Thursday	*jeudi*	March	*mars*
Friday	*vendredi*	April	*avril*
Saturday	*samedi*	May	*mai*

June	*juin*	morning	*le matin*
July	*juillet*	noon	*midi*
August	*août*	afternoon	*l'après-midi*
September	*septembre*	evening	*le soir*
October	*octobre*	night	*la nuit*
November	*novembre*	today	*aujourd'hui*
December	*décembre*	yesterday	*hier*
day	*le jour*	tomorrow	*demain*

Numbers

1	*un/une*	18	*dix-huit*
2	*deux*	19	*dix-neuf*
3	*trois*	20	*vingt*
4	*quatre*	30	*trente*
5	*cinq*	40	*quarante*
6	*six*	50	*cinquante*
7	*sept*	60	*soixante*
8	*huit*	70	*soixante-dix*
9	*neuf*		(except Belgians
10	*dix*		who say *septante*)
11	*onze*	80	*quatre-vingt*
12	*douze*	90	*quatre-vingt-dix*
13	*treize*		(except Belgians
14	*quatorze*		who say *nonante*)
15	*quinze*	100	*cent*
16	*seize*	1,000	*mille*
17	*dix-sept*		

Appendix 2

FURTHER INFORMATION

ESSENTIALS
Lille Tourist Office   w lilletourism.com

ENTERTAINMENT *Sortir* magazine (page 51) has weekly entertainment listings. Daily free newspapers at métros and stations also have the latest listings and reviews. Check the day's *La Voix du Nord* (page 51) at your hotel.

LOCAL TRANSPORT
Eurostar   w eurostar.com

Ilévia   w ilevia.fr

SNCF   w sncf-connect.com

TER   w ter.sncf.com/hauts-de-france
(local trains)

TRAVELLERS WITH LIMITED MOBILITY   See page 32.

LGBTQIA+ LILLE   No more magazines or websites. Just as Lille was early to embrace gay and lesbian culture and bars, the wider LGBTQIA+ and feminist movements have integrated into the mainstream. Lille Pride is practically a civic event these days, but organisers may advise on sympathetic businesses and accommodation. Bars and clubs are on page 151.

Lille Pride   w lillepride.org

MAPS   Michelin's *Regional Map 511* covers the Hauts-de-France region and the larger-scale *Local 302* features greater Lille (including Belgian towns). Online map sources include w viamichelin.com and w mappy.fr.

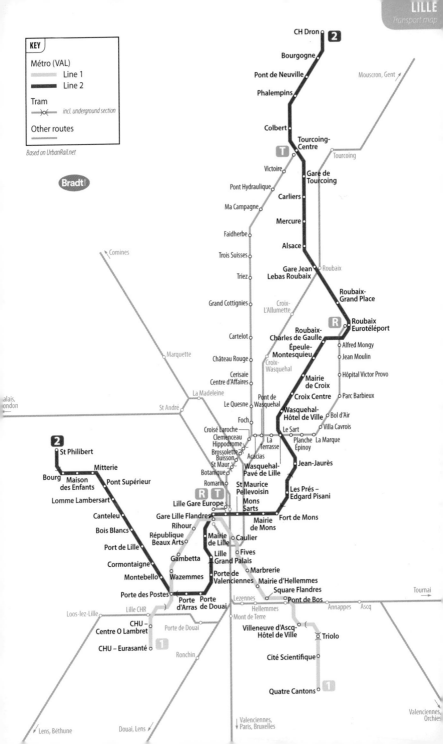

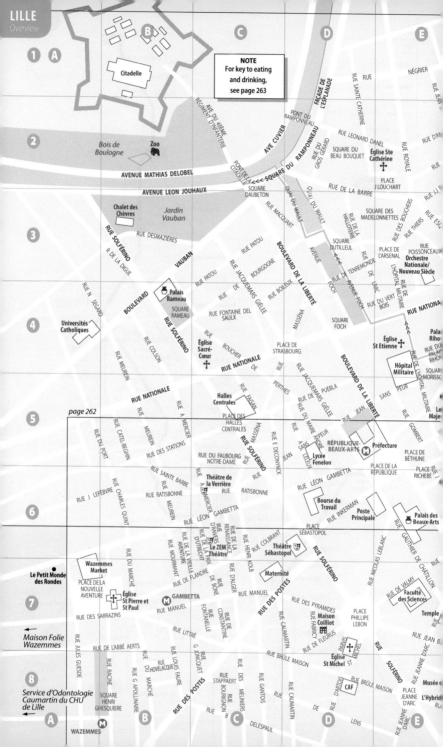

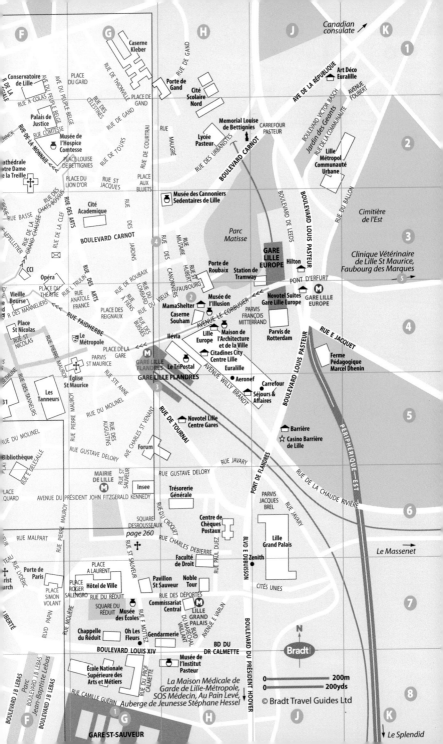

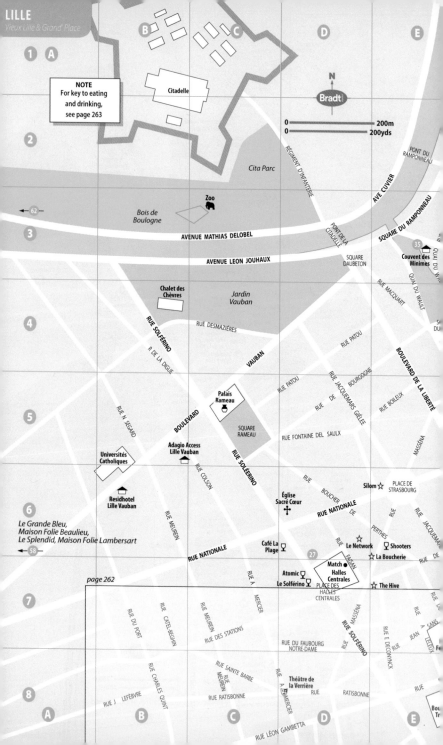

LILLE
Vieux Lille & Grand' Place

NOTE
For key to eating
and drinking,
see page 263

Citadelle

Bradt

N

0   200m
0   200yds

Cita Parc

RÉGIMENT D'INFANTERIE

PONT DU RAMPONNEAU

AVE CUVIER

Zoo

Bois de
Boulogne

SQUARE DU RAMPONNEAU

PONT DE LA CITADELLE

AVENUE MATHIAS DELOBEL

QUAI DU WAULT

SQUARE DU RAMPONNEAU

AVENUE LEON JOUHAUX

SQUARE DAUBETON

35   Couvent des Minimes

QUAI DU WA

RUE MACQUART

QUAI DU WAULT

Chalet des Chèvres

Jardin Vauban

RUE DESMAZIÈRES

RUE SOLFÉRINO

R DE LA DIGUE

VAUBAN

RUE PATOU

S DU

BOULEVARD DE LA LIBERTÉ

RUE PATOU

RUE JACQUEMARS GIÉLÉE

RUE DE BOURGOGNE

RUE BOILEUX

Palais Rameau

SQUARE RAMEAU

RUE DE

RUE FONTAINE DEL SAULX

MASSÉNA

BOULEVARD

RUE SOLFÉRINO

Universités Catholiques

RUE N SÉGARD

Adagio Access Lille Vauban

RUE COLSON

RUE BOUCHER

Silom ☆

PLACE DE STRASBOURG

Église Sacré Cœur ✝

Residhotel Lille Vauban

RUE MEUREN

RUE NATIONALE

DE

RUE

RUE JACQUE

PERTHES

Le Grande Bleu,
Maison Folie Beaulieu,
Le Splendid, Maison Folie Lambersart

Café La Plage ♀

RUE FA

Le Network ☆

♀ Shooters

58

RUE NATIONALE

27

☆ La Boucherie

RUE DE

Atomic ♀
Le Solférino ♀

RUE A

Match ●
Halles
Centrales

PLACE DES HALLES CENTRALES

☆ The Hive

MASSÉNA

RUE SOLFÉRINO

page 262

RUE DU PORT

RUE CATEL-BEGHIN

RUE MEUREN

RUE MERCER

RUE DES STATIONS

RUE DU FAUBOURG NOTRE-DAME

RUE E DECONNYNCK

RUE

JEAN

SANS

RUE LEF

Fe

RUE CHARLES QUINT

RUE SAINTE BARBE

RUE MEUREN

Théâtre de la Verrière

RUE

RATISBONNE

RUE

RUE J LEFEBVRE

RUE RATISBONNE

RUE MERCER

Bou
Tr

RUE LÉON GAMBETTA

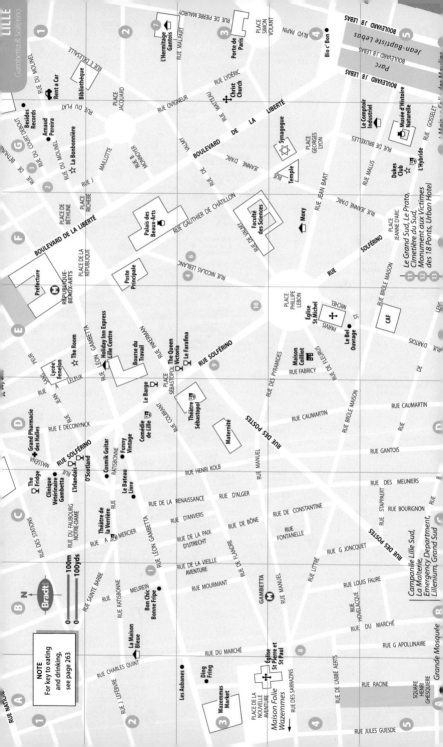

Appendix 2 FURTHER INFORMATION

A2

Index